Populism in Peru

Populism in Peru

The Emergence of the Masses
and the
Politics of Social Control

Steve Stein

The University of Wisconsin Press

Published 1980

The University of Wisconsin Press
114 North Murray Street
Madison, Wisconsin 53715

The University of Wisconsin Press, Ltd.
1 Gower Street
London WC1E 6HA, England

First printing

Printed in the United States of America

For LC CIP information see the colophon

ISBN 0-229-07990-2

Publication of this book was made
possible in part by a grant
from the Andrew W. Mellon Foundation.

For Pilar

Contents

List of Tables

List of Figures and Charts

Charts

Preface

JULY 12, 1979, and I am in Lima for a few days to see family and friends. While doing my research for this book I lived in the Peruvian capital for nearly two years between 1969 and 1971, and I have been back a number of times since. But this week is different. I cannot remember any previous moment when there was so much uncertainty in the political air. The new constitution is about to be promulgated by the constituent congress, and no one is certain how the military government will respond. There is also the threat of a serious general strike for next week. But even such a potentially momentous event as the enactment of a new national charter or the prospect of a total disruption in their daily lives appears to interest people only marginally. Public attention is sharply focussed elsewhere, on the fate of one man, Víctor Raúl Haya de la Torre. The founder and "supreme chief" of Peru's Apra party is dying. The individual who more than anyone else has dominated Peruvian politics for the past half century seems finally to be passing from the scene. Questions and rumors are flying back and forth. How sick is Haya? Is he too sick to sign the constitution whose writing he supervised as president of the constituent congress? Maybe he is already dead and the Aprista leaders are covering up the fact in order to buy political time. Whatever the case, it seems clear that Haya de la Torre's days are limited. What is less clear is the effect Haya's death will have on the future of Peruvian politics. Luckily historians are not often called upon to predict the future, perhaps because we do so poorly at it.

I will be sorry to see Haya go. I remember distinctly our first meeting in the Casa del Pueblo, Apra's party headquarters. I had been in Peru for nearly a year, and after extensive research into primary and secondary materials, I found that there were still a number of open questions about the early years of Apra. Haya was the logical person to provide some answers. I cannot say that I went to see the man actually expecting to like him. Indeed, I had formed quite a negative opinion of the Aprista leader

xiii

while sifting through the sources on him and his party. And as I was issued into his presence that night in the Casa del Pueblo, I saw nothing to change my opinion. The party faithful that filled the building almost to overflowing seemed to regard him as a near deity, and I was frankly uneasy about such uniform and visible adulation.

In the following months I interviewed Haya de la Torre a number of times in the Quinta Mercedes, his large, villa-style house in Vitarte, a small town on the outskirts of Lima which, thankfully, was far from the noisy distractions of the Casa del Pueblo. I must admit that during those sessions I genuinely came to like the man and, more importantly, experienced at firsthand the enormous appeal of the Aprista leader. I was able to observe some of those elements that made up that intangible quality of "charisma" which had been central to Haya's long-term political success. I will not say that my analysis of Haya's political style is based on my personal impressions of his warm and affable manner, but I have no doubt that my understanding of the man and his popularity was increased by my extensive contacts with him.

But Haya de la Torre is only part of the story of the emergence of the masses and of their political "integration" in twentieth-century Peru. This book is the product of over two years of research in the libraries, archives, and streets of Lima. A major source of material for all aspects of the work was the extensive collection of newspapers, periodicals, political pamphlets, and secondary materials held by the Biblioteca Nacional del Perú. The Biblioteca's handbill and photographic holdings provided highly interesting information on both the Sánchezcerrista and Aprista movements. I spent many months working in the Biblioteca's Sala de Investigaciones Bibliográficas and owe a special debt of gratitude to the head of the Sala, Graciela Sánchez Cerro, for facilitating my access to the Biblioteca's fine collection in addition to providing interesting background on her uncle, Luis M. Sánchez Cerro.

The use of personal letters, memoranda, mementos, and photographs from the Archivo de Luis M. Sánchez Cerro, previously unavailable to scholars, enriched the chapters on Sánchezcerrismo. Pedro Ugarteche, who passed away shortly after I left Peru, made a particularly valuable contribution to this book by opening the Sánchez Cerro Archive to me. Materials consulted in the personal archive of Arturo Sabroso, who has also since died, plus the many hours spent with Sr. Sabroso discussing the early development of organized labor and Apra, contributed significantly to my discussion of those movements. Manuel Bustamante de la Fuente graciously permitted me to use his archive, which contains a fascinating series of personal letters and telegrams from prominent figures reflecting the response of the elites to the emergence of populism and providing important background information on the politics of 1930–31. The Archivo del Jurado Nacional de Elecciones was consulted extensively in the preparation of the chapter on the election. Architect and urban historian Juan Gunther, the possessor of probably the finest library in Peru on the history of Lima, patiently allowed me to work for nearly two months in his home and offered important insights into the problem of urban development and change. The private library of Félix Denegri Luna contains valuable material on a number of aspects relating to early-twentieth-century Peru.

After spending some months in Lima it became increasingly apparent that interviewing some of the prominent participants in the events of the 1920s and 1930s could illuminate various questions left unanswered in the printed and manuscript sources as well as add a human dimension to my study. I wish to thank the following individuals who devoted many hours of their valuable time to my seemingly endless questions: Víctor Raúl Haya de la Torre; Alfonso Llosa G. P.; Luis Alberto Sánchez; Arturo Sabroso; and Pedro Ugarteche. Interviews of working class participants in the Sánchezcerrismo and Aprismo movements were also highly productive, and my talks with them remain highpoints of my stay in Peru. I wish particularly to thank Alcides Carreño, Máximo Ortiz, and Próspero Pereyra.

Numerous other Peruvians contributed significantly to my work. During my initial twenty-one months in Peru I was affiliated with the Instituto de Estudios Peruanos, an independent research institute devoted to social science studies on contemporary Peru. The staff of the Instituto, particularly Julio Cotler, Giorgio Alberti, and José Matos Mar, provided invaluable critical analysis of various aspects of my research. Jorge Basadre, the dean of modern Peruvian historians, gave generously of his time and offered much fascinating information and encouragement.

Many scholars and friends in the United States have been extremely helpful at various stages of this work. I wish especially to thank Thomas Davies, Paul Drake, Henry Dietz, John J. Johnson, Robert Levine, Robert Slenes, John Wirth, and Gary Wynia. While those who aided me in my endeavors bear no responsibility for the views which follow, they share credit for any merits this book may have. Also deserving of thanks are Lydia Ostenson and Dianne McGann. Their painstaking editorial work was extremely helpful.

The original research for this work was made possible by a grant from the Foreign Area Fellowship Program. Additional study was supported by the Center for Latin American Studies at Stanford University and the Research Foundation of the State University of New York. All state-

ments and conclusions contained in this book are those of the author and
do not necessarily reflect the opinions of any of the above organizations.

Finally, I want to thank, above all, my wife, Pilar, who introduced me
to Peru and who provided a constant stimulus for the study of its history.
Her tireless help in all stages of this work from its first conception
through the typing of manuscripts to its final proofreading have been
invaluable. To her this book is dedicated.

S. S.

Lima, Peru
July 1979

Populism in Peru

1

Populism and Social Control

THE FUNDAMENTAL distinction between the twentieth century and preceding ones in the history of Latin America has been the growth of the popular masses in size, in importance, and as a potential threat to the status quo. National populations have expanded spectacularly, communications networks from roads to radio waves have begun to crisscross nations, bringing new awareness to formerly isolated peoples. Huge numbers of men, women, and children have streamed into Latin American cities, which in turn have become ringed with squatter settlements that have arisen to house the new arrivals.

With conditions of unremitting poverty for most of the new masses and in the face of social and economic inequalities seemingly as eternal as they are profound, many observers have reasoned that established structures and institutions would be subjected to intolerable pressures; some predicted that violent revolutions must soon engulf the whole of Latin America. When Fidel Castro took power in Cuba in 1959 and less than three years later defiantly identified his nation with Marxism-Leninism, his movement seemed only the first manifestation of a larger revolutionary process. Latin America's move to the left appeared inevitable; the outstanding issues were how far, how fast, and by what means?

Yet events subsequent to the inititation of the Cuban Revolution have negated these predictions. The "enforced stability" of countries like Chile, Argentina, Uruguay, Bolivia, and even Mexico has confirmed a rightward trend in Latin America, with nations ruled by socially conservative and politically authoritarian regimes. And, upon reexamination, even when authoritarianism has not come to the fore the expected buildup of popular pressures for revolutionary change has not occurred.

3

Major questions remain as to how societies essentially oppressive of large portions of their populations have survived intact in most countries, or why, in other words, Latin America's ferment has not boiled over into more far-reaching transformations. Why have genuine popular revolutions been the exception rather than the rule in contemporary Latin America? This extremely complex question has no easy answers. For most Latin American nations any approximation about the absence of expected popular disruptive activity would have to stress the various mechanisms of social control that have long helped maintain the status quo throughout the Continent.

With the upsurge of repressive governments in contemporary Latin America, physical repression clearly emerges as a major form of social control. At various times in Latin American history when groups and individuals have attempted to change existing structures or conditions they have been met with force. Repression has been exercised in many ways in modern Latin America, from the primitive *hacendado* who personally chastises "misbehaving" peons to the sophisticated military units trained in counter-insurgency and mob control who root out guerrilla bands or torture political prisoners. Despite the effectiveness of repression, to view Latin American countries historically as a series of armed camps is highly misleading. For mass social control, the general climate of fear created in all societies where extensive repression has taken place has proven more important than isolated repressive acts. When the powerful, whether individuals or governments, can and have shown that they will summarily punish signs of dissent from below, those with less power must think twice about manifesting or acting upon their dissatisfaction with the existing system.

By focusing on Latin America's present wave of political authoritarianism one might tend to exaggerate the long-term importance of physical coercion as a form of social control. At the same time that the high concentration of power in the hands of narrow elite groups has for centuries made varied forms of repression possible in Latin America, it has also helped spawn a system of patrimonial values and institutions that have strongly supported basic inequalities and worked to defuse mass protest. As an ideology originally produced by the semifeudal colonial systems of Spain and Portugal in America and continually buttressed by official and folk Catholicism, patrimonialism has stressed hierarchy and organicism. To the powerful it has taught charity; to the powerless, dependence on the charitable. As an extensive network of reciprocal patron-client relationships between actors of highly disparate power and status, patrimonialism has provided a framework for vertical personal dependence by offering concrete channels, commonly in the form of ceremonial kinship, through which working class men and women have "private" access to those above them. As an institutional framework for politics, patrimonialism has appeared in the form of party machines and corporatist governments in which elaborate patronage organs have exercised a seminal role in linking together the rulers and the ruled. In all its forms, patrimonialism has encouraged the popular masses to look upwards, to reject individual, group, or class protests of adverse conditions in favor of dependence on forces more powerful and influential than themselves for the amelioration of immediate or prolonged suffering.[1]

The pervasiveness of clientelism in all its forms is a palpable indication of the elites' inclination to rely on the more "benign" forms of social control except in times of perceived emergency. During this century at least, flexibility and/or the propensity to coopt has been the most characteristic elite response to potential challenges from new forces.[2] In 1930 the Brazilian Liberal Alliance leader Antonio Carlos Ribeiro de Andrada expressed in simple and direct terms the idea of flexible preemption of threats to the status quo with his classic slogan: "We must make the revolution before it is made by the people."[3] A prominent example of how the old order has carried out Antonio Carlos's dictum by bending to accommodate possible "dangerous elements" has been its cooptation of rising middle sectors. Viewed initially as the forces of modernity that might lead European-style bourgeois revolutions in Latin America, these groups have been successfully absorbed without upsetting the existing system. The absorption process has proceeded in various contexts. Forsaking the perpetuation of a closed aristocracy, upper class families have allowed and even encouraged social contact to the point of intermarriage with the "recently arrived," especially if there were some economic benefit in the bargain. Particularly in the depression years of the 1930s, when old agrarian fortunes were hard hit by the decline in export markets, the upper strata turned to middle sector individuals for the capital and expertise needed to diversify into new activities, notably industry. On another level, and counter to many early predictions, traditional elites have warmly supported the growth of modern states in Latin America, captained not by themselves but by the middle sectors. These enlarged public administrations have materially contributed to the maintenance of social peace, at least as far as middle groups are concerned, by providing an abundant source of employment for the growing numbers of ambitious graduates from secondary schools and universities. Also, by encouraging the development of governments led and staffed by nonelite individuals over which they nevertheless retain considerable control through their huge economic resources and their continued high social status, Latin America's upper classes have been able to give the middle sectors a sense of exercising power while continuing themselves to set the basic rules of the game.[4]

In twentieth-century Latin America the single institution that best demonstrates the interaction of the various elements for social control is populism. Urban-based populist movements were a conspicuous feature of Latin American political life between the 1930s and the 1960s to the point that this whole era of the Continent's development has been called "populist." As James Malloy has written, "in one manner or another all political forces from left to right have been forced to structure their behavior in response to the populist challenge. For good or ill, populism has, since its inception, been the major political force in Latin America."[5] To appreciate the impact of populism as a political force one need only enumerate some of the most prominent movements commonly labeled as populist: Peronismo in Argentina; the administrations of Getúlio Vargas and João Goulart in Brazil; the Cárdenas government in Mexico; Peru's Apra party, the regime of Manuel Odría and the Acción Popular party of Fernando Belaunde Terry; the presidencies of Arturo Alessandri, Jorge Ibañez, and Eduardo Frei in Chile; the Acción Democrática and COPEI parties of Venezuela; the followers of Jorge Eliezer Gaitán and Gustavo Rojas Pinilla in Colombia; and the brief regime of Juan Bosch in the Dominican Republic. The term continues to be applied to certain contemporary institutions, notably the Peruvian military government in the 1968–75 years.

One immediately distinguishing feature of populist movements is that they have arisen at times of profound discontinuities in the political and social systems of their respective countries. Populism constituted a political response to the severe structural crisis that accompanied Latin America's transition from a series of agriculturally centered export societies in the nineteenth century to the rapidly urbanizing, massifying societies of the twentieth century. That crisis contributed to the political bankruptcy of a traditional elite political system which seemed incapable of neutralizing large concentrations of working class people that had emerged in modernizing and increasingly complex nations.

In bridging the gap between orderly oligarchy and mass society, populist movements have constituted the principal political form of social control in modern Latin America. With their strikingly patrimonial style they have provided an effective political blend of the hierarchical, elitist modes of the past and the new currents of mass society. Easily outpacing and directly helping to undermine autonomous worker parties which sought to oppose lower class interests to those of other social classes, populists built vertical coalitions whose very *raison d' être* was the integration of the masses into national politics without greatly disrupting the existing system. Through the distribution of material and symbolic concessions by a group of highly charismatic, personalist leaders, these movements succeeded, for a time at least, in bringing ever larger numbers of lower class elements into politics while preventing them from "subverting" the process of national decision making. In the very act of providing a form of structured participation to working class people, populist movements have functioned as an institutional restraint to those sectors of society with the greatest potential for social explosion, converting them instead into a new base of support for an established system in crisis.[6]

Despite the continuous presence of populism in recent Latin American history, few movements have been the subject of extended analysis, and considerable confusion has arisen over an accepted definition of the phenomenon.[7] Existing literature on populism often contains contrasting, even contradictory arguments regarding the nature of populist movements. Some observers stress the extreme dependence of lower class groups on the higher class leaders of populist coalitions and the ad hoc, transitory nature of populist organization. Others affirm that populism has involved genuine political mobilization, pointing to the establishment of mass-based parties and unions and to a new sensitivity of populist decision makers to the needs of those below them. Still others combine both views in the same analysis. Given such a diversity of approaches, should the term *populism* be retained in the Latin American political vocabulary?

Before speculating on the existence or lack of a common populist tradition, new studies are needed on specific populist experiences. This book on the origins of populism in Peru is a response to that need. Populist parties appeared in Peru during the 1930s, a period considered to have been a major turning point in the country's history. More than the ravages of the Great Depression, it was populism's initiation of an era of mass politics that marked a definitive change in the course of modern Peruvian history. In the previous decade the capital city of Lima, more and more a powerful magnet for waves of rural migrants, had grown spectacularly; and the decline of the nation's traditional political elite seemed to keep pace with the expansion of the urban masses. These two critical developments merged in 1930 when the definitive political ouster of the last representative of the orderly oligarchy coincided with the emergence of Peru's first populist movements, Apra and Sánchezcerrismo. On the surface at least, each of these movements represents a distinct type of populism. Sánchezcerrismo, epitomized by the charisma of its dominant *caudillo*-like leader Luis M. Sánchez Cerro, stands as an archetypical example of the dependent variety. Apra, in contrast, emerging out of Peru's early union movement and led by one of Latin America's first politicians to preach social justice, Víctor Raúl Haya de la

Torre, seemed to exemplify the populism of mobilization and organization. By comparing these apparently diverse models of populism, this study suggests a new basis for assessing the validity of contrasting views of populism and of the whole populist construct. The book should also provide a useful framework for larger comparative studies of populism while offering new insights into modern Peruvian history.

Many of the most salient transformations of twentieth century Peru revolved around the fierce contest between Apra and Sánchezcerrismo for power in the 1931 presidential election. One of the parties involved, Apra, went on to become Latin America's first enduring populist movement. Although these mass organizations came to dominate the political stage in Peru before the most active years of populism elsewhere in Latin America, it is evident that they shared numerous traits with later populists. The study of the Peruvian case should, therefore, help illuminate the internal dynamics of the phenomenon throughout the area and begin to answer the seminal question of how these movements have bridged the gap of social discontinuity by introducing new forms of social control.

To place the detailed examination of the Peruvian case into the Latin American context, some preliminary defining of populism is desirable. The term *populism* is hardly limited to Latin America. In fact, it has become widely used as a classification for political movements in various parts of the world. In the study of populism two basic types stand out: the classical variety, exemplified by rural populism in the United States and socialist populism in Russia; and the third-world examples, most significantly communitarian populism in Africa and Latin American populism. Most of what has been written to date about the phenomenon deals with its classical forms. Hence, one sees populism defined along the lines of the following list of meanings:

> One was that populism was any kind of movement aiming at the redistribution of wealth regardless of how this was done. The second that it must be some movement of protest or social claims on the part of the lower masses. A third meaning was that it was a movement of protest of the rural classes in particular. A fourth meaning was that it was peasantist in character, according to the traditional pattern. The fifth that it aimed at the preservation of a rural way of life, not just at an improvement in the peasants' status. The sixth meaning was that it was some kind of idolization of the traditional peasant way of life.[8]

What is immediately evident about these definitions is that they widely miss the Latin American mark, particularly in their emphasis on the affirmation of the life-styles of rural small producers against the encroachments of bigness and centralization from the modern urban world. The same problem arises when trying to compare Latin American populism to the African brand, which elevates the tribal village to the status of ideal social model. Consequently, studies of North American, Russian, or even African populism, referring to areas at widely different stages of sociohistorical development, generally add little to the understanding of the phenomenon in Latin America. While one could attempt to fit the Latin American experience into the larger analytical category of populism by drawing parallels such as the movements' glorification of the simple people or their leadership by nonmass elements on behalf of the masses, such an exercise would probably confuse more than enlighten. As British sociologist Peter Worsely has perceived somewhat sarcastically, the tendency at one point to use the term too widely encouraged the belief that "populism was the biggest growth industry. It led everywhere. It was an exploding universe and it would continue to explode sideways unless the problem of conceptualization was tackled."[9]

Even within Latin America literal comparisons are difficult to draw between movements which have appeared in different contexts yet which are equally classified as populist. The prospects for mass recruitment by populists in post-World War II Peronist Argentina, for example, with its relatively high level of urban industrial employment were quite different from those that Apristas faced when they began seeking a following in post-World War I Peru, where only a minimal development of an industrial labor force had occurred. Mexico's or Bolivia's revolutions, which acted as preludes to populism, had no parallels in either Argentina or Peru. And the case of Brazil, where the foundation of populist institutions if not an actual movement under Getúlio Vargas in the 1930s seemed to predate rather than react to a social crisis, does not fit any of the above instances.

Given such diversity of circumstances, should the term *populism* be thrown out entirely as a proper classification for these movements? I think not, for at least three reasons. First, it has been commonly utilized both in and outside of Latin America to refer to movements like Peronism, Apra, the MNR, etc. Second, many of the disparities between populist experiences are attributable to the different historical contexts in which they emerge, that is, to the varying levels of national development or specific international economic and political conditions affecting single countries or Latin America as a whole. Third and most important, though these groupings are hardly identical, a number of basic commonalities exist among them. While a strict definition of populism in Latin America is risky as it surely would fail to contend with innumerable exceptions, a discussion of commonalities is a useful tool for understanding the movements' internal dynamics and their place in history as well as providing a start down the rocky road of conceptualization.[10]

Most Latin American populist movements have exhibited several common traits: (1) the formation of electoral coalitions of upper, middle, and lower social sectors with potentially conflicting interests; (2) the appearance of a popularly exalted leader figure capable of appealing to the emotions of large portions of the citizenry; (3) an overriding concern for gaining control of the existing state for power and patronage without envisioning a major reordering of society; and (4) the explicit rejection of the notion of class conflict with the advocacy instead of the creation of a corporate-style state to rule the national family hierarchically. Each of these populist parallels is worth discussing at greater length.

Latin American populist parties have developed mainly in large cities,[11] with their members drawn from all levels of the urban social pyramid. In terms of their composition, two sectors have habitually predominated: middle and upper middle class groups that have assumed leadership positions and working class groups that have formed a mass electoral base. In nearly all cases members of the middle sectors initiated the movements and then attracted the lower class contingent into them. From the standpoint of middle sector populists, the impetus to form such coalitions stemmed from a complex set of factors. As a general rule, they were individuals discontented with their circumstances. Perhaps they were *nouveaux riches* still to be accepted by the reigning social elite. Or they may have been the offspring of the wealthy families of old who had been unable to keep up with the changing conditions of dependent development and had consequently fallen into relative poverty. Then again, they may have been counted among the increasing numbers of highly educated individuals for whom the existing system had not expanded fast enough to offer an occupational status to fit their aspirations. For all of these men, politics offered a way of improving their circumstances. Perceiving that the working classes were increasing in size and importance, it became obvious to prospective middle sector leaders that the masses were the indispensable basis for political legitimacy, especially on the backdrop of the decline of traditional elite rule. Furthermore, there was a pervasive feeling on the part of both working and middle class groups that acting independently would be less effective than working in alliance. Finally, it was to the decided advantage of many of the more privileged strata to direct the masses' integration into politics rather than risk a buildup of popular political frustration that could lead to a "revolutionary" situation.

One of the most striking facets of populist movements is that they derived their real cement from the presence of a strong leader with whom people could identify above all in emotional terms. These leaders have generally built their appeal by effectively translating a series of positive individual traits into a personal political style. Many have been ideal *"macho"* types; strong, authoritative, *simpático*. Their special leadership qualities have often seemed to make them particularly effective guides in times of distress, men with an unusual practical talent to achieve concrete ends. Successful populist leaders have not spontaneously arisen by virtue of their "exceptional qualities." Nor has their ascendance rested on traditionalist legitimacy or hereditary claim. Rather they have been men who, more than others, have consciously exploited their personalities and their surroundings to build a special rapport with large segments of the population.

The relationship between the leader and his mass followers has been the key to understanding populist political dynamics in Latin America. The most striking feature of that relationship has been its personalism. The working class participant identified with his leader not in class or interest terms but as one individual to another, without institutional mediation. Most often assuming the role of protector along traditional patron-client lines, the leader was seen as a particularly benevolent man who *donated*[12] his help, often before it was asked, because he intimately understood the needs of the masses. He was perceived as a generous father figure who could capably direct the political affairs of his less sophisticated children. In large part, the success of the populist leader depended on his ability to extend this paternalistic relationship into the formation of a political movement. Or in other words, he used loyalty to and indentification with his person for the creation of a vertical political coalition able to incorporate individuals from diverse sectors and levels of society.

The tutelary nature of populist politics has severely limited the possibilities of autonomous mass participation. Entering into patently dependent relationships with their leaders, working class populists have remained essentially passive with regard to the administration of political power. It was expected that, allowed free rein, the leader would make the correct decisions on the basis of those special properties which qualified him for political leadership. The subordinate position of the working class populist suggests that at the same time these movements have contributed to the integration of specific sectors of the popular masses into the political system through their utilization of mass followings in the pursuit of power, they have also limited the impact of that integration by severely constricting the political activities of their followers to the realm of leadership support. Indeed, on a superficial level at least, many populist parties seem to have been simple conglomerations of the personal adherents of the leader figure. This support role has been especially visible on the occasions of mass demonstrations that have been a prominent characteristic of populist politics. At Perón's "17th of October" or Haya de la Torre's "Día de la Fraternidad," communication has flowed in a single direction, producing forms of adhesion as uncritical as they were fervent.[13]

In short, the tie between populist leader and masses constituted a dominant or "authority-dependency" relationship.[14] Under these conditions the leader committed himself to the satisfaction of a constellation of desires held by his constituents. But it was the leader who determined when, how, and to what extent those desires were to be fulfilled. In contrast, the dependent number of the populist coalition maintained an attitude of appealing for rather than demanding action. Whatever perceived or real benefits did accrue came not as the product of a sustained effort on the part of the troops but at the behest of the general. Some followers may not have agreed with their leader on every occasion, but all, by virtue of their perceptions of his extraordinary qualities, surrendered to him the power to formulate the objectives and strategies of their movement.

The goals of populist movements have been generally amorphous with the exception of the immediate and concrete enterprise of getting their leader into office. Once this goal was attained it was expected that the leader would employ his power, in a usually undefined way, to better the existence of his supporters. The role of the leader figure as the central uniting force of the populist movement implies that his political style may indeed have been more important than issue-oriented political platforms in the workings of populist politics. It follows that to understand populist dynamics one must concentrate more on the political symbols generated by the movement than on the stance a populist party might have taken on specific issues.

Where populist parties have elaborated explicit programs of action, they have seldom proposed a major transformation of economic and social structures. On the contrary, they have generally made little pretense of radically changing the shape or mixture of the existing social and economic pie, being content to seek a larger piece of that pie in order to provide top-down payoffs to their followings. Commonly in these movements the populist leader's appeal has revolved in part around his perceived ability to ameliorate the real discontents and grievances of his political clientele by distributing jobs, material rewards, and other payoffs. Whether this political clientelism resulted in any concrete redistribution of income by populist governments towards the popular sectors depended in large part on prevailing economic conditions. Juan Perón, for instance, was able to raise workers' real wages perceptibly during the first years of his presidency (1946–50) by dipping into the large surpluses generated by Argentina's wartime trade. When those surpluses ran out and the economy began to decline, the workers' real wages followed suit. In Mexico under Lázaro Cárdenas the picture was even more spotty, with rises and falls in real wages occurring throughout his administration.[15] More evident than any identifiable redistributive trend is that those changes in the status quo produced by populists in power have focused on the expansion of the administrative state, particularly its patronage mechanisms. In this respect populist governments have closely resembled the old political machines of large cities in the United States, stressing short-term, particularistic handouts and functioning as informal welfare agencies for their loyal supporters.[16]

The content of populist ideology distinctly reflects these movements' reluctance to come to grips with the kinds of social costs required in a program of substantial national restructuring. The supreme importance of the personalist leader has militated against the generation of ideology, "in the sense of codified, rationally elaborated systems of thought which illuminate the causes of man's problems and describe paths of action for remedying them."[17] Nevertheless, these movements have made more or less coherent statements of their beliefs about the nature of society and the basis of political action. The recurring theme of those statements has been the simultaneous rejection of class antagonisms and fostering of social collaboration, not surprising in the light of the multiclass composition of populist coalitions. Equating the concepts of people, family, and nation, populists have denied the existence of irremediable conflicts between the social classes that make up the citizenry. Since all "the people" belonged to the same family, differences, inequalities, and competition between groups were said to be outweighed by their common interests. All potential discord was to be eliminated, or at least smoothed over, by the emphasis on the fraternal and filial over the more conflictive prospects implied by workers versus owners, peasants versus landlords, or consumers versus producers. The unity of the family was provided by the Nation, a construct within which all groups could find mutual identification. In the context of Latin America's long-standing condition of dependency, the populists' insistence on national solidarity also accentuated the idea of class harmony as imperative for the defense of the fatherland against threats of domination by the world's more developed countries.

Thus far my analysis of the creation and political course of populism in Latin America has emphasized the seminal role of the leader figure in everything from recruitment to ideology. But the leader's preeminence cannot take away from the fact that without the existence of certain objective conditions populist movements would never have evolved so extensively. The presence of an organizable mass as a source of populist support and legitimacy was a first necessity for the emergence of populism. Historically in Latin America this populist following has appeared in major cities as a result of substantial discontinuities in social structure touched off by rapid urbanization. Some agrarian forms of populism have developed, as in the cases of Mexico and Bolivia, where national revolutions forced the incorporation of large population sectors from the interior. But it was mainly in the major cities that the process of intense rural-urban migration led to the compact massification necessary for populist mobilization. That same massification brought to bear growing pressures on traditional institutions whose resilience determined to a great extent the point at which populist movements eventually arose. When the closed elite political systems born in the nineteenth century found themselves in crisis, whether the result of a loss of internal cohesion or of their inability to handle the expanding masses—in most instances a combination of both—a power vacuum originated at the national level. The decline of traditional politics provided a point of entry for populist movements.

Social scientists have for years tended to downplay the role of political parties in Latin American development. And they appear correct in asserting that for many countries parties have had only a minimal impact on the basic facts of social and economic life. But it would seem that in their oft-stated disappointment with and consequent belittling of these institutions for failing to either advance the growth of democracy or affect significant change, many have ignored the enormous importance of some parties—perhaps more movements than parties—as effective elements of cooptation. In the region's expanding mass societies, where the process of cooptation can no longer proceed on an individual level, populist organizations have repeatedly taken the place of person-to-person clientage by creating clientelist systems, and in some cases clientelist states, to act as decisive conservatising agencies.

To summarize briefly, Latin American populist movements have been socially multiclass, structurally hierarchical and authoritarian, and ideologically nationalistic and semicorporatist. Their central dynamic has been the personalistic particularistic ties between powerful leaders and dependent followers. They have appeared in conjunction with large-scale social massification generally brought on by rapid urbanization. They replaced traditional political elites whose ability and legitimacy to rule had been seriously eroded by the social discontinuities attendant on the massification process. The primary impact of most populist movements in terms of political development has been to increase popular participation while at the same time directing it into paternalistic forms that have served to bolster an exploitative status quo. Hence, populism has been a major force throughout modern Latin America for the reduction of pressures on established social structures, for the management of potential and real conflict, and for the maintenance of passive, nonrevolutionary popular masses.

Many of the specific characteristics of individual populist movements have been influenced by the international context in which those movements arose, their political antedecents, and their social composition. In post-World War II Argentina, for instance, a rapid rate of industrialization and the existence of a large industrial working class encouraged Peronismo to favor import substitution industrialization as an economic and political response to the growth of the masses. Fifteen years earlier, in a largely preindustrial Peru with only a small industrial proletariat, industrialization was given relatively minor emphasis in the political programs of the two populist movements that vied for power. And in the Mexico of the 1930s, populist politicians faced the aftermath of what was in some areas of the country a peasant revolution by making agrarian reform a mainstay of their rule. Also, the final outcome of populism has depended on certain special conditions. When accepted by the powerful, populist movements have commonly promoted the political pacification outlined above. If, however, they have been repressed by inflexible ruling sectors, these movements have sometimes given rise to a greater radicalization of the working classes. This latter situation has been a particularly strong possibility in those countries where populist parties were dismantled after exercising some measure of political power. After Perón's ouster in 1955, the Peronista worker groups in Argentina moved increasingly leftward as their high expectations formed during the Perón presidency were ruthlessly quashed by successive military and civilian regimes. And in the Dominican Republic in 1965 the aroused followers of former populist President Juan Bosch battled U.S. Marines in the streets of Santo Domingo in the name of their exiled leader. But even in those cases where "radical populists" have gained office and wielded their power to alter positively the lot of the popular masses, those advances have often been short-lived. Achieved through the beneficence of paternalistic leaders as opposed to autonomous effort or within an institutional framework, working class populists generally have lacked the united resolve to preserve their attainments when the leader-figures departed the scene. A case in point is post-Cárdenas Mexico where government-sponsored unions for years have presided over a steady decline in the real wages of organized labor without significant protest. As Paul Drake has observed, populism "is likely to be more effective at mobilizing protests by the underprivileged than at securing their organized participation in national decision making or at delivering substantial benefits to them."[18]

My analysis of the emergence of Peruvian populism and the principal features governing its development is divided into three sections. The first, chapters 2–3, treats the conditions which facilitated the formation of populist movements in the Peru of the early 1930s. More specifically, chapter 2 closely traces the slow disintegration of the traditional political elite from 1903 through 1930, especially concentrating on how that process contributed to the creation of a power vacuum which opened the road for populism. Chapter 3 identifies those changes in urban social structure from the outbreak of World War I through the depression which contributed to the appearance of a politically mobilizable mass and to the crisis of the old order.

The second section, chapters 4–8, examines in depth the two populist movements, Aprismo and Sánchezcerrismo, which gained prominence in 1930. The focus is on questions of origins, composition, leadership, structure, and ideology. Placing particular emphasis on the way in which these movements integrated the masses into national politics, this section discusses working class responses to the political styles and appeals of populist leaders; the ways in which populist movements helped shape popular mass assumptions regarding the nature of the political system and their role in it; the means working class populists found most effective for gaining access to authority; and to what extent they felt able to influence decision making. The 1931 election signaled a decided watershed in Peruvian politics, and chapter 8 reviews this suffrage process in which for the first time the popular masses cast secret ballots for the direct election of a president under the supervision of an independent electoral bureaucracy. The chapter directly confronts the question of the degree of fraud in the 1931 process and presents a social analysis of voting patterns in Lima.

The final section, chapter 9, attempts to gauge the ultimate impact of populism on political and social change in twentieth-century Peru. After summarizing the chief innovations made by the populist movements, especially in terms of mass participation and the distribution and exercise of political power on the national level, it traces the persistence of populist modalities from the 1930s through Peru's present military government.

This book is first and foremost a detailed case study of two populist movements. It will serve not only to illuminate important facets of modern Peruvian history but also to help in the assessment of the shape and context of Latin American populism in general. A fundamental institution in the area's twentieth-century development, populism represents a subject ripe for further social scientific inquiry. While limited to the Peruvian experience, this work touches on wider issues of crisis and change present in a variety of third-world societies. By exploring the conditions underlying the political emergence of the masses and the mechanisms through which mass pressures on existing systems have been controlled and diffused, this work provides one important perspective on the course of lower class politics in developing nations.

2

The Desertion of the Elites

EARLY ON the morning of August 22, 1930, in the provincial city of Arequipa in Peru a little known army major, Luis M. Sánchez Cerro, aroused his troops and ordered them to march to an open field a short distance from their barracks. Once assembled, Sánchez Cerro, with a riding crop in one hand and a pistol in the other, exhorted the troops to join him in a revolt against the president of Peru, Augusto B. Leguía (1919–30). Greeted by almost unanimous cheers of approval, he ordered his men to take control of Arequipa with the assurance that all of them would soon be in Lima to celebrate the political funeral of Leguía. The rebels easily scattered weak resistance, and the revolt quickly spread throughout the southern part of the Republic. Three days later Leguía, president for eleven years, resigned and left the government palace, accompanied by a small group of faithful followers and relatives. The rebel forces claimed total victory, and Sánchez Cerro flew immediately to Lima to assume the duties of chief executive.

Most observers, regardless of their political preferences, sensed that with Leguía's flight and Sánchez Cerro's arrival in Lima, Peru was about to enter a new political era. Events in Peru seemed to fit into an international panorama of rapid political change, as during the same period established regimes were also overthrown in Spain, Bolivia, Argentina, the Dominican Republic, Guatemala, Panama, and Brazil. And while the changing of governments by military coup was hardly a new experience in Peruvian history, the establishment of political peace and order that had generally followed military *golpes* in the past appeared to contrast sharply with the uncertain conditions after Sánchez Cerro's rebellion in Arequipa. The backdrop of the Great Depression added an important economic dimension to the situation in 1930 that had been absent in most similar occurrences of previous years, but it was the particulary acute political chaos that most disturbed the majority of commentators: "Although it is painful for us to confirm it," wrote Peruvian Army General and future President Oscar Benavides, "unfortunately it appears as if a streak of ignorance, of madness, has invaded us, wresting from us our innermost feelings of nationality."[1] The political disorganization following the revolt in Arequipa produced a climate of fear and despair so intense that many predicted Peru's extinction as a nation-state. In this vein recognized conservative intellectual and politician Víctor Andrés Belaúnde lamented that "the very bases of our civilized life threaten to disappear."[2] Even some left-wing elements that might have welcomed a political crisis as an important element on the road to a social revolution cried with alarm, "the people move to and fro, confused and aimless, on the perilous precipice of a social order in decline, an order in a profound state of decomposition and decadence."[3] To Peruvians on various levels of the social and political spectrum, the political system may indeed have seemed the threatening monster pictured on a handbill widely distributed at the time (see figure 1).

Figure 1. "The Political Situation." From Archivo Sánchez Cerro (ASC), Lima, Peru.

The alarm expressed about the new political situation proceeded, to a large extent, from the visible increase in political activity among the working class elements of Peru's major city, Lima. From the very day of Leguía's ouster, working class groups in the capital played a perceptible part in public affairs. Beginning with mass demonstrations and rioting which resulted in the destruction of the residences of various prominent Leguiístas including that of the ex-president, the Lima working classes in succeeding months dominated the urban political scene. The use of the terms *"pueblo," "masas,"* and *"elementos populares"* ("people," "masses," and "popular elements") which had in previous years been largely absent from the political vocabulary, held prominent places in the speeches and writings of nearly all public figures in 1930–31. Aware of the newfound importance of the urban masses, Lima's major newspapers joined the trend by devoting increased attention to working class affairs and introducing special sections dealing with the problems of the laboring man. Clustered together in large numbers for the first time, the urban popular elements had become a clearly visible social and political force.

The mass political activity of 1930–31 contrasted sharply with previous decades when working classes had generally counted for little in the national political equation.[4] In the past they seemed most in evidence at times of religious processions and Independence Day celebrations. The popular elements had played a marginal role in certain elections, but even in those they were largely limited to roaming around the city as members of gangs hired by individual candidates seeking to make sure that the ballot boxes would declare the appropriate results.[5]

After Leguía's downfall, however, the urban masses were no longer regarded as a kind of innert substance to be used and discarded at will. The most concrete indication that they had indeed become interested in some new form of political participation was the dramatic appearance of two populist political movements formed around a pair of commanding personalities. Competing with one another in their efforts to capitalize on mass political mobilization were Luis M. Sánchez Cerro, the upstart army major who had overthrown Leguía, and Víctor Raúl Haya de la Torre, the young politician who was the founder of the Aprista movement. Popular sector groups responded to both of these men by demonstrating an enthusiasm unkown in past Peruvian politics. They formed committees, organized political clubs, printed and distributed propaganda, and filled public *plazas* nightly with demonstrations for their political favorites. And in the October 1931 presidential election the urban masses clearly took advantage of a new electoral law that eased enfranchisement and provided for the secret ballot to give the Sánchezcerrista and Aprista movements a virtual monopoly of national politics.

Not unexpectedly, individuals belonging to Peru's traditional elites were most alarmed by this first substantial massification of politics in Peruvian history. Perceiving that those whom politics had served in the past would suffer the most in the new order, they warmly recalled the times when the popular masses seemed to accept their lot with humble resignation, times when the able few could rule without pressure from below. The "old rhythms," the "dignified traditions" of the past—what had been politically familiar and reassuring to the elite sectors of Peruvian society—seemed to have been irrevocably lost in the uncontrollable "anarchy" of the present. Again, the words of Víctor Andrés Belaunde express this sense of loss, "The noble beings have disappeared, leaving a profound emptiness in the atmosphere."[6]

The strongly rooted legitimacy that Peru's traditional governing clique had enjoyed in previous decades seemed in 1930 to have been yanked from the political earth. Standing in the background of the pervasive mass presence, formerly dominant upper classes could not see anywhere an "acceptable" political group with the potential for effective leadership, and they who had once guided Peru's fortunes found themselves in most cases not only too weak to resume their traditional roles but also hesitant to demand any voice in public affairs. Viewing the decline of the internally divided and disorganized traditional political elite, Peruvian historian Jorge Basadre wrote in 1930: "People have spoken of the 'rebellion of the masses . . .' In Peru it would be more appropriate to speak of the rebellion or desertion of the elites."[7]

The traditional governing elites, on the defensive in 1930, had first gained political hegemony in the 1850s. In the initial postindependence years (1824–45), instead of being a unified nation, Peru, like most Latin American countries, was a series of regional societies connected superficially by a single colonial heritage. In the political sphere this period was characterized by contests for power between rival *caudillos* based in distinct regions who demonstrated a far greater interest in personal plunder than in any form of national government. Hard hit by the physical destruction and economic chaos of the independence wars, no single group of men, a region, or a city was able to claim effective administrative supremacy over the rest of the country for any length of time. The intra-elite conflict that *caudillo* warfare represented was hardly conducive to the kind of political consensus among the leading elements of society necessary for orderly upper class rule.

To a large extent events outside of the country's borders were responsible for the attenuation of this anarchic political situation. Since independence, Peru, as did most of Latin America, found itself with a depressed economy. Peru's privileged position in the Spanish imperial trade had been lost with the coming of independence, and no other nation had replaced Spain as an active buyer of exports or supplier of imports. By the mid-1840s, however, Great Britain, with the repeal of the Corn Laws, finally resolved to become the world's major industrial and commercial power, thereby bringing to fruition an ideology that had steadily gained influence since the publishing of Adam Smith's *Wealth of Nations* some seventy years earlier. Propounding an economic system referred to as the international division of labor Britain, and to a lesser extent other western European countries plus the United States, worked to establish a system of world trade in which they would supply manufactured goods in exchange for raw materials from less developed countries. The industrial nations of western Europe, they argued, would play their natural role as factory countries, while the nonindustrial areas of Europe and Latin America would play their natural and complimentary role as producers and providers of raw materials to fuel the industrial machine. An important contributing factor to this development was the radical improvement in the conditions of transoceanic shipping that the introduction of clipper ships and steam nagivation created. The most striking immediate result of this economic awakening was a notable increase in the European demand for Latin American exports.

In Peru increased European demand was reflected in the growth of an export economy based principally on the exploitation of guano. The abundant droppings of guano birds that lived on desert islands off the Peruvian coast had been accumulating for centuries into deposits hundreds of feet thick. With its high concentration of nitrogen, guano represented one of the most abundant supplies of high grade fertilizer known at the time. When Europe's renewed midcentury industrial push occasioned a visible decline in both labor and land devoted to food production, guano took on an ever greater importance as a fertilizer used to stimulate the productivity of European agriculture. Consequently, the demand for and price of Peruvian guano rose sharply, beginning in the 1840s. The spectacular growth of the guano trade meant an unprecedented economic boom for Peru. The possibilities for prosperity that accompanied the boom brought home to important sectors of the Peruvian elites the need for an ending of political conflict, instability, and regional disarticulation. The localistic and particularistic orientations of the old highland *latifundistas* rapidly gave way to the consolidationist views of the rising export sector. While bitter disagreements surfaced between individual members of the new elites about how guano production should be managed and financed, all appeared to agree that its exploitation was of primary importance and that without internal order such an enterprise was impossible. Important segments of the country's upper classes had found a common economic ground upon which to reach political agreement: the necessity for political order to achieve economic prosperity. At the same time revenues from the guano trade would provide the economic resources necessary for the formation of a national government.

Beginning in 1845 under the astute leadership of President Ramón Castilla, considered the founder of the Peruvian nation, powerful elements of the upper classes began to build a centrally administered state with an executive and a congress designed to represent the diverse interests within the elite. Peruvian governments for the first time had national budgets, and a relatively stable bureaucracy was created to administer public expenditures and to regulate at least marginally agriculture, mining, industry, and commerce. Particularly sensitive to the internal disorders of the postindependence period, Castilla channeled a large portion of guano profits into the creation of a national army to insure order and the establishment of a growing public bureaucracy to service his large personal clientele among the country's elite. Military strength and an effective patronage system were essential elements for the maintenance of stability by his and future regimes. Guano revenues also permitted Castilla and his successors to undertake the construction of numerous public works including port facilities, roads, and railroads which explicitly facilitated export economic growth as well as gaslight, water, and sanitation facilities in the major cities. Most important, the whole concept of government in Peru changed as radically as her economic prospects in the guano era. Castilla's actions and words revealed the basic transformation the state had undergone since the *caudillo* days: "Our military forces are not the instrument of tyranny or the enemies of society. . . Imbued with a sense of the importance of their noble destiny, they are the conservers of public tranquility, the custodians of external and internal peace, and the loyal defenders of the Constitution and the laws."[8]

In the decades following Castilla's second presidency (1856–62) the formula of an orderly oligarchical state under the political hegemony of a cohesive social and economic elite gained currency. The upper classes had gone about consolidating their position by employing part of their profits from the guano boom in the purchase of large coastal plantations devoted to export agriculture. These plantations not only provided them a more secure economic base than the increasingly erratic guano trade but also gave them a kind of territorial support for their political and social ambitions. In addition, Peru's orderly oligarchical families branched into banking and finance. During the 1860s they established the country's first banking institutions, thereby uniting commercial and financial capital under their control. In the latter part of the century they would further extend their activities to the mining sector, which had begun a rapid process of recuperation thanks to the infrastructural and technological advances of the time. The coastal elites' superior economic resources and their direct ties to a dynamic and expanding export economy provided them with sufficient power to extend their hegemony over the rest of the country through the strengthening of the central state. While their concept of the role of government was severely limited by their liberal economic view, which condemned administrative tampering with market forces that could make foreign commerce the dynamo of national development, they nevertheless relied on their control of the public administration to maintain their own economic and social supremacy. This group suffered a temporary erosion of its position during the war with Chile (1879–83); the economic and political chaos of the war and postwar years directly threatened their interests, and Peruvians blamed them for defeat at the hands of the Chileans. During a brief period the civilians who had governed before the hostilities were content to withdraw from politics and let the soldiers pick up the pieces of a shattered nation. But Peru's rapid economic recovery, beginning in 1890, permitted the reemergence of a united group of elite politicians determined to confirm decisively the political supremacy of their class. They successfully ousted the military from power in 1895 and initiated a period of relatively stable government referred to by historians as the *República aristocrática.*[9]

The *República aristocrática,* which lasted from 1895 through the 1920s, epitomized those "dignified traditions" that the elites remembered with such reverence in 1930. The administration of the state during this period was dominated by the members of a family-like group of upper class politicians who could claim membership in the social and economic as well as the political elites of the country. In control of the agrarian and commercial sectors of a preindustrial Peru, this group projected its influence over the rural and urban spheres of national life. Their economic power afforded them similar social preeminence, which in turn reinforced their access to and virtual monopoly over the mechanisms of national political rule. Their success at preserving at least superficial political stability and a high degree of consensus in their own ranks was the result of various interrelated factors: their common economic interests; their close personal ties through extended families and ceremonial kinship; their membership in the same prestigious social clubs such as Lima's Club Nacional; their direction of exclusive economic societies including the Sociedad Nacional Agraria (National Agrarian Society) and the Lima Chamber of Commerce; their control of banks and corporations through participation on interlocking directorates; their embracement of Europe for culture, style, and travel; their attendance at the same upper class churches; their education in the same upper class schools; and their relatively uniform views of the world.

These men were, in the words of one of them, the "elements of order and hard work who at the same time bring about the happiness and greatness of the people."[10] Similar to the elite governments of Julio Roca in Argentina, Federico Errázuriz in Chile, Rafael Reyes in Colombia, and Manoel Campos Sales of Brazil, the *República aristocrática* implied the rule of an oligarchy of men with a particular vocation for political affairs. Presidents and other high officials were chosen from their ranks with elections carried out mainly through networks of patron-client relationships linking the national and local levels. These networks not only provided the channels for formal political succession but also helped hold the system together by extending the influence of the elites to the local level.

The major features of national policy were as likely to be mapped out by this political elite in the elegant salons of the most exclusive social clubs as in the government palace or the Chamber of Deputies. Decisions concerning which individuals were to obtain political power and how that power was to be exercised were made within the confines of a relatively small directing council of the major political parties of the period. The size of these councils was aptly described by one prominent politician of the day who remarked that the total membership of any given political party in Peru could easily fit into one railroad coach. Mass participation in this system of manipulative formal democracy was limited to a minimum. The proponents of the *República aristocrática* rejected popular campaigns, arguing that any form of concurrence of the general public in government was unnecessary since paternalistic rulers could minister to their needs from above and furthermore that the rule of the people "would not be government but disorder."[11] The viability and legitimacy of such a system depended on the continued existence of a highly stratified society divided between the privileged few and the marginalized majority.

To the leaders of the *República aristocrática* there was a close relationship between political and economic power. In their eyes the duty of the state was to protect and reinforce existing economic privilege. Identifying politically and intellectually with European liberalism, they conceived of economic growth as the expansion of the export sectors to maintain a favorable balance of trade. They found few disadvantages in the fact that the control of the principal export products was in the hands of foreign interests and openly encouraged capitalists from abroad to exploit Peru's rich resources. In an era of expanding world trade and a growing demand for their country's exports, this group derived economic profit as well as intellectual satisfaction from the politics of laissez faire.

The career and words of Manuel Candamo, one of the most important spokesmen of this elitist political-economic system, are instructive in the understanding of the *República aristocrática*. Born into one of the richest families in the country, he worked as a young man for Lima's major newspaper, *El Comercio,* and spent time in the diplomatic service. Though Candamo was not himself a large landholder like most of the prominent politicians that surrounded him, he had strong connections to the planter elite through his presidency of the Anglo-Peruvian Bank and his activities on the boards of directors of various other important credit institutions that directly subsidized agriculture. Candamo began to take an active role in national politics as a member of the powerful Partido Civil. When he became president of his party in 1896, he jointly held the post of president of the Lima Chamber of Commerce, which represented the interests of the nation's most influential economic sectors. In 1903 he was elected president of Peru. Shortly after taking power he spoke to his old friends at the Chamber of Commerce and declared that in his view the objectives of the state and of the country's economic elites were one and the same:

> The new president of the republic will not profess different principles in matters of commercial freedom and privileges, nor will he view the relations between commerce and the exchequer with a different criterion than that which he held as president of the Chamber of Commerce . . . The well-being and prosperity of modern nations is connected to the development of their commerce, and, for Peru, the development of its foreign commerce is almost a vital necessity. To protect it is one of the most imperative obligations of the government, and you may be assured, gentlemen, that my government will do all that is possible in this sense. Besides its supreme economic importance, foreign commerce has been and will continue to be for Peru one of its most powerful mediums of civilization and culture . . . Believe me gentlemen that I express myself thus because thus I believe, because these are my profound convictions, and I ask you to accompany me in toasting to the prosperity of commerce and for the personal happiness of each one of the gentlemen present today.[12]

In many ways the model of the *República aristocrática* represented the renaissance of the governing style of the colonial period in Peru. Throughout much of the nineteenth century the nation's upper classes had waged war against *mestizo caudillos* in an attempt to consolidate anew the forms of political elitism which had prevailed under Spanish rule. The initiation of the *República aristocrática* seemed to be the final victory in that war. At last the descendants of the creole elite of 1810 and those who later had been absorbed by that elite held the most important posts in all sectors of government. The country was once again to be ruled by a strong executive with ample powers. Consolidation of the elites at the top would insure the exclusion from political participation of the propertyless and impoverished people at the bottom. And as in preindependence Peru, the care of the majority of the population – of the *gente sin razón* in the terms of colonial law – would be entrusted to a small segment of "philosopher kings" of European background. Government would again function politically under the same rules as the exclusive clubs that regulated the elites' social existence: a limited membership well represented with good names, an acknowledged hierarchy largely guaranteed against sudden shocks, dangerous ideas, unfamiliar experience, and discomforting change.[13]

The men that ruled this neocolonial model of government came from Peru's two major opposing political parties, the Partido Civil and the Partido Demócrata. The alliance of these two groups in 1895 to support the presidential candidacy of Nicolás de Piérola constituted the closest political consensus on the national level since independence. It had been achieved only by the successful setting aside of deep personal hatreds that had arisen between these two competing political movements since the guano era. From the Civilista side, prominent party leader Francisco Rosas provided the justification for an alliance with their Demócrata enemies. In a meeting of the party directorate he convinced his colleagues that "only a man who can ride a horse could be president of the Republic." He went on to argue that the only civilian he knew capable of filling the *caudillo* role was Nicolás de Piérola, the head of the Partido Demócrata. On his part Piérola justified an alliance with the Civilistas by saying simply that "without the Civilistas, it is impossible to govern."[14]

More basic to the formation of the Civilista-Demócrata coalition than the argument of Rosas or Piérola was the lack of profound discrepancies between the two organizations. As Piérola himself pointed out, "it would be very difficult to distinguish between the differences of the principles of the two parties."[15] The platforms of both groups advocated the same general principles, including the conservation of institutional order, the maintenance of civilian rule, dedication to the progress of the nation, insistence on respect for the law, a pledge to promote the alleviation of poverty, and a commitment to honest public administration. In short, they viewed the political role of the state as the protection of existing interests from potential elements of rural or urban dissidence – whether upstart *caudillos* or unruly mobs – and its economic role as the support of elite material progress. In basic agreement on social structure, political action, and economic development, the antagonism between them arose from competition over the exercise of political power, over which leader and which party would occupy the government palace.

Since these traditional groups were separated by their support of political personalities and not by their advocacy of distinct ideologies, alliances between them were made with relative ease. Government during the *República aristocrática* functioned as a kind of "traditionalistic, patrimonial clientage system"[16] in which rulers or ruling groups competed for power in order to favor their faction with political and administrative sinecures. Using the mechanisms of clientage in an era of economic expansion, the elites were able to minimize repressive actions by absorbing newcomers and potential competitors into their ranks. Under these conditions the role of political parties was to gain office in order to obtain a share of national political power; or in other words to obtain the most favors from the state for their particular oligarchical clan. Coalitions were possible to the extent that they were able to distribute political favors satisfactorily to their constituent groups.

Despite the basic elite consensus on laissez-faire economics, social privilege, and oligarchical politics that underlay the *República aristocrática,* the stability of this neocolonial government model was continually threatened. In fact, the system began to show signs of stress and disintegration almost as soon as it was inaugurated. The first threat to the ideal was the breakup of the Civilista-Demócrata coalition, which had constituted the cornerstone of the elite government edifice. The animosities between the parties, which had been placed aside in the coalition of 1895, began to reassert themselves during the first presidential administration of the *República aristocrática.* Although civilian rule began under the presidency of Demócrata Nicolás de Piérola (1895–99), the members of the rival Civilista party gradually took over the positions of influence in the national administration. Under the next president, Demócrata Eduardo López de Romaña (1899–1903), they succeeded in nearly monopolizing important political offices. In reaction to these events Piérola openly broke with his ex-allies in 1900, vowing to once again seek office in order to assist his party. But the Civilistas' effective control of the critical posts in the power structure, particularly the powerful Junta Electoral Nacional, reduced to a minimum Piérola's chances of making good on his promise of political resurgence. After the election of Civilista Manuel Candamo to the presidency in 1903, the history of Peruvian politics through 1919 was essentially the history of the Partido Civil.[17]

It could not be said that the supremacy per se of the Partido Civil truly damaged the prospects of elite rule in Peru. After all, the party was made up of men that belonged almost exclusively to Peru's highest social and economic classes. The richest and most prestigious elements of the Peruvian elites were Civilistas, including wealthy bankers and businessmen from Lima, the owners of the large sugar and cotton *haciendas* of the northern coastal area, most of the successful doctors and lawyers, the country's most influential newspaper editors – in sum, those people who had "done well" in life. The congregation of these economically and socially powerful elements under the single roof of the Partido Civil, combined with the political ascendancy of that party, should have assured the hegemony of the oligarchy in Peruvian politics for many years. Yet schisms which began to develop within the very confines of the Civilista governing elite, becoming increasingly serious after 1903, ultimately constituted an important factor in the eventual demise of the Partido Civil in 1919 and the decadent state in which traditional politics found itself in 1930.[18]

The first major crack in the edifice of the Partido Civil and consequently of the *República aristocrática* coincided with the initiation of Civilista dominance in national politics. It took the form of internal party conflict revolving around competition between two distinct generations of Civilista leaders for party control. The older generation, led by party president Isaac Alzamora, argued that their seniority in the Civilista movement qualified them for the job of leadership. On the other hand, the younger generation, with José Pardo, son of the first Civilista president Manuel Pardo, at the head, maintained that the infusion of youthful blood and ideas was necessary for the long-term regeneration of the Civilista movement. Ultimately the differences between these two sectors were reduced to who would control party affairs. Neither Pardo nor Alzamora envisioned any major changes in the party program.

When Candamo assumed the presidency in 1903 these two factions came into open conflict over the selection of his first cabinet. But party unity was seriously threatened only when Candamo's health failed and he died in May 1904. Manuel Candamo had been the Civilistas' most important unifying element; largely through his efforts the internal harmony of the Partido Civil had been forged in the first place. With his passing, conflict between old and young intensified, notwithstanding the insistence of both Alzamora and Pardo that they would not allow their differences to endanger Civilista hegemony.

The immediate problem generated by Candamo's death concerned who would represent the party in the coming election, called to fill the vacant office of the presidency. The "young Turks" immediately declared that their chief, José Pardo, should be the Civilista presidential choice. Claiming that the "old guard" had outlived their usefulness and controlled party politics long enough, Pardo's followers praised the "constructive" role their man had played in the Candamo government. The "old guard" meanwhile worked diligently for the elevation of party head Isaac Alzamora to the candidacy. One spokesman for Alzamora bitterly rejected Pardo's bid, declaring: "To back Mr. Pardo as a candidate to the presidency of the Republic is the most anti-political act that Civilismo

could commit and the most effective means of killing the party."[19] Most
Civilistas disagreed with the somber predictions from the Alzamora
camp, however, and made Pardo their choice. While this turn of events
meant a fall from leadership for the members of the "old guard," the
principle of party unity above all internal squabbles was strong enough
to prevent any formal division within the Civilista ranks. Alzamora's
followers could have formed a separate party to oppose the candidacy of
Pardo, or they might have joined with the rival Partido Demócrata. Instead, they eventually supported the election of Pardo at the insistence of
Alzamora himself, who did not wish to endanger in any way the political
supremacy of Civilismo.[20]

After his election Pardo was largely able to smooth over the generational conflict which had been stirred up by his candidacy. Indeed
Pardo's first presidential term (1904–8) was a time of almost unequaled
internal political peace within the governing party. The gravity of the
conflicts of 1903–4 should therefore not be exaggerated. Nevertheless,
the very existence of seemingly profound splits within the dominant
party of the period from the beginning of that party's rule cloud the ideal
image of the *República aristocrática* as an era of perfectly stable governments, free from turmoil of any kind. Only four years after these initial
problems the election of Augusto Leguía to the presidency would bring a
new series of internal conflicts which this time were not to be healed by
cries for "party unity above all."

When Leguía assumed the presidency in 1908 his administration
appeared at first glance to be a simple continuation of Civilista hegemony
along the lines that Pardo had established. Leguía had been Candamo's
Ministro de Hacienda, and after Candamo's death the defender of the
Pardo candidacy in the debates with the "old guard." Under Pardo he
was returned to the Ministerio de Hacienda and became the president's
top political advisor. During that time Leguía won his party's respect as
both an intelligent and energetic cabinet officer and a man who could be
counted on for his loyalty in party affairs.

In spite of these impressive credentials, not all Civilistas were satisfied
with Leguía's choice as presidential candidate. The more aristocratic
thinking and conservative members of the party, who took pride in calling attention to their "noble" lineages, objected to the elevation to the
highest post in the land of a "middle class upstart" who had gained prominence through his hard work and resourcefulness in the business world
rather than through the use of elite family ties. Furthermore, Leguía
himself never felt at ease in the company of this group and did not
hesitate to let his feelings be known.[21] Pardo's insistence on Leguía's candidacy, however, silenced the objections from these sectors, who not

only respected the president's authority in party decision making, but also felt that it was important to maintain party unity in the face of competition from the Demócratas. They clearly opted to accept Leguía rather than risk a return to power of their old political nemesis, Nicolás de Piérola.

After four years of Leguía rule most of those Civilistas that had supported his candidacy must have agreed with their originally skeptical colleagues that the medicine was probably worse than the illness it was supposed to cure. Stung by the insults of certain high-society-minded Civilistas, President Leguía from the first revealed not only his scorn for them but also his resolve to snub all forms of party control. Throughout his first four-year term the man who was supposed to reinforce Civilista political predominance through the establishment of a carbon copy of the Pardo regime ended up bitterly attacking most of the leaders of his own party. So strong was Leguía's attack that some individuals who had previously argued for the unity of the Civilista party above all other considerations came to fight the Leguía regime with every means at their disposal, thereby occasioning a profound and irreparable split in the Civilista ranks.

Leguía's progressive alienation of his fellow Civilistas began shortly after his election in 1908 when he passed over many prominent party leaders in the selection of his cabinet. One became a member of the cabinet, it seemed, on the basis of his personal loyalty to Leguía rather than in recognition of either his particular abilities or his good works in the name of Civilismo. The private grumblings of many Civilistas over Leguía's cabinet selections quickly turned to unconcealed wrath when the president, in what he called the spirit of "conciliation," ousted close friends of ex-President José Pardo from important government posts only to replace them with members of the opposition Partido Demócrata. While the political heresy of "conciliation" came to an abrupt end in 1909 when a group of ungrateful and overly impatient Demócratas revolted in an unsuccessful attempt to take power by force, Leguía continued to pursue policies unacceptable to the mainstream of Civilismo. The battle between the pro- and anti-Leguía factions shifted to the national Congress, where each group fought for dominance. Both sides became more and more rigid in their rejection of each other's policies, leading in 1911 to a move on the president's part to gain control of the legislature by openly interfering with the 1911 congressional elections. Leguía's Civilista opponents responded by uniting with two opposition parties to form a parliamentary coalition called the "Bloque."[22]

That the mainstream of Civilista leadership would make formal alliances with former political enemies for the purpose of fighting former political friends demonstrated how deep the divisions within the Partido Civil were becoming. Only three years after Leguía's inauguration the conflict between the president and his Civilista foes came to a head on July 13, 1911, when pro- and anti-Leguiísta groups clashed violently at the Chamber of Deputies building over the seating of new congressmen in the aftermath of the government-controlled election. These agitated incidents were the last straw for the anti-Leguiísta members of the Partido Civil. They formed themselves into a new body called the Partido Civil Independiente and severed all ties with the government. In their desperation to defend themselves against Leguía, they went to the extreme of making concerted efforts to gain the backing of their arch enemies, the Demócratas. In September of 1911, on the occasion of the imprisonment of a young Civilista leader, José de la Riva Agüero, Lima awoke with amazement to the cries of "Viva Piérola! Viva Pardo!"

The divisions within the Partido Civil which occurred during Leguía's first presidential term were of a much more serious nature than the generational fight of 1903–4. No longer were the participants in the dispute willing to sit down around a table and bury their differences in the name of party unity. One important parallel between the conflict of the Leguía period and the earlier generational division within Civilismo was that neither split centered on ideological, economic, or social differences between the two opposing sides. In both cases conflict revolved around which particular group within the Civilista elite was to hold political office. During the Leguía regime the president had attempted to elevate his own personal circle of friends to the top rungs of the administrative ladder while at the same time embarking on a series of highly unorthodox policies such as the conciliation with the Demócratas. It was Leguía's independence in his use of political power that particularly vexed the hierarchy of his party rather than any significant change in the social or economic direction of the nation.

The upshot of Leguía's actions was the substantial weakening of Civilismo as a political force. He had demonstrated that a government could rule not only without the support of the Partido Civil, but indeed with their opposition. As Manuel González Prada caustically wrote in 1914: "Thanks to Leguía, Civilismo stopped being the strong wood of construction, becoming converted instead into a weak and worm-eaten stick only good for throwing into the fire."[23]

The seriousness of the Civilista debacle became clearly evident in the events surrounding the election of a new president in 1912. Leguía placed his half-hearted support behind old line Civilista Antero Aspíllaga, who, as president of the Senate in 1911, had seconded the administration's attempts to control the Congress. The rest of the divided Civilistas, under the rubric of the Partido Civil Independiente, decided to back their former political enemy, Guillermo Billinghurst of the Partido Demó- crata. They based their decision on the belief that they lacked sufficient political power to launch a candidate from their own ranks and on their unwillingness to accept Aspíllaga, whom they accused of aiding Leguía to foster the division within the party. This choice was not an easy one for the Independent Civilistas, as Billinghurst had in the past shown himself to be an aggressive enemy of Civilismo. But in the face of Leguía's challenge, Billinghurst seemed the least dangerous alternative. Even ex-President Pardo instructed his followers from Paris to support the candidacy of Billinghurst. Lima's two leading newspapers, the Civilista *El Comercio* and the Demócrata *La Prensa,* which had fought each other for years over political questions, buried their differences and joined in the promotion of Billinghurst's candidacy.

On the eve of the election national politics was in a state of chaos. Seasoned observers commented that they could not remember having seen the political elites of the country so divided. Those who later decried the chaos of 1930 might well have looked back to 1912 for a preview of their situation. Although not nearly as grave as the conditions of elite disintegration in 1930, the apparent irreconcilable differences in 1912 between the former rulers of the *República aristocrática* also reflected the development of a power vacuum at the highest levels of national politics. And on the occasion of the 1912 election, as eighteen years hence, that vacuum was partially filled by the entry of the masses into the political scene. A kind of early populist, Billinghurst had begun to gain working class support on the basis of his sympathetic treatment of the urban poor during his tenure as mayor of Lima in 1909 and 1910. He reinforced that support during his campaign by making his symbol a low-priced large loaf of bread and threatened that an Aspíllaga victory would mean a smaller loaf at four times the price. Hearing rumors that the president's control of the electoral machinery would assure the election of Aspíllaga, the Billinghurst camp held a mass demonstration six days before the voting, both to show the popularity of the candidate and to convince the government that any tinkering with the suffrage mechanism would pro- voke a large-scale violent reaction on the part of the Lima proletariat. On election day groups of working class Billinghurst supporters roamed through the streets of the capital breaking up polling places and dispers- ing electoral officials. Their actions effectively prevented the voting from taking place, and the selection of a new president was thrown into the Congress, which proceeded to choose Billinghurst as the country's next first executive.

The popular masses' assertion of their political voice which contributed so visibly to Billinghurst's election proved to be a continuing feature of his presidency (1912–14). Without basically challenging the premises of elite rule, the new president portrayed himself as the friend of the working man in speeches and public acts. He intervened on the side of labor in various work disputes during his term, including the important longshoremen's strike of 1913. Lima's streets were often seen filled with working class demonstrators who, in their fervent and active support of the regime, disrupted the traditionally tranquil atmosphere of the city. Furthermore, not only did the president's working class followers exhibit open and often violent hostility toward his adversaries, but the masses, "ordinarily tranquil or at least respectful, well-mannered in their relations with other social classes," also acted aggressively "against all the so-called decent persons and those considered to be wealthy."[24]

Galled and frightened by this situation of "instability" and incipient conflict attributed to Billinghurst, the old governing class of the *República aristocrática,* which at first had accepted and even backed the new president, anxiously began to seek a new unity in the face of the "undesirable" turn of political events. When Billinghurst appeared to reaffirm his antielitist tendencies with a frontal attack on the National Congress, which was controlled by oligarchical elements, the members of the traditional ruling groups once again began to collaborate in order to curb tendencies that they considered dangerous to their very existence. Initially they criticized the "demagogical and personalist" Billinghurst from their seats in the Congress. With their verbal protests going unheeded and still weak from internal squabbling during the recent past, the elites soon began to seek aid from an outside party to oppose the president. They perceived that only the military boasted sufficient power to return the country to its "normal" course, and they decided to call upon the armed forces despite their long-standing distrust of that institution. As the president moved to dissolve the Congress, military forces under the command of then Colonel Oscar Benavides, with the support of a preponderant portion of the traditional elites, abruptly ended the Billinghurst regime. The masses, that had only one day earlier marched through Lima's streets cheering Billinghurst, offered no resistance. The country had been returned to an "orderly path." And the *República aristocrática's* most prominent politicians, in the words of one of them, had at least momentarily "reacted and unified in the face of the crisis of what are irremediable evils."[25]

In spite of fears voiced by many elite politicians, the Billinghurst experience did not mark the end of the *República aristocrática.* Considering the damage done to Civilismo during Leguía's presidency,

Billinghurst could not have been called a cause but rather a symptom of the disintegration of the political system. Indeed, it could be argued that by helping to create a troublesome situation to which the elites reacted by momentarily closing their ranks, the upstart president had actually infused new life into the *República aristocrática* and provided a stimulus to the maintenance of elite politics for at least one more presidential term. As one elite politician reflected: "In nations, as in individuals, when they suffer great perturbations in their life, there awakens within them, stronger than ever before, a deep desire for peace, for security, and for well-being."[26]

By supporting the 1914 military coup, elite politicians fought the symptoms of the disease which plagued their preferred political order. In the following year they attempted a more permanent cure by calling on the leaders of all of Peru's major political parties to join in proclaiming a single candidate for the presidential election of 1915. Obtaining support for this proposal was not an easy task. The divisions within the Partido Civil, which had been encouraged by Leguía, persisted through 1915. In that year one could count three major Civilista factions. After private deliberations in an attempt to agree upon a single candidate for the Partido Civil, they reluctantly admitted their failure. It appeared that the only workable solution was President Benavides's suggestion that the most influential of the country's politicians representing all existing factions call a formal convention to arrive at the choice of a candidate.

The so-called "Convención de Partidos" met in 1915, with former president José Pardo emerging on the third ballot as the agreed-upon candidate. The Civilista newspaper *El Comercio* voiced what must have been the feelings of most of the traditional elites in rejoicing at Pardo's nomination and praising the convention for having reached a degree of political consensus necessary for the avoidance of "uncultured" disturbances which might have otherwise accompanied the choice of a presidential candidate. The outcome of the convention, they maintained, showed that Peru had returned to the road of civic culture, political progress, and national accord and solidarity. They envisioned the nation entering a new era of tranquility and political consensus which they considered necessary to "reconstruct the national edifice so seriously damaged by those strong jolts that have disturbed it recently."[27]

Many times before opposing parties had entered into coalitions and formed at least temporary alliances. Every regime of the *República aristocrática* reflected in varying degrees these types of political agreements. But never before had the political elites held a public convention to choose a single presidential candidate. In 1912 those groups opposing Leguía had attempted a similar arrangement, but their efforts had stimulated little enthusiasm. Comparable efforts in subsequent years were also doomed to failure.

The 1915 "Convención de Partidos" had three specific conditions that augured for its success. First, it was called in response to the conditions of uncertainty created by the presidency of Billinghurst. Second, its sponsors could count on the presence of a relatively small and still cohesive group of elite politicians who collectively had the power to control national politics. And third, the political system did not yet have to face serious demands from the masses for increased political participation.[28]

After the nomination of Pardo, the elites readily turned their backs on the military, which they had utilized only to avert the immediate dangers of disorder posed by the Billinghurst regime. They put their trust in a known political quantity rather than seeking new men or new directions in elite rule. They remembered the "happy days" of Pardo's first presidency before the alteration of the rules of the elite political game by the ungrateful, personalistic policies of Leguía and by the quasi-populism of Billinghurst.

When José Pardo entered his second presidential term, prominent Civilistas expressed the hope that his prestige and his name would serve to heal old wounds and quiet personal hatreds, thereby bringing about a return to the hegemony of their party in national politics. But seemingly insensitive to the strong undercurrents of division within the *República aristocrática* that had been barely covered over by the Convention of 1915, Pardo emulated the policies of the Civilista nemesis Leguía by imposing the rule of men particularly loyal to his person in party and national affairs. The unity momentarily achieved at the 1915 convention had been lost by 1917, and the Partido Civil found itself divided into four warring factions. A handbill distributed in Lima on the occasion of Pardo's birthday in February 1919 demonstrated the extent of the president's failure to reconstruct the elite political model represented by the *República aristocrática*. According to its author, the Civilistas had anticipated that on the heels of the 1915 convention "there would arise, above the remains of the old fatherland of our elders, a new phoenix, the grand nationality united once again, briming over with force. . . ." But "the much desired unification of the Peruvian family" had not occurred. The author concluded with the lament that "division kills us."[29] Pardo also found himself alienated from potential middle and working class supporters who saw their economic circumstances deteriorating in the midst of wartime prosperity due to rapid inflation and a depreciated currency. No longer the "young Turk" of 1904, Pardo brought few innovations to elite poltics during his second term and failed to achieve the elite political unity that he and his followers had so ardently desired. By the time he left office, public confidence in Civilismo had all but disappeared.

If the disappearance of a strong and united Partido Civil was largely responsible for the disintegration of the *República aristocrática,* also important in the process was the weakness of other elite political groups that might have saved the traditional system. The party that appeared to have the best possibility to take over the reins of government from the declining Civilistas was the Partido Demócrata. Unlike the Partido Civil, which produced a series of prominent leaders over the years, the Partido Demócrata was composed of the followers of one man, the civilian *caudillo* Nicolás de Piérola. In a real sense the Partido Demócrata was Piérola and the admirers of Piérola. As their leader aged and was progressivly excluded from political power by the ruling Civilistas, the Partido Demócrata had declined in importance from the high point of 1895–1903. By controlling the electoral machinery, the Partido Civil was able systematically to curtail the influence of the Partido Demócrata. First they thwarted all of Piérola's attempts at the presidency and then consistently reduced the number of Demócrata congressmen until by 1910 the Demócratas had disappeared almost entirely from the country's legislative body. When in 1912 Piérola broke with party cohort and former friend Guillermo Billinghurst over his presidential candidacy, the future of Demócrata politics appeared sealed. One observer of the period remarked: "The presidency of Billinghurst was in reality the political death of Piérola."[30] Piérola's physical death came a year later, and with it the Partido Demócrata virtually disappeared from the scene of Peruvian politics. The party died with its leader.

Both of the other major parties of the *República aristocrática* had also depended for their existence essentially on the political acts and style of their respective leader figures. The Partido Constitucional had formed around the figure of one of Peru's most prominent military heroes, Andrés Avelino Cáceres. And, as in the case of Piérola, the problems of an aging leader combined with the Civilista dominance of national politics seriously limited the Constitucionalistas' potential for becoming an important political force or for even maintaining the influence they had gained by use of Cáceres's heroic image. The weakest political organization of the *República aristocrática* was the Partido Liberal, led by its own civilian *caudillo,* Augusto Durand. Along with most of those who would later be his supporters, Durand had fought with Piérola in 1895 against the military rule of Cáceres. Originally members of the Partido Demócrata, they broke off from that group in 1899 and thereafter never exhibited the sufficient strength to supersede their status of junior partner in various coalition governments during the *República aristocrática.*[31]

One final group which might have succeeded the internally disrupted Civilista party into a position of political prominence was the Partido Nacional Democrático. Led by intellectual José de la Riva Agüero, this organization was made up mainly of younger Civilistas who were dissatisfied with their status within their own party and to a lesser extent by prominent Demócratas who saw little political value in continuing their ties with the aging Piérola. While the Nacional Democrático leadership contained some of the most talented intellects in the country, the party never achieved political success. The high command of the party found itself rebuked by both Leguiísta and anti-Leguiísta Civilistas as well as by the majority of the Partido Demócrata and finally gave up the political battle, recognizing that intellectual prowess was no substitute for the political savvy of their more seasoned opponents. Instead of laying the groundwork for a possible Civilista resurgence, the Nacional Democráticos' actions only served further to disturb the internal unity of the Partido Civil.[32]

In an important sense the inability of the younger generation of Civilistas to take over the political reins later abdicated by their elders doomed to failure attempts at a future regeneration of Civilismo. That failure constituted a significant expression of the frank process of disintegration of traditional politics under the *República aristocrática* mold. The once omnipotent Partido Civil had been reduced to a club of elderly oligarchs that had lost their political prestige and were barely able to hold on to the last vestiges of a "glorious" past. The Partido Demócrata had died with its leader, Nicolás de Piérola. The Nacional Democráticos resembled more a society of scholars than an entity dedicated to political action. The Constitucionalistas appeared to be an association of tired war veterans who had tried without success to transplant their military successes of yesteryear into the field of politics. The Liberals had never shown any vitality. Thus, on the eve of the 1919 election, all these elite political parties were in a state of near collapse. They resembled the imposing colonial houses still owned by many of their most prominent members; impressive façades that hid aging structures beset by internal decay.[33]

The definitive decline of traditional elite rule occurred on a backdrop of augmented social and economic stresses arising from the effects of World War I on Peru. Coinciding with the first years of the *República aristocrática* Peru had begun to experience a significant increment in its involvement in the international economy, with new British and American investments the rule of the day. Foreign capital had flowed particularly into Peruvian export agriculture, mining, and petroleum.

The coming of World War I and the opening of the Panama Canal in 1914 increased demands for Peruvian exports beyond the expectations of even the most optimistic observers. During the war years the nation's elites expanded to include new wealth, particularly in the urban commerce sector, while established landed fortunes grew apace. World War I also marked the growth of new industry, the dramatic intensification of organized labor protest, and the beginnings of the massification of urban society that would characterize the decade of the 1920s.

Both the greater integration of the country into the world market system and increasing social pressures at home brought Peru the need to modernize the state's administrative machinery. It was during this period that Peruvian public administration took the form of a so-called "service state" dedicated to "fostering institutional and material change through governmental action."[34] The growth of the export economy, with the attendant rise in tax revenues, helped stimulate a visible increase in the size of the public bureaucracy, particularly after 1918. New governmental departments were established to administer agriculture, statistics, labor, Indian affairs, mines and petroleum, communications, and immigration. The number of public employees needed to man this enlarged and more complex system jumped spectacularly from 975 in 1920 to 6,285 in 1931, an increase of 544.6 percent. Government expenditures for the maintenance of the expanded state apparatus grew steadily, nearly tripling between 1919 and 1929.[35]

In part, the decline of the traditional politicians was tied to their unwillingness and apparent inability to adapt themselves to the requirements of administrative modernization resulting from the country's growing commercial export activities and the profound social changes occurring in both urban and rural areas. Indeed, the *República aristocrática* was designed more with an eye to upholding established interests than to responding effectively to changes in economic, social, and political conditions. While flexibility, particularly in the opening of their ranks to upwardly mobile individuals, had been a hallmark of elite behavior and a major ingredient in their resiliency over the years, they failed to make the political transition demanded by the new economic and social orders. The model of a dynamic state apparatus staffed by men sensitive to the daily fluctuations of the international economy and the internal society was distasteful to the rulers of the *República aristocrática*. In previous years the governing elite had found public administration to be a relatively uncomplicated affair. Without serious protests they had limited access to government to a group of like-minded friends. Their job had consisted for the most part in granting favors to *latifundistas* and businessmen whose major worry seemed to be to assure themselves a fixed income. But by 1919 these relatively uncomplicated times seemed over; it was the moment of more dynamic sectors, of a new political elite made up of "modern men," of financiers rather than aristocrats, of social engineers rather than politicians of privilege. The preparation and attitudes of the old leaders seemed irrelevant in a setting of increased international ties and rapid social change. Under these circumstances, traditional leaders found themselves no longer able to claim a useful or legitimate role in the national political system.

Within the oligarchy new divisions began to appear between those closely linked to the tradition of Civilista political rule and those who pushed for the modernization of the state to allow Peru to take greater advantage of its new and augmented foreign commerce. The conflict between the two groups focused on the 1919 presidential election. Under the leadership of José Pardo, old-line Civilistas who continued to grasp at the remnants of *República aristocrática* rule forwarded the candidacy of Antero Aspíllaga, a wealthy coastal landholder who had been Leguía's unsuccessful presidential choice in 1912. The more "modern-minded" members of Peru's elites, accompanied by the discontented members of the masses and by the fledgling middle sectors, overwhelmingly rejected Aspíllaga and threw their support behind the opposition candidacy of former president Augusto Leguía. They saw in Leguía a political heretic of sorts who, operating outside of the structures of traditional parties, had the best chance of firmly guiding Peru into the modern world.

Leguía seemed particularly well suited to the role of modernizer with his extensive background in world trade, his ties during his business career with various foreign companies, and his reputation as an expert financier gained as Ministro de Hacienda to Candamo and Pardo. Under his guidance, according to his supporters, Peru would be a *"Patria Nueva"* characterized by the politics of pragmatism as opposed to the inflexible and highly conservative rule of *"doctores"* and dilettante theoreticians.[36]

Leguía's political style reinforced his image as a modern man able to deal with modern problems. Asked to describe his technique of government, Leguía replied on one occasion:

> Out of necessity, as Cabinet Minister in 1903 and President in 1908, I had to meditate many times about what exactly is the art of government and about what is the best way to govern Peru. My meditations convinced me of the uselessness of the theoretical systems that use logic to organize powers and establish functions on the dead leaves of a book without being attentive to their applicability to real life, as is the case of certain constructions designed by architects that ignore the superior laws of balance. The problem of government, in its philosophical aspect, consists of adapting authority to the geographical, technical, and sociological conditions of a people.[37]

·During the campaign of 1919 he assured the citizenry that he would stimulate the creation of a strong state to promote national prosperity, foster rapid economic growth, especially in the export sectors, by forging closer ties with the outside world, and open the interior to the fruits of this new economic progress through massive road- and railroad-building projects. The promise of development and prosperity must have held a special appeal to many who saw their privileges potentially threatened by the heightened labor and university protests during the first months of 1919. As election day approached the public mind was filled with the image of Leguía ending wartime economic instability and fulfilling the hopes raised by Peru's new role on the international trade scene; he was, in sum, the man destined "to save the nation."[38]

Plagued by internal discord and a candidate unacceptable to the majority of their own party, there was little doubt that the Civilistas faced certain defeat at the ballot box. But fearing that his enemies were prepared to take extraordinary measures to keep him from the presidency, Leguía decided to take power by force and plotted a military *golpe* in his favor before the votes were counted. Within a year of taking office he initiated a series of repressive moves against Civilismo that lasted throughout his three successive presidential terms (1919–30). The regime sent out a constant stream of anti-Civilista rhetoric in speeches by pro-Leguía politicians and through the government-controlled press. On the president's authority the police forcibly broke up meetings of opposition parties. Government-instigated mobs assaulted anti-Leguía newspapers and set fire to the homes of prominent Civilista politicians. Without making formal accusations or carrying out judicial proceedings, the administration exiled potential troublemakers and major political figures who publicly criticized the executive. Silencing most and deporting those whom he could not tolerate, Leguía successfully dispersed Peru's traditional ruling class both politically and geographically. Those members of that class that remained in the country desisted almost entirely from overt political acts which might have been judged subversive. Under these conditions the Civilistas as well as the other traditional parties were unable to continue even publishing their programs much less resisting the regime in an active or organized way.

Leguía had various reasons for pursuing his harassment policy against the rulers of yesteryear. He had based a considerable part of his campaign propaganda on the issue of ending Civilista rule. During his presidency he continually attacked the Partido Civil and its major leaders as a means of maintaining his own popularity. Leguía's energetic stand against Peru's traditional rulers also emerged from his fear that, allowed free rein, they might successfully conspire to overthrow him. These fears were probably groundless given the weakness of the Civilismo after 1919, but Leguía could not have failed to look back to his first presidency, during which various plots were hatched against him, one of which in May of 1909 was almost successful. The president considered the repetition of an ouster attempt a real possibility and believed his attack on Civilismo to be a necessary precaution. He was reported as having said to an aide, "They will only trap the cat once."[39] In a more formal but no less frank statement, Leguía summarized the reasons for his repressive stance, declaring in a 1928 interview: "Up to the time I took power the country had been governed by an oligarchy, imbued with absurd prejudices dating from colonial times. It was essential to dispose of these positions of privilege which had endured for so many years. Despite the fact that public opinion favored the new regime, such men did not conform, and their attempts to change the order were numerous. It was difficult to govern under these conditions."[40]

Leguía's virulent attacks on the traditional parties of the *República aristocrática* earned for him the reputation of having destroyed them. According to one prominent Civilista leader, the president's actions caused the "inactivity of the Party, converted later into cataplexia, and finally produced the death of the organization."[41] In a similar vein the cartoon in figure 2 shows Leguía delivering a funeral oration before the recently erected tombs of various of those parties. Given, however, the debilitated state in which he found these institutions at the initiation of his rule, he only administered the *coup de grace* to a dying political order.

While Leguía's suppression of elite political privilege helped reduce the traditional parties to a state of inactivity, he did not mount similar attacks on the social and economic privileges of the nation's upper classes. They were for the most part excluded from the *Patria Nueva*'s bountiful patronage handouts, but neither their property nor their fortunes were threatened. The new Leguiísta elite of businessmen, bankers, and landowners found it unnecessary to challenge established wealth; they made their way by simply garnering a piece of the growing economic pie. Even the headquarters of traditional upper class social prestige, the Club Nacional, remained largely inviolate during the *oncenio* (Leguía's eleven-year rule), as the new Leguiísta leaders tended to become members of the Club de la Unión, an organization of decidedly lesser stature.[42] Indeed during his presidency Leguía explicitly allowed the nation's economic oligarchs to thrive, especially those connected to the expanding export sector. By thus demonstrating to this group that they could not only maintain but actually improve their economic positions without the aid of a Civilista government, the president threw new earth on the grave of the *República aristocrática*. Under Leguía the oligarchy came to the realization, perhaps for the first time, that economic hegemony was not inexorably tied to traditional political hegemony, and therefore they concurred that Civilismo had ceased to fulfill its function as the agent of oligarchical dominance. Such a realization would also make them more open to the alternative form of government represented by populism in the 1930s and afterward. Indeed the elites' malleability in giving the reins of government to nonelite, mass-based movements marks an interesting contrast to their oft-repeated refusal since World War I to guide directly a process of conservative modernization.

Figure 2. The Funeral of Traditional Politics. From *Mundial* 4, no. 181 (November 2, 1923): unpaged.

The economic hardships posed by the depression served to strengthen the resolve of the elites to desist from supporting outmoded politicians and political organizations. Among those sectors hardest hit by the economic crisis were the sugar and cotton *hacienda* owners, who saw their international markets evaporate, mining interests, and groups involved in international commerce and finance. Precisely the elements which had in the past invested in traditional politics, they now pulled in their belts in reaction to the real or perceived straits of the depression and argued publicly for an end to "superfluous" spending. One wealthy *hacendado* with financial and industrial interests proposed, for example, "austerity of life, austerity in all aspects, in all orders, using all possible means to achieve it. . . ."[43] At least in the initial period following the overthrow of Leguía in August 1930, a sharp restriction on elite investment in politics was one of the areas directly affected by the insistence on austerity.

"Where do the dead go, Lord, where do . . . the cadavers of those that were political parties in Peru go?" So questioned one journalist as he surveyed the political scene five months after the revolt in Arequipa in 1930.[44] With the disappearance of Leguía those parties which he opposed did not automatically reorganize. Men who had expected that the end of the "tyranny" would bring a return to the politics of the *República aristocrática* were sorely disappointed by the events following the demise of the Leguía regime. The internal divisions since 1903 and the various periods of official repression culminating with the politics of the *oncenio* had resulted in the extinction of the Partido Civil, the cornerstone of traditional politics. Moreover, the increasing evidence that Peru's oligarchical rulers were unable to deal with the demands of administrative modernization and the emergence of middle and working class groups on the social and political scene called into serious question the viability of the *República aristocrática* as a model of effective government.

The idea that it was unrealistic to hope for a revival of the traditional political system, much less of the Partido Civil, was one shared by friends as well as enemies of that system. Only three weeks after the end of the *oncenio* two of Civilismo's most prominent leaders, José Matías Manzanilla and Manuel Vicente Villarán, publicly concurred that the Partido Civil was dead, that it "pertains to the past and new parties should emerge with political, economic, and social programs based on democratic and human renewal which can inspire confidence in the country."[45] Those who would attempt to revive it, in the words of the Civilistas themselves, would be undertaking an absurd and quixotic enterprise. Aristocratic politician José de la Riva Agüero summarized the futility of promoting the resurgence of a political system which seemed to belong to the past: "It seems to me both irrational and childish to try to revive the traditional parties of the late nineteenth and early twentieth centuries . . . Although I have a historical bent, I do not share these illusions of an antique dealer."[46]

An additional ingredient in the pessimism about the political future of Peru's traditional ruling elites was the recognition that public hostility toward that group had greatly increased over the years. Although the voice of Leguía, the single individual most responsible for the increasing hostility, had been stilled, the end of his rule marked no letup in the opposition to the politicians connected to the *República aristocrática*. Given the joy with which Leguía's downfall was greeted, it might have been expected that his most long-standing political foes would have been received as heroes rather than being condemned as useless old men. But Leguía's anti-Civilista rhetoric had made sense to many who were resentful of the political limitations of the *República aristocrática*. Furthermore, Civilismo had suffered a tremendous loss of prestige as a result of its inability effectively to oppose Leguía during the *oncenio*. Many Civilistas could and did maintain that they deserved respect for having constantly fought the regime, suffering prison and deportation for their efforts. But exile in a European capital such as Paris or London had aspects of luxury and the good life that considerably deflated claims to political martyrdom. When these politicians returned from abroad and it was rumored that they would attempt to regain their former political positions, a formidable reaction occurred. They were openly vilified at public demonstrations, in street corner discussions, in newspaper editorials, and in numerous political cartoons. As example of this harsh treatment is the cartoon in figure 3 which displays three undernourished and unattractive showgirls that represent the three strongest traditional political parties in the process of being violently repudiated by a loudly screaming public. Waiting in the wings are the populist parties that will soon take over the stage.[47]

In the face of the antagonism that they encountered, traditional politicians, not only as groups but also as individuals, desisted from making any claims to re-initiate their participation in government and quietly withdrew from politics. Surprisingly few took an active part in the overthrow of Leguía, nor did they hold posts in the subsequent administration of Sánchez Cerro. They left both areas almost exclusively to the military. Instead of politics the overriding concern of most former party leaders appeared to be putting their own personal affairs in order after having suffered the rigors of political repression during the *oncenio*. While the upper classes as a whole prospered under Leguía, the most prominent members of the traditional political elite had been the targets of the regime's dictatorial policies. For eleven years these individuals had been on the political defensive. Many had also suffered professionally and economically. Upon returning from prison or exile, their main concern was the recovery of their jobs and their re-entry into the Peruvian upper class community. As José Matías Manzanilla, a man who under other circumstances would have been a logical Civilista presidential candidate, said in 1930:

> All of us who have suffered, not only in our own lives but also for Peru, should dedicate ourselves at this time to take advantage of the return to normal conditions and the restitution of personal guarantees and improve our professional circumstances . . . Furthermore, in this moment for Peru, I think that we must suspend the reorganization of the parties . . . For now let us enthusiastically support the government junta.[48]

The inability on the one hand, and the reticence on the other, of traditional politicians to assume the leadership of the new state contributed substantially to the creation of a power vacuum after the downfall of Leguía. Also significant in this regard was the gradual loss of power that all political institutions, with the exception of the presidency, had experienced during the *oncenio*. Since the initiation of republican rule in Peru, both the legislature and the judiciary had been subordinated to the

Figure 3. "The Reappearance of an Old Company." From *El hombre de la calle* 1, no. 2 (September 27, 1930): 5.

executive branch. Congress in particular had functioned more as a clearing house for presidential patronage and as a rubber stamp for official policy than as a legislative body. But during the *oncenio* public faith in the prerogatives and abilities of the parliament and the courts reached a new low. Laws and judicial decisions were arrived at openly in the government palace. Congressmen and judges dedicated their activities to making flattering remarks about the president. They outdid each other in their competition for Leguía's favor, which could result in jobs for their friends and economic benefits for their own pockets. Indeed a majority of them had themselves obtained their positions in return for political favors tendered to the regime. By 1930 their situation had deteriorated to such an extent that the parliamentary and judicial branches could claim little legitimacy and less public respect as exercisers of political power. Local government suffered a similar loss of power during the *oncenio*. The departmental and provincial councils and municipal elections that had contributed in the past to a modicum of local autonomy were suspended by the regime; the selection of all local officials took place in the capital.[49]

Leguía's extremely personalistic rule during his *Patria Nueva* only exacerbated the impotence of the traditional political elites and of other branches of government. During the *oncenio* one-man rule had reached heights reminiscent of Bolívar's "Presidency for Life" of 1825–26. After taking power by force in 1919, Leguía justified his two successive reelections with the argument that only his presence made the state function. And this affirmation must have seemed highly accurate to many who saw during the *oncenio* the clear development of an identification between the government and the personality of the president, between the nation and the man. Leguía himself sarcastically summed up the omnipotence gained during his eleven-year presidency as he renounced his office in the face of the military coup of 1930 with the words: "If they believe that the Country can proceed without me, they can have it."[50]

During his government Leguía made only half-hearted attempts to institutionalize his personalism through the creation of a formal party mechanism. While fostering the formation of a Leguiísta political organization called the Partido Democrático Reformista, he never transferred to it substantial power. During the *oncenio* it became clear that the very existence of the party depended upon the personal stature and political influence of Leguía, its self-stated *"jefe nato"* ("born chief"). Insofar as Leguía attempted to create a base of support for his politics, he concentrated his efforts on the recruitment of individuals whose worth could be measured by the degree of their loyalty and subservience to him. He had attempted a similar enterprise during his first presidential term, but at that time his success was blunted in some measure by the oppo-

sition of the still powerful Civilistas. During his second, third, and
fourth terms, the absence of opposition made it easy for the president to
fill the ranks of public administration with personal friends.

After Leguía's ouster the populace rejected all claims of the ex-
president's "morally corrupt" and never particularly powerful former
supporters to a continuing role in politics. Moreover, the new regime
created a special tribunal to investigate the political and economic dealings of the most highly placed Leguiístas. Harrassed by new president
Sánchez Cerro and having in many cases squandered personal fortunes
made during the *oncenio,* this group lacked the potential to attenuate the
power vacuum of 1930. In short, when he vacated the government palace
in August, Leguía left a clean political slate for the later emergence of
populist parties.[51]

Direct government by a limited and identifiable oligarchy has occurred
few times in Peruvian history. Most historians have pointed to the
República aristocrática as the most successful example of stable elite rule
in the country's past. But even the *República aristrocrática* was hardly a
period of unruffled elite political hegemony. From its very initiation, internal party fissures — the product of a lack of cohesion among political
leaders who frequently refused to place loyalty to the system above their
personal ambitions — produced periodic crises. The absence of unifying
party principles and growing unwillingness among the men at the top to
compromise revealed an underlying flaw in the whole conception of the
República aristocrática. And finally, the deliberate attempts of one man,
Augusto Leguía, to create his own support base at the expense of traditional politics contributed to the creation of a serious impasse for the first
time in 1912, a development which foreshadowed a similar phenomenon
in 1930.[52]

3

Enter the Masses

IN BOTH 1912 and 1930 the urban popular masses emerged to play an important role in national politics. The political eruption of the working classes was facilitated in part because the traditional elites, fully preoccupied with their own internal battles, failed to notice any significant change in the balance of political power. In their first experience with "popular participation" during the Billinghurst period, the elites awoke in time to the "threat" of the masses, glossed over their differences, and called in the military to save the system from any immediate danger. They then institutionalized their momentary solidarity in the party convention of 1915. Fifteen years later the elites again welcomed military intervention as an effective defense against the "menace" from below. But in 1930, unlike 1914, the traditional governing class had lost the manipulative ability, internal unity, and self-confidence necessary to replace a military *junta* with their own convention-type formula. Neither were they strong enough to prevent a shift in politics from a family-style government run by political aristocrats and based on highly limited participation to one of populism, which sought an enlarged power base in the lower sectors of society. Traditional politicians, the mention of whose names in another day might have elicited an almost superstitious respect from the populace, found themselves without prestige and looked upon with indifference if not hostility. Under these circumstances, a return to the solutions of 1912 seemed beyond the realm of the possible. No bourgeois or mass revolution had toppled the *ancien régime*. To a large extent it finally fell in 1930 because for some time it had been only a shell of its former self.

An equally important factor which prevented a rebirth of elite

dominance along the lines of the 1915 convention was the development
which the urban masses had undergone in the intervening years. In part,
upper class politicians had been able to regain leadership positions after
the overthrow of Billinghurst because of the relative weakness of his
mass base. By 1930, the working classes were not so easily isolated from
politics. As the cartoon in figure 4 shows, in 1930–31 it was perceived
that the masses had replaced the so-called cardboard politicians of yesteryear in the center of the political scene.

Figure 4. The Unsuccessful Political Resurrection. From *Libertad,* December 1, 1930, p. 1.

Contemporary observers advanced various explanations for the sudden emergence of the popular elements after the downfall of Leguía.
Some affirmed that the masses had been anxiously awaiting the end of the
"tyranny" to express political attitudes which they had repressed during
Leguía's regime. Others cited the destructions of traditional political institutions by the ex-president as the major cause for the mass eruption.
Still another group explained that the entry of the working classes into
national politics simply reflected a trend toward democratic government
throughout the world. They asserted that a democratic demonstration effect had filtered into Peru and stimulated increased mass participation.[1]

By failing to account for the significant changes in urban social structure from 1915 to 1930, all of these explanations ignore the most fundamental factors in the emergence of popular politics. Most important,
during that period Lima underwent dramatic growth. In the eleven years

from the beginning of Leguía's government in 1920 to the emergence of mass politics in 1931, the city's population jumped 68 percent from 223,807 to 376,097, far outstripping the demographic expansion of preceding decades and of the 1930s. In the twelve-year interval between the 1908 and 1920 censuses, for example, Lima's total population rose only 29.4 percent from 172,927 to 223,807, while between 1931 and 1940 it grew 53 percent, reaching 577,070.[2] The significance of the population increase during the *oncenio* relative to the evolution of previous years is graphically demonstrated in chart 1.

Forces at work in the world outside of Peru were largely responsible for the demographic and attendant social-structural changes in the capital city. During the nineteenth century Peru, along with large areas of Latin America, Asia, and Africa, was incorporated into the economic orbit of the world's more developed nations, a process which led to far-reaching changes in social and political life. Responding to the demands of European and North American industrial economies, these regions of what is presently called the third world began building export economic structures to supply the so-called factory countries with primary products in return for manufactured goods. In Peru the initial stages of this development came in the guano era from 1840 to 1880; it continued into the twentieth century with the emphasis changing to agricultural and some mineral exports. The sudden strengthening of the export economic thrust, which came with World War I, constituted the first major development in the evolution toward eventual mass political mobilization. The demand for Peruvian products jumped sharply after 1915; and during the war the country's links to the international market system multiplied. Simultaneously, the Panama Canal was opened, shortening the distance betwen Peruvian producers and prospective buyers. Now Peru was firmly anchored on the world's trade routes. While the rate of development hardly rivaled the growth of certain other Latin American economies during this period — Argentina and Brazil most notably — the export sectors took advantage of what was in the Peruvian context a true boom to extend their activities and take an even more prominent role in the national economy.[3]

Indicative of the new importance that was assigned to the role of Peruvian trade in the world market was the expansion in the number of production units and the amount of land under cultivation in the agricultural export sector. In the case of sugar production, for example, the number of plantations rose by over 30 percent between 1914 and 1919 from 89 to 117; the total number of hectares in production climbed some 20 percent from 202,086 to 248,390. Cotton underwent an even more spectacular expansion. The sum total of landholdings jumped 300 per-

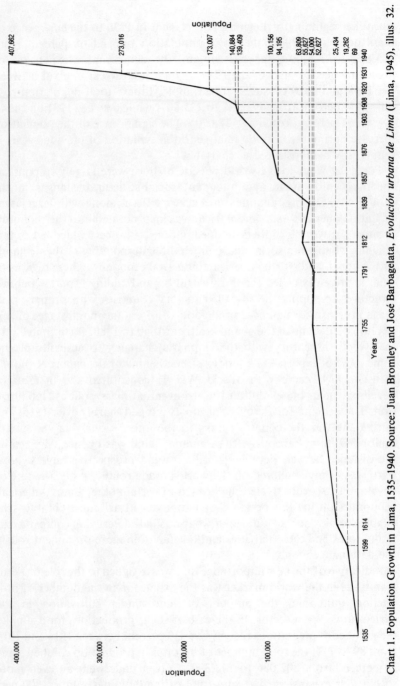

Chart 1. Population Growth in Lima, 1535–1940. Source: Juan Bromley and José Barbagelata, *Evolución urbana de Lima* (Lima, 1945), illus. 32.

52

cent from 226 in 1915–16 to 674 in 1917–18; in the same period hectares
in cotton rose nearly 60 percent, from 55,635 to 88,863.[4]

At the same time that the more dynamic sectors of Peru's economic
elites pushed for the expansion and transformation of national production to meet the increased demand from foreign markets, they looked
abroad for the capital and technology they considered essential to continued rapid growth. Traditionally Peru had depended upon Great Britain as its major market, investor, and supplier. But the wartime
difficulties faced by the British merchant marine due to German sub-
marine attacks plus the capital drain experienced by Great Britain and
other European belligerents resulted in the rapid rise of the United States
to a dominant position in Peru's—and generally Latin America's—
foreign trade. The strengthening of trade ties between Peru and the
United States in turn brought a substantial expansion of American
capital investment. In short, the general accentuation of the American
presence in Peru, particularly in the agricultural export and mining sectors, served to reinforce the movement of the South American republic
towards greater dependence on the developed world.[5]

The intensification of American participation in the Peruvian economy
reached new heights during the 1920s. Peru's dynamic economic elites,
awakened to the promise of rapid economic growth resulting from increased links to the United States, pressed for their country to continue
to take full advantage of the new relationship. The most powerful
representative of this thinking was the president of Peru, Augusto
Leguía. Placing foreign-sponsored economic development at the top of
his priorities during his eleven-year regime from 1919 to 1930, Leguía
made an all-out effort to attract trade, capital, loans, and technology
from abroad by offering extremely favorable terms. As he declared to
The West Coast Leader, the newspaper that represented foreign business
interests in Lima, "during my administration foreign capital will be given
facilities and opportunities for the development of Peruvian resources
which have never heretofore been accorded and which may never be accorded again."[6] Noting that foreign capitalists sought a tranquil
economic and political climate for their investment, Leguía tried to
create stable conditions in Peru by repressing all real or potential
troublemakers. His most extreme attempts to attract investors ranged
from the lavish entertainment of important American businessmen and
diplomats to the establishment of the fourth of July as a Peruvian national holiday in honor of the United States.

A further indication of Leguía's "Yankeephilism" was his recruitment
of United States citizens to head numerous governmental offices. During
his regime North Americans were placed in charge of the customs service
and the tax bureau, directed the Department of Education and the Cen-

tral Reserve Bank, and played a major role in training naval and aviation corps officers. "My hope," Leguía affirmed at one point, "is to put an American in charge of every branch of our Government's activities." And it appears that he nearly accomplished this feat.[7]

Stimulus for American invesment in Peru did not come from Peru alone. In the United States as well the 1920s were times of considerable interest in overseas economic ventures. Victory in World War I had led to an increased sense of importance for America in the affairs of the rest of the world. In the 1920s that sense was transformed from the wartime provision of arms to the peacetime provision of dollars. Now it was American businessmen and bankers who would lead an international offensive. Various factors encouraged these groups to extend their foreign activities. During the war the United States had responded to increased demand for its products in Europe by greatly expanding production in both the agricultural and manufacturing sectors. After the end of the hostilities, businessmen feared that large surpluses would clog the American market and force a hard and costly adjustment for the economy. Most economic experts agreed that foreign investment could solve the problem by enlarging markets for United States products overseas. For their part, formerly reserved bankers and financiers virtually begged foreigners to utilize their credit facilities in order to stimulate a "healthy" outward movement of capital. Besides the general belief that there was a quick profit to be made, investors were encouraged by the American government to place large amounts of their capital in foreign areas. Herbert Hoover remarked in 1928 that "we must find a profitable market for our surpluses." And in the same year John Foster Dulles declared: "We must finance our exports by loaning foreigners the where-with-all to pay for them."[8] America was the richest nation on the globe and would, therefore, as President Warren G. Harding had earlier said, "go on to the peaceful commercial conquest of the world."[9] Also, anxious to discourage revolutions and to defend against threats from political and ideological competitors, American policy makers pushed for the expansion of the nation's economic power as an antidote to dangerous instability abroad.

In the case of Peru, extensive United States investment led to the creation of something of an American economic empire, although British capital continued to be important in the overall economic picture and even German investments remained after World War I, playing the dominant foreign role in sugar production. New United States capital entered Peru in various forms. Private banks loaned large amounts of money to the Peruvian government mainly for the financing of extensive public works built, for the most part, by United States contractors. The American-owned Cerro de Pasco Copper Corporation invested heavily in the mining sector, while the London and Pacific Petroleum Company, a subsidiary of Standard Oil, came into control of most of Peru's oil production. In agriculture, W. R. Grace Company was the largest United States investor with its giant sugar complexes at Paramonga and Cartavio.

Peru's increased integration with the developed world which accompanied the growth of foreign investments had profound and long-lasting effects on the nation's economic and social structure. One particularly visible consequence of expanded foreign investment and wider Peruvian participation in world trade was the rapid urbanization and modernization of the country's capital city, Lima, and its adjacent port, Callao. From the colonial period power had been urban-based in Peru, and with the rise in the nineteenth-century export economy Lima's primacy increased further. The city grew as a commercial-bureaucratic center to service the export economy and regulate national affairs. Large supplies of imported manufactured goods financed by exports flowed into Peru, and Lima benefited substantially by serving as a distribution center for the trade. The city also rose in size and importance in this period because it was able to appropriate much of the government revenue derived from export and import taxes. With the advent of World War I, and as mining and export agricultural production in the interior attained augmented economic importance, Lima was forced to expand at a still higher rate in order to carry out efficiently its role as an intermediary between rural producers and foreign markets. The commercial, banking, service, and industrial establishments which grew in response to the new demands on the nation's export economy located their offices in Lima. For reasons of practicality and pride the capital city could no longer be, in the slightly exaggerated terms of one observer, a "dirty, miserable little hamlet . . . without water, without light, without pavement; a sad leftover of what was colonial grandeur."[10] In the eyes of the Leguía regime a new Peru that would proudly face the outside world must boast a capital with wide boulevards, beautiful parks, modern public buildings and elegant shops and hotels. Furthermore, Lima must make itself particularly attractive during the centennials of Peru's independence in 1921 and 1924 when particular attention from abroad would be focused on the nation. Individuals closely tied to the president, anxious to gain economically as well as politically under the regime, enthusiastically supported urban construction enterprises in which they held a major share.[11]

The combination of these factors led to the transformation of Lima during Leguía's eleven-year rule, the so-called *oncenio,* into a modern city. The noise of construction machinery dominated the urban atmosphere. The American-based Foundation Company laid an extensive network of asphalt streets and avenues to handle the increasing quantities of newly imported motor vehicles. Several of these new avenues led to the modern suburbs which grew up on the edges of traditional downtown Lima. As the city spread outward, the leading families, many of whom in the past had clung to colonial mansions, abandoned their old homes for palatial residences in the outlying areas. Individuals with political influence and economic resources competed hotly for the quick profits to be made in the building of upper and middle class housing. Although working class living areas generally deteriorated during this period, parts of the older sections of the city directly benefited from the construction boom. Twelve new plazas, scores of stone and cement buildings with bronze and marble decorations, and extensive public recreation facilities were built to grace the old colonial center. The main shopping streets were cleaned up and the sanitation system renovated. The government directly encouraged urbanization by enacting laws explicitly favorable to the construction industry and by itself engaging in the acquisition of large amounts of foreign credit to promote public works. In the space of eleven years the face of Lima had changed more completely than at any time in the preceding century, and the city became known as one of the most modern and beautiful capitals in South America.[12]

Closely related to the urbanization of the *oncenio* was a substantial increase in the flow of rural migrants to Lima. In large part the dramatic numerical growth of the city's working class was the result of this migration process. One indicator of the importance of migration for urban growth is that by 1931 nearly 40 percent of the capital's population originated from the provinces. The movement of peoples from the interior to the capital city was not a new phenomenon in Peru. The instability of the country's independence struggle had early stimulated geographic mobility. Particularly after the political consolidation of the 1850s with the attendant growth of government bureaucracy and elite educational institutions in Lima, the offspring of provincial upper and middle sectors traveled to the capital to take advantage of its relatively wide range of political and cultural possibilities. By the turn of the century a railroad connected Lima to the mining center of La Oroya, thus opening the central Sierra[13] as a source of migration, and the Juliaca-Cuzco Railroad made it possible for people from the heavily populated Department of Cuzco to reach the capital by journeying to Mollendo and from there to Callao by steamship. While clearly noticeable, these early migrations were, however, a mere trickle compared to the flood of the 1920s. As well as showing an enormous increase in intensity of movement, that decade marked a visible change in the social composition of the migrant population, with working class people substantially outnumbering those from upper and middle strata.[14]

As Leguía built up Lima and further concentrated economic and political power there, the popular refrain, "Peru is Lima," appeared increasingly accurate. To the inhabitants of the interior, Lima represented a vibrating and exciting urban center. Life in the countryside seemed drab and monotonous by comparison. Peruvian novelist and anthropologist José María Arguedas, who himself grew up in a small rural town, described well the desire to see the modernized and beautified capital city which ran through extensive parts of the interior:

> To arrive in Lima, to see, even for one day, the government palace, the stores, the cars that hurtled down the streets, the trolley cars that made the earth tremble, and afterwards to return home! This was the greatest aspiration of all the people from Lucanas . . . It was to Lima that the headmen drove all the hundreds of calves that had been fattened in the valleys; it was to Lima that the hundreds of pounds of wool went after having been collected from the bleak highland plateaus by the peons, driven on by the whip and the gun; it was for Lima that the herds of mules went from the mines of Papacha don Cristián. From Lima came the packages of fine cigars, the yardgoods that filled the windows of the local shopkeepers; from Lima came steel cooking pots, sugar, porcelain plates and jars, bottles, colored ribbons, sweets, dynamite, matches . . .[15]

Relatives of the people who lived in the provinces wrote or returned with stories about the great progress of the capital, of the marvels to be seen there, of Don Augusto Leguía's great works. To the arriving migrant Lima was no longer the dusty and decaying provincial city of the past. Now everything was concrete and steel; in the bustling capital every day was like attending a fair.[16]

Rural migrants were attracted to Lima not only by its external glitter but also by the increased economic opportunities offered by a rapidly burgeoning urban center. While the Leguía regime and private capitalists poured millions of dollars into new construction, legions of *provincianos* left their homes to fill the ranks of workers engaged in building the new ministries, luxurious homes, and elegant avenues that graced the city. The majority of those migrants who sought better economic opportunities in Lima saw their expectations fulfilled. Despite substandard living conditions in Lima, the *provincianos* generally had little trouble in finding jobs which in most cases paid them at least twice as much as they had earned in the countryside, and they experienced a substantial rise in their general standard of living. The following statement of one man who migrated during the *oncenio* summarizes well the various facets of the Capital's magnetism for the *provinciano:* "I came to Lima in the year of 1921, because there were greater opportunities to work and to learn. The ambition to see Lima, the Capital. There was the grand Paseo Colón. You felt, Ah! Lima! The Paseo Colón! Many fellows came as I did. There were more opportunities in Lima, above all in construction work."[17]

While a modernized Lima attracted thousands of migrants, other factors were also at work in inducing people from the interior to move to the capital city. And, as in the case of increased urbanization, these factors also largely resulted from Peru's increased dependence on the developed world. Rushing to meet the augmented demands for its exports during World War I and afterwards, the country found itself slowed by the lack of an adequate communications network. If Peru was to enrich itself by exploiting its mineral and agricultural raw materials for the world market, it would have to forge infrastructural links between the urban commercial groups and the export production areas of the interior. Upon assuming the presidency, Leguía surveyed a country with tremendous geographical barriers between coastal deserts and Andean heights. The entrepreneur-minded first executive also noted that, with the exception of the mining-linked railroads of the late nineteenth century, previous administrations had done little to surmount the difficulties of transportation between rural and urban areas. In response to Peru's infrastructural deficiencies, Leguía made highway construction a top priority of his regime. He proclaimed October Fifth the "Day of the Road," and in many of his speeches equated national progress with the development of an internal communications network. In his address on one such Day of the Road, Leguía stated: "Yes, my fellow citizens; the campaign for roads is the crusade for the great Peru of tomorrow. He who fails to support it is a traitor to the splendid future of the fatherland. . . the Incas carried civilization from Cuzco to every corner of their vast empire on those stupendous roads whose vestiges we still admire today."[18]

During the *oncenio* Leguía's roads were extended to the hinterlands and with them went the "Western civilization" of the new international empire—of the new Incas. The government completed substantial stretches of two parallel highways that were projected to run the length of the country on the coast and through the Andes. At the same time penetration roads were built to join specific port cities with interior mountain towns. In eleven years the regime more than doubled the extension of the country's roads. From 1926 to 1930 alone the length of roads in use jumped from 10,643 kilometers to 19,465 kilometers.[19]

Encouraged verbally and materially by the Leguía government, a road building fever swept through the interior of the country. In the northern, central, and southern Andes the inhabitants of whole towns held meetings in the main *plazas* to plan cooperative road construction projects. In his novel *Yawar fiesta* José María Arguedas presents a fascinating description of one such meeting:

But in the month of January of 192[?] . . . the news arrived in Puquio that in Coracora, capital of Paranicochas, the whole population had held a meeting.

That the priest had spoken in Quechua and then in Spanish, and that everyone had agreed to open a highway to the port of Chala in order to travel to Lima in five days and to show the people of Puquio that they were better men. The work would begin in March. Indians, *cholos,* and tenants became angry in Puquio . . . "People of Puquio opening street in great mountain, just like butter! . . ." The last Sunday in April the great *ayllu* [Indian communal organization], Pichk'achuri, commissioned its chiefs to go and talk to the Vicar. They wanted him to give a sermon about the Coracoras, that the four *ayllus* wanted to open a highway road to Nazca to arrive to "la mar k'ocha" [the Pacific Ocean] in one day, and so that the vehicles of the foreigner, the trucks, would belch their smoke and rumble in the streets of Puquio. The Vicar accepted . . . He said his whole sermon in Quechua, the Vicar did. The Indians stood up, even the women stood up . . . When the Vicar said that the men of Puquio could, if they agreed to it, make a tunnel from within the mountains up to the sands of the Coast, the sixteen headmen could not contain their happiness: "of course, *tayta* [revered one]! Of course!" they exclaimed . . . The tenants and the authorities filed out of the church, and they shouted in the square, they cheered Puquio and the four *ayllus.*[20]

After agreeing to build a stretch of highway, telegrams were sent to Lima confirming the decision. In return the government often sent engineers, money, and equipment. Interior settlements and *hacienda* owners frequently fought over the routes of the new roads in their attempts to insure that they would directly benefit their particular interests. As a result, many roads twisted and turned for miles in order to pass through a maximum number of *haciendas.*

The roads which were originally built to open the hinterlands to commercial exploitation also permitted the diffusion of new cultural norms in many areas of rural Peru. Numerous small Sierra towns and Indian communities that formerly had lived in isolation from the European-based coastal civilization now became aware of the outside world. In many cases that awareness brought uneasiness about the limiting conditions of rural life, conditions that in most areas, despite the new roads, did not change for the better. As peasants and small town inhabitants widened their geographical and cultural horizons, their traditional societies began to undergo profound transformation. The very impetus to build roads and to see the products of modern civilizations, as described by Arguedas, was symptomatic of a general breaking down of local barriers. The trucks which carried produce and minerals from the countryside to Lima returned with manufactured goods and periodicals which proclaimed the grandeur of urban life in the capital. The meeting of coast and Sierra that resulted from Leguía's road construction projects is graphically, if somewhat ideally, represented in a popular magazine cover of the era[21] (see figure 5).

The most visible feature of the changes brought to the hinterland by the new roads of the *oncenio* was the radical increase in the number of people who left their traditional homes for new lives in Lima. After centuries of geographic inertia, the *serranos* began to move. At the same time that increased communication links made rural inhabitants aware of

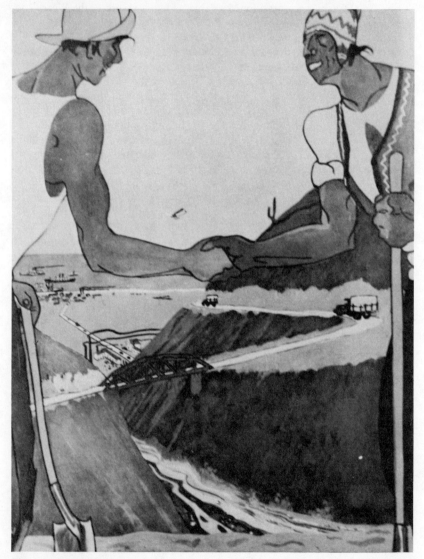

Figure 5. A Meeting of Cultures. From *Ciudad y campo y caminos* 5, no. 41 (August–September 1928): cover illus.

the "advantages" of the capital, the new roads provided them with the means to reach the city. Some returned by those same roads to their villages to tell of the marvels of city life. Dressed in new Western-style clothing and bringing rubber balls, toy trains, and even bicycles, they must have seemed like new men to many of their former neighbors. Their stories of the buildings that looked as if they were reaching the sky, paved streets filled with people and automobiles, and the beautiful and elegant women that inhabited the capital in turn served to encourage others to exchange their less attractive rural existence for a new one in the modern city.[22]

Although many of the new roads of the *oncenio* were built voluntarily, as Arguedas described, or by the state, the Leguía regime also instituted a system of forced labor for highway construction in order to take some strain off the public works budget. Referred to as the *"Conscripción Vial,"* this procedure established obligatory service for construction and repair of roads throughout the country. All males between the ages of eighteen and sixty were subject to the provisions of the *Conscripción Vial,* with the exception of those that could either pay a small amount of money equal to the value of their labor on the roads or find someone to send in their place. In effect, this latter provision limited the *Conscripción Vial* system to the rural poor who lacked the financial resources to pay their quotas. Legally conscripts were required to work only six to twelve days each year, but in reality the great majority of them labored for considerably longer periods.

In its original conception the *Conscripción Vial* law was designed to be a just and expedient way of moving forward on highway construction, but in practice it brought considerable suffering to large sectors of the Peruvian peasantry. Indians were forced to leave their homes and travel many miles over difficult terrain to the construction sites. Telegrams from bitter peasants to the government in Lima tell the story of men forced to work the year round on the roads, notwithstanding provisions to the contrary in the original law. Generally the workers received little, if any, food and no medical attention; deaths among the *conscriptos* were not uncommon. In order to keep workers on the job, the local authorities often confiscated parts of their clothing and other possessions and returned them only when the work was terminated.

Under these conditions it was little wonder that large numbers of peasants attempted to flee from their obligations under the *Conscripción Vial*. In response to the veritable manhunts that were organized to round up workers for the forced labor road projects, many peasants traveled to Lima, where it was rumored that one could lose himself among the masses of the city and thereby escape from his duty. The *Conscripción*

Vial also contributed to the destruction of the bonds of traditional Indian society by forcibly moving men out of the isolated communities and exposing them to the influences of the larger nation. At the same time that the system meant physical bondage, it freed the conscripts' minds to the possibility of different life styles and made them aware of the alternative of migration to the cities as a way to attain those styles.[23]

The changes in Peru's economic relationship to the developed world that ultimately encouraged internal migration by stimulating rapid urbanization and infrastructural modernization also contributed to the rural-urban movement of population by generating an alteration in the ownership patterns of property in extensive sections of the interior. At the beginning of the twentieth century most cultivated agricultural land was still devoted to subsistence production to support the rural population. But with the expansion of the export sectors in the war and postwar period, land that could be put to commercial use increased in value. Fallow areas, mesquite thickets, sandy patches, salt grass swamps, and other areas previously left to peasant communities for subsistence agriculture almost overnight became the sought-after prizes of land-hungry entrepreneurs striving to obtain their share of the export barbecue. On the coast the new landowners concentrated on sugar or cotton production, while in the Sierra new land was usually acquired for livestock grazing or for commercial food production to support the growing coastal population in the cities and on the plantations. The development of better communications throughout the country reinforced the upward revaluation of rural property by making it more accessible to profitable exploitation.

The headlong rush to obtain new land and the conversion of production to meet the export demand gave rise to a veritable social and economic revolution in many interior regions. Generally that revolution occurred at the expense of the rural peasantry, resulting in the disintegration of a series of time-honored social structures and relationships. Particularly in the Sierra, commercially minded landowners extended their holdings by stripping peasant communities of their most productive parcels. Traditionally peasant communities had been organized on the basis of collective property. The land, the water, and other fundamental resources were administered by a communal government council which regulated the access of individual *comuneros*. The system functioned through the reciprocal exchange of goods and services between different members of the community. These peasant communities began to undergo a process of disintegration in the late nineteenth century to the extent that by the 1920s for many their major functions consisted of fighting a losing battle with encroaching *hacendados* to defend their members' lands and preserving remnants of traditional Indian culture such as language, dress, and certain social customs. Population growth played a major role in their decline. Turning around the long demographic depression of the colonial years, Peru's population approximately tripled from the end of the independence period in 1824 to the beginning of the twentieth century. In the rural areas this increase placed real pressure on the land base of the Indian communities that had been relatively fixed since the sixteenth century. Increasingly the rural poor found themselves forced to move to more marginal lands and higher altitudes. Some communities even had to give up agriculture altogether and take up grazing on the arid plateaus only adequate for pastoral pursuits. Within communities tensions grew between *comuneros* who fought for subsistence, and communal lands became progressively parcelized into individually controlled plots. The new *latifundistas* took advantage of the situation, often attempting to encourage individual *comuneros* to sell property in the name of the community as a whole. When bribery failed, the aid of cooperative local authorities was enlisted to cut off vital irrigation water in numerous instances to take communal lands by force. The *comuneros* reacted to these incursions with surprise and sorrow:

> . . . from as far back as anyone can remember all the inhabitants of the settlements indicated above have possessed in common the lands which we now inhabit, traditionally known as the Community of "Todos los Santos." We have never been dispossessed in law or in practice. But now we live under the constant threat that we will be thrown off of the small parcels of land that we have worked our whole lives, as did our ancestors who passed them down to us . . . Those who would take the lands find any individual, he that most readily accepts their plan, and they have him sign a bill of sale; and with this false title we are deprived of our lands. This is what they have tried to do with the Community of "Todos los Santos."[24]

The largely ineffectual provisions of the 1920 constitution, which recognized the legal status of indigenous communities, were unable to stem the tide, as *haciendas* formed of land usurped from peasants and small private farmers began to appear all over rural Peru during this period. Although the *latifundio* had colonial roots, it became a dominant institution in the interior only after Peru's increased integration into the world market made commercial farming more profitable. One *latifundista* coldly chronicled the growth of *haciendas* in the area of Lake Titicaca:

> Some twenty-five years ago the *haciendas* of the Department of Puno were not considered commercially exploitable lands; what was produced on them such as livestock, wool, cheese, butter, etc., was sold at extremely low prices, so low that they were less than half of present day prices; and with the rise in price that

has become felt from year to year, this situation has brought with it as a consequence an awakening of interest in the acquisition of plots of land in the backlands; but since with few exceptions the landowners would not sell their plots, they thought of buying the communal lands of the Indians, and since these plots were generally small, it became necessary to join together various of them until a large enough extension of land could be had to graze some thousands of sheep, and when accomplished they were given the name of *haciendas*.[25]

Other developments occurring roughly at the same time as the expansion of *latifundios* also had important effects on the changes in rural social structures. During the Leguía period many political friends of the president took advantage of their newly acquired political and economic power to displace traditional landowners in hinterland areas who had failed to respond to changing economic conditions. *Patrón*-client relationships that had lasted through generations of *hacendados* and peons were suddenly transformed by new owners. A large proportion of these new owners as well as the old *hacendados* who remained on their lands instituted changes in technology and modes of production aimed at modernizing their operations to compete in the export economy. Laborers were often displaced by the introduction of agricultural machinery and more capital-intensive techniques. Even those who remained adapted to the commercialized *hacienda* with great difficulty.[26]

In short, the land-hungry *hacendados* pushed peasants in ever greater number from their ancestral homes. No longer wedded to a parcel of land, which they had lost, or to an agricultural community, whose reason for existence had been eliminated, these peasants for the first time in centuries found themselves adrift and forced to seek new life styles. For most the loss of land and community signified an immediate descent in economic status to more extreme conditions of poverty than they had previously experienced. Even those communities that had successfully retained a part of their original property faced each year the hardships of having to eke out an existence on a diminishing per capita quantity of land. The rural poor that lived in provincial towns also suffered from the growth of the *latifundios*. Particularly hard hit were those engaged in petty commerce and peddling. Many were driven out of business by the *hacienda* stores that monopolized the commerce in the areas they controlled. "All of us that are in commerce have lost much," one small businessman declared. "The *haciendas* close their doors to the peddler, to the small shopkeeper in the nearby town so as to benefit their own stores that exploit the peon and his family without competition or control."[27]

While most of the rural poor passively accepted this new situation and went to work as peons for the *latifundistas,* a large number also sought to escape by moving to more promising areas. Indeed, the flow of rural-urban migration during the 1920s was substantially augmented by displaced *comuneros* and dissatisfied peons.[28]

The expansion of mining in the Sierra and the growth of sugar and cotton plantations on the coast were two other developments which helped break down the cement of traditional society and thereby contributed to increased internal migration. Initiated in large part between 1880 and 1910 both of these activities experienced phenomenal growth in the 1920s. Their expansion called for an ever larger labor force. The most common form of procuring the needed workers was known as the *"enganche"* system (literally, "hooking" system or "recruiting through devious methods"). Mine owners and *hacendados* sought out the services of a labor contractor who would guarantee to provide a requested number of laborers. The contractor, or *enganchador,* then traveled to provincial communities and attracted recruits with the promise of fantastic job opportunities and offers of immediate cash or consumer goods. The majority of those who accepted the *enganchador's* terms and signed a contract could not read the terms to which they had committed themselves, and they soon found themselves working in mines or on plantations as debt laborers whose long work hours went to paying off the original advance of the *enganchador.* In spite of the injustice involved in most of these operations, a large proportion of the debt laborers found their new conditions and pay superior to their former circumstances. This was particularly true of those who had lost their land and been forced to work on Sierra *latifundios.* As word of these "benefits" spread throughout rural Peru, periodic migrations, especially at harvest times, became a fact of life for the populations in many regions. Freed from the geographic immobility of their former milieu and introduced to a universe of new perceptions and experiences on the plantations and in the mines, a further migration to the city for this group seemed a much less serious undertaking than it would have been in the past.[29]

A glamorous and modern capital, new roads, and strong pressures on the life of the rural population combined to produce a significant increase in the flow of migration to Lima during the 1920s and a consequent jump in the size of the urban population. Between 1919 and 1931 some 65,000 *provincianos* came to live in the capital. The number of new arrivals alone exceeded by over 30 percent the total number of migrants residing in Lima in 1908. By 1931 over 19 percent of the city's inhabitants had moved there from the countryside in the preceding eleven years. At the same time that Lima had experienced a natural population increase of 1.3 percent per annum, the overall increase reached 6.2 percent. Rural migrants made up over 30 percent of the city's gain in population during the 1920s.[30]

Migrants streamed into Lima during the 1920s from all areas of the country, coming in largest numbers from regions with the best road systems and the most intense growth of *latifundios*. Approximately 60 percent of all migration originated in the central and southern regions of the Sierra, and 80 percent of that number came from the four departments of Junín, Ancash, Arequipa, and Ayacucho. Although coastal migration accounted for a smaller proportion of those who made the move to Lima, it followed the Sierra in importance with 30 percent. The departments of Ica, which borders Lima, and La Libertad provided the largest number of coastal migrants. A graphic representation of the distribution of migration is represented in chart 2.[31]

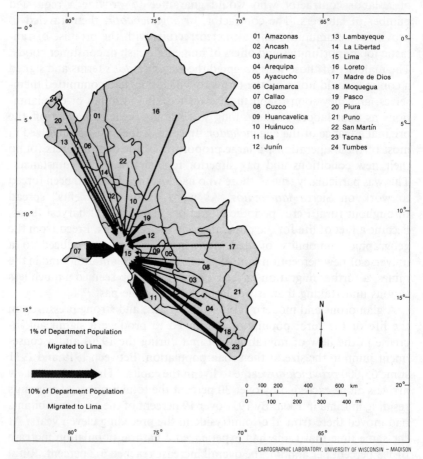

01 Amazonas	13 Lambayeque
02 Ancash	14 La Libertad
03 Apurimac	15 Lima
04 Arequipa	16 Loreto
05 Ayacucho	17 Madre de Dios
06 Cajamarca	18 Moquegua
07 Callao	19 Pasco
08 Cuzco	20 Piura
09 Huancavelica	21 Puno
10 Huánuco	22 San Martín
11 Ica	23 Tacna
12 Junín	24 Tumbes

1% of Department Population
Migrated to Lima

10% of Department Population
Migrated to Lima

0   100 200   400   600 km
0   100   200   300   400 mi

CARTOGRAPHIC LABORATORY, UNIVERSITY OF WISCONSIN – MADISON

Chart 2. Relative Intensity of Rural-Urban Migration to Lima, 1920–1940. From Roque García Frías, "Intensidad absoluta y relativa de la emigración provinciana al departamento de Lima," *Estadística Peruana*, vol. 3, no. 5 (July 1947): 57.

Just as rural-urban movement population occurred in nearly all geographic regions of the country, so did migration proceed from diverse economic areas. Although there are no figures that compare the levels of economic development of different Peruvian provinces in the 1920s and 1930s, the correlation of migration data by province from the 1931 census with a developmental factor analysis of provinces based on the 1960 national census permits some speculation concerning what types of economic circumstances most migrants left behind. The results of this correlation show that migration to Lima flowed largely from the middle economic range of Peruvian provinces; strikingly few people seem to have come from the poorest regions. In large part the lack of movement from the least developed zones is explained by the absence of communication facilities and the lack of pressure from *latifundistas* to obtain the generally poorer quality lands of these areas.[32]

After arriving in the city, most migrants settled into one of various forms of lower class housing: a *callejón*—a blind alley lined generally with one-room dwellings and with a single water tap at one end; a *solar*—a dilapidated mansion abandoned by its former wealthy owners and subdivided into a series of small rooms; or a *casa de vecindad*—a two-story working class apartment house near the downtown area. While their living conditions were clearly substandard, they were nevertheless superior to the even greater hardships that the migrant left behind. The *provinciano* could generally find a job without difficulty in the capital during the 1920s, a job which paid considerably more than he could hope to make in the countryside. He could also send his children to at least a few years of primary school, something that constituted a luxury throughout much of the interior. Furthermore, in cultural terms most rural migrants were *mestizos*. Their Western dress and ability to speak Spanish greatly facilitated their adjustment to urban ways.

For many migrants entry to the city was eased by close relationships they formed with people already living in Lima. Some had relatives or friends in the city who could be relied upon to provide various forms of aid including at least temporary shelter until more permanent housing could be secured. These people often had played a part in the initial decision to migrate by sending passage money and promising assistance. Ties of kinship which facilitated the migrants' assimilation were soon institutionalized, taking the forms of sports clubs and regional associations. Composed mainly of working class individuals from the same town or province, these associations often had hundreds of members. Some amassed sufficient capital to purchase or build headquarters. By 1928 there were forty-four regional societies in the capital. The territorial base of these clubs helped establish regional lines for the integration of migrants. An individual belonging to a particular association was likely to seek employment through others from his home province, to find a prospective spouse from among its ranks, and to establish clientage relationships with its upper strata members. These societies also facilitated the adjustment of migrants by acquainting them with the unfamiliar features of urban life from Western dress versus the Sierra poncho to the proper forms of social etiquette. At the same time they ameliorated the break with life in the interior by sponsoring traditional fiestas that featured regional food and music. In short, they functioned as social centers and meeting places and served as substitutes for the complex web of relationships that the migrants had left behind in the provinces.[33]

Despite the relative ease with which most migrants integrated themselves into the life of the city, adjustment to urban ways that differed significantly from those of their rural homes was not accomplished entirely without problems. A Lima folk song by Laureano Martínez entitled *Provinciano* expresses well the bittersweet experience of many migrants:

> Las locas ilusiones
> me sacaron de mi pueblo
> y abandoné mi casa
> para ver la capital.
> Como recuerdo el día
> felíz de mi partida,
> sin reparar en nada
> de mi tierra me alejé
>
> . . . . .
>
> Ahora que conozco la ciudad
> de mis dorados sueños
> y veo realizada la ambición
> que en mi querer forjé
> es cuando el desengaño
> de esta vida me entristece
> y añoro con dolor mi dulce hogar!
> Luché como varón para vencer
> y pude conseguirlo,
> alcanzando mi anhelo de vivir
> con todo esplendor;
> y en medio de esta dicha
> me atormenta la nostalgia
> del pueblo en que dejé
> mi corazón![34]

> I was pulled from my hometown
> by crazy illusions
> and I abandoned my home
> to see the capital.

How well I remember
the happy day of
my departure,
I left my home
without even looking around
.   .   .   .   .   .
Now that I know the city
of my golden dreams
and I find my ambitions
fulfilled
now is when the disappointment
of this life makes me sad
and I recall with pain my sweet home!
I fought like a man to get ahead
and I was successful,
fulfilling my desire to live
in great splendor;
and in the midst of this happiness
I am still tormented by the nostalgia
for the home where I left
my heart!

As Lima's population grew rapidly during the 1920s, the city underwent a period of remarkable social change. The urban masses and middle sectors grew during these years to unprecedented numbers. Transformed in size, makeup, and importance, they could no longer be ignored and were about to assume new roles in the nation's political life as participants in the populist movements of the 1930s.

Detailed social data contained in the 1920 and 1931 censuses permit reasonable estimates of the proportions of middle and popular sector expansion. One gauge of the increasing importance of these groups is obtained by measuring the alterations in the occupational structure of the capital during the *oncenio*. In the case of the lower strata, construction workers engaged in the building of a modern Lima constituted the largest single segment of the male urban working class at the end of the 1920s. Following them in importance were large numbers of men in semi- or unskilled occupations that involved little or no training and were often the most poorly paid as well as the most precarious in terms of job security. Undoubtedly, many rural migrants who were lured to the city by the possibility of construction jobs and yet were unable to find work in that sector filled the ranks of this kind of *lumpenproletariat*. They included peddlers who went from door to door selling foodstuffs or cheap consumer goods, vendors in the various open markets of the city, street peddlers, sellers of lottery tickets, gardeners, waiters, deliverymen, and simply unskilled manual laborers who gathered at the train station to carry bags, at construction sites to haul water and bricks, and in the city streets to run errands, help with parcels, or sing for a few pennies. This group underwent the largest numerical and percentage increase during the postwar period, perhaps in part due to the onset of the depression in 1930 that forced scores of men to seek marginal forms of employment. Next in numerical importance came the more traditional artisan class and laborers who worked at a trade. These were the tailors, the shoemakers, the carpenters, the bakers, and the mechanics. They generally had their own tools and equipment, possessed some specialized training, and could maintain a modicum of economic independence. While this group continued to be an important component of the popular classes throughout the 1920s, it grew at a slow pace over these years. Interestingly, the working class segment that showed the smallest increase during the *oncenio* was the industrial labor force. Industrialization, which had expanded substantially in the war years to make up for the diminished flow of imports from European suppliers, slackened in pace in the succeeding period with a consequent decreased growth in industrial employment. Working class women continued to fill the menial and poorly paid occupations of laundress, seamstress, and domestic servant.

In all, approximately 110,000 individuals held working class-type jobs in 1931, by far surpassing the number of people (66,000) who had the same occupational status in 1920. Those with working class occupations in 1920 had represented 58.47 percent of the city's total employed population; the passage of eleven years saw that ratio rise to 67.62 percent. Table 3.1 shows that the growth of specific lower class occupational groups clearly outpaced the 60.89 percent increment in the economically active population and the 44.35 percent advance in overall employment between 1920 and 1931.[35]

Two other indications of the expansion of Lima's working classes during the *oncenio* were the changes in the racial composition of the city's inhabitants and the exceptional population growth in lower class neighborhoods. Similar to other areas of Latin America, in the Peru of the 1920s there was a close correlation between race and social class. In the eyes of the society as a whole and the census taker in particular, the more upper class strata were classified as whites and the more lower class generally as *mestizos*. Only those unable to speak Spanish were defined as Indians, and they had been actually declining as a percentage of the urban population since the turn of the century. The variations in the proportions of different racial groups in Lima between 1920 and 1931 reveal a profound transformation of the city's social mix. In 1920 *mestizos* and whites were nearly equal in demographic importance, accounting for 39.9 percent and 38.0 percent, respectively, of the population. By 1931,

Table 3.1. The Growth of Selected Lower Class Occupations in Lima, 1908-31

Occupation	Number employed			Percentage increase	
	1908	1920	1931	1908–20	1920–31
Construction workers	2,080	3,291	5,857	58.22	77.97
Mechanics	709	1,973	3,347	178.28	129.09
Chauffeurs	–	715	3,979	–	456.50
Food vendors in markets	316	359	1,314	13.61	266.01
Street vendors	552	185	862	- 66.49	365.95
Lottery sellers	110	73	253	- 33.64	246.58
Domestic servants	3,935	5,920	16,202	50.44	173.68
Day laborers	1,613	1,778	3,224	10.23	81.33
Peddlers and small merchants	–	380	5,448	–	1,333.68
Bakers	644	892	1,620	38.51	81.61
Carpenters	2,520	2,901	3,744	15.20	29.06
Tailors and seamstresses	8,410	11,246	13,037	33.72	15.93
Textile workers	575	1,959	2,411	240.70	23.07

Sources: Perú. Dirección de Salubridad Pública. *Censo de la Provincia de Lima (26 de junio de 1908)* (Lima: Ministerio de Fomento, 1915), 2:1906-43; Perú. Ministerio de Hacienda. *Resúmen del censo de las Provincias de Lima y Callao levantado el 17 de diciembre de 1920* (Lima: IMP. Americana, 1927), pp. 163-82; Perú. *Censo de las Provincias de Lima y Callao levantado el 13 de noviembre de 1931.* (Lima: Torres Aguirre, 1932), pp. 192-241.

however, the situation had changed markedly, with whites dropping to 32.7 percent and *mestizos* reaching an absolute majority with 51.1 percent.[36]

As Lima's *mestizo* working class contingent grew, so did those neighborhoods with high *mestizo* populations, notably the districts of Rimac and La Victoria. With 58.9 percent *mestizaje* for Rimac and 58.7 percent for La Victoria as compared with 51.1 percent for the Province of Lima as a whole, they ranked as the most nonwhite and most working class urban area. At the same time, these were the very districts which experienced the highest population growth in the 1920s (see chart 3).

Besides race, other measures of the working class makeup of Rimac and La Victoria are data on the population density of these neighborhoods compared to other urban zones of Lima and figures on the attendance of local children in primary and secondary schools. In population density Rimac and La Victoria were substantially more crowded and had

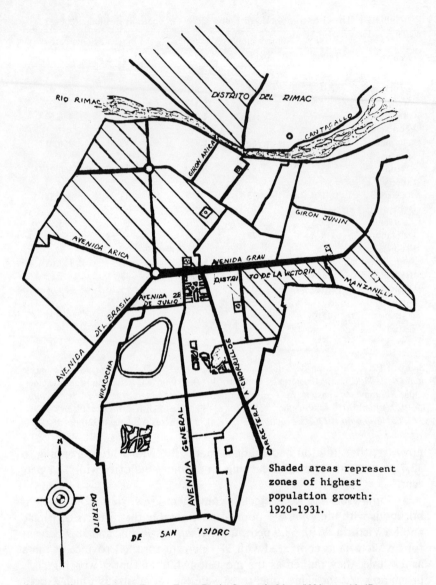

Shaded areas represent
zones of highest
population growth:
1920-1931.

Chart 3. Lima by Census Zones. From Perú, *Censo de Lima 1931*, pp. 46–47.

poorer quality living areas, with 2.10 people per room and 2.03 per room, respectively, than, for example, did the center of Lima, with 1.49 per room. Regarding school attendance they also ranked lower than the center of Lima with 28 percent of the six-to-fourteen age group out of school in Rimac and 25.27 percent out in La Victoria as compared to 19.01 per cent out in Lima. School attendance reflected economic status to the extent that children from lower income households were forced to leave school and work for their families more often than those belonging to households with greater economic resources.[37]

In sum, during the decade of the 1920s Lima had undergone a process of massification. The working classes had grown from their position as a mere component in the urban scene to domination of that scene demographically and socially. The populist movements of 1930-31 would be the political expression of their "dominance."

The substantial growth of Lima's middle sectors accompanied the expansion of the urban proletariat. Middle groups had begun to merge since the middle of the nineteenth century as part of the bureaucratic and commercial expansion arising from Peru's initial export economic experience. In those years Lima saw increasing numbers of goverment and commercial employees, students and educators at all levels, independent merchants, and military officers — all of whom contributed to middle sector expansion. During and after World War I the increase in economic and political activity produced by the country's assumption of a new role in the world market fomented middle sector development to new heights. White collar employees in large public and private organizations were the most visible evidence of this growth. They were the office workers, the petty bureaucrats, the retail clerks, and the bookkeepers among others. Also, increasing numbers of lawyers, doctors, engineers, storekeepers, teachers, and university students swelled the ranks of this strata. Employment in all these areas was virtually assured by the economic boom of the Leguía years and the growth of the state budget, which nearly tripled between 1917 and 1929. Such in fact was the demand for these occupations that middle sector growth had difficulty keeping pace. Certainly, part of the flow of migrants from the interior was made up of middle sector individuals expecting better opportunities in Lima.

The expansion of middle sector occupations in Lima during the 1920s is traced in table 3.2. Besides the demographic rise indicated by census figures, other factors point to the growth of this group. Banks increased from four in 1897 to twelve in 1928 at the same time that their deposits jumped fivefold. There were only two insurance companies in 1899; by 1928 the number had risen to thirteen. Road and railroad building had become important activities in the first decades of this century. In politics as well the middle sectors had become an increasingly important force. Some of their number formed the backbone of the Leguía regime, which had explicitly favored the new salaried classes by passing legislation that protected their jobs and required their employers to provide pensions and special life insurance policies. Others actively supported and in some cases led the populist movements that sought to integrate politically the newly incremented urban masses after 1930.[38]

One element that specifically affected the massification of Lima was the expansion of the city's industrial sector. But industrialization exerted a more qualitative than quantitative influence. The events of World War I played a major part in stimulating the intensification of the industrialization process. Previous to 1914 domestic workshops were largely limited to the manufacture of those fairly rudimentary articles not provided by imports. Nearly all local industries were of the artisan type, producing such things as flour, biscuits, soap, candles, glass bottles, beer, soda water, cigarettes, candies, and liquor. They operated with a minimum of capital and utilized simple technology. The exceptions to this rule were the small number of textile plants founded for the most part by British and American interests beginning in 1896. The majority of these manufacturing activities were directly connected to Peru's primary producers. This was the case, for instance, for the textile industry, which acquired abundant raw materials from cotton growers and wool producers.[39] In the first decade of this century small manufacturing firms received some impetus from the increasing domestic demand for consumer goods that accompanied the growth in the urban population. This initial industrial push was, however, modest compared to the boom that began in the war

Table 3.2. The Growth of Selected Middle Sector Occupational Groups in Lima, 1920–31

	Number employed		Percentage increase
Occupation	1920	1931	1920–31
Commerce	12,667	25,481	99.01
Public administration	898	5,313	491.65
Legal profession	460	848	84.35
Medical profession	932	2,408	158.37
Engineers and technicians	536	915	74.07
Writers and newspapermen	137	341	153.28
Accountants	492	1,124	128.46
Students	8,643	17,067	97.47

Source: Perú, *Censo de Lima 1931*, p. 206.

years. A general decline of consumer production in the nations that traditionally provided Peru with manufactured goods, the difficulties involved in maritime shipping, and the new limitations placed on credit all combined to push up dramatically the prices of many imports while totally cutting off the supply of others. Local entrepreneurs responded to the demands for manufactured goods by expanding existing industrial facilities and founding new plants. In the textile sector, for example, the total number of looms increased nearly 150 per cent between 1906 and 1918 from 1,050 to 2,588. More industrial production required a larger labor force, and the Lima working classes involved in manufacturing grew apace. Those employed in the textile industry registered the most dramatic increase, gaining 240 percent from 575 laborers in 1908 to 1,959 in 1920.[40]

Industrial growth continued after World War I, but at a slower rate, as Peruvian consumers were eager to buy foreign goods once again after the wartime hiatus in imports. The sectors that expanded the most were those related to construction, notably lumber mills, brick factories, plumbing concerns, carpentry shops, and a cement plant. The numerical importance and economic impact of these industries should not be exaggerated. Even after the expansion during the war and succeeding years, in 1930 most manufacturing enterprises in Lima were still small artisan establishments. And the bulk of the capital's industrial laborers were not factory workers but manual artisans.[41]

While the growth of manufacturing in Lima did not lead to the creation of a modern industrial proletariat, it did, on the other hand, contribute significantly to the rise of the organized labor movement. Those unions that in the 1920s and 1930s would play an important part in populist politics[42] were virtually nonexistent before the industrial boom of the war years. In Peru, as in most of Latin America, mutual assistance societies that grouped small numbers of the most privileged members of the working class by individual trade were the initial forms of labor organization, preceding the appearance of the union movement by several decades. The first such organization, the Confederated Universal Union of Artisans (CAUU), was founded in 1884 and was followed in 1901 by the Assembly of United Societies. These guild-like institutions brought together employees and owners of small artisan shops more than factory workers. Explicitly rejecting confrontations with either management or the government, their major functions were to provide some measure of social security from funds collected as monthly dues and to act as social clubs where members could play soccer, dance, or simply meet together.

Visible if relatively weak shifts toward labor militancy first occurred in

1905 when Lima's bakers, the city's premier union organization founded in 1887, took the lead in revising their charter to include specific demands for higher wages and shorter hours. Later, during the presidency of Guillermo Billinghurst (1912–14), working class organization seemed to be moving towards a more radical posture. Billinghurst, who had gained office with the help of working class street demonstrations in Lima, had promised a sympathetic ear for labor in the goverment palace. Hopes for presidential aid spurred a series of walkouts shortly after Billinghurst's inauguration, and in November of 1912 the stevedores in the port of Callao, demanding and eight-hour work day, initiated the largest strike in the history of organized labor in Peru to that date. Billinghurst ultimately took the side of the strikers and officially declared an eight-hour day for all port workers.[43]

In spite of the demonstrated effectiveness of confrontation tactics, the great majority of Lima's workers remained quiescent through 1914. Mutual aid societies maintained their commanding position in the labor movement. In general management continued to be confident that "the social question that agitates almost all the peoples of the world does not exist as an issue among us."[44] Their "optimism" may have grown out of the observation that nearly all unions, even the Federación de Obreros Panaderos, which had the longest tradition of militancy, continued after the eight-hour decree of Billinghurst to consider personal recourse to the president to be a more practical strategy than the resort to coercive measures. One veteran labor leader attested to the relative lack of interest in the understanding of union organization on the part of most workers in his description of the offhanded manner in which one union was founded in 1914: "At that time nobody knew what a union was. That a union be formed, that this was the modern form of worker organization and that it was the only way to support workers' interests, that this and that. So, it was agreed that a union be formed."[45]

World War I and the accompanying boom in domestic industry marked a definite change in the course of labor organization. As larger numbers of workers gathered under one roof in new factories and shops, union organizers were able to reap an abundant harvest. Their task was made still easier by the rise in the cost of living in Lima that stimulated suffering workers to enter unions in order to defend themselves against increased economic burdens. Unions grew more rapidy in number between 1910 and 1920 — with most expansion occurring in the war years — than either in the preceding or succeeding decades. Furthermore, nearly all those unions that later made up the vanguard of labor organizations were founded during or shortly after the war. These included the Federación

Textil, the Federación Obrera Regional Peruana, the Federación de Choferes, and the Federación Gráfica del Perú.[46]

Two high points of this period of labor organization growth were the general strike in Lima for the eight-hour day and the formation of the Federación Textil, both in January 1919. The eight-hour strike constituted the first massive show of strength by organized labor in Peruvian history and marked the initiation of ties between the union movement and groups of university students, most notable among them Víctor Raúl Haya de la Torre.[47] Following on the heels of the eight-hour victory, the creation of the Textile Federation served to confirm the leadership position of those workers that had been the most active in promoting unionism in the past. At the time of this founding the Federación united eight different factory unions, with a total membership of approximately 1,200 individuals.[48]

During the years of union ascendancy groups representing three distinct ideological persuasions vied for control of organized labor: the traditional proponents of mutual aid, the anarchists, and the syndicalists. With extensive government support, the mutual aid advocates that had dominated the labor movement since the mid-nineteenth century remained strong through the first two decades of the twentieth century despite concerted attacks by anarchist and syndicalist newcomers. As for the anarchists, their "golden age" lasted from 1906 through 1918. During that time they received the encouragement of prominent local idealogues like Manuel González Prada and foreign anarchists with extensive previous labor experience in Spain, Argentina, and Italy. Native-born anarchist workers began the publication of *La Protesta,* the most widely read labor newspaper in the country, and they formed Peru's first modern working man's federation, the Federación Obrera Regional Peruana (FORP). Preaching unlimited individual liberty and the abolition of all forms of sovereignty including the state and private property, the anarchists produced the majority of the leaders of the union movement through 1931.[49]

It was from within the very ranks of the anarchist leaders, however, that syndicalism received its major impetus. With diverse occupational backgrounds and clashes between strong personalities, the anarchists had never been able to present a united ideological front even in their most successful years. And they had always been more effective as newspapermen than as union organizers. Wartime conditions induced some anarchist leaders to move towards more immediate and concrete forms of syndicalist tactics which promised security and higher wages, issues largely ignored in the past. As much of the labor movement retreated from a pure anarchist position, the new label of anarcho-syndicalist began to be applied to the mainstream of organized worker groups. The eight-hour general strike and later actions demonstrated that the syndicalist element progressively received more emphasis as anarchism receded. In the opinion of veteran labor leader Arturo Sabroso, no matter how deep their commitment to their original ideals, the anarchists invariably "ended up surrendering to reality."[50]

After the impressive victories of 1919, union leaders held high hopes for the future of their movement in the coming decade. The founding of the Federación Textil seemed only the first step in the total unionization of urban labor. During the initial years of Leguía's administration their optimism appeared justified. With the textile workers in the vanguard, the unification of the entire labor movement was attempted in 1922 when the Federación Obrera Local de Lima (FOL) was established. Various new worker newspapers came into existence, unions set up libraries, and leaders attended "Popular Universities" to improve themselves "intellectually and morally."[51] By 1923, however, the panorama began to darken. The government that had at first tacitly supported unions turned repressive, closing down worker newspapers and harassing "Popular Universities." In 1927 Leguía finally decided to end decisively the "threat of organized labor," and he banned all union activities while ordering the arrest of the most prominent labor leaders. After that date syndicalist activities were forced underground until 1929 when the Confederación General de Trabajadores del Perú (CGTP) was founded to replace the old FOL.[52]

On the basis of the CGTP's claims that it had a membership of 19,000 workers in 1930, it would seem that the expectations of 1919 had not been unrealistic. These claims were, however, largely unfounded, and their defenders were unable to produce concrete evidence to support them. In fact, the overwhelming majority of the urban working classes remained unorganized. The group included an enormous number of workers in artisan shops, small industries, most of the construction sector, the urban services, and those without steady employment. Moveover, the same men who proudly boasted of the CGTP's extensive membership complained in the same breath that the union movement continued to be weighed down by strong artisan traditions and government repression, both of which acted to hold back the development of a true industrial proletariat.[53]

During the *oncenio* organized and unorganized workers benefited to some extent from the prosperity and full employment of the Leguía administration. But for both groups the Great Depression abruptly ended the gains of the "golden decade." Initially most Peruvian observers took scarce note of the potential effects on their own economy of New York's

"Black Tuesday." It soon became evident, though, that those same augmented ties of dependency to the world market that had brought economic growth in times of plenty would now be instrumental in involving Peru in an international economic crisis. First to suffer was the nation's foreign trade. Agricultural and raw materials exports had actually been on unsure footing since 1926. With the depression the prices of basic export products including sugar, cotton, and wool began to drop even more sharply than before, the total value of Peruvian exports declining 59 percent in two years from $134,032,000 in 1929 to $55,277,000 in 1931. The import sector suffered even more. Reflecting both a cutback in the supply of manufactured goods from developed countries and a scarcity of foreign exchange in Peru, the total value of imports plummeted 63 percent between 1929 and 1931 from $75,914,000 to $28,694,000. Local commerce incurred particularly heavy losses as a result of the shortage of imported goods as well as from a steep plunge in the purchasing power of consumers, the devaluation of the national currency, and increasingly strict limitations on credit. The public sector was no better off. Much of the funding for Leguía's large-scale public works

Figure 6. "Sunday's Tragic Bullfight." From *Mundial* 10, no. 508 (March 15, 1930): no page given.

projects and expanded bureaucracy had come in the form of loans from American banks and other Wall Street investors. No longer able to obtain foreign loans after 1929 and without the usual earnings from custom receipts, the government found itself on the verge of financial bankruptcy. The solvency of banks was seriously threatened, and many, including Peru's largest, failed to survive. Like people in other parts of the world, Peruvians reacted to the deteriorated economic situation first with disbelief, then with panic, and finally with despair. To many the depression must indeed have seemed like the savage bull depicted in a popular cartoon of the time, destroying all in its path[54] (see figure 6).

Lima's working classes were especially hard hit by the economic crisis. The most serious consequence for the masses was a radical downswing in the rate of employment. By November 1931 31,139 men between the ages of fourteen and sixty-nine were without jobs in Lima—a full 25 percent of the city's labor force. All occupational sectors were afflicted to a greater or lesser degree. Those in the construction industry suffered most. The public works and private building projects that had boomed during the *oncenio* ground to a sudden halt, forcing 70 percent of the men employed in the building trades out of work. Next came craft industries that closed their doors, filling the ranks of the unemployed with artisan laborers. It appears that, in general, unionized workers were more successful in retaining their jobs than the nonunionized. In the case of the highly organized textile workers, for example, only 12 percent were unemployed as compared to the overall rate for Lima of 25 percent. Also unemployment was less critical among native residents of the capital than among migrants from rural areas. A large proportion of the migrants worked in unskilled occupations or in construction and were, therefore, the first to be laid off. The unemployment problem among migrants was so severe that many, with a great deal of urging from the government, decided to return to their original homes in the interior.[55]

High as they were, unemployment figures did not fully reflect the difficulties sustained by Lima's working classes during the depression. Having lost their original jobs, scores of individuals sought to attain a minimal level of subsistence for themselves and their families by taking up marginal forms of employment. Former construction workers, plumbers, and skilled artisans walked the downtown streets trying to sell a few pieces of fruit candies, collar stays, or lottery tickets to passersby. Others, without sufficient funds to buy even a few trifles for resale, resorted to begging from house to house for bread or scavenged through the city dump for pieces of food left by garbage trucks.[56]

Under these circumstances, those who retained their jobs could consider themselves fortunate. But their lot was by no means an easy one.

Across the board, employers reduced salaries, and workers, moreover, found that the money they did receive purchased less goods as a result of the devaluation of the national currency. Also many factories shortened their work week to four days in an attempt to remain in business, thereby reducing even more the income of their laborers. Some workers voiced complaints that the hard-won gains of the past two decades had suddenly been wiped out by selfish employers. Nevertheless, expressions of protest on the part of the discontented seemed fruitless, as management could easily replace "troublesome" individuals with someone from the legions of unemployed that often formed lines at factory entrances in hopes of obtaining a job. The events of the Lima transit workers' strike in August 1931 provide a striking demonstration of the power of management over labor during the depression. Two hours after the workers walked off the job the transit company's buses and streetcars were back in circulation with new drivers and conductors. On the day following the strike, in order to keep mobs of job seekers away from their doors, the company placed an announcement in the city newspapers stating that all positions left vacant had been filled and entreating people to desist from asking for employment. Finally the strikers' original demands for better wages dissolved into appeals to be allowed to return to their original duties under the former conditions.[57]

These workers could hardly be blamed for their apologetic pleas, for they merely represented an appraisal that their best chance for survival in this critical period lay in returning to their jobs. Even in better economic times most members of the urban masses had earned barely enough to live on. Saving for emergencies was a luxury they simply could not afford. As salaries diminished or disappeared entirely, hunger became an everyday fact of life for the urban poor. A 1931 study of Lima public school children found that 62 percent were considerably undernourished, eating only one meal per day that often consisted solely of thin soup. The problem of deficient caloric intake was probably even more serious among the less privileged children that did not attend school. Also housing conditions became progressively worse. Many individuals without the funds to pay their rent regularly were evicted from their homes by landlords unwilling to extend to them a period of grace. Already overcrowded dwellings that had been single-family residences in the past were now occupied by two or three families who attempted between them to meet rent payments. As 1930 moved into 1931, predictions in the local press by businessmen and bureaucrats of an economic recovery proved unfounded. For the urban masses misery actually became more prevalent as the months went by.[58]

In the midst of these times of economic crisis, the Sánchezcerrista and

Aprista populist movements came to dominate national politics. Captained by a new breed of politicians who portrayed themselves as uniquely
qualified to relieve the hardships of the poor, these movements clearly saw
the opportunity for political control open to those prepared to grasp the
potential support of Lima's enlarged and impoverished working classes.
Under the conditions of a crisis in the hegemony of traditional forms of
government and of the dominant sectors of society, the presence of
numerous and highly visible urban masses plus ambitious charismatic
figures to lead them changed the face of Peruvian politics in the years
following the collapse of the *oncenio*. From 1930 on, the legitimacy
necessary for rule would be sought repeatedly in the creation of populist
alliances on the Sánchezcerrista-Aprista model, alliances that appeared
able to produce a new harmony between society and politics without
essentially changing economic and social structures in Peru.

4

Sánchezcerrismo I:
The Hero Appears

LIMA REMAINED quiet—business as usual—that Saturday the 23rd of August 1930 in spite of news that the previous day a movement to overthrow President Leguía had broken out among elements of the military in the country's second largest city, Arequipa. The morning papers published short articles stating that the revolt was led by a commandant named Luis M. Sánchez Cerro and that, notwithstanding some initial rebel victories, the government was confident order would soon be reestablished. The next day the official newspaper displayed bold headlines announcing that: "The country returns smoothly to normal as if on railroad tracks."[1] By then, however, the surface optimism of the regime contrasted markedly with the first visible signs of support for the revolt in Lima. As rumors multiplied that the entire southern part of the country supported the movement, small numbers of individuals banded together and marched down city avenues shouting their hatred of the regime. Streetcorner orators urged bystanders to join them. All thoughts seemed to focus on the rebellious commandant of Arequipa. "Sánchez Cerro!" "Who is he?" "A brave man." "He'll finally get rid of that old man Leguía." "I hope so." "Have you heard? The cabinet is going to resign. Leguía will have to resign now." "Viva Sánchez Cerro!"[2]

At first Leguía himself appeared unworried by the events in Arequipa. On the same day that Lima reverberated with the name of Sánchez Cerro the president attended the afternoon horse races as was his custom. Only when booed by large portions of the crowd did he seem to waver in his confidence, leaving the track earlier than usual. That night the lights of the government palace burned for many long hours as Leguía attempted to survive the crisis by forming a new cabinet of loyal military officers. At the same moment, groups of younger officers met in the General Staff headquarters and resolved to prevent Leguía from remaining in power. In the dawn of August 25 they marched to the palace and confronted the chief executive. At first courteously and then with increasingly violent language, the young officers finally bullied Leguía into renouncing the presidency. Momentarily a *junta* of senior military officers led by General Manuel Ponce presided over the nation, but they quickly retreated in the face of unfavorable public opinion in Lima and Sánchez Cerro's strongly worded telegrams from Arequipa in which he threatened to punish severely anyone who failed to submit to his authority. When two days later he flew from Arequipa to Lima, no one openly disputed that Sánchez Cerro would be the new president of Peru.[3]

Sánchez Cerro arrived in Lima on August 29 to be greeted by the largest public demonstration in Peruvian history up to that time. This tribute to Peru's "second liberator" was all the more impressive because it was largely spontaneous. As Sánchez Cerro stepped off his plane he was immediately surrounded by a delirious mob of people vying to touch or at least catch a glimpse of the new president. After being carried around the airport on the shoulders of the multitude, he was able only with great effort to reach the vehicle that would transport him to the government palace. Along the way a true hero's welcome awaited him. Huge crowds lined the streets along his route. Church bells rang. Women showered the rebellious commandant with flowers as he passed under their balconies. Flags and pictures of Sánchez Cerro appeared everywhere. The noise of the cheering throngs was deafening. Standing firmly erect in his open car, Sánchez Cerro waved and smiled in response to the acclaim of the people. In these moments the so-called "Hero of Arequipa" seemed to personify the elements of a new Peru. He still wore the dust-covered military uniform he had used on the first day of the revolt. In one hand he carried a bouquet of flowers given to him by a poor market vendor; he rested his other hand on the butt of a revolver strapped to his side.[4]

Sánchez Cerro's fervent reception in Lima represented more than a momentary outpouring of mass emotion. On that day, with the recent events of Arequipa dominant in the public consciousness, ties were forged between large segments of the Lima populace and the revolutionary hero that would later form the basis of the political movement to elect Sánchez Cerro to the presidency in 1931. Almost overnight a once obscure army commandant had become the incarnation of the hopes of the nation. The story of how Sánchez Cerro gained such immediate popularity in the minds of individual Peruvians is perhaps best told by one working class man present at the demonstration of August 27:

I went to see Sánchez Cerro's arrival from Arequipa in August of 1930. I was in the Plaza Washington. Sánchez Cerro came down the Avenida Arequipa in a car. And since I saw such a large number of people, then and there I came to take a liking to Sánchez Cerro when I saw him come by. Right then I liked the man. It was a great feeling. Seeing every bit of the street filled with people, right then I got the feeling to support the man. From that very moment I came to favor the man, to favor him strongly, very strongly. Before that I had no idea who he was. He had never been in politics before. And I had never supported anyone before. But then I immediately became a Sánchezcerrista. Everybody was a Sánchezcerrista. Blacks, whites, *cholos.* The people cried, they applauded, they embraced him. It was something fantastic. I have never seen anything like it. He was a hero, and we did not even know him.[5]

This individual's reaction was not unique. To those who applauded him on his triumphant parade through the city, Sánchez Cerro approached the stature of a superman. He was the valorous hero who had come victorious from a war fought to save the very life of the nation. The appearance of Sánchez Cerro on the national scene made a lasting impression on Peruvian political life. As Víctor Andrés Belaunde commented, it signified the emergence of an important political archetype, "a sort of resurrection of the romantic *caudillismo* that characterized the first years of the republic."[6]

There was one person whom these dramatic events did not take by surprise, and that was Sánchez Cerro himself. At various times during this life he had explicitly revealed his desire to become the president of Peru. Racially and socially a *mestizo,* Luis M. Sánchez Cerro was born to a middle class family of moderate means in the northern Peruvian city of Piura on August 12, 1889. He lived in relative poverty during his first years; his father was barely able to scrape together enough money from his meager earnings as a notary to allow him to complete a primary and secondary education in Piura's public school system. When at age sixteen Sánchez Cerro expressed a desire to continue his education and seek a career, the most viable step seemed to be entry into the national military school at Chorrillos. He finished his studies there in 1910, and when four years later he advanced in rank from lieutenant to captain, he did so having obtained the highest score on the examination taken by all candidates seeking promotions.

Since his childhood Sánchez Cerro had shown an avid interest in the exercise of power. His fellow schoolmates called him "El Dictador" because of the way he authoritatively directed their youthful games. The first record of Sánchez Cerro speaking openly about his ambitions to become president dates from 1919. When stationed in the government palace he startled a complaining orderly by declaring: "When I am president, I'll take care of such things."[7] Although this could be considered simply an innocuous jest, later that same year Sánchez Cerro expressed in writing his serious intent to attain the presidency. On September 27, 1919 he wrote in the yearbook of a fellow officer:

> With a smile, reflect, pause for a moment, and when you hear a story about me or you see me lashing the indolent and lazy rabble, with a piece of bread in one hand and a whip in the other, say that it is Sánchez Cerro who is trying to put the masses on the right track . . . say that Sánchez Cerro, convinced that the germ of cowardice has disappeared from the masses, believes that the opportune moment has arrived to direct the masses on the right path, the path that we should be marking out.[8]

In addition to Sánchez Cerro's extremely pejorative characterization of the masses at this early date in his evolution, what is particularly striking about this declaration is that in it he even predicted that he would revolt in the general area of Arequipa, telling his friend to take special note, "when there, from the extreme south, you see this Piurano advancing and advancing. . . ."[9]

In the 1920s Sánchez Cerro twice showed that he was prepared to convert his ambitious words into action. Apparently disregarding his prophecy of an emergence in the South, he rebelled first in the Amazon town of Iquitos in 1919 and later in the former Inca capital of Cuzco in 1922. Initially punishing the rebellious officer with imprisonment and then with assignments in some of the most inhospitable military outposts of the interior, Leguía finally decided to remove him from the Peruvian scene by sending him to Spain, Italy, and France for further professional training. Sánchez Cerro finally returned to Peru in the last months of 1929, and, his political ambitions undiminished by previous setbacks, he reaffirmed to friends his confidence that he would soon become the president of his country. In a conversation held at the home of José Carlos Mariátegui, he is reported to have said: "I must be president; I must overthrow this wretch . . . These are not idle boasts; what I say I do . . . I swear by my mother that you will continue to hear about me."[10] And soon thereafter when speaking to a fellow plotter about who would assume the presidency upon the fall of Leguía, Sánchez Cerro resolutely affirmed: "The president will be me."[11]

Sánchez Cerro's final success in the attainment of this presidential goal was the culmination of long and careful planning. Having failed in two previous ouster attempts in 1919 and 1922, he initiated serious conversations with civilians and military men in Lima about a third effort to depose Leguía in the first months of 1929. At that time Sánchez Cerro contemplated using the national military school at Chorrillos as his rebel base but was forced to change his tactics when transferred to Arequipa in the month of June. Armed with recommendations from his fellow conspirators in the capital, Sánchez Cerro found fertile soil for his scheme in Arequipa. He was able to capitalize on the friction that had already built up since 1927 between the military establishment in Arequipa and the political administration in Lima and quickly gained the support of a group of young officers. Sánchez Cerro brought into the conspiracy a group of liberal intellectuals who had not only been alienated by the tyrannical aspects of Leguía's rule, but also shared the widely held opinión that Arequipa had been neglected if not maligned by the administration. Beginning in April or May of 1930, the plotters met weekly in a private home on the outskirts of the city to discuss alternative forms of action. In order to insure the success of his attempt it is reported that Sánchez Cerro also carried on secret talks with Foción Mariátegui, a highly placed member of the Leguía regime and a relative of the president. Finally the date was set: on August 30, 1930, the Arequipa garrison under Sánchez Cerro's command would rise against the government. But when it was learned on August 21 that Leguía had discovered their intentions, the conspirators hastily decided to move the next morning.[12]

In the early hours of August 22, 1930, Sánchez Cerro led his troops through the streets of Arequipa to take control of the city. As news of the movement spread, small groups of people began to follow the rebels and applaud their progress. It immediately became obvious that the rebellion was directed at the overthrow of the government, but what was its program? To predict that Sánchez Cerro would take a "military" position in politics clarified little, as the armed forces had largely stayed out of the political arena after Benavides's short-lived government in 1914–15. During the *oncenio* the military was hardly visible in public life and clearly lacked the cohesion and sense of direction necessary for the formulation of a blueprint for socioeconomic reform or even for a major political overhaul. How, then, did Sánchez Cerro intend to govern? These questions were answered, at least in part, by the *"Manifiesto de Arequipa"* which the rebels distributed the afternoon of August 22. Signed by Sánchez Cerro, the *"Manifiesto"* was mainly devoted to explaining the motives of his movement; over half of its contents contained a strong attack on the Leguía government for its "corrupt and inefficient politics." In powerful and direct language the *"Manifiesto"* promised to end the tyranny and repression of the regime and thoroughly to moralize the state. Except for a brief reference to the need for freeing the nation from the yoke of foreign creditors, the document projected no revolutionary changes in economic or social structures. Instead, the few concrete policies enumerated included a return to freedom of the press, thrift in public administration, public works, and free elections.[13]

When they first met, the military rebels who wrote the *"Manifiesto"* and committed themselves to the overthrow of "the tyrant" might indeed have been skeptical about predictions of an easy victory. Throughout most of his eleven-year rule Leguía had demonstrated an uncanny ability to maintain public support. In the eyes of large segments of the population the president had set Peru on the road to "progress." He built roads and railroads, and, as if with a magic wand, transformed a decaying colonial Lima into a modern metropolis. Furthermore, diverse social strata seemed to benefit from "Leguía's prosperity." The demand for manual labor increased in a rapidly urbanizing Lima; professions grew at a spectacular pace. The government built schools and hospitals that served both middle and popular sectors. Peruvians were proud of Leguía's promotion of two gaudy centennials that attracted people from around the world, who, it was said, "doubtless were amazed by the splendor they saw."[14] The president's closest supporters spoke of the "Century of Leguía" and boasted that Peru had entered into a totally unprecedented period of national progress and greatness. As one commentator wrote, "Peru lived through these years in a dream straight out of the Arabian Nights . . . Everything went perfectly. Everyone was thankful to Leguía."[15]

To guard against those who refused to recognize the benefits of the *oncenio* and instead publicly protested or tried to overturn the government, the president created an elaborate system of surveillance and repression. A reorganized national police force watched cafés, restaurants, churches, union halls, and military barracks for any sign of antigovernment activity. Suspected subversives were harshly dealt with, usually ending up in prison or in exile without trials.[16]

It was only when the most important pillars of the regime—the military and the majority of the nation's economic elite—withdrew their support from Leguía that the *oncenio* truly began to falter, making possible the impressive victory of Sánchez Cerro. Throughout his administration Leguía had taken great pains to insure the support of the country's highest ranking military officers. Loyal servants of the regime received promotions and special economic benefits. Hence, when elements of the armed forces determined to overthrow the president, they sought support only among younger officers as yet untouched by government patronage. A degree of anti-Leguía sentiment in the military began to crystallize around the signing of the Tacna-Arica settlement with Chile in 1929. In the young officers' eyes the "surrender" of Peruvian territory under the terms of the treaty constituted an act of treason, and Leguía was to be held responsible. In addition, members of the military were disturbed by the president's large-scale harassment and imprisonment of army officers following an unsuccessful *golpe* attempt in September of 1929 and by a general lowering of salaries during the first days of the depression. In spite of the growing unrest within the armed forces, it appears that Leguía maintained the backing of the majority of the officer corps up to the revolt of Arequipa. And the military as a body backed the *golpe* only when it became evident that the regime was on the brink of collapse. It was largely from the younger officers that Sánchez Cerro received wholehearted support, as he symbolized to them a heroic "new man" who, uncontaminated by the corruption of the *oncenio* had shown the courage to stand up to Leguía on more than one occasion.[17]

During the *oncenio* Leguía had also made a concerted effort to curry the favor of Peru's economic oligarchy. Although the president overtly worked to undermine the traditional elite politically, at the same time he repeatedly made it clear that in their economic affairs large landowners, bankers, and businessmen had nothing to fear from his regime. Moreover, he pointed out that this group could expect to be one of the major beneficiaries of the economic progress during his government. Serious cracks in a previously smooth relationship started to appear in 1928 when Peruvian producers and exporters began to suffer from a decline in world sugar prices. In increasing numbers landowners and businessmen blamed the government for having failed to act promptly and effectively in their support. Instead of trying to mollify these sectors, the regime reacted to criticism by threatening the water supplies and the very existence of the *latifundistas* with talk of the desirability of irrigation projects leading to the creation of numerous small, diversified farms. The administration also moved to enforce existing water distribution laws for the first time, while the official press belittled the protests of the Sociedad Nacional Agraria with suggestions that the planters put their own houses in order rather than seek aid from the government. The depression acted to deepen the existing rift between the president and the economic oligarchs who objected to various restrictions placed on their financial activities to ameliorate the effects of the crisis. When Sánchez Cerro revolted in August, he acted with the approval of most elements of the nation's upper classes.[18]

Throughout Peruvian society dissatisfaction with the government mounted as the depression became more serious. The 1920s image of prosperity became increasingly eroded. A regime based on the constant flow of capital from abroad could not function effectively in times of an international economic crisis. Failing to see the international scope of the deteriorating economic picture, the general public held Leguía accountable for the growing problems. His ministers reacted slowly and unimaginatively to the changing economic situation. And Leguía, faced with the imminent destruction of his *Patria Nueva,* seemed to have become physically and mentally worn out after eleven years in the presidency. The man who had claimed as his own the material progress of the past could not now escape being held responsible for the crisis of the present. As the administration proved unable to moderate the effects of the repression, many pointed to the military *golpes* that had occurred early in 1930 in Bolivia and Argentina as appropriate forms of solving Peru's problems. When it became known in Lima that Leguía had definitely stepped down, the outpouring of public enthusiasm was enormous. Workers, aristocrats, and students joined together to celebrate the fall of the tyrant. Large mobs sacked and burned the homes of prominent Leguiístas.[19]

Once in the government palace Sánchez Cerro based much of the legitimacy of his rule on his predominant part in the ouster of Leguía. He was aided by the fact that in the months following the downfall of the previous government all Lima seemed obsessed with exposing the corruption of the *oncenio*. Eleven years of censorship and growing repression gave way to a veritable public witch hunt of "wicked" Leguiístas. The newspapers with the highest circulations were those that crowded into their pages the largest number of stories about the wealth accumulated by the fallen malefactors, the luxurious life led by the ex-president's closest cohorts and relatives, and the details of specific cases of graft and underhanded financial dealings. A group of men that had been political prisoners under the previous regime formed the Committee of Public Safety and Revolutionary Consolidation that investigated and leveled accusations against ex-public administrators on the basis of individual denunciations. From the beginning Sánchez Cerro was identified in the public mind with this anti-Leguía sentiment. In the press, in street demonstrations, and in personal letters praise was heaped on the new president for his redemption of a people that, it was alleged, had "lost all notions of dignity, of pride, of virility."[20]

Sánchez Cerro consciously exploited to his own political advantage the atmosphere of hatred toward the fallen "tyrant." Nearly all his public speeches contained numerous references to the Leguía regime, to his own part in its overthrow, and pledges of continued dedication to the elimination of all vestiges of the shameful past. In actions, as well as in words, he perpetuated the connection between his ascendancy and the extermination of Leguiísmo. One of his first acts as president was to order the imprisonment of Leguía along with the detention of prominent politicians associated with the fallen "tyrant." Next he formed the Tribunal of National Sanction, whose sole function was the trial and punishment of members of the former government. The vehemence with which he attacked the Leguiístas was in part the product of Sánchez Cerro's personal anticivilian bias, an attitude nurtured during his army days. To the Hero of Arequipa and to his military associates, the corruption of Leguía's rule must have represented all that was wrong with civilian politics in Peru.[21]

Sánchez Cerro governed Peru as the president of a military *junta* for a period of six months, from September 1930 through February 1931. During that time the persecution of ex-functionaries of the *oncenio* was a prominent feature of his regime. But other policies undertaken by his "Government of Six Months" served to strengthen even more directly the bonds forged in August between the rebellious *caudillo* and the urban masses. The favorable impression created would be of particular value to him during his subsequent electoral campaign in 1931. While still in Arequipa Sánchez Cerro initially buttressed his popular support by decreeing the abolition of the hated program of forced labor for road construction. Although the *Conscripción Vial* was most rigorously applied in the interior, Lima too had witnessed the organization of road gangs made up of men who had been unable to pay their highway tax quotas. In the capital as well as in the rest of the country the working classes rejoiced at Sánchez Cerro's ending of the forced labor system. Another move that gained the new president considerable favor was the establishment of civil marriage and divorce. With the exception of weak protests from the Catholic hierarchy and scattered traditional groups, Sánchez Cerro's divorce law was greeted with almost unanimous approval.[22]

Sánchez Cerro's efforts aimed at the alleviation of the suffering imposed on the urban poor by the depression probably contributed most to the reinforcement of his popularity among members of that sector. Three weeks after assuming power, in response to entreaties for help from Lima's hungry, the president ordered the distribution of food rations in the city's police stations. Long lines of anxious men and women, often with children in their arms, pressed close to the stationhouse doors to claim their share. and after collecting their bundles "innumerable words of praise have rushed out of those hearts for the magnanimous man who protected them thus. Those virgin lips now have learned to pronounce with affection the name of the person who has favored them . . . the people join together in acclaiming their affection for the brave and honorable soldier who threw out tyranny."[23]

In 1914 Guillermo Billinghurst's government had distributed food in response to the momentary crisis provoked by the outbreak of World War I. But no administration had ever undertaken this procedure on such a large scale. The editorials in the local press jubilantly applauded Sánchez Cerro's initiative, affirming that "it is the first instance in recent times that a chief of state has assumed such a generous and gentle attitude."[24] They further suggested that the people acclaim and, what was more important, reward Sánchez Cerro's beneficent works: "From this day on the people now know that you cannot trick them with words or promises, as was the custom in the era of the dictatorship: real deeds are what reveal the good works that inspire the new regime."[25]

Many of Sánchez Cerro's measures to help the needy in Lima were carried out in conjunctiom with the city's mayor, a close political collaborator of the president, Luis Antonio Eguiguren. Backed publicly by the chief executive, Eguiguren proceeded to launch a tenacious campaign to lower the cost of food and other items essential to the subsistence of the population in the capital. The city government established "popular fairs" in which meat, lard, potatoes, rice, and other articles were sold to the public at cost. A rapidly decreed emergency law prohibited the proprietors of working class dwellings from evicting tenants who had fallen behind in their rent payments. Eguiguren also met frequently with local businessmen and industrialists and attempted to convince them, in the name of the president as well as his own, to cease laying off more workers, to maintain salary levels, and to donate food and clothing for allotment to the most poverty-striken segments of the populace. Soon daily lists of contributors began to appear in the morning newpapers alongside stories about how the mayor had convinced the electric company or the millers or the local dairies to reduce their rates to the public. On Christmas Eve both Sánchez Cerro and Eguiguren handed out toys to poor children in hospitals and at City Hall. In return they received tearful tributes of thanks for their "noble sentiments."[26]

At the same time that Sánchez Cerro gained the loyalty of a large part of Lima's working class population during his presidency of the *junta,* he also revealed certain of his fundamental ideas about how Peru should be ruled. And if his charitable deeds quickly found favor with nearly the totality of the urban masses, other of his policies soon alienated specific working class groups. One most prominent target of the new president's hostility was the organized labor movement. In a communiqué sent from Arequipa on August 27, Sánchez Cerro gave indications of his distaste for "radicalism" with the statement that "Communist excesses, all types of misbehavior will be repressed with force, with energy."[27] Nevertheless in the first weeks of his regime many prominent labor leaders continued to admire the rebellious *caudillo* for having ousted Leguía. Any hopes that these men might have had for favorable treatment from Sánchez Cerro were, however, quickly dissipated by his relentless suppression of strikes and his outlawing of the Confederación General de Trabajadores del Perú (CGTP) on the heels of violent disturbances in the interior mining centers of La Oroya and Malpaso. Heated protests of labor and stu-

dent groups alleging that the government had become the brutal instrument of foreign imperialism and despotism fell on deaf ears as Sánchez
Cerro stood firm in his intention to put down any movements that in his
view might be obstacles on the road to national recovery.[28]

The new president's harsh treatment of organized labor was but one
example of the generally conservative orientation towards the solution of
Peru's problems that he revealed during his "Government of Six
Months." Upon first assuming power Sánchez Cerro was an unknown
quantity in ideological and policy terms. Unencumbered by commitments to specific political factions and surrounded by a *junta* made
up totally of military men that had seconded him in the Arequipa revolt,
it seemed to many observers that the *caudillo*-president might indeed
represent a new kind of reformist element in the armed forces similar to
the Prestes group in Brazil. But Sánchez Cerro quickly destroyed these
illusions by enacting policies that were, for the most part, highly
favorable to the interests of the established elites. In October 1930, for
example, the government moved rapidly to satisfy the National Agrarian
Society which represented the country's large landholders, in its requests
of the lowering of fertilizer prices, the elimination of property taxes on
land devoted to sugar and cotton production, the increase of agricultural
credits, the temporary subsidization of the sugar industry, and the adoption of irrigation policies in line with the needs of *latifundistas*. One
month later Sánchez Cerro invited a relatively conservative economic
mission from the United States, headed by Princeton professor Edwin
Kemmerer, to visit Peru in order to recommend remedies for the nation's
fiscal problems.

Another indication of Sánchez Cerro's conservative bent was his
dependency on members of the traditional oligarchy for advice. From
the beginning of his regime he had solicited the aid of individuals identified with the country's elites, and their dominance seemed well
established when the new president reorganized his cabinet for the first
time in November 1930 to include men clearly identified with the political
leadership of the *República aristocrática*.[29] Sánchez Cerro's
demonstrated affinity for these elite elements may be attributed to
various factors. Most important, there is considerable evidence that the
president himself was a committed political conservative. We are
reminded of his references to the lower classes in his yearbook entry
where he defined them as "the indolent and lazy rabble" he would rule
with "a loaf of bread in one hand and a whip in the other." Perhaps
influenced in part by his experiences as a military officer, Sánchez Cerro
expressed similar views in another early statement included in a 1916
letter to his brother Antonio. Commenting on an oil strike that year, he
wrote:

I have always affirmed and continue to affirm that this poorly understood system of strikes—typical of the rabble—is the worst of those evils recently introduced in this already degenerated and convulsive country. The imbecile mass only yields when the cudgel enters into action . . . It truly irritates me, as if it were an attack directed against me personally, every time that these horrid events occur.[30]

In an important sense Sánchez Cerro had nowhere else to turn than to the old political pros of the *República aristocrática*. The military as an institution had failed to develop a unified approach to government, and the new president's personal conservatism kept him from seeking advice from the more progressive sectors of the bourgeoisie. What was worse, many of the "progressives" were closely identified with Leguiísmo. Acutely conscious of his inexperience in the art of government, Sánchez Cerro concluded that he would rule most effectively with the assistance of men who themselves had exercised power in the past. And the oligarchical veterans were among the first to offer publicly their aid to the new regime. With their own political organizations in disarray, certain traditional politicians sought to ingratiate themselves with the *junta* as a means of retaining some measure of political influence.[31]

When Sánchez Cerro first assumed power at the end of August he gave only vague indications of how long he intended to retain the presidency, remarking that the *junta* would resign at the time it considered the country ready for civilian government. Three months later, however, when the government decreed the formation of a constituent assembly charged with the election of a provisional president, it became apparent that the Hero of Arequipa had begun to make concrete plans for his political future. The new law effectively centralized the electoral machinery in the hands of the executive and created a legal façade for the retention of power by Sánchez Cerro. Those favorable to the *caudillo*-president openly rejoiced that "the constituent assembly in May will simply confirm a fact about which all of us Peruvians are in perfect agreement: that is that Commandant Sánchez Cerro is the supreme chief of Peru."[32] Spurred on by the prospect of an upcoming election, enthusiastic backers of the president began to promote the publication of telegrams and proclamations in the Lima newspapers urging the reaffirmation of Sánchez Cerro's rule by means of the suffrage process. The majority of these documents reasoned that the nation owed the rebellious commandant a debt of gratitude for his overthrow of the tyranny. They suggested that his election to a six-year term of office would constitute a proper form of payment.

From his seat in the government palace, Sánchez Cerro actively encouraged these efforts. When presented with the proclamation of his candidacy, he accepted willingly. At the same time he materially assisted in the campaign by personally soliciting the cooperation of prominent men throughout the Republic. In a telegram sent to future president David Samanéz Ocampo in Cuzco, for example, Sánchez Cerro wrote: "Those who are frankly in agreement with my politics should proceed immediately to proclaim my candidacy . . . Please show these originals to the prefect and the rest of our friends that meet at the prefectura. Here there is perfect common agreement among my friends."[33]

Seemingly not content to wait until May 1, 1931, when the Constituent Assembly was to hold the elections, the Sánchez Cerro government enacted still another electoral law in February calling for elections within six weeks. The *junta* argued that this policy change resulted from "the wishes of the nation that a true plebiscite should issue forth to record the unanimity of the people of the Republic."[34] With the reference to a plebiscite and given the short time between the issuance of the decree and the projected date of the election, which made it nearly impossible for opposing candidates to mount campaigns, it seemed clear that Sánchez Cerro expected the upcoming vote to bring about an extension and further legitimation of his rule. By all appearances, Sánchez Cerro was fully set on retaining power and was loath to make any moves which might jeopardize his electoral enterprise. As he bluntly responded to one individual who suggested that he step down as president before pursuing his candidacy in order to avoid the possibility of an election controlled from the government palace: "I would not step down from power even if I was asked to do so by my mother standing naked."[35]

Sánchez Cerro's determination to remain in office was not accepted as a forgone conclusion by all. A powerful offensive against the president was mounted initially by a group of young intellectuals that had founded the Acción Republicana movement in January of 1931. They vigorously attacked Sánchez Cerro in the press, in public speeches, and at times in personal confrontations, charging that his attempts at an *"autoelección"* ("self-election") had led to the suppression of political opposition and the rigging of the suffrage process. They added that his continuation in government was undesirable because his own administration had been riddled by vacillation, uncertainty, and outright mistakes.[36]

Their campaign against the *autoelección* of Sánchez Cerro appears to have played an important role in influencing key national figures to reconsider their previously unconditional support of the Hero of Arequipa. A particularly important faction of this growing opposition was made up of high ranking military officers who never could fully accept being subordinate to a mere commandant. As Sánchez Cerro's electoral schemes became an increasingly important issue, the formerly frag-

mented opposition to the regime unified behind the call for fair elections
and finally turned to armed rebellion. Generals, colonels, majors, and
sergeants led a series of disjointed movements in the northern, southern,
and central regions of the country. In the space of two weeks seven
different revolts broke out, and for a short time the nation was ruled
simultaneously by two "revolutionary" governments, one in Arequipa
and another in Lima. In the last days of February 1931 Peru experienced
a level of political chaos that was strongly reminiscent of the most
agitated moments of the nineteenth century.

The first attempt to oust the president by force came close to undermining all subsequent efforts. Led by Leguía's chief of police, General
Pedro Pablo Martínez, a small number of rebels rose in Callao with the
ostensible intention of taking advantage of the atmosphere of criticism
of the regime to initiate a Leguiísta renaissance. Loyal government
troops easily put down the revolt amidst the approving cheers of sympathetic crowds in Callao. Nearly all sectors of public opinion repudiated
this endeavor to return to the policies of the *oncenio,* including the
members of the Acción Republicana, who were particularly anxious to
disassociate themselves from any hints of ties with the previous regime.[37]

The very night that Sánchez Cerro proudly credited himself with having defeated the revolt in Callao while promising to "punish today and
always all traitors,"[38] another rebellion broke out in Arequipa that was
to spell the end of his "Government of Six Months." In spite of the cool
reception afforded the rebels by the populace of Arequipa, which, for the
most part, repudiated the move against the *caudillo*-president, it had the
backing of the majority of the local military command and of numerous
prominent civilians. One factor which reinforced these civilians' opposition to Sánchez Cerro was their feeling that he had failed to carry out his
promise of increased local autonomy contained in the *"Manifesto de
Arequipa."* Indeed, various of the conspirators participated in the
rebellion only on the condition that the presidency and the cabinet posts
of a new governing *junta* would go to men from southern Peru, essentially Arequipa and Cuzco. Notwithstanding these strong regional concerns, on the night that the insurgency broke out its leaders decided to
muffle anything that might detract from the national image of their
movement. Realizing that opposition to Sánchez Cerro's *autoelección*
had made unity possible in the first place, they resolved to "raise as a banner of the revolution Sánchez Cerro's failure to keep the promises he
made upon assuming power and his intention to campaign for the
presidency, retaining the power of government in order to impose
himself in the coming election."[39] Moreover, they promised that their
first act upon taking power would be the calling of fair elections in which

the vote by secret ballot would insure the final elimination of tyranny in Peru. Soon after the outbreak in Arequipa military units in the northern part of the country revolted against the government and proclaimed similar goals.[40]

There is evidence that unfulfilled personal expectations to obtain concrete benefits from the original August revolution in Arequipa may have been a fundamental consideration in the decision of many military men actively to seek the ouster of Sánchez Cerro. Even at the height of his prestige during the first weeks following the overthrow of Leguía the *caudillo*-president could count on only the partial support of the armed forces. Officers at the top of the military hierarchy who had been excluded from power and humiliated at having to obey younger colonels and majors never smiled upon the new government, and many tirelessly plotted its overthrow. More importantly, Sánchez Cerro steadily lost the cooperation of a large segment of his original following because he not only failed to honor the traditional custom of promoting confederates but also indignantly berated those that appealed for advancement on the basis of their collaboration in the Arequipa movement. One of the leaders of the attempt to overthrow Sánchez Cerro in February 1931 gave vent to his feelings of unfair treatment at the hands of the president in a telegram urging officers in Cuzco to join the rebellion: "For Commandant Sánchez Cerro, the resignations of those of his *compañeros* who were the soul of the August 22nd movement have meant nothing. He has preferred to ignore those men who had a high concept of the meaning of the overthrow of the Leguía regime. . . ."[41]

Sánchez Cerro followed two lines of action in his attempt to suppress the threat to his regime. He first tried to retain power by retreating from his intransigence on the question of the presidential plebiscite. On February 23 he canceled the impending election and also withdrew his presidential candidacy. Shortly thereafter, when it became evident that this momentary show of weakness on his part only served to strengthen the determination of the rebels, Sánchez Cerro decided to use force and dispatched expeditionary forces to put down the disturbances in the South and in the North. But these troops never reached their respective destinations. Shortly after the forces sent south left the harbor of Callao aboard two troop transports, the commander-in-chief of the navy issued a proclamation announcing that he had ordered the ships to stop in order to prevent the eruption of a civil war. Out of options and faced with the fact that his power base had been significantly weakened, Sánchez Cerro called a meeting of the leading representatives of the country's corporate groups and, proclaiming his desire to spare Peru from bloodshed, resigned from the presidency.[42]

The announcement caught those present totally unprepared, and initially it was uncertain who would govern the nation. For a few short hours the Apostolic administrator of the Lima Archdiocese presided over the country, but he quickly gave way to a provisional administration headed by the president of the Supreme Court, Ricardo Leoncio Elías. Elías's presidency lasted only four days. Gustavo Jiménez, commander of the troops originally sent south by Sánchez Cerro, provoked the precipitous downfall of the provisional regime when he disembarked with his men in Callao and marched boldly on the government palace. At first it was generally believed that the action of Jiménez, a collaborator of Sánchez Cerro and member of his first cabinet, represented the restoration to power of the fallen *caudillo*. Even the troops that Jiménez led from Callao believed that he had the intention of replacing Elías with his old associate Sánchez Cerro. But Jiménez had other plans. Initially intending to retain the presidency for himself, Jiménez was immediately confronted with the opposition of the rebels in Arequipa. After feverish negotiations by telegraph with the insurgents in the South, Jiménez finally agreed to accept the powerful post of minister of war in a new *junta* made up of civilian elements representing five different regions of the country, under the presidency of an old-line politician from Cuzco, David Samanéz Ocampo.[43]

The groups that had worked against Sánchez Cerro were eminently pleased with the relatively easy success of their enterprise. Virtually without bloodshed they had been able to displace a *caudillo*-president known for his almost blind personal courage and his inclination to resort to violent actions. But if they thought that by removing Sánchez Cerro from the government palace they had also accomplished his exclusion from politics, the public reaction to his overthrow must have caused them considerable concern. Before and after his resignation the streets of Lima were the scene of impassioned mass demonstrations in his favor. In the moments when Sánchez Cerro was relinquishing the office of president, fiery orators in public plazas, to the applause of large crowds, pledged their undying loyalty to the "only head of the revolution of Arequipa, because if it had not been for him, we would still have the rule of the Leguía tyranny, and therefore all the gratitude of our people is for him."[44] Outside the balcony of the suite at the Hotel Bolívar, where Sánchez Cerro lived after leaving the government palace, sizable groups composed mainly of working class people kept day-long vigils on their beloved *comandante:* "Old women in *saya* and *manta* [the traditional feminine dress of Lima], young girls in high-heeled shoes and sheer silk stockings, workingmen collarless and in shirt sleeves, people of all colours and complexions and conditions of life. Among them the small urchin who tries to sell me 'huachitos' ['sections'] of lottery tickets on Wednesdays and Saturdays."[45] All patiently waited together for an opportunity to hear Sánchez Cerro speak, or just to catch a glimpse of him. Never before in the memory of contemporary observers had the citizenry gathered in such a manner to acclaim a fallen president.[46]

It appeared that not only had the admiration of the masses for Sánchez Cerro remained intact, but his popularity had probably grown in response to the attack upon his right to rule. He continued to be the "Hero of Arequipa," the man who had risked all for the salvation of his country. And now he could add the laurels of a martyr to his political portfolio, of one who had sacrificed his political ambitions for the well-being of the nation — this time to prevent the outbreak of a bloody civil war. In his communiqués and speeches throughout the period of crisis Sánchez Cerro effectively bolstered this image by comparing his own "unquenchable faith as a soldier and pure patriotic spirit" with the actions of his enemies, whom he termed a "group of reprehensible elements that want to finish sinking the fatherland into the mire of their bastard ambitions."[47] Once having unseated the tyrant, Sánchez Cerro claimed that his only ambition had been "to work for the greatness of the fatherland and carry out the words of the 'Manifiesto de Arequipa' over which I am a watchful sentinel." But he had been thwarted in his righteous task by "a Leguiísta reaction paid for by the corrupting gold of Leguiísmo."[48] On the day that he finally left the country for a self-imposed exile in Europe, Sánchez Cerro promised to return to take an active part in national politics: "In the meantime, my heart, my brain, and my muscle remain loyal at the altar of the fatherland, ready as always to make the sacrifices imperiously demanded by the nation. Fellow citizens: in this farewell embrace, receive all my affection; and the great desire that I have to contribute, upon my return, to the realization of your just aspirations."[49]

Mobs of demonstrators accompanied Sánchez Cerro's motorcade as it slowly drove through the streets of Lima, and in the port of Callao they sadly witnessed the parting of a man whom they still considered a hero and now a martyr. This emotional send-off contrasted sharply with the muted reception of Samanéz Ocampo some four days later; and even greater was the difference between Sánchez Cerro's original arrival in August to take the presidency when he was greeted by 100,000 people and Samanéz's arrival at the capital, which only attracted 2,000 onlookers. Some observers ignored these events and rejoiced that Sánchez Cerro's ouster meant that "with his stepping down from the presidency he has been politically flattened, and he has absolutely no future."[50] Other more thoughtful commentators did not allow themselves to be blinded by the seeming ease of the ex-president's over-throw. As one anti-Sánchezcerrista sourly remarked, Sánchez Cerro's momentary loss of power did not mean his political funeral. Judging by the extraordinary outpouring of support on the part of "the people of Lima, who if they lack political ideals and spiritual profoundness, do possess a sharp instinct for events and personalities," it appeared evident that the "Hero of Arequipa" remained a major political force in the country, one certainly to be reckoned with in the upcoming contest for the presidency.[51]

5

Sánchezcerrismo II:
The Hero Campaigns

FROM THE early morning hours scores of people started their short journey from Lima to the neighboring port city of Callao. By train, by streetcar, by bus, by truck, by car, or if all else failed, on foot the faithful slowly gathered to greet the returning hero. Sánchez Cerro was back after four months of exile in Europe.

The large majority of the crowds were working class people: "stevedores, fishermen, millhands, unemployed and unemployable, women with sleeping babes in their arms. . . ."[1] The Samanéz *junta* had tried to limit the political impact of Sánchez Cerro's reception by cutting off all rail and automobile traffic from Lima to Callao after 12:00 p.m. But their efforts were to no avail. The men and women who in the days since learning of his impending return had envisioned grandiose scenes of welcome were not to be denied. By 2:00 p.m. on July 2, a waiting multitude filled the piers jutting into the Pacific. "Viva Sánchez Cerro!" "Forward the victor of the Revolution!" "The tyranny is ended!" "Viva Sánchez Cerro!" Applause. All promised that the event would be a splendid fiesta.

But gradually a sharp tension began to invade the jubilant atmosphere. Since mid-day, the site where Sánchez Cerro would land was guarded by military and police troops. In the early afternoon these forces began to cordon off the area, but people continued to stream in and noisily force themselves through the lines of armed men. As the crowds and troops jockeyed for position, the Italian steamer *Orazio,* carrying Sánchez Cerro, finally appeared on the horizon and dropped anchor in the harbor. The ecstatic multitude would not, however, see their idol that afternoon. In the midst of the excitement the soldiers and policemen received orders to dissolve the demonstrators. Many in the crowd stubbornly stayed in place, and some began to pelt the troops with stones. Swords were unsheathed. Gunfire broke out. The people ran terrified in all directions. Men and women sought safety by diving to the ground or jumping into the sea. In the face of these disorders, Sánchez Cerro decided to wait until early the next morning to disembark in order to avoid further violence.[2]

This confrontation was not easily forgotten. A baker, a construction worker, a taxi driver, a peasant, and two market vendors lay seriously wounded in the streets of Callao. Together they represented a kind of microcosm of the people Sánchez Cerro could expect to be his working class followers in the approaching campaign. Numerically speaking, that mass following was to constitute the major force in the populist coalition formed to support his bid for the presidency. In the three months following his stormy return from Europe Sánchez Cerro mounted a vigorous campaign during which he successfully transformed an originally amorphous group of working class sympathizers into an effective political force.

Sánchez Cerro's political style was the all-important foundation upon which he proceeded to build his political edifice. Believing that he was dealing with a citizenry better prepared to accept the relatively simple force of a personality than the abstract language of a political platform, the "Hero of Arequipa" carefully constructed his appeal around the projection of an attractive self-image. But to say that Sánchez Cerro worked to present a favorable picture of himself does not mean that the picture presented was necessarily a false or artificial one. On the contrary, his style represented the manifestation and emphasis of specific character traits that he already possessed. Those traits, more than his explicit stands on political issues, were fundamental in determining the character of his movement.[3]

One immediately visible trait which had particular importance in capturing the working class vote was Sánchez Cerro's physical appearance. Short of stature and weighing slightly over 110 pounds, his most striking feature was his dark skin, revealing a definite *mestizo* racial background (see figures 7 and 8). Sánchez Cerro skillfully capitalized on his racial makeup to underline his identification with the urban masses. In numerous instances during the campaign his working class supporters could be heard boasting that "he's a *cholo* like us."[4] While many upper class Peruvians were scandalized by the possibility that a man of humble social origins could dominate a political stage previously occupied almost exclusively by white members of the national aristocracy, the urban poor saw in his dark face one of their own that had successfully scaled the political heights. The common man could indeed take pride in seeing an individual physically similar to himself, "flattered by the solicitude of learned lawyers and fanned by the coquetry of the most aristocratic ladies."[5] Moreover, ostensibly of the same extraction as the majority of the urban masses, Sánchez Cerro was a figure of special trust who could be counted upon to work in government particularly hard for those of similar lineage. "He was of our race," reflected one of his working class followers, "and because of that all us working people supported him. Our feelings, his race—together they combined to bolster the man. We had confidence in him."[6] Irrespective of the true mixture of blood that ran through his veins, Sánchez Cerro was a *cholo,* an Indian, a black to his various working class sympathizers.

The commandant-candidate strengthened his association with the urban masses by maintaining frequent personal contact with them. Daily

Figure 7. Luis M. Sánchez Cerro. From ASC.

his campaign headquarters was filled with working class individuals seeking an audience, and he usually obliged them, telling his aides, "don't
turn the people away, because they have to come to me to shake my
hand. Let them all embrace me. I want to embrace them too."[7] Sánchez
Cerro tried to attend popular celebrations often, where, side by side with
common laborers, he danced the *marinera*,[8] and apparently with genuine
gusto joined in all aspects of the festivities. Those who observed Sánchez
Cerro's face-to-face encounters with the masses commented that he
treated them with visible affection, as if they were his children. In the
words of a working class follower, he was considered, in fact, "a father
for us all."[9]

Sánchez Cerro's experience as a troop commander probably had an
important influence on the development of a paternalistic relationship
with his mass supporters. He had learned in the military that an officer
was responsible for his men just as a father was for his children, and this
posture was easily extended to the popular masses in general. Stationed
in isolated small town garrisons during much of his career, Sánchez
Cerro had undoubtedly been called upon to play the *patrón* before. His
dealings with the poor as a chief figure in the local hierarchy had

Figure 8. Sánchez Cerro Speaks. From Archivo Gráfico, Biblioteca Nacional del Perú, Lima.

prepared him to mix closely with his working class followers while retaining his professed conservative, even disdainful, view of society's lower strata. At the same time that he may have thought of the poor as "lazy and indolent," the candidate encouraged them to approach him personally and ask for favors. Sánchez Cerro invariably responded by patting his humble supplicants on the back, writing down their names, and at times taking money from his pocket for them or even giving them articles of clothing from his own wardrobe. Always employing the *tú* form and speaking to them in simple language, he would say, "Toma hijo, toma hija. Hijito, hijita, sí, ya vamos a ver" ("Take this son, take that daughter. My little son, my little daughter, yes, yes we shall see.")[10] It might have seemed to many that the words of a song that became popular during the campaign constituted an accurate indication of what could be expected of Sánchez Cerro once in power:

> Cuando suba Sánchez Cerro
> no vamos a trabajá
> pue nos va a llové todito
> como del cielo el maná.[11]

> When Sánchez Cerro is in power
> We won't work
> 'cause every little thing's going
> to rain on us like the manna from heaven.

Disturbed by what he saw, one observer wrote the following picturesque account of how some members of the elite viewed Sánchez Cerro's relationship with the masses:

Sánchez Cerro has offered to pull the mob out of its present situation as is evident in cases like the following: a family, the head of the house is an aunt of mine, has gone down socially and economically, and when she was trying to sell her possessions in order to go to England, the native country of her husband, she received the following offer from her butler: "Don't sell anything, don't go to England and wait for a short while until Luis takes power, he is my friend. I will get a job in the post office and I'll get a good job for the *patrón*." You can laugh about that offer. A vegetable seller in the market says to a client of hers: "As a vegetable seller I have trouble finding good husbands for my daughters, but now we can start looking for better candidates, because when Luis Miguel is in power I will be the head of the state shops, my daughter who's a midwife will have a good job and my other daughter will be an accountant in a ministry." These cases are counted in the hundreds.[12]

Sánchez Cerro's political style, eminently personalistic and paternalistic, had a significant impact on potential working class voters. It seemed that the *mestizo* candidate, with his kind manner and simple language, understood the masses well. Assuming the characteristics of an authoritative and beneficent father figure, Sánchez Cerro appeared particularly qualified to both comprehend and solve the problems of his lower class followers. His successful building of a profoundly personal relationship with the humble gave his campaign an aura of responsiveness to popular needs; his person was seen as a sympathetic link between the powerless and the power structure.

The commandant-candidate's protective stance was only one facet of his fatherly role. As a fervent working class Sánchezcerrista declared: "He was a father both to punish and to give; for both things. He gave and he was stern too."[13] Sánchez Cerro revealed a particular severity bordering on violence in his treatment of those who displeased him, and he would not tolerate abuse from any sector. When part of the audience began to boo his words during one of his speeches, an infuriated Sánchez Cerro abruptly stopped their protests by harshly commanding the crowd to silence. On another occasion when he still headed the "Government of Six Months," the president is reported to have angrily rebuffed a hostile demonstration of striking laborers by shouting, "Carajo, no sigan fregando!" ("Shit, stop bothering me!").[14] More than once after assuming the office of first executive in 1931, Sánchez Cerro personally whipped servants in the government palace that failed to carry out his orders properly.[15]

As a candidate Sánchez Cerro made no attempt to cover up these more violent aspects of his personality. In fact, there is evidence that he made considerable political capital of his strong language and actions.[16] In his campaign propaganda Sánchez Cerro's excesses were interpreted as the outward expressions of a powerful and authoritative individual overflowing with the inner toughness and self-confidence necessary to rule the national household effectively. In addition, Sánchez Cerro's staff insisted that these very characteristics had made it possible for him first to mount his successful attack on Leguía's seemingly impregnable political fortress and then properly to punish the "criminals of the tyranny." It was not to be forgotten — Sánchez Cerro would certainly not allow it — that the commandant-candidate was a military officer, a patriotic man of action in whom any sign of weakness or timidity would have tarnished an impressive masculine image. He stressed his past acts of seemingly boundless physical courage and exhorted the multitudes not to forget "the man who repeatedly risked his life for the liberty of the people and for the honor and future of Peru." Throughout the campaign he explicitly portrayed himself to be a supreme *caudillo* who combined the strength, courage, audacity, and authority necessary to "clear the path with his invincible sword" and thereby do for the people that which they were incapable of doing for themselves."[17] In short, Sánchez Cerro nurtured his image of the man who "llevaba los pantalones" ("wore the pants," or clearly was in charge), a valuable attribute in a culture that highly prized *machismo.*

An extraordinarily gifted orator, in his public speeches Sánchez Cerro effectively reinforced the belief that he was above all a straightforward man of action. His addresses usually lasted only five to ten minutes and seldom contained complex ideas. As he remarked on one occasion to his personal secretary: "You must not fill your speeches with phrases that might be very beautiful for the university but that the people do not understand."[18] Better suited to the spoken than the written word, his discourses were virtual harangues that exploded forcefully upon his listeners. With a voice that resounded over the crowd, Sánchez Cerro enjoyed drawing sharp contrasts between his enemies — the "horrid tyrants," "scoundrels," or "flea-filled rats" — and himself — the determined savior of his country guided by a "patriotic dream." In his own words, he was a simple man for whom "there is no effort, no sacrifice of which I am not capable. Every night when I close my eyes and every morning when I awaken, I renew my vows, before the altar of the fatherland, to carry on my duties as ruler with the purity of the priesthood."[19]

Also mixed into his oratory were striking expressions of compassion for the multitudes: "I love the masses with gratitude and conviction. I desire their betterment and their well-being, and I expect to attain them. . . ."[20] When speaking in public Sánchez Cerro rarely sought to inform his listeners or to convince them that he was right about a specific point. Instead he tried to inspire the populace with admiration for him as an individual. Hardly position papers or ideological statements, his orations were the vehicle by which a *caudillo* communicated to masses of people what he considered to be the most positive aspects of his personality. And if the cheers that greeted nearly his every phrase were any indication, Sánchez Cerro was eminently successful at this undertaking.[21]

To fully understand Sánchez Cerro's successful projection as a charismatic *caudillo,* the perceptions and attitudes of his followers must be examined. To a large extent, the charismatic figure is a creation of his supporters. As Max Weber has argued, rather than conforming to a set of universal charismatic characteristics, "it is the recognition on the part of those subject to authority which is decisive for the validity of charisma."[22] Without that recognition, the leader will be unable to exercise charismatic authority, notwithstanding his desire to convince all of his personal superiority. In the case of Sánchez Cerro the study of those aspects of his style that most appealed to the masses is facilitated by a seemingly endless series of letters, speeches, and proclamations that were written by members of working class Sánchezcerrista clubs and published daily in the Lima newspapers during the campaign. Their content overwhelmingly reflects an unquestioning faith in the candidate as a man who, by virtue of his innate superiority, could singlehandedly solve Peru's and their problems. Variously referred to as a *"patrón"* or a *"padre protector"* ("protective father"), he was remembered as the president of the "Government of Six Months," who had carefully tended to the needs of his poor children by providing them with their daily bread.[23] According to his working class supporters, he was a man who, guided by his particularly strong sense of *"fé, cariño, y amor"* ("faith, affection, and love"), would save the country from all present and future dangers. Furthermore, time and again he was referred to as the virile *"macho"* who, "with a strong fist, at great cost," had risen up to cure a sick nation of the ravages of the Leguía tyranny.[24] For that act, his supporters affirmed that the Peruvian people owed him their gratitude, their affection, and their political backing.

The words written on a homemade election poster (see figure 9) summarize well the qualities that Sánchez Cerro symbolized in the popular mind. The "Hero of Arequipa" is pictured in military uniform cutting the chains that bind a helpless Peru. Wrapped in the Peruvian flag, he is shown to embody the positive virtues of "honor, patriotism, heroism, sacrifice, and abnegation." On his sword appears the word "liberty," and it is clear that Sánchez Cerro is in the process of freeing the nation from the tyranny and corruption of Leguiísmo. The caption at the bottom reminds us that August 22 was the day on which liberty and individual rights had been returned to the republic. Judging by their seemingly boundless admiration for him, Sánchez Cerro's followers must have considered him to be gifted with powers bordering on the supernatural. He had, they maintained in numerous statements with distinctly charismatic overtones, "emerged through an invincible effort, led to his new duties by the supremely ordained will of the Universe."[25] A crude handbill, widely distributed among the Lima populace, effusively summarized the powerful personal impression communicated by the commandant-candidate:

CREDO CERRISTA

I BELIEVE in "cerrismo," all powerful, creator of all the liberties and all the claims of the popular masses; in LUIS M. SÁNCHEZ CERRO, our hero and undefeated paladin, conceived by the grace of the spirit of patriotism. Like a true Peruvian he was born in Holy Democracy and in the nationalist ideal; he suffered under the abject power of the *"oncenio";* he was persecuted, threatened, and exiled, and because he gave us liberty he shed his blood in the sacrifice of his being; he descended triumphant from the peaks of the Misti (Arequipa) to give us liberty and teach us by his patriotism, rising thusly to Power, glorious and triumphant. . . ."[26]

One important lesson to be learned from these accolades was that political ideologies were generally overlooked in favor of total person-to-person commitments to the *caudillo*. In weighing the relative importance of the electoral platform and the man in the Sánchezcerrista campaign, one working class backer affirmed in a letter to the candidate:

Figure 9. Sánchez Cerro in the Popular Mind. From ASC.

We are so sure, sir, that, about political creeds and doctrines, many thousands of electors . . . know and understand nothing, they only know that you have done well for them; because of this disinterested, blind faith in your steering of the destiny of the beloved fatherland, we pray that you be the man illuminated by the Almighty and that He grant you many years of life for the good of Peru.[27]

For his part, Sánchez Cerro plainly mounted a campaign in which the consideration of issues received little emphasis. An editorial published six days before the election in the major Sánchezcerrista newspaper unabashedly stated that political propaganda had clearly taken a back seat to the concrete accomplishments of the "Hero of Arequipa." The editorialist confidently predicted that the masses would be guided by a "sure intuition" rather than by any ideological commitment because,

As in the case of a Roman victor, among the triumphant cheers and acclamations of the citizens, thus, Sánchez Cerro, the hero of liberty, the strongest of the strong by virtue of the vigor of his own forceful life and the support of his fellow countrymen, has been carried forward by the vast multitude . . . Sánchez Cerro stands within the popular soul, very deep . . . because the people have understood that in Sánchez Cerro they have a chief capable of sheltering them . . . .[28]

Sánchez Cerro's working class supporters echoed the view that political propaganda was relatively unimportant in their decisions to vote for the commandant-candidate. They asserted that attendance at a rally, for example, was not for the purpose of hearing partisan discourses, but rather that "the people went to see him, nothing more. To touch the man, nothing more. It wasn't for his speeches or anything like that. His name alone was enough. Sánchez Cerro, that was all there was to say."[29]

During the campaign Sánchez Cerro hardly made mention of his political platform or his plans for Peru. Apparently in disregard of the fact that he had actually made his platform public some days earlier, the candidate replied at one point when asked about his program by an English journalist: "I have drawn up a scheme for the moral and economical regeneration of Peru. At the present moment nobody knows anything at all about it except myself. But I believe it will be found to meet the needs of the country."[30] Those who tried to pin him down about his plans for governing Peru were generally told that his own moral integrity and hard work were the best assurance for the nation's future. When particularly pressed by one individual who demanded to hear his views on the economic problems faced by the country, Sánchez Cerro is reported to have angrily answered: "The day when I have a couple of hours of free time I will solve Peru's economic problem."[31]

Sánchez Cerro's assertions to the contrary, his movement did take formal stands on a series of issues during the campaign, perhaps because such stands might help to legitimize the intense personal clash between competing electoral candidates.[32] As might be expected from the preceding analysis of Sánchez Cerro's political efforts, the major thrust of his rhetoric was directed at what the commandant *had done* in the past for Peru and not what he *would do* upon becoming president. The most commonly repeated theme and in a sense the symbol of his campaign was Sánchez Cerro's role in overthrowing Leguía. In nearly every public speech and daily in the Sánchezcerrista press the populace was reminded that with a single stroke of his glorious sword the commandant-candidate had broken forever the oppressive chains of the eleven-year tyranny. Popular songs praised the "Spartan soldier . . . with a warrior's breast" who had made his country free.[33] Satirical cartoons favorable to the "Hero of Arequipa" asserted that the brilliant light of the revolt of August served exceedingly better to show the way for the nation than the faint glow emitted by the competing Apra party's oversized "ideological lanterns" (see figure 10). The Sánchezcerrista electoral platform, published on the very day of the first anniversary of the revolt in Arequipa, began with the reminder that the candidate had by his heroic actions recovered for all Peruvians the dignity of a free people. On election day the party newspaper summed up its vindication of Sánchez Cerro by telling voters that it was their sacred duty to remember the man who had liberated Peru after eleven years of slavery and to express their gratitude properly by casting their ballots for him.

But a vote for Sánchez Cerro, it was argued, would mean more than an expression of thanks. In a direct appeal to the working class voter, campaigners for the commandant-candidate explained: "and it is the humble, those who most need a wave of relief from their situation, who have the highest hopes in Sánchez Cerro; because a marvelous intuition allows their rude consciousness to perceive that the same man that saved them once from the savage and bestial oppression of Leguiísmo can save us now once again."[34] As evidence for their claims of Sánchez Cerro's superior abilities to alleviate the suffering of the masses they pointed to the candidate's good works during his truncated "Government of Six Months." Newspaper articles and handbills cited the importance of "deeds and not words" and boasted that Sánchez Cerro had successfully fought the hunger of the people by "paternally" feeding the unemployed, had abolished the hated *Conscripción Vial* law, and had imprisoned Leguía and punished his corrupt collaborators.[35] Finally, the Sánchezcerristas declared that their candidate's labors could be completed only by his election to the presidency.[36]

The only major document produced by Sánchezcerrismo that contained indications of what Sánchez Cerro might do after being elected

was his platform, which, as may be recalled, the candidate himself overlooked on occasion. Conservative in tone, it called for the creation of a
regime of order, liberty, and hard work to accomplish the rebuilding of
the nation ravaged by the Leguía tyranny. Pronouncing the necessity that
class conflict give way to social unity, the platform took to task those
who it claimed were seeking to exploit existing social and economic
differences between Peruvians to create chaos. On the whole the document offered no radical departures from the past. It demonstrated that
the Sánchezcerristas had an essentially corporatist view of politics and
society and that they equated national progress with the rejuvenation of
traditional social and economic structures rather than the introduction of
new ones.[37]

   To different groups in the country the program promised specific

Figure 10. Words vs. Deeds. From *La Opinión,* September 10, 1931, p. 1.

benefits. Blue and white collar workers were offered a social security system to protect them and their families in cases of sickness, accident, physical handicap, old age, and death. Indians were told that under the Sánchez Cerro regime they would be considered full citizens with the same rights and duties as the rest of the population. Also usurped lands belonging to Indian communities would be returned to their rightful owners, plots would be distributed to the landless, cooperatives would be encouraged, technical aid would be made available, and special agricultural education would be disseminated through a new system of rural schools. The most radical sounding part of Sánchez Cerro's program was its discussion of land reform. The platform pledged legislation to restrict the formation of *latifundios* while protecting the small holder. But in the same breath it toned down this seemingly bold step by asserting that with extensive colonization of new lands, every rural family could own land without altering the existing distribution of property.[38]

While only a minor portion of Sánchez Cerro's campaign rhetoric was devoted to positive policy statements, considerably greater emphasis was given to attacking the candidate's real and supposed opponents. By accusing opposition politicians of everything from Leguiísmo to communism, a series of negative references[39] were propagated which served to elevate Sánchez Cerro by comparison. The negative reference most frequently employed corresponded to a political force that had already ceased to exist in Peru: Leguiísmo. And indeed those parts of Sánchez Cerro's speeches in which he vilified the "odious tyranny" of the former regime elicited the most enthusiastic response from his audiences.

Aware of the depth of anti-Leguiísta feelings in the populace, the Sánchezcerristas were also quick to use the issue of the fallen dictator against their major competitor in the election, the Aprista party. A frequent theme of their campaign was the tying of Aprismo to the defunct regime of the *oncenio*. Citing early contacts between Apra's leader and founder, Víctor Raúl Haya de la Torre, and Leguía and the fact that part of the financing for the Aprista campaign was provided by members of the former government, the Sánchezcerristas published fliers that blared: "Workers remember!! APRA is just a screen for Leguiísmo." Speeches and newspaper articles contained lurid details of Haya's dealings with the former president, and false handbills were distributed, purportedly signed by the Aprista leader, in which he was represented eagerly accepting Leguiísta support.[40]

The linking of Apra with Leguía was part of a larger effort aimed at the creation of a general climate of fear at the prospect of Haya de la Torre attaining the presidency. The Sánchezcerristas proclaimed that their opponents were anti-Catholic, antimilitary, antinationalist, and therefore against Peru's deeply ingrained values, which the commandant-candidate was said to represent. The public was told that an Apra victory would mean the outlawing of organized religion, the dissolution of the family, and the total disintegration of the social order. Underscoring the Apristas' display of the flags of all the Latin American republics and their elevation of a party song, the *Marseillese-Aprista* over the *National Anthem* at public demonstrations, the Sánchezcerristas dubbed Apra the "anti-Patria." They accused its leaders of criminally renouncing their own country in an attempt to "destroy the ideal of nationality and the concept of the fatherland."[41]

In contrast to this dark portrayal of their political opponents, the Sánchezcerristas depicted themselves as confirmed nationalists who would initate a revival of a "grand Peru, the proud master of its own destiny."[42] In most of his speeches Sánchez Cerro told of his overriding desire to regain Peru's prestige as a sovereign nation and to raise the country to a respected place in the international community. He also assured the people that he would be guided in all his acts by the symbols of the fatherland, "the hymn and the flag of our country that our mothers taught us to love when we first opened our eyes to the light of the Peruvian sky."[43] Although Sánchez Cerro condemned any form of political, diplomatic, or economic submission to other powers, his nationalism contained little hint of antiforeignism. He took special pains to assure prospective foreign investors that their interests would be safeguarded and insisted he would make every effort to attract new capital from abroad to contribute to Peru's development.[44]

Those socioeconomic groups that most favorably reacted to Sánchez Cerro's political style and campaign rhetoric were, as one observer contemptuously remarked, "the dregs of the upper and lower classes."[45] In terms of his mass support in Lima the commandant-candidate appealed principally to the most deprived members of the working classes. Belonging essentially to a *lumpenproletariat,* lower class Sánchezcerristas were humble vendors in markets and on the streets, construction workers, street cleaners, and laborers in small artisan industries. A sizable portion of them were recent migrants to the city, some of whom still wore traditional provincial dress. As a whole this group was characterized by extreme poverty, a high degree of unemployment, and a notable lack of union organization. Often barely able to read and write, their painfully composed letters to Sánchez Cerro were filled with misspelled words and nearly incoherent sentences.[46] The enemies of the commandant-candidate constantly made fun of his humble followers, painting them as poorly dressed illiterates attracted to Sánchezcerrismo only by the promise of abundant alcohol and a good meal (see figure 11). A more

Figure 11. "Declaration of Principles": "I swear to you, Hombre de la Calle, that not one coin has passed through my hands." From *El hombre de la calle* 2, no. 56 (October 10, 1931): 32.

accurate impression of the physical appearance of Sánchez Cerro's working class sympathizers may be obtained by examining actual photographs of demonstrations and marches in which they participated (see figures 12, 13, 14).

Sánchez Cerro's other major support group, made up of the upper strata of Peruvian society, at first withheld backing from all of the major presidential candidates. They mistrusted Sánchez Cerro from the beginning. To them he was a socially inferior *cholo,* both too unpredictable and too inexperienced to exercise the presidency over a long term. When the *junta* in Arequipa rose against him in February, Peru's major landowners, businessmen, and professional men supported the rebels. As the presidential race became reduced to two populist politicians, they marked time and waited for the emergence of an acceptable upper class figure. In June and July they enthusiastically underwrote unsuccessful

Figure 12. Sánchezcerrista Demonstrators. From ASC.

Figure 13. Sánchezcerrista Demonstrators. From ASC.

Figure 14. Sánchezcerrista Demonstrators Carrying Sánchez Cerro. From Archivo Gráfico, Biblioteca Nacional del Perú, Lima.

attempts to launch a single candidacy through the mechanism of a convention of parties modeled on the convention of 1915. Even in mid-September, only one month before the election, numerous members of the oligarchy flocked to support the moribund campaign of the Peruvian ambassador to Brazil, José María de la Jara y Ureta, in spite of overriding evidence that his chances for victory were remote.[47]

In the end, however, their dislike of Sánchez Cerro was momentarily set aside in the face of what they perceived to be a dangerous turn of events. From the mass demonstrations and marches in favor of Sánchez Cerro and Haya de la Torre that daily filled the Lima streets, it was evident that the working classes had become integrated into the political process and that, barring unforeseen circumstances, they would play a decisive role in the selection of a president. Out of touch with these sectors and unable to find their own candidate, the oligarchy realized that they could only hope to exert a measure of indirect control over the masses through one of the two candidates with mass followings. It was at this point that the Sánchezcerrista scare campaign bore fruit, convincing the majority of the elites that Sánchez Cerro was manifestly the lesser of two evils. They began to fear "the iconoclastic furor of the fickle multitude," which represented a "serious threat to our persons and interests." They worried that the emerging masses could be easily swayed by a "tumultuous and deafening demagoguery of sticks, stones and tin cans." In a letter to an associate one member of Peru's traditional elites summed up well the logic of upper class support for Sánchez Cerro during such uncertain times:

> Those of us who have interests to conserve and protect, "WE ARE WITH THE RIGHT WING . . ." Sánchez Cerro is with the right wing, his principles and his government program ARE CONSERVATIVE . . . Since Sánchez Cerro is the candidate with conservative principles, he therefore has the support of those who are of the right wing since there is no other candidate who has done so well with the masses as Sánchez Cerro.

His associate replied in kind, affirming that, given the existence of grave threats to the established order, "hopefully Sánchez Cerro will use the whip and the sword, because it is clear that there is no other way to govern this country." In opting for the rule of a military officer over the dangerous excesses of a "youthful demagogue," many might have thought back to the year 1914 when, under similar circumstances, Peru's civilian oligarchy turned to the armed forces as a temporary guarantee against anarchy.[48]

The upper classes finally decided to back Sánchez Cerro, but they were never comfortable with the "upstart *caudillo*." Having given their support, they concentrated their efforts on insuring that Sánchez Cerro would not turn his back on them once in power. They pressed the new president to appoint a cabinet of men sympathetic to their interests, hoping that he might thereby "govern well because those who would advise him knew well his personal deficiencies of temperament and character."[49] Sánchez Cerro fulfilled their expectations by choosing his first cabinet from the ranks of the pre-*oncenio* Civilista party. Three of the seven ministers had actually held cabinet posts previously under Civilista administrations.[50]

Sánchez Cerro recruited old-line Civilistas to advise him for various reasons. In addition to the pressure from the oligarchy to establish a regime along traditional lines, the new president had once before depended on men from this group during his "Government of Six Months." After his election in 1931 he continued to apply the same criteria as previously, finding the Civilistas to be not only the most experienced politicians in the country but also men with conservative ideas similar to his own. Furthermore, whether inwardly they scorned him or not, from the time when he first became president, elite elements constantly fawned over Sánchez Cerro. They flattered his ego, invited him to their parties, and admitted him to their most exclusive social clubs. He plainly enjoyed this treatment and invariably sought out the company of the upper classes. Finally, Sánchez Cerro received a considerable proportion of his campaign funds from members of the oligarchy. Elevating them to important political office was a fitting way to repay their support.[51]

While Sánchez Cerro relied on old-line Civilistas for financial support and for a degree of political advice, the backbone of the leadership for his movement came from a group of right-wing nationalists whose political philosophy was closer to a kind of creole-fascism than to the liberal Civilista ideal of the *República aristocrática*. Sánchez Cerro maintained particularly extensive contact with this group during the presidential race. Generally individuals from upper middle or upper class backgrounds, many were related to the first families of the *República aristocrática*. They had become interested in politics as university students during the 1920s when, united by their opposition to Leguía, they had organized a series of antigovernment demonstrations. Their hostility toward the *Patria Nueva* had sprung from a distaste for dictatorial methods which they perceived to be directed against members of their own social class. At one point in 1924 they declared open warfare on the regime and promised to second all acts of rebellion against the tyranny. They took as a banner their protest of Leguía's *"entreguista"* policy on the question of Tacna and Arica, insisting that Peru recover her status as a sovereign nation by defending her rightful territorial claims against the Chilean enemy to the south. Angered by Calvin Coolidge's apparent intervention on the side of Chile in the dispute, they sharply criticized the president for allowing Peru to be governed by Yankee imperialist policy made in the State Department in Washington. Notably, this antiimperialist rhetoric was rapidly dropped after the fall of Leguía.[52]

Previous to their entry into national politics behind Sánchez Cerro in 1931, the right-wing nationalists had taken an active role in university politics during the 1920s. According to their own admission, they saw student political activities as "a kind of preparation for the larger national political arena."[53] In the university they formed a compact group that vied for leadership with another faction, led by Víctor Raúl Haya de la Torre, whose most prominent members would direct the Aprista campaign in 1931. The right-wing nationalists took issue with the Hayistas on various grounds. As early as 1920 they opposed the university reform movement, in which Haya participated, because it threatened Civilista professors with whom many had close personal ties. In 1921 and 1922, when the right-wing nationalists supported the closing of the university to protest the deportation of various upper class intellectuals by Leguía, they clashed with the Hayistas, who argued that the continued interruption of classes was placing a terrible strain on their limited economic resources. Furthermore, both bands realized that they had substantial ideological differences. The right-wing nationalists saw themselves as wise political realists, while viewing their opponents as utopian dreamers whose social projects could only lead to disaster. They were particularly incensed by what they considered to be a lack of patriotism among the future Apristas. When Haya de la Torre, back from a trip to Chile, declared his solidarity with the Chilean student movement, the right-wing nationalists bitterly accused him and his followers of sympathizing with the enemy. And underlying the whole conflict was a deep thread of personal hatred towards the figure of Haya. In university politics the right-wing nationalists were, more than anything else, anti-Hayistas. As one member of the faction commented:

> Our group was anti-Hayista because Haya had become a kind of professional politician within the university. Since he first entered, he had not advanced in his career. He remained a first-year student. He did not study. For him the idea was to make himself known, to make himself known in proletarian and student circles, and he went about forming his group which was larger than ours. Therefore, all this awakened a certain resentment, a certain hatred towards Haya de la Torre. In Haya's case, the resentment was mostly the product of personal consideration.[54]

In 1930 and 1931, when national politics was reduced to a battle between the populist forces of Sánchez Cerro and those of Haya de la Torre, there was no question whom the right-wing nationalists would support. In addition to their long-standing animosity towards the Aprista leader, they found in the "Hero of Arequipa" a man with whom they could concur on almost every major issue. He had rid the nation of their mortal enemy Leguía. He was a patriotic soldier who promised to defend Peru's sovereignty and recover her lost dignity in the community of nations. To them, Sánchez Cerro "was the founder of an integral Peruvian nationalism, both fervent and belligerent . . . he created that nationalism with his blood, with his heroism. . . ."[55]

When still conspiring to overthrow Leguía, Sánchez Cerro had maintained contacts with some members of the right-wing nationalist group. Upon taking power he appointed their leader, Alfredo Herrera, his private secretary. In turn Herrera, accompanied by former Civilista leader José Manuel García Bedoya, went about exhorting his long-time cohorts from university politics to work for Sánchez Cerro. In the "Government of Six Months" this group was a major force behind the movement to proclaim Sánchez Cerro's presidential candidacy, and when he left the country for his short exile in Europe, they began actively preparing his upcoming electoral campaign almost singlehandedly. Later they acted as the commandant-candidate's principal political strategists. Drawing upon their past experience in student politics, they first founded the Partido Unión Revolucionaria to serve as an organizational base for the electoral race. Within the party they established and partially manned a "Directing Council" and a "Central Committee," set up a campaign headquarters, decided on lists of congressional candidates, wrote and disseminated propaganda, placed advertisements in the local press announcing important events, supervised the allocation of campaign funds, assured the distribution of ballots, and coordinated the activities of local Sánchezcerrista organizations. They also launched their own political newspaper, *La Opinión*, which regularly printed tributes to the commandant-candidate and publicized the most important aspects of the campaign. Furthermore, they planned trips for the candidate to the interior. They supervised the distribution of a constant stream of handbills to the general public. They made sure that at each party rally at least one working class man and woman spoke. To further the identification of their candidate with the masses, they began to publish articles in the party newspaper supporting the demands of labor for higher wages and better working conditions. Unlike Sánchez Cerro, they had little direct contact with the working classes, whom they considered distinctly inferior: "Thus the masses became transformed, in fact, into the soldiers. We were the officers."[56] Those who watched Sánchezcerrista demonstrations were indeed struck by the contrast between the majority of the rather poorly dressed demonstrators and the leaders of each section that stood out with their elegant clothing and their aristocratic manner.[57]

Two valuable sources of aid for this young and energetic group of party leaders were the former Lima mayor Luis Antonio Eguiguren and the city's most prominent newspaper, *El Comercio*. While himself running for a seat in the Constituent Congress, Eguiguren closely linked his image as a charitable public official who had materially helped the urban working classes in the midst of the depression with the aura of the "Hero of Arequipa." His campaign headquarters was infinitely better organized than Sánchez Cerro's and largely through his labors partisan propaganda was effectively distributed to the Lima populace. Eguiguren also contributed large sums of money to cover the costs of rent, light, and furniture for sixty local clubs and from his personal fortune paid for over 18,000 photographs to be affixed to the voter registration cards of Sánchez Cerro supporters in Lima. Since the *caudillo's* return from Europe and with increasing insistence as the election approached, *El Comercio* featured news about Sánchez Cerro's campaign activities, his major speeches, and the doings of his local clubs. It also printed without charge large advertisements announcing major public demonstrations. Of even greater political consequence than its praise of Sánchez Cerro was *El Comercio's* hard-fought war against the Apra. The paper became the major vehicle of Sánchez Cerro's concerted negative reference campaign.[58]

The most effective piece of campaign strategy in Sánchez Cerro's bid for the presidency was the mounting of popular demonstrations in support of his candidacy. These events had a massive quality about them designed to convince the public of the power of the Sánchezcerrista movement. While large demonstrations to establish popular legitimacy were not new in Peruvian politics, those of the 1931 campaign dwarfed previous efforts. They were usually planned to coincide with special occasions like the celebration of the first anniversary of the rebellion in Arequipa. Preceded by feverish efforts to assure good turnouts, they constituted the largest public outpourings that Lima had ever seen, with the single exception of Sánchez Cerro's reception after his victory in Arequipa. They were arranged in order to show off the candidate in the best possible light. Compact masses of people, with pictures of Sánchez Cerro and miniature flags pinned on their lapels, filled the streets through which the *caudillo* would pass. Sánchezcerrista clubs carried huge banners identifying themselves and expressing their adherence to the candidate. Sánchez Cerro, standing in an open car or riding on a white horse, traveled to a central meeting place, generally one of Lima's two largest squares, amid the wild cheering of his followers: "Sánchez Cerro, presidente! El Apra su sirviente!" ("Sánchez Cerro, president! Apra his servant!")[59] The candidate's address to crowds ranging up to 50,000 people was the highlight of these events (see figures 15, 16, 17). The Sánchezcerrista leadership was fully aware of the political impact of these mass demonstrations. In their newspaper they graphically expressed pride at their achievements in a cartoon portraying Sánchez Cerro as a soccer player scoring two goals against Haya de la Torre (see figure 18). Each ball represented a Sánchezcerrista mass demonstration.[60]

Although highly successful at mounting mass meetings, in general the Sánchezcerrista leadership carried on a relatively disorganized campaign characterized by confusion and improvisation in most areas. Only the figure of Sánchez Cerro seemed to hold everything and everyone tenuously together. But what the commandant-candidate's followers lacked in organizational talent and financial backing they made up in enthusiasm. Sánchez Cerro was able to generate a fervor in his supporters beyond all expectations. It was this ardor for the candidate that gave birth to the working class Sánchezcerrista neighborhood clubs that proliferated in the preelection period. These institutions were formed spontaneously, mainly in June and July, without instigation or aid from the central Sánchezcerrista headquarters. The Central Committee of the Unión Revolucionaria learned of their existence in most instances only after they had been founded. At all times the mass-based local clubs

Figure 15. Sánchezcerrista Mass Meeting. From ASC.

Figure 16. Sánchezcerrista Mass Meeting. From ASC.

Figure 17. Sánchezcerrista Mass Meeting. From ASC.

Figure 18. The Mass Meeting Game. From *La Opinión,* October 6, 1931, p. 1.

overtly maintained a high degree of autonomy, manifesting a certain mistrust toward the central headquarters: "Those of us who were the most enthusiastic formed our own political clubs without help from anyone. In the central campaign headquarters, we did not have a dominant position. People of another social class dominated. These were two distinct organizations."[61] The presidents of the clubs were well-known men in their respective neighborhoods who used their personal influence and contacts with relatives and *compadres* to gain adherents. Located in the lower class *barrios* of Rimac, La Victoria, and Barrios Altos, these clubs generally had memberships ranging from 100 to 150 persons. Most clubs met at least weekly in the house of the president, where they heard speakers sent by the central headquarters and planned their campaign activities. In addition to their fervor for Sánchez Cerro the promise of free alcohol seems to have been a powerful attraction to attend meetings.[62]

No complete list of these institutions exists, but by counting the clubs mentioned in the political sections of the Lima daily papers during the campaign, a total of 155 formally established local Sánchezcerrista organizations emerges. Calculating a membership of 100 to 150 people for each club, as they claimed, one arrives at a total of nearly 20,000 working class Sánchezcerristas in these local organizations previous to the election.[63] The examination of a list of selected club names confirms allegations of contemporary observers that they were located in the poorer areas of the city and that their members, in the main, belonged to the Lima working classes (see table 5.1). Of particular interest is that many club names contained terms — *liberty, savior, sword, peace, order, work* — that corresponded to the major symbols emphasized in Sánchez Cerro's political style and campaign rhetoric. Their appearance indicates that the commandant-candidate was extremely successful in the communication of his desired image among large sectors of the urban masses.[64]

A number of Sánchezcerrista clubs were also founded by groups of recent migrants to the capital. Including in their appellations the name of a specific province or department in the interior, they appear to have originated from the migrant associations of the 1920s. Appealing to provincial loyalties and often holding special celebrations with musical groups from the interior, they represented a concerted effort to exploit regional ties for political advantage. The largest number of these institutions aggregated individuals from the Department of Ancash, the very area that had contributed the largest quantity of migrants to the Lima population.[65]

The working class clubs drummed up support for their candidate on the neighborhood level by word-of-mouth canvasing. They worked hard to enlist people for attendance at mass demonstrations. They carried out registration drives of potential Sánchezcerrista voters. Women members made campaign posters and badges, while the men distributed handbills and put up election posters. Each club was responsible for getting out the vote in its area on election day. The clubs were aided in all these tasks by a group of political intermediaries between the candidate and the working classes known as *capituleros*. A fixture of Peruvian electoral politics in the past, they had been previously employed to buy votes and organize demonstrations. By 1931 the mass nature of politics in Lima put the buying of individual votes beyond the financial resources of all candidates. But *capituleros* were still used by the Sánchezcerristas to exert their influence on their traditional constituencies. It was the specific job of the *capitulero* to assure that printed propaganda continually flowed between the central headquarters and the local organizations and to provide alcohol for club meetings and mass demonstrations. In return for their labors they generally received the promise of some form of government

Table 5.1. Indicators of Social Class and Appeal of Candidate Image
in Selected Names of Sánchezcerrista Clubs

CLUBS	KEY INDICATOR WORDS	
	Ideological	Occupational and Geographical
Club Adictos Sánchez Cerro La Victoria No. 1		Victoria–working-class district
Club Defensores de la Patria No. 1	Defenders of the fatherland	
Club Femenil Espada de Sánchez Cerro Infantas No. 1	Sword	
Club Industrial Obrero Manco Capac		Industrial workers
Club Infantil Grito de la Libertad Sánchez Cerro No. 1	Liberty	
Club Invencible Cahuide Sánchez Cerro No. 1	Invincible	
Club Lealtad y Patriotismo Sánchez Cerro Lobatón No. 1	Loyalty and patriotism	
Club Libertador Sánchez Cerro No. 1	Liberator	
Club Nacionalista Pro Candidatura Sánchez Cerro	Nationalist	
Club Paz Orden y Trabajo Sánchez Cerro	Peace, order, and work	
Club Político Artesanos y Obreros—Candidatura Pro Sánchez Cerro		Artisans and workers
Club Político Obrero Pro-Elección Luis M. Sánchez Cerro		Worker
Club Propaganda Obrero Sánchez Cerro No. 2		Worker
Club Reacción Sánchez Cerro No. 1	Reaction	
Club Rimac Sánchez Cerro–Eguiguren		Rimac–working-class district
Club Sánchez Cerro No. 10 de la Victoria		Victoria–working-class district
Club Señoras de la Parada del Mercado Central de Lima Sánchez Cerro No. 1		Market vendors
Club Señoras y Señoritas "El Salvador" 22 de Agosto	The savior	
Club Triunfo de la Opinión del Mercado de la Aurora Sánchez Cerro No. 1		Market vendors
Comité Nacional de Señoras del Distrito del Rimac		Rimac–working-class district
Comité de Propaganda de los Barrios Altos y Defensor del Sufragio		Barrios Altos–working-class district

employment after the election.[66] In all of these ways, the working class clubs, more than the central headquarters or the official party, brought the Sánchezcerrista campaign to the masses. Sánchez Cerro's victory in the 1930 election clearly reflected the appeal of his personal style and the success of his supporters' vigorous campaign for votes, particularly their efforts at the grass roots level of working class Lima.

6

Apra I:
The Birth of an Alliance

IN THE months preceding the 1931 presidential election the Partido Aprista Peruano, ultimately to be Peru's longest lasting populist movement, emerged to share political dominance in Peru with the supporters of Luis M. Sánchez Cerro. Under the undisputed leadership of Víctor Raúl Haya de la Torre, the Apristas hotly contested the 1931 presidential election with the Sánchezcerristas and subsequently loomed as the most significant political force in the country from the 1930s through the 1960s. Unlike Sánchezcerrismo's almost overnight appearance on the Peruvian political scene, the development of Apra came about gradually as a result of over a decade of personal contact between Haya de la Torre and key members of both Lima's university student community and its industrial proletariat. The primary elements that made up the cement of Apra's populist coalition in 1931 cannot be understood without first undertaking an extensive look into the formative years of the movement previous to its entry into electoral politics.

Apra's beginnings date back to 1919 when Haya de la Torre first became associated with the Lima working classes. In early January of that year, against a background of increasing labor discontent touched off by a noticeable deterioration of the living conditions of the urban masses, the capital's newly incremented labor organizations went on strike in an effort to win an eight-hour working day and an increase in hourly wages. To cries of, "On your feet, *compañeros!* Long live the eight hour day!" the first to walk off their jobs were the weavers in the W. R. Grace Company's Inca Textile Factory. The movement spread rapidly to other textile plants; soon the powerful bakers' union joined

129

and was followed by the shoemakers, tanners, public transport workers, longshoremen, and printers.[1]

As the strike gained momentum and support, several labor leaders carried on a series of secret meetings with the then twenty-three-year-old university student, Víctor Raúl Haya de la Torre. Some of them had previously visited the future leader of the Apra Party after reading his proposal in a Lima newspaper for the establishment of a "popular university" in which college students would undertake the education of manual laborers. Now, in the heat of the strike, and on the heels of an assault on the strikers' headquarters by government troops, they worked through Haya de la Torre to strengthen their cause by gaining the backing of the university student community in the hope that the regime would show greater tolerance to a movement supported by an influential faction of the country's middle and upper classes. Haya brought the workers' plea for student cooperation to the Peruvian University Student Federation. At first the students balked at the idea of cooperation, demonstrating a visible lack of sensitivity to social issues. But the efforts of Haya and his supporters finally met with success nearly two weeks after the strikers' original request. Haya de la Torre was named, along with two others, to represent the students before the workers.[2]

On the same day that the Student Federation publicly announced its decision to cooperate with the workers, the eight-hour movement attained the proportions of a general strike. For weeks management and government had steadfastly refused to consent to the demands of labor. Finally, the strikers felt compelled to bring Lima to a standstill. The total shutdown of the capital lasted three days as factories and businesses were forced to close their doors to avoid attacks by the striking workers. Public transportation was halted. Army units patrolled the streets and protected the groups of people that formed in front of the few stores that remained open to sell basic necessities. At night Lima was in darkness; the municipal authorities made no effort to replace the street lights shattered by bricks thrown by irate laborers.[3]

When it became evident that the strike was succeeding and that the longer it persisted the greater were the prospects of increased violence, the government, through the office of the Ministro de Fomento, decided to form a commission to negotiate a settlement. The strikers sent the student delegates as their representatives before the new government commission. They chose this approach because they felt that working class negotiators might be singled out for repression, but that the government would use greater restraint in dealing with students, almost all of whom came from more privileged backgrounds. As their chief negotiator, the strikers selected Haya de la Torre, the person most responsible for securing student support in the first place. His efforts on their behalf earned him an extraordinary degree of admiration from the workers. During three days of seemingly nonstop activity Haya held ten meetings with the Ministro de Fomento, Manuel Vinelli. His lively reports on the progress of the negotiations made him the center of attention at strike meetings. Time and again he affirmed his loyalty to the cause of labor and in return received the enthusiastic approval of the assembled workers: *"Compañeros:* I have dreamed of this for a long time. To see myself participating in a workers' fight, to participate in it and to incorporate myself forever into the cause for the workers' noble and just aspirations." And when on one occasion he shouted, "Here with you to the death or to victory!"[4] his words were greeted with a thunderous ovation. Such were his oratorical powers that some old-line anarchists who had feared the possible consequences of the students' participation from the beginning expressed trepidation that Haya might seize control of the movement from its "true working class leaders."[5]

In the light of subsequent events the anarchists' concerns were warranted. Working with men of considerable prestige in the labor movement, Haya rose to a position of leadership even before the issues of the eight-hour movement were resolved. His presence dominated the strike meetings, and it was he who formulated the strikers' position in the negotiations with Vinelli. Haya reinforced his authority among the workers by openly defying government troops at several points during the conflict. In one instance, when the soldiers surrounded the meeting place of the strikers and threatened to open fire, Haya faced the heavily armed men alone and defiantly challenged: "Do what you wish, but the strike will not end." And on the following day, when it again appeared that the government troops were about to fire on the strikers, Haya and the other members of the student delegation averted the danger by standing in front of the laborers and daring the soldiers to kill students. Haya is reported to have exclaimed: "Let them open fire; we will die arm-to-arm with the workers."[6]

Haya's prestige among the workers was sealed when on January 15, 1919, he personally brought them the news that they had achieved victory in their fight for the eight-hour day. Carrying a copy of the presidential decree which had been sent to him by Vinelli, he stood before the striking workers and in exultant tones read the terms of the settlement: a maximum work day would thereafter consist of eight hours instead of ten, and the laborers would receive the same pay as they had for ten hours on the job. Perhaps afraid that the general strike in Lima might degenerate into the same kind of bloody confrontation as had occurred in Argentina's *"semana trágica"* just one week earlier, the government had given in to the workers' demands. By personally presenting the decree to the strikers, Haya consummated his identification with the eight-hour victory and with the cause of organized labor. And when he ended his presentation with the hoarse cry, "We have triumphed, *compañeros!,*" the strikers broke into cheers for the students. Haya was lifted onto the shoulders of the workers, and a triumphant demonstration ensued which lasted a full thirty minutes.[7]

For organized labor in Peru, the eight-hour movement was a true milestone, demonstrating unequivocally that the urban working classes were a force that could no longer be ignored. In the history of party politics as well, the strike marked the beginning of a new era. By successfully associating himself with union leaders and rank-and-file workers alike, Haya de la Torre started to lay the foundation of the Apra party.

Although like Sánchezcerrismo, Apra developed as a vertical movement with a mass base, at first glance it would seem that these two organizations were different animals. Sánchezcerrismo consisted of a loose, ad hoc structure held together by a charismatic leader. Apra became one of the most highly organized political parties in the history of Latin America. Sánchezcerrismo rejected the need for political platforms, emphasizing instead the intuition of the leader. Apra fashioned a series of highly complex party programs and never ceased referring to them as well as printing innumerable copies. Sánchez Cerro was a political conservative and openly antilabor. Haya de la Torre referred to himself at times as a revolutionary, and the very origins of his movement were tied to the creation of a labor alliance.

Indeed, the story of the origins and growth of Aprismo is the story of the careful building of bonds of loyalty between the future Aprista leader and the urban labor groups that would later constitute the mass base of his populist movement. And it was these bonds — equally at the heart of Aprismo and Sánchezcerrismo — and the systems of political clientage they evolved into that constituted the essential cement of both movements; this basic similarity ultimately overshadowed the apparent differences between them.

It might seem strange that an individual of Haya de la Torre's middle class background would have assumed the championship of labor's cause in 1919. Haya was born in Trujillo in 1895 to a family that, particularly on the maternal side, had close connections to various sectors of Peru's economic and political elites. Although his father, Raúl Edmundo Haya, was not one of the most wealthy men in Trujillo, the family lived well in a large and comfortable house in the city. The senior Haya's income as the editor of one of the most important local papers, *La Industria,* plus his varied business activities — including the foundation of the Trujillo

Chamber of Commerce — permitted him to maintain an enviable lifestyle and send his son Víctor Raúl to the Seminario de San Carlos, the preferred educational institution of the Trujillo elite. Also, Raúl Edmundo Haya had the sufficient social and political prominence on the local scene to be elected to the National Chamber of Deputies for Trujillo between 1904 and 1908.[8]

When the young Haya arrived in Lima in 1917 to take courses at the University of San Marcos, he had numerous useful contacts with individuals in the "establishment" through his family connections. His first stopping place in the capital was the home of his uncle, Amador del Solar, a leading Civilista and president of the Peruvian Senate at the time. Another uncle, Agustín de la Torre González, was a member of the other principal faction of the Peruvian political elite, holding the office of second vice-president of the country under Augusto Leguía between 1919 and 1923. Haya's first employment in the capital was in the law office of Eleodoro Romero, also a front-line Leguiísta and cousin of the president. Haya described the impact upon him of his initial experiences in the capital, writing: "At that time I was a little *criollo* brat, sick to my bones with that epidemic frivolity — the plague of the people of high status . . . Because of this I arrived in Lima thinking about the immense honor of seeing myself in the classrooms in contact with certain personages who were so frequently mentioned in the press."[9]

It is difficult to determine just when and how Haya de la Torre underwent a transformation from a "sickly *criollo*" to a determined representative of labor in the university community. Haya claims to have been moved for the first time in his life to direct his efforts at helping the less fortunate on a trip to the old Inca and colonial town of Cuzco in 1917, the same year he arrived in Lima. After seeing there levels of suffering worse than anything else he had previously imagined, Haya asserts that he was cured for good of his *"criollo"* frivolity.[10]

Another important stimulus for Haya's gaining of a "social awareness" appears to have been the ideas of Peru's leading nonconformist intellectual, Manuel González Prada. Like many of his fellow students, Haya avidly read and discussed González Prada's works. Particularly taken by González Prada's essay on the intellectual's role as the guide of the working man, Haya began to see himself as able to "instruct the masses in order to transform the most humble worker into a conscious collaborator."[11]

A final clue to Haya de la Torre's interest in representing labor on the occasion of the eight-hour movement may be found in his youthful experiences in Trujillo. From his early years Haya admits that he had a passion for political organization and an interest in social movements.

His childhood games were, in fact, devoted to these central interests. As he recalled:

> Wc had some very spacious rooms to play in, and we created a republic there. We had a president, we had cabinet ministers, deputies. We had politics. And there we practiced. And we were twelve-year-old kids. And we practiced at reproducing the life of the country with spools of thread. All my brothers, I got them into the game. I used to receive very nice toys: locomotives, trains. But I was not interested in these things. What interested me was to have an organized setup, like a country . . . When I recall this, you can see how early I had a political imagination. It was quite noteworthy, because we imitated life, but we assured a life of order. Now I tell myself, how I've always had this thing about organizing. We directed political campaigns.[12]

For Haya, participation in the eight-hour movement was vitally important in determining what direction his penchant for leadership and political organization would ultimately take. Haya recently summarized the significance of his first active participation in a labor cause, stating: "I took advantage of the eight-hour strike to forge ties with the workers."[13] And ensuing events reflected his considerable success in that endeavor. The extent of Haya's ascendancy with the labor groups that participated in the eight-hour movement was evident on the day following the end of the strike when he presided over the birth of the Federación de Trabajadores de Tejidos del Perú (Federation of Peruvian Textile Workers), an organization which in the following decade would constitute the most powerful force in the Peruvian labor movement. Two primary considerations led to the elevation of Haya to the chairmanship of the meeting and that established the Federación Textil. First, the workers wished to honor him for his role in the eight-hour victory. When Haya, observing that he was not a textile worker, initially showed some reluctance to accept the post, one union leader who participated in the foundation of the Federación Textil is reported to have insisted that the student accept the honor, declaring, "you have been the valuable director of an important social triumph."[14] Second, Haya had taken the lead in efforts to create a unified organization of textile workers. Anxious to make the most of the unity and enthusiasm generated by the eight-hour victory, he had called together the most prominent union leaders from each textile factory and proposed the creation of a federation. He argued that only by fashioning an association that would coordinate the activities of the formerly decentralized factory unions could the workers hope to preserve the fruits of victory and go on to greater labor conquests. In reply to the affirmation by certain leaders that such an arrangement should be formed by unions from all industrial sectors, Haya held that a more inclusive organization could come later. For the moment, however, the textile workers, being the most numerous and the best prepared labor group in Lima, would be well advised to work independently. Haya added that "since you spend months and years together in your work places, you know who are the best friends and the best *compañeros,* and you can make them your leaders."[15] Building on the links of friendship and personal loyalty that existed both between the laborers within the textile sector and between their leaders and himself, the student delegate drafted the constitution for the new Federación Textil and coordinated the formation of its governing body.[16]

Haya relinquished the presidency of the Federación Textil immediately following its foundation, but in the coming months he made a concerted effort to maintain and strengthen the ties he had forged with labor in the critical days of January. He remained in contact with many of the union leaders whom he had met during the eight-hour strike, and he soon began to offer classes in psychology to a group of them. Those classes were the precursors of the "Universidad Popular González Prada," an institution that would serve to strengthen and widen Haya's contacts with labor throughout the 1920s.

Haya's name had originally been linked to the idea of a school for workers manned by university students when he supported the creation of popular universities in August 1918. And at every step of the way leading to the eventual establishment of the Universidad Popular in January 1921, his personal leadership was the decisive element. Haya encouraged the labor leaders with whom he had worked in the eight-hour movement and the formation of the Federación Textil to spread the idea of a popular university among their peers. He pressed for the formation of committees in Lima's largest factories to forward the idea of a workers' school. He arranged for the publication of letters in the capital's working class newspapers urging labor to reinforce the solidarity between workers and students by supporting the Universidad Popular. And in 1921 Haya further stepped up his efforts on behalf of the workers' school by initiating a kind of "whistle stop" campaign: from atop a horse-drawn carriage, which he had rented for the purpose, Haya spoke daily to union meetings and to groups at factories, entreating workers to use their free hours to advance themselves culturally in the classrooms of the Universidad Popular instead of squandering their time and money in taverns and bordellos. Every weekend he went by train to the town of Vitarte, a textile center outside of Lima, to organize soccer matches among workers. Laboring groups from Vitarte had played a prominent role in the eight-hour movement, and Haya hoped to secure their backing for the Universidad Popular. His appeals were greeted with such enthusiasm that he decided to set up a separate workers' school in Vitarte.

According to one member of the Vitarte working class community, Haya's resounding success there was the product of "the friendship he had forged" with the proletariat elements of the town during and after the eight-hour movement.[17]

At the same time that he proselytized for the Universidad Popular among urban laborers, Haya de la Torre worked within the Student Federation to gain the backing of the university community. Elected to the Federation's presidency in October 1919, to a large extent thanks to his prominence in the eight-hour movement, he was able to exert considerable influence over his fellow students. At the First Congress of Peruvian Students held in Cuzco in March of 1921 Haya used his power successfully to push through, over strong conservative opposition, a resolution decreeing the official assistance of the students for the establishment of a popular university. The wording of the resolution contained a clear portent of the future path of Haya's workers' school. While affirming that the school was to pursue an essentially educational mission, the Congress followed the precedent set by the eight-hour movement in stipulating that the Universidad Popular should intervene in all future labor conflicts. Within this conception of a workers' school as a political as well as educational institution, ultimately the political side would prevail as the Universidad Popular became the organizational and spiritual base for the Aprista party.

Following the adjournment of the Cuzco Congress, Haya de la Torre returned to Lima and immediately set to work enlisting students to teach in the projected workers' schools. He moved from classroom to classroom, telling the students that as a privileged educated minority it was their duty to share their learning with the members of the working classes. He offered them no remuneration for their time and efforts. Personal satisfaction would be their only reward. When San Marcos was closed down by the government in 1921 and 1922, Haya found it substantially easier to find instructors for the Universidad Popular; the students, unable to pursue their studies in San Marcos, could readily devote their time to teaching in the schools for workers.[18]

It was from among this group of university student-professors of the Universidad Popular that the nucleus of Aprista party leadership later emerged. Many of these youths had middle and upper class backgrounds similar to that of Haya de la Torre and were often motivated by the same kinds of social and political concerns. The first indication of the emergence of an anti-status quo and socially concerned faction among the nation's youth coincided with the initiation of the University Reform movement in Peru. Inspired by the reform of the University of Córdoba, Argentina, in 1918 and specifically by the visit to Lima of Alfredo

Palacios, one of the leaders of that movement, a substantial proportion of the student body at the University of San Marcos went on strike in June 1919. They were led in the main by youthful members of the middle sectors in rebellion against a university geared to the education of a social and political elite. The striking students demanded a part in the government of the institution, the opening of San Marcos to the middle and lower classes and the retirement of various "incompetent" professors. These demands were implicitly political in nature, as the university in the years previous to the reform had been essentially a training ground and an employment agency for the career politicians of the ruling Partido Civil. The men on the faculty constituted a Civilista oligarchy in miniature. In many cases they owed their positions to political influence rather than to personal ability. Not surprisingly, the majority of the repudiated professors were those most closely connected to the "governing caste." When the students criticized the *"esclerosis de la docencia"* ("teaching sclerosis") within the university, they were at the same time attacking the foundations of the *República aristocrática* on the national level.

Despite the caustic tone and content of their declarations, in the beginning these students were not totally alienated from the traditional political system. They strongly supported the presidential bid of veteran politician Augusto Leguía in 1919. The previous year, when it seemed evident that Leguía would be an opposition candidate to the ruling Partido Civil, the university youth bestowed upon him the title of *"Maestro de la Juventud"* ("Mentor of the Youth"), seeing him as a champion of "antiestablishment" forces and as a potential advocate of their interests once in power. For his part Leguía enthusiastically sympathized with the aims of the reform-minded students, and shortly after taking office he granted the demands of their movement. When a year later Leguía reversed himself and made the university a major target in a widespread wave of repression, the students were shocked and outraged. Their hopes for the new president vanished as it became obvious that he was more closely tied to the social and political status quo than to their concerns. The disillusionment of the students was made particularly sharp by the high expectations for reform under Leguía that they had previously held. Increasing numbers of young people came to reject the established political system out of hand and began to seek other alternatives, principal among them the Universidad Popular and later the Aprista party.[19]

For this growingly dissatisfied group of middle and upper class students, the rejection of Leguía was part of a larger repudiation of the older generation. At the beginning of the 1920s the Peruvian youth enthusiastically proclaimed their own incorruptibility and portrayed themselves as the only force capable of regenerating the political system of their country. Various circumstances encouraged these students to see themselves as missionaries of social and political reform for their country. World War I, the promise of the Wilsonian Doctrine and the Peace of Versailles, the Mexican and Russian revolutions — all produced in certain segments of student population an awareness of great social "evils" while at the same time holding out great hopes for near miraculous solutions. And in their eyes the particular "purity" of youthful men and women suited them well for taking on the heroic mission of transforming the political and social fabric of their country. They were encouraged in this belief by the teachings of various prestigious figures from the intellectual community, chief among them Manuel González Prada. The scholar's oft-repeated phrase, *"los viejos a la tumba y los jovenes a la obra"* ("the aged to the tomb and the youth to work"), had become a watchword of those who advocated youthful self-affirmation. When in one of his most famous esays, entitled "Propaganda y ataque," González Prada incited his readers to open the eyes of the masses and prepare them for the dawning of a new social order, he seemed to be putting into words the role that many young students, Haya de la Torre among them, had begun to envision for themselves.[20]

The masses that González Prada referred to had become a more visible force in Peru after the industrial boom of World War I and the accompanying development of union organizations. With the appearance of industrial laborers in larger numbers and a labor movement increased in size and in audacity, university students became aware for the first time of the "social question." In many cases their recognition of that problem led them to support the workers in their conflicts with employers, as was the case with the eight-hour movement. After 1921 the labor contacts of this newly politicized group of students multiplied considerably with the establishment of the Universidad Popular — the concrete response of the youth to González Prada's plea for the guidance of the popular masses by dedicated intellectuals.

A further possible cause of the emergence of a fairly coherent group of politically minded and socially conscious university students was the element of social resentment. Various observers have characterized the future leaders of Aprismo as a frustrated middle class group whose families were socially and economically on the decline. According to this line of thought, these nascent politicos found themselves unable to gain the desirable social, economic, and political positions to which they aspired within the established system. They translated the resulting status anxieties into a kind of "class resentment," which led them to resort to opposition politics as a mechanism for social and economic advancement.[21] Although these considerations may have operated in the lives of certain persons, clearly they were not a major element in the majority of cases. Most of the students who ultimately followed Haya de la Torre into the Aprista movement simply would not have encountered formidable barriers to their inclusion in the "establishment" had they chosen that path. Their university education, for example, a highly valued commodity in the existing system, would have generally sufficed to afford them access to some of the best jobs in the public bureaucracy or in the private sector. Many came from well-to-do families like Haya. Most had excellent political connections, particularly with the Leguía regime. Yet they too, out of choice rather than necessity, elected to accompany Haya initially into the Universidad Popular and later to join in the formation of his mass political movement.[22]

The student activists and industrial laborers — the two eventual pillars of Aprismo — first came together in an institutional context at the inauguration of the Universidad Popular held at the headquarters of the Federación de Estudiantes on January 22, 1921. The atmosphere was charged with excitement. In a hall filled to the point of overflowing, one by one the leaders of Lima's important labor organizations stepped on stage to declare their support for the newly founded school. They were followed by those students who had pledged to act as professors, each of whom outlined the program of his specific course. Haya de la Torre then stepped to the podium. With emotion in his voice he declared: "I have dreamed of this for a long time!" He went on to outline the difficulties and rewards involved in the launching of the Universidad Popular: "this task requires a firm will, unfailing doggedness, genuine modesty, profound enthusiasm, and an intelligent and serene patience; all heroic qualities." He concluded by stating that the school "represents a crusade against all moral evils, against the mental and psychological weaknesses inherent in our deficient education."[23]

In these pronouncements Haya touched on various of the concepts that would later shape his political career. In the 1931 presidential campaign, for instance, he would project the values of heroism, enthusiasm, and resolution as prominent elements of his political style. And his portrayal of the Universidad Popular as a moral crusade was the prelude to the veritable missionary fervor that later characterized the Aprista movement.

Designated the rector of the Universidad Popular by the unanimous vote of students and professors, Haya continued to be the dominant force in the workers' schools after their foundation. He personally taught courses in geography and social history, appointed professors, developed the curriculum, arranged for speakers, planned special cultural and social activities, drew up propaganda, and personally signed the identifi-

cation card of each matriculated student. It was little wonder that one
working class student publicly affirmed in *El obrero textil* that without
the presence of Haya de la Torre there would be no Universidad
Popular.[24]

The schools operated three nights weekly in Lima and twice weekly in
Vitarte from approximately 9 to 11 p.m. The curriculum placed a heavy
emphasis on practicability with classes on hygiene, anatomy, arithmetic,
grammar, and geography. Morality campaigns were also a salient feature
of the education in the Universidad Popular. Responding to the initiative
of Haya de la Torre, the workers and professors joined in a common
effort to eradicate alcoholism and to curb disease. The educational functions of these schools also extended to proceedings outside of the classroom. The Universidades Populares organized regularly scheduled sport-
ing events, hikes into the countryside, and special musical programs.
Medical school students who donated their time to the Universidad
Popular established popular clinics, diagnosed illnesses, and prescribed
remedies. Workers and their families were urged to attend numerous
dances and other social events organized under the auspices of these
schools. One of the most spectacular of these "extra-classroom" expressions of the Universidades Populares was the annual "Fiesta de la
Planta" ("tree celebration"). Held in Vitarte during the Christmas
season, this celebration involved the planting of trees in the main square
of the town. Through all these activities the Universidades Populares
transcended the status of pure educational institutions to become true
community organizations that addressed themselves to the personal,
social, and cultural problems of Lima's working classes.[25]

It is impossible to determine exactly how many students regularly
attended the Universidades Populares, as class lists were never kept.
According to Haya de la Torre, the schools had 5,000 registered students
by 1923, and on some nights fully one thousand working class men and
women would meet to hear their rector speak on the issues of the day.[26]
More important than the sheer number of people in the student body was
that most of the leadership of the capital's organized labor force studied
there at some time between 1921 and 1924. Men who conducted the
major unions in this period and who would direct labor in the 1930s and
1940s shared a common experience in the classrooms of Haya's schools.
In fact, these sixty to eighty leaders dedicated so much of their activities
to the Universidad Popular that one workers' newspaper complained that
it seemed about to replace the union as the directing force of the organized laboring class.[27]

The constant contact between the university students and the labor
leaders in the Universidad Popular led to the generation of deep ties of

friendship and a perceptible *esprit de corps* between these two groups. The origins and ultimate impact of these ties are well characterized in a comment made by Haya de la Torre: "We were much more than professors. We were friends; everything in their family lives. And at times we even slept in their beds. In Lima as well as in Vitarte there existed the same kinds of ties. There we formed great friendships."[28]

The laborers who attended the Universidades Populares confirmed Haya's view. To these individuals who had received little or no formal education before entering the Universidad Popular, it constituted an unforgettable cultural awakening. In the words of one labor leader: "My case is a clear example. In the poverty and harsh condition of my *callejón* home, my educational fortune consisted of a third grade education . . . Being lost thus in this nebulous ignorance, the Universidad Popular was for me my guide toward wider horizons . . ."[29] The university student-professors were invariably singled out for special praise. They were seen as a "bunch of good and disinterested fellows from the University," leading a new crusade to bring "the rays of learning to our dark minds."[30]

While the faculty of the Universidades Populares was admired as a group, the only individual name that appeared time and again in workers' references to these schools was that of Haya de la Torre. Called *"El Maestro,"* the soul of the Universidad Popular, and *"el compañero Rector,"* Haya was not only looked up to for his "intellegence, sincerity, and spirit," but also because he had abandoned the aristocratic world of the University of San Marcos for the world of proletarian Lima. The workers continually demonstrated their confidence in Haya by asking him for aid in the resolution of various of their personal problems. In addition to his responsibilities as a teacher and administrator, he became the arbiter of numerous quarrels between parent and child, husband and wife, friend and enemy.[31]

The bonds of friendship and personal loyalty established in the Universidad Popular were the most important elements in the emergence of a coalition of university students and workers between 1921 and 1923 that ultimately took the form of the Aprista party. In the classrooms of the Universidades Populares professors from middle and upper social strata and their worker-students became acquainted for the first time. A visible solidarity between these two groups—a sort of reciprocal trust—grew out of their common educational experience. The "frente de obreros manuales e intelectuales" ("front of manual and intellectual workers"), Haya's favorite title for the Aprista movement, was the offspring of the workers' schools he formed in 1921. And in the particular case of Haya de la Torre, doubtless many of the techniques that he used as a populist leader in attracting urban laborers to his cause were first learned in the Universidad Popular.[32]

In May of 1923 Haya's manual and intellectual worker front faced its first critical test, a test that would contribute significantly to the shaping of its trajectory in the coming years. Early in that month President Augusto Leguía made known his plan to consecrate Peru to the Sacred Heart of Jesus, purportedly in order to gain clerical backing for his imminent re-election attempt. Shortly after the news of the consecration became public, Haya, as the head of the Universidad Popular, began to work secretly against the maneuver. Not wishing to identify the workers' school with the opposition to Leguía's move for fear that he would alienate potential middle and upper class allies, Haya began his protest campaign by arranging the publication of editorials attacking the consecration in various widely read Lima newspapers and magazines. From the beginning the rector of the Universidad Popular took on the full burden of leadership of the protest, traveling from university classroom to Protestant church, from union hall to the Y.M.C.A., drumming up support. Haya charged the professors and students of the Universidad Popular with providing an organizational base for the protest movement. It was their job to coordinate the various participating groups, to print and distribute propaganda, and to mobilize large numbers of laborers for mass demonstrations. On May 19, only after Haya had secured firm backing, the Universidad Popular openly took a stand by flooding the streets of Lima with handbills invoking the support of all free-thinking men in fighting "the imposition of clerical anachronisms" on Peru.[33]

On the afternoon of May 23, 1923, the protest was officially launched with a public meeting in the assembly hall of the University of San Marcos. Crowded with students and workers, the session began with the election of Haya de la Torre to lead the movement and went on to declare that the consecration of the Republic to the Sacred Heart of Jesus constituted in both spiritual and political terms a reactionary act which threatened freedom of thought. Then, with Haya at its head, an ardent multitude numbering approximately 5,000 people erupted from San Marcos to exhibit their indignation in the streets of Lima. When they saw their progress blocked by mounted government troops, the demonstrators broke into smaller groups in order to continue through side streets toward their objective, the presidential palace. Unable to contain the protestors, the troops charged them with swords drawn. Fire from soldiers' rifles echoed in the streets. Soon the word was passed from group to group that Salomón Ponce, a trolley car motorman, and Alarcón Vidalón, a university student, had been killed by the onrushing troops. When groups of demonstrators succeeded in reaching Lima's central square, Haya de la Torre, with gestures reminiscent of the eight-hour movement, faced the menacing soldiers and harangued the crowd. Pointing to the troops he declared: "The man who murders students and workers is not among you, soldiers. You are acting under the reign of terror." And then turning toward the presidential palace he shouted: "the real villain is the tyrant that is hiding there!"[34]

The events of May 23 — the aggressive spirit of the San Marcos assembly, the violent encounters with government troops, the deaths of a worker and a student, Haya's bellicose speech — all had a profound effect on those who participated in them. Eudocio Ravines, a university student, who at first worked with Haya and later, as a leader of the Peruvian Communist party, against him, described in glowing terms the emotions of May 23, which were not easily forgotten:

> A street battle is a magnificent thing! Magnificent above all for the individual who feels like a protagonist in it, facing the mouths of the rifles and the edges of the swords with his fists. It is like being in ecstasy, because the participant comes to forget his fear, that is, he forgets he is risking his life, and he enters the icy summit, wild yet serene, of heroism. The youthful heroism of that night intimidated the cavalry.[35]

The dogged resolve of the students and workers in the face of the government troops brought added cohesion to the protest and gained for it the sympathy of diverse sectors of the Lima populace. On May 24, in a sensational move, a group of protestors with Haya in the lead stole the cadavers of Ponce and Vidalón from the city morgue and carried them to the university. That night San Marcos girded itself for an armed assault after it was learned that the minister of interior had ordered an attack to recapture the bodies. Again Haya was in the forefront, organizing the fortification of the university and encouraging its students and worker defenders to resist to the end. The expected attack never came, apparently called off at the last minute by Leguía himself. The next morning, with authorization from the police, Ponce and Vidalón were buried in the Lima cemetery. A crowd estimated at 30,000 witnessed the ceremony, at which Haya de la Torre was the principal orator. Speaking in the name of the Universidad Popular, Haya based his presentation on the Fifth Commandment. He repeated over and over again, "Murderers, the Fifth means Thou Shalt Not Kill." The impact of his words was enormous. As one Lima daily wrote:

> And everyone heard — clear, rotund, dominating — the vibrant voice of Víctor Raúl Haya de la Torre. Magnificent, the speech that he made. A magnificent attack on those reponsible for the murder of the youth and masses of Lima . . .

To the entreaties of his words of admonition and battle, the human mass that listened to him swore in a thunderous response not to desert the ranks . . . to persist until the sacrifice of all their lives in the work already begun of throwing off the ominous yoke of all tyrannies from the body of the nation.[36]

On the same day as the funeral, the archbishop of Lima announced the suspension of the consecration effort. The protest movement had been victorious. The events of May signified much more than the victory of a multiclass campaign of dissent against the political-religious stategy of the Leguía regime. In the longer view the consecration protest marked the definitive consolidation of bonds between university students and workers later to be translated politically into the Aprista movement. The well-known Peruvian ideologue José Carlos Mariátegui emphasized the significance of the movement when he wrote: "the 23rd of May revealed the social and ideological extent of the rapprochement of the vanguard of university students with the working classes. On that date the new generation had its historical baptism and, under the aegis of exceptionally favorable circumstances, began to play a role in the very development of our history."[37] Haya de la Torre echoed Mariátegui when he affirmed: "if the birth of Aprismo comes in 1919 with the eight-hour movement, its baptism of fire occurs in May of 1923."[38] The blood of the "martyrs" Ponce and Vidalón had cemented the concord between workers and students, making it, according to a San Marcos student assembly the following year, "indissoluble . . . strong, and inflexible against all political tyrannies."[39] In individual terms the most direct beneficiary of the sentiments produced by the consecration protest was Haya de la Torre. The undisputed "soul of the triumphant movement," Haya was a national hero, and more important, in the eyes of the Lima proletariat "the responsible guide of the working class of which he had already become *Maestro*."[40]

The 23rd of May movement signaled a profound transformation within the ranks of Lima's organized labor force: the departure of labor from apolitical traditions to the acceptance and even advocacy of politics as a necessary activity for the betterment of daily existence. With some hindsight it may be said that the politicization of these workers was imminent from the instant that they joined the Universidad Popular. The anthem of these workers' schools, for example, which exhorted "Awake slaves! Already the rays of a new sun are bright in the East . . . The more ignorant the worker, the more impossible it will be for him to conquer his liberation,"[41] expressed the necessity of taking concrete actions to gain personal advancement. But it was the unity of the Sacred Heart protest and its aftermath of repression of the movement's most prominent leaders by the government that convinced workers their fight was with the rulers of the state, and hence a political fight. During the months following the 23rd of May protest various prominent labor leaders approached Haya de la Torre about the creation of a formal political entity. They argued that, whether they liked it or not, they constituted a political force: "they treat us as politicians. They persecute us as politicians. And we don't have the advantage of being a political movement. We should form a political movement."[42] These same leaders urged Haya de la Torre personally to undertake the founding of a political party. By his own admission, Haya had long considered the conversion of the worker-student coalition into a party but had desisted from proposing such a move because he had originally promised to keep the Universidad Popular apolitical.[43]

There is evidence, however, that Haya took to heart the overtures of these individuals and began immediately to plot against Leguía's re-election to a second term in 1924. A letter from exiled politician Arturo Osores to Haya in July 1923 stated that it was imperative to end Leguía's rule, by force if necessary, and admonished Haya to be prudent in carrying forward the conspiracy he had already initiated.[44] Both this anti-Leguía movement and the establishment of a political organization remained, however, in the planning stages when the government jailed Haya de la Torre in the first days of October 1923. Although large numbers of workers in the Capital and in Vitarte responded wholeheartedly to the call for a general strike to protest the imprisonment of the *"maestro,"* and two laborers were killed by repressive government troops, Leguía held firm in his resolve to remove Haya from the scene and sent him out of the country to Panama.[45]

Shortly before being deported Haya embellished his sympathetic image by embarking on a dramatic hunger strike. In an emotion-filled message smuggled out of his prison cell and published in Lima's most widely read proletarian newspaper, he underscored his own "heroic martyrdom" and at the same time boldly predicted his eventual return to Peru:

> "I do not know what will happen to me, and I am not interested in thinking about it . . . If I have to go into exile, some day I will return. I will return in my own time, when the hour of the great transformation has arrived. I have said and I repeat: only death will be stronger than my decision to be untiring in the liberation crusade that America expects of its youth in the name of social justice."[46]

With his exile in 1923 the legend of the eternally persecuted Haya was born. From that year to date, the "martyr" image has constituted a vital element of Haya's political style. This image is related to another element that emerged from the events of 1923 to reappear throughout the subsequent development of Apra: Haya's moral-religious tone. Whether by chance or out of conscious choice, the future Aprista leader had electrified his followers time and again using a language filled with religious symbolism. Terms like *apostle, mission, crusade,* and *faith* proliferated in public references to Haya during his exile and later set the tone of much of Apra's 1931 campaign rhetoric.

The government's attack did not end with Haya's exile. In the succeeding months and years, the regime made the Universidad Popular and Lima's labor unions its two principal targets. The workers' schools and labor organizations alike had not only refused to compromise with the government, but, worse, had become ever more determined and open in their opposition. Through the second half of 1924, one by one the workers' schools were forcibly closed down, and Leguía ordered the imprisonment and in some cases deportation of professors of the Universidad Popular and labor leaders. These actions were directed precisely at the most prominent members of Haya's nascent student-worker movement. Undaunted by the repression, labor leaders who had managed to elude the police reopened the Universidades Populares in union halls, and when discovered there, they moved to the entrances of major factories with blackboards and chalk. Finally they were forced to form into small groups that set up classes in the dwellings of individual working class students. In 1927 Leguía finally dealt a paralyzing blow both to the Universidad Popular and to the union movement. Alleging the existence of a "Communist plot" against the state, the secret police made the largest raid to that date, imprisoning all of the best known worker and student leaders—some 200 in all—still left in the country. The Second Workers' Congress of the Federación Obrera Local which was in session at the time continued to function behind bars on the prison island of San Lorenzo in the Bay of Callao.[47]

Repression by the government had effects unforeseen by those who planned it. Most important, the events of these years deepened the attachment, now political in nature, between Haya de la Torre and Lima's industrial workers. As Haya observed in a 1970 interview when referring to the Sacred Heart protest and the ensuing period of repression: "with the 23rd of May movement and with my exile, my relations with the workers were strongly reinforced. That is the base. This solidarity appeared at that time because we all contributed, we all fought, and afterwards, we all suffered repression."[48] Seeing themselves as the victims of the same outrages as the rector of the Universidad Popular, urban workers identified themselves more closely with him and announced their intention of carrying on his fight while anxiously awaiting his return. The name of Haya, while prominent in the labor press before 1923, came to dominate the pages of working class publications after his deportation. He was even recalled in songs written after his exile in 1923 and sung at meetings of worker groups during the years of persecution. One such composition entitled "Vals ideal" and dedicated to the "absent *maestro*" recounted his "glorious deeds" and affirmed the faith of the workers in his abilities:

> Haya de la Torre, joven estudiante
> sincero y decidido, como no ha habido otro igual,
> ha sido deportado por una vil calumnia
> del clericalismo canalla y ruin:
> por el único delito de enseñar al pueblo
> el camino de la Luz y la Verdad.
>
> . . . .
>
> En nuestra mente tendremos el recuerdo
> del Apostol de la nueva humanidad.
> Y sirviendo de acicate a sus palabras
> a su regreso más fuerte nos encontrará.[49]

> Haya de la Torre, young sincere and decided
> student, the likes of whom there has never
> been another, has been deported through a
> vile lie of low and base clerical forces;
> his only crime was to teach the people the
> path of Light and Truth.
> In our mind we will have the
> memory of this Apostle of the new humanity.
> And with his words to stimulate us,
> he will find us stronger upon his return.

The repression had transformed a relatively amorphous student-worker alliance into an incipient political party and had secured for Haya de La Torre the leadership of that party by strengthening the ingredient of personal loyalty in his relationship with the members of the Lima proletariat. When in 1924 Haya officially founded the Aprista movement during his residence in Mexico City, the most influential members of the Lima proletarian community promptly declared their adherence to the new organization. Seven years later many of these same men formed the backbone of Haya's popular support in the 1931 presidential campaign.[50]

Haya's rise in popularity during his exile years was also the product of a diligent effort on his part to make sure that in his absence his name would not be forgotten by his working class followers. To this end he launched an active letter writing campaign to key individuals in the Lima proletarian and intellectual communities. The recipients of these messages were generally men who later became Aprista leaders. In these messages Haya pledged to continue steadfast in his "apostolic crusade" to bring culture and justice to the forgotten laboring classes of his country. Although exiled to foreign lands he would, in his words, continue to dedicate his entire existence to the social revindication of the proletariat in Peru. Of his worker followers he asked that they keep faith with the martyrs of May and October 1923 by constantly "renewing our promise of unshakable loyalty." He usually concluded by affectionately writing: "Te agradezco. Un abrazo, Víctor Raúl" ("I thank you. An embrace, Víctor Raúl").[51] Even more than the founding of Apra, Haya's letter writing campaign shows that by 1924 he had become committed to the life of a full-time politician.[52]

The men to whom Haya directed his voluminous correspondence were also those responsible for keeping his name before the Lima working class during his exile years. Writing in labor publications and producing myriads of handbills, they circulated news about the absent leader. Whole issues of working class newspapers were dedicated to Haya de la Torre, with articles about his leadership in the eight-hour movement, the Universidades Populares, Sacred Heart protest, his "martyrdom" at the hands of the "tyrant" Leguía, and his exciting travels through the capitals of Europe. Columnists exuded affection and praise for the *"compañero"* and *"maestro,"* who was classified as the "only honorable and sincere defender of the people."[53] Time and again working class writers affirmed that although Haya was not physically present in Peru, he continued to be the moral guide of the working classes. As one "disciple" announced in 1924: "Haya lives among us in spirit, his teaching is the beacon that guides us, his fighting words vibrate in our lives, bringing the promise of a hope for the future."[54] Imaginary dialogues were published between Haya and laboring men and women in which the absent leader was depicted admonishing followers: "Do not tire, continue onward: fear not the darkness in which you live because soon the day of eternal light will arrive."[55] In nearly every meeting of organized workers extensive mention was made of "nuestro querido ausente" ("our beloved who is absent").[56]

At the same time that Haya worked to maintain his influence among the ranks of Lima's laboring groups, during his exile he also sponsored the organization of Aprista cells in various Latin American and European countries in order to unite behind his leadership other men who had been deported by Leguía. Led by individuals of recognized prestige in the student-worker coalition, these cells publicized Haya's doctrines and prepared leaders for future political roles in a party apparatus in Peru.

Not fully content to sit on the sidelines and await Leguía's political demise, Haya considered from Europe the undertaking of a revolution in his native land. He had been approached on various occasions by men who suggested that he initiate and lead such a movement, and he finally decided to make the attempt in June 1930, after talking in Berlin with Leguía's ex-minister of foreign relations, Alberto Salomón. According to Haya, Salomón had realized the weakening effects of the depression and eleven years in office on the Leguía regime. In Haya he saw the hope that the aging president might be removed without bloodshed. The Aprista leader's account of their conversation is of particular historical interest:

> Then I said to him, "You know that the regime is doomed." Then he said to me, "And why don't you return to Peru?" I replied, "No, I will not be bought." "No," he said, "No, no." I said to him, "Look, the only way for you to save yourselves, and if you see Leguía tell him so, is that he himself make the revolution." Then I proposed to Salomón, I said to him, "Look if Leguía permits me freedom of action and I enter Peru from the North as the head of the Aprista party, and I make a call for action, and he gives me the freedom to make an opposition movement against him, but of course one of democratic opposition, then I arrive in Lima, and if I make it, fine, well then Leguía steps down. That is the revolution." Then he responded, "I really like the plan, because the situation is very bad." "Good," I told him, "You go and tell Leguía." Then he said, "Breaking all speed records, I will travel to Lima." "When are you leaving? When do you think you will arrive?" "The fifth of August," he told me. "Be careful, it may be too late," I said to him. "Because I think that events are moving quickly. And Leguía is going to be the victim of Civilismo. Because those men will react with incredible furor and vengeance. And what we need is another type of movement, a social movement, a democratic movement, and that is Apra." Then he replied, "Breaking all speed records I will go to Hamburg to see my nephew and from there to London and from there to Peru."[57]

Salomón arrived in Lima on the very day that Sánchez Cerro rose in Arequipa, too late for Haya's plans to come to fruition.

In the period between his first contact with the Lima proletariat in 1919 and his projected revolution in 1930 Haya de La Torre twice faced serious challenges to his position of influence with the urban working class. The first attack on his ascendancy came from a group of prominent anarchist labor leaders who questioned his motives and generally resented his accumulation of authority. To them Haya was an "outsider," a member of a distinct social class whose interests were "opposite to those of the man that suffers and lives in ignorance due to the following trilogy: State, Capital, and Religion."[58] They suspected that the university student's only interest in helping the workers was to gain a popular base for the subsequent launching of a career in politics, a pursuit which they viewed with disgust.[59]

In his battle to gain the acceptance of the anarchists Haya's most effective weapon was his own repeated promotion early on of principles that closely paralleled the anarchist position. From the time of his introduction to labor in the eight-hour movement through the Universidad Popular, Haya deliberately "took as my norm the apolitical stance of the anarchists."[60] Whenever the anarchists tried to pin the student leader down concerning the ideological orientation of the Universidad Popular, he affirmed that the only uniting precepts of the institution were social justice and proletarian culture. To a considerable degree the practical orientation of these schools had grown out of Haya's efforts to gain the confidence of the anarchists. At the same time he had made it a point to exclude any teachings which might have been construed as ideological or political, he also dedicated various of his own lectures to attacks on politicians whom he blamed for the deplorable state of Peru in general and of the working classes in particular. Furthermore, many of Haya's personal traits helped break down the resistance of the anarchists. His puritanism, evident in his fight against alcoholic beverages in the Universidad Popular, his extreme moralism, and his advocacy of the need to lead a "clean life" free from temptations greatly appealed to anarchist workers who espoused many of the same ideas and who also considered themselves purists. Finally, Haya upped his stock among the anarchists by adding the name of González Prada to the Universidades Populares shortly after their foundation. Manuel González Prada had been the most successful of the few Peruvian intellectuals who had attempted to approach and gain the favor of working class elements in Lima. Through his writings and public discourses he had become the intellectual leader of Peruvian anarchism. Haya's identification of González Prada with the workers' schools was a master stroke in gaining anarchist support.[61]

Another important factor which aided Haya in overcoming the objections of the more hard-line anarchists was that he came into contact with the urban proletariat when anarchist influence was declining within the labor movement. Particularly after the eight-hour strike, in which unionist tactics were used effectively to gain immediate demands, the traditional anarchists' position was considerably weakened. Indeed, they could not avoid comparisons between the successful eight-hour movement, in which Haya and other bourgeois elements had played an important role, and the failure of another general strike called in May of the same year to protest the spiraling cost of living. Under the leadership of veteran anarchists, the second movement was broken after a week of violent encounters with government troops. Contrasting the dismal results of direct confrontation in the May 1919 strike with the apparent success of conciliation in the eight-hour movement, increasing numbers of workers came to reject as highly utopian the position that only a revolutionized, stateless, and propertyless society could bring well-being to the laboring man.

Hard-line anarchists soon found themselves supplanted by enthusiastic pupils of the workers' schools, who were the most committed advocates of a united front of students and laborers. By 1923 the few holdouts who continued to oppose the prospects of class cooperation and reform embodied in the Universidad Popular had become marginal to the labor movement as a whole. According to one textile worker, they were considered "incompetents or egotists who withhold their support of the well-understood interest of the collectivity that they boast so of defending."[62] After the Sacred Heart Protest, even the most suspicious of the traditional anarchists admitted to the authority of Haya de La Torre. In a front-page story, *La Protesta,* the spokesman of hard-core anarchism in Peru, renounced its past opposition to the student leader and praised his enthusiasm, nobility, and decision in the defense of the workers' cause. Recanting on its previous allegations that the actions of Haya and his fellow students stemmed from impure political ambition, the labor newspaper threw its full support behind the alliance of "the university youth and the workers, the two vibrant and dynamic forces on the side of the spiritual and economic development of the people."[63] The anarchists had come full circle from opposition to praise of Haya, whom they now called "friend and comrade." A man that epitomized "all sincerity, bravery, and sacrifice, he was and is the only great leader to come out of the university classrooms."[64]

Towards the end of Haya's exile he sustained another serious threat to his political ascendancy, this time from within the leadership ranks of Apra. At the head of the movement against Haya was José Carlos Mariátegui, who had inherited the mantle of leadership of the worker-student movement with the exile of the *"maestro."* Later the founder of the Partido Socialista, which after his death became the Partido Comunista, Mariátegui is considered the father of Peruvian socialism. Although the struggle between these two men was carried on almost entirely within the middle and upper class ex-student faction that claimed a directing role in the Aprista alliance and had only a minimal effect on the movement's labor following, Haya's loss to Mariátegui would have constituted a serious impediment to his future political ambitions. As it was, the conflict profoundly affected the future of socialism as a working class movement in Peru.

Mariátegui's initial contact with the student-worker front came largely through the influence of Haya de la Torre, who personally invited him to lecture in the Universidad Popular. When during his first lecture Mariátegui was booed by workers calling him a Leguiísta in disguise,

Haya himself calmed the crowd and convinced them to accept
Mariátegui. Upon his deportation Haya left the direction of the student-
worker periodical *Claridad* to Mariátegui and warmly supported him
when he founded his widely read monthly *Amauta*. Four years later in
1927 a visible rift developed between the two former friends and co-
workers. Mariátegui, the confirmed socialist, had never been satisfied
with the Universidad Popular's failure to develop proletarian class consciousness and apparently had mainly participated in the student-worker
front to disseminate his own ideas and ultimately to create a class party.
Hence, almost inevitably a split began to appear within the workers'
school, with a "Hayista" group who portrayed themselves as the paladins
of social justice ranged against those who sided with Mariátegui in
advocating frankly Marxist revolutionary ideas. On the occasion of an
antiimperialist conference in Brussels in 1927 these divisions came into
the open when several Apristas publicly abandoned the movement and
attacked Haya de la Torre.[65]

The next year Mariátegui, in Lima, openly broke with Haya. The
exiled *"maestro"* had proposed the creation of the Partido Nacionalista
Libertador del Peru (PNL) to back his candidacy to the presidency
against Leguía in the 1929 election. Although Haya insisted in a letter to
Mariátegui that the PNL was solely a maneuver to give symbolic support
to a military revolution being prepared in the north of Peru, Mariátegui
claimed never to have received his message and accused Haya of having
betrayed the original principles of Apra. He contended that Apra had
been established as a kind of popular front which included men of different classes and ideological backgrounds united by their opposition to
imperialism in Latin America. It would be a tragedy, he declared, to
substitute a vulgar electoral machine for this noble alliance designed to
make people aware of the dangers of imperialism and feudalism.
Mariátegui specifically objected to the multiclass, populist nature of
Haya's political conception, affirming that the Peruvian bourgeoisie was
incapable of generating revolution; for the socialist leader the only true
revolutionary party was one directed by and made up of the proletariat.[66]

The conflict with Mariátegui significantly weakened Haya's position
with relation to the rest of the Aprista leadership group. Doubtless with
some exaggeration, prominent Aprista Luis Alberto Sánchez, in commenting on the fight over the alliance versus party question, has affirmed
that "there was one moment during the schism that the whole of Apra fit
into a sofa."[67] What was apparent was that notes of doubt and defection
issued from nearly every Aprista cell outside of Peru and from various
important leaders in Peru. Haya reached the point of offering to resign as
head of Apra and return to the ranks as a simple soldier, a gesture that

was promptly rejected by the pro-Hayistas to whom the Aprista leader expressly directed his resignation offer. Manuel Seoane, Haya's second in command within the movement, was so deeply impressed by Mariátegui's attack that he observed: "Apra consisted of just him, Víctor Raúl."[68]

Behind the language of alliance versus party or communism versus Aprismo was the personal battle between Mariátegui and Haya. A series of letters written by Haya and Mariátegui between 1928 and 1930 in which the two men freely traded personal insults demonstrated the depth of the enmity that had grown between them. Mariátegui accused Haya of trying to fulfill his own political ambitions by launching arbitrarily and opportunistically an old-style liberal movement based on the traditional "criollo" devices of caudillismo, empty rhetoric, fanfare, bluff, and outright lies.[69] Haya replied that Mariátegui's objections were solely based on his profound hatred for the Aprista leader: "I know that in reality—subconsciously Freud would say—you are reacting against me. Haya is the target of your hidden suspicions." And he added that he considered Mariátegui a tropical demagogue, filled with impractical European ideas. In his letter to Mariátegui, Haya repeatedly advised, with no little sarcasm, "Calm yourself friend Mariátegui! . . . you are really hurting yourself with your lack of calm."[70] In the heat of the fight Mariátegui and his followers sent messages to Apristas in various European and American cells criticizing Haya as a childish "jefe ofendido" ("offended chief") with proto-fascist tendencies and petit bourgeois ends. Haya responded with calls for unity to prevent the further weakening of Apra by the divisionism of Mariátegui's revolutionary puritans and pseudo-socialists in Lima.[71]

In all of Haya's statements he implied that one was either fully behind him or against him; agreement with the Mariátegui group on any of their contentions meant the full repudiation of his leadership. And when the "votes" began to come in, it quickly became apparent that Haya would be the victor. Some of the same men who in preceding months had criticized Haya for launching his electoral candidacy rapidly returned to the fold when the loss of their time-honored leader seemed a distinct possibility. Friends and enemies of Haya alike commented on the central importance of his past deeds and his personality in the maintenance of his supremacy within Apra. One individual who first criticized and later supported Haya reflected about the incident: "We always had the idea in our minds that Haya would be the leader of any movement. It was the force of Haya that kept the movement united. We were loyal to the leadership of Haya."[72] An inveterate enemy of the "maestro" concurred with the above evaluation. When trying to explain Mariátegui's defeat he wrote: "The ties of personal friendship with Haya, or his caudillo

qualities, were more powerful than ideas in many of us."[73] His past acts
and his propagandistic abilities had led to the creation of a veritable
legend around Haya's name, and his opponents, to their dismay, found
that the legend was more powerful than any of their derisive charges.

Apra did not take the form of a national political party until October
1930, after the downfall of Leguía. But as the *oncenio* approached its
end, Aprismo manifested all of the elements that would distinguish it
during Sánchez Cerro's "Government of Six Months" and in the later
presidential campaign. On the basis of the experiences of the previous
decade, the movement appeared in the form of a political coalition
between separate socioeconomic groups: the middle and upper class
leadership with its core of ex-Universidad Popular instructors and their
proletarian supporters who belonged in most cases to the ranks of
organized industrial labor in Lima. The nexus between these different
strata of Peruvian society was the element that had been instrumental in
establishing the alliance in the first place, Víctor Raúl Haya de la Torre.

The political joining of "la juventud del brazo y del cerebro" ("the
youth of muscle and the youth of brains"), as Haya enjoyed referring to
his creation, was necessary, according to the Apristas, because of "the
ignorance that predominates in our working classes." Given this relatively negative view of the capacity of the Peruvian working class for
self-government, the balance of power between the two factions of
Aprismo regarding decision-making was predictably unequal. The
Aprista leaders reasoned that, since the workers lacked the consciousness
and ability necessary for independent political action, the government of
the party and eventually of the nation would be left to the middle and upper class intellectuals who were the best prepared for the requirements of
ruling. These men would be the specialists, the political technicians who
would direct the management of the state with the interests and the
defense of the masses in mind. Early in the 1931 election campaign Haya
confirmed the hierarchical structure of Apra in a pamphlet designed to
serve as an organizational blueprint for the party. Entitled *Vertical
Organization of the Peruvian Aprista Party,* it began by stating unequivocally that "the very size of the Peruvian Aprista party and the enormous potential for action of its masses demand an increasing technifica-
tion of its functions; that its structure be vertical in order to make the
greatest use of the energies of its followers, channeling their activity into
a series of specialized tasks."[74]

This doctrine of the uneven division of power within the vertical mold
was accepted and even advanced by the proletarian members of the
Aprista coalition as well as by their upper and middle class leaders. From
the days of the Universidad Popular the workers had considered that the

university students were, "the best prepared to bring us light . . . We always need a shepherd."[75] And in the 1931 campaign this group continued to insist on the guidance of former university students instead of men from their own socioeconomic level. The most prominent Aprista labor leader, Arturo Sabroso, described the workers' view of party and national leadership:

> A government totally made up of people from the proletariat was never considered as a possibility. Precisely when we became convinced of this a few fellow workers said, fine, we will join the party, but fifty percent workers and fifty percent intellectuals in everything: deputies, senators, everything. Others of us reasoned that no, impossible to have half workers. In a parliamentary block you have to have professional men, technicians, doctors, engineers, economists, lawyers, professors, workers, and employees. For study and consultation on many problems you need experts in their field. This will assure that all the studies can be more effectively carried out. It is not a question of demagoguery. This is being realistic.[76]

At the top of this hierarchical framework was Haya de la Torre. Accorded the title of *"Jefe máximo"* ("highest chief"), his right to the position of supreme interpreter and director of the "vague and imprecise desires of the multitude"[77] was disputed by no one who still called himself an Aprista. No other individual could aspire to the ultimate direction of the party. That position belonged to Haya by right, as he was considered "the creator of the doctrine and its principal instrument and [deserved to lead] for having done what he has done."[78]

Haya's dominant relationship with the masses of his party displayed definite similarities to Sánchez Cerro's omnipotence within his political movement. Like the "Hero of Arequipa," the Aprista leader and his followers considered themselves members of a single large family in which parents were to be respected and emulated by their children. As one piece of Aprista propaganda urged: "Aprista: Your party is a great family in which whoever knows, teaches and whoever does not know, learns."[79] United more by the affection and mutual obligations inherent in a family-type situation than by the political principles suggested by a political party, Apristas declared that they were more interested in how the followers *felt* than how they *thought*.[80]

In contrast to Sánchez Cerro, the Aprista chief was never explicitly referred to as a father by his followers, but rather called "the older brother." In describing their movement the Apristas repeatedly referred to themselves as a great brotherhood in which party members were treated as individuals and not just as votes. Notwithstanding this emphasis on the brotherliness of the party in general and of Haya as the "older brother" in particular, the Apristas bestowed on their leader all the attributes of a political patriarch. Haya himself warmed to his fatherly role. He viewed the working class contingent of his party as a child: "A child lives, a child feels pain, a child protests because of the pain; nevertheless, a child is not capable of guiding himself."[81] On another occasion Haya referred to himself as a "curious father" who in the times of trial for Apra, especially after the 1931 election, "wants to test his son or opus against all that resist."[82] In a 1970 interview Haya outlined the nature and origins of his paternalism by comparing in ideal terms the leader-follower relationship in Aprismo to the social relations that characterized the traditional *casa grande* or seigniorial house in his native city of Trujillo:

> In Trujillo there existed the very highest nobility . . . These ties are very strange because they come from the family. Aristocratic ties were conserved in Trujillo . . . I was nurtured in this aristocratic tradition . . . One inherited this like a kind of code of conduct. This aristocracy was closer to the people. It was an old tradition. They treated the people very well. In Trujillo the good treatment of the servants is traditional. The families that lived in what were called the *casas grandes* obeyed this rule. That the children wait on the servants on their birthdays, that they do all these things; be the godfather of their marriages, all this sort of thing . . . And you have to go up to each one of the servants and greet them and kiss them . . . It's a different spirit. And we who come from the north, for example, with the blacks, very affectionate, and everything. At the same time there was always something very cordial with the people. That is Apra! The Aprista masses have seen in their leaders people who had come from the aristocracy . . . We were educated in that school . . . People who don't know the inner workings of the party don't understand these things . . . We were born of this stock . . . In a country which was not an industrialized or bourgeois country, still a patriarchal country, these ties meant much. And Apra owes its success in its first years to this fact.[83]

Considering the source and substance of the alliance between the socioeconomic groups that made up Apra, the party could hardly be judged as the expression of the revolutionary interests of a particular social class, whether the proletariat or the bourgeoisie. Rather it involved an approach to politics and social change which posited a beneficent minority at the top directing the less-favored majority towards what was good for them. Not only was this approach evident in statements of Haya but also in the whole evolution of the Apra movement. The popular universities, for example, represented the establishment of a series of vertical, patron-client relationships through which intellectual elites locked the masses into dependent relationships by providing non-material benefits, that is, education. Later these same relationships would be used to create the kind of mobilizable mass following necessary for the successful launching of a populist party. Cooperation between the different strata was the watchword of that party. Class distinctions were replaced by identifications with the person-to-person relations of trust, dependency, and obedience between a charismatic, upper middle class leader and his mass following. As it stepped on the political stage in 1930-31, Aprismo did not represent, as many terrified members of the elites thought at the time, the beginning of the class struggle in Peru or even an attempt at structural change, but instead an effort on the part of certain sectors of the urban masses to gain more desirable lifestyles by tying themselves to a man whom they considered their protector and benefactor. Ten years of intimate contact with those followers had gained for Haya de la Torre the distinction of assuming the position of leader.[84]

7

Apra II:
The Alliance in the Campaign

WHEN AUGUSTO Leguía fell from power in August 1930 the Aprista faithful joined Peruvians of all political persuasions in jubilantly celebrating the end of the *oncenio*. Finally Víctor Raúl Haya de la Torre's painstakingly formed alliance of manual and intellectual workers would be able to participate openly in Peruvian politics. It appeared that over ten years of hard work in the creation of a polyclass coalition might at last bear political fruit. Shortly after Leguía's ouster the Aprista leader was confidently predicting the emergence of moral and progressive politicians untarnished by any past role in government who would head a new type of popular regime.[1]

Unfortunately for the politically ambitious Apristas, Sánchez Cerro's lightning takeover of the national government stood as an effective barrier to any immediate fulfillment of their high hopes. Haya himself was quick to realize that the new president might impede Apra's political ascendancy. Writing from Berlin on the very day Sánchez Cerro triumphantly entered Lima, the Aprista leader darkly warned his followers of the imminence of a military dictatorship in Peru. He predicted that "the second stage of the movement will entail, without doubt, the battle against the generals,"[2] thus early on drawing the lines of combat between himself and Sánchez Cerro that would become the dominant note of the 1931 electoral campaign.

Haya lost no time in preparing his own forces for the coming political "battle." From his Berlin home in the weeks following the Revolution of Arequipa he oversaw the first steps in the construction of an Aprista political machine in Peru. Ex-university students returning from exile formed the nucleus of that machine. Their central concern was to make

158

Haya de la Torre a viable candidate in a hoped-for presidential contest. The Aprista leader had been absent from Peru for seven years, and the first priority of his representatives in Lima was to refresh the public's memory about the rector of the Popular University and the "hero" of the Sacred Heart protest. While this fledgling organization rapidly set up grass roots branches, printed handbills, disseminated Haya's writings, and promoted the publication of stories about him in the Lima press, the "first chief" remained in Berlin, cautiously awaiting the right moment to return to his country. Haya's caution seemed justified when only two months after the political demise of Leguía the Sánchezcerrista regime initiated a systematic attempt to repress all opposition groups. Top Aprista leaders were deported, the weekly party magazine was closed down, and political meetings were declared illegal. Not until March 1931, after Sánchez Cerro was replaced in government by the Samanéz *junta,* could the Apristas openly resume what they considered the all-important task of party organization.[3]

The Apristas' deep concern over elaborate organization, clearly apparent in their political efforts previous to Sánchez Cerro's clampdown on opposition activities, became a trademark of their campaign for the presidency in 1931. Haya himself was the most decided advocate of a well-planned party organization. In the early political games of his childhood he demonstrated an overriding interest in bringing order to his imaginary republic. Later, in the Popular University, Apra's founder stressed time and again that discipline was an indispensable ingredient in any enterprise devoted to the accomplishment of social change. His penchant for order became even greater during his exile years. At the same time that Haya was deeply impressed by the methodical operation and rigid stratification of European Fascist and Communist parties, he also endured a dangerous challenge to his own leadership of Apra from the "undisciplined" Mariátegui group in Lima. To Haya, the implacable combating of all signs of internal divisions within his movement became a top priority for the building of a smoothly functioning political machine.

Spurred on by Haya's organizational obsession, the Aprista leadership group in Lima began feverishly to build organizations to recruit followers from the ranks of the urban proletariat. They spawned a large number of working class branches bearing a myriad of titles, including committees, subcommittees, cells, *juntas,* federations, and unions. As in the case of the Sánchezcerristas, Apra's leaders also made a concerted effort to tap the potential political resources represented by the recent migrant population in the capital. They established an elaborate web of regional party organs to attract adherents from those provinces with the highest percentage of residents in Lima. In addition, the Apristas resurrected the Popular Universities of the 1920s and gave them an explicitly political role by making them appendages of the Aprista party.

Most of these Aprista working class organizations convened regularly two or three times per week. Meetings centered around various types of activities. Often the central attraction of these get-togethers was a speech by a middle class or labor leader sent by the National Executive Committee. Also, campaign strategy for the local level was mapped out, the distribution of propaganda discussed, and Aprista songs practiced. Often these sessions ended with the shouting of party slogans and street demonstrations.[4]

While in name and in function many of the Aprista working class organizations appeared similar to the local clubs of the Sánchezcerristas, there were important differences which reveal sharp contrasts between the campaign styles of these two populist parties. An initial difference involved the amount of central control exercised over grassroots proletarian branches. The followers of Sánchez Cerro generally formed their local clubs spontaneously, without the direct intervention of the party leadership. Once in existence, they continued to maintain a large degree of autonomy from the "directing council" of the party. Aprista committees and cells, on the other hand, were in the majority of cases first set up and then closely coordinated by the central core of middle and upper class party leaders. A further indication of the varying degree of centralized organization practiced by the two movements was the type of locale chosen for working class group meetings. While nearly all of the Sánchezcerrista clubs gathered in the homes of their presidents, most of Apra's proletarian assemblages convened in the party's central headquarters, the so-called Casa del Pueblo (House of the People).

The Apristas' emphasis on a centrally controlled organization was also apparent in their repeated insistence upon the necessity of party discipline, a consideration conspicuously absent from the Sánchezcerrista camp. Throughout the campaign the movement's leaders were extremely sensitive to any noticeable deviations of rank-and-file Apristas from the party line. They argued that political success was possible only through strict obedience to the dictates of the party. Individual followers were permitted to make suggestions about policy still in the formative stage, but once that policy had been determined, no dissent was tolerated. Given their faithful compliance to a central chain of command, the Apristas' characterization of themselves as a civilian political army was not inappropriate. Every Aprista organization, from the National Executive Committee to the smallest local cell, had a disciplinary commission that was charged with maintaining central control. Clothing themselves in secrecy, these disciplinary commissions studied "the work of all the groups and members of the party to uncover all actions that diverge from our doctrine and our rules; they study the backgrounds and activities of the members. . . ." Although rarely invoked, the penalty for deviation from party norms was immediate expulsion.[5]

The orderly party meetings and mass demonstrations that immensely impressed the friends and foes of Apra constituted tangible evidence of the movement's concern over individual and collective discipline. Advance preparations for large public meetings included exhaustive attention to the smallest of details. Special commissions supervised the manufacture of banners, the choice of speakers, and the rehearsal of cheers and songs. Only standards and signs approved by the party's disciplinary commission were allowed to be carried. Only approved speakers could individually voice their support for Apra. Special committees carefully planned the routes marchers would take, and appropriate maps appeared in the party newspaper, *La Tribuna,* on the day of the demonstration. Apra directives even stipulated that a distance of thirty meters be kept between groups of 2,000 demonstrators in order to facilitate cross traffic.[6]

Like the Sánchezcerristas, the Apra leadership considered mass demonstrations to be of vital importance for their campaign, and the party press claimed turnouts to major events ranging from 40,000 to 60,000 people. While these estimates may have been somewhat inflated and according to most observers Aprista demonstrations were slightly smaller and more restrained than those of the Sánchezcerristas, they were nevertheless impressive affairs. The demonstrators began by marching through the streets from various geographic points in Lima to a central meeting place, usually a public plaza. There, amidst a veritable sea of party flags, the crowd joined in a series of prerehearsed unison shouts of "A . . .! PRA . . .! A . . .! PRA . . .!" They intoned numerous Aprista songs and formally initiated each rally with the singing of both the Aprista hymn, the *"Marsellesa Aprista,"* and the national anthem. These preparations all led up to the dramatic entrance of Haya de la Torre. Preceded by shouts of "Víctor Raúl! Víctor Raúl!" Haya suddenly stepped on to the speakers' platform, and with his left arm extended in the air, greeted the crowd with the Aprista salute. There was surprise, an instant of silence, and then an enormous ovation. Middle class and labor leaders made preliminary speeches, punctuated by songs and shouts. Then came Haya's address, the high point of the event (see Figure 19), more songs and unison shouts, and the end of the rally, with Haya's followers slowly filing away.[7]

Apra's most important public gathering during the campaign was on the occasion of Haya de la Torre's presentation of the party program. Since the initial formation of the movement in Mexico, the Apristas had widely publicized the five basic aims of their continental alliance. They included: (1) action against Yankee imperialism; (2) the consolidation of Latin American political unity; (3) the nationalization of industries and lands; (4) the internationalization of the Panama Canal; and (5) the solidarity of Latin Americans with all oppressed peoples and classes of the world. But as a campaign platform these general and in some cases revolutionary principles regarding the whole of the Latin American continent were hardly appropriate, and pressures built up to produce a "realistic" program directly tied to Peru's needs. In his speech on August 23, 1931, Haya answered these pressures and outlined his party's *"programa mínimo"* ("minimum program"), which he contrasted to the movement's original five points, now referred to as the *"programa máximo"* ("maximum program"). Sounding more like a university professor than a political speaker, Apra's leader devoted the first half of his address to the enumeration of the principal problems facing Peru. With language that recalled the kind of developmental nationalism that many of Apra's middle class leaders had learned during their university days, Haya explained that economic factors were at the root of the nation's difficulties. He placed most of the blame on existing forms of foreign economic

Figure 19. Víctor Raúl Haya de la Torre Speaks. From Archivo de Víctor Raul Haya de la Torre (AdHT), Vitarte, Peru.

penetration plus the extreme backwardness that characterized the non-foreign-controlled parts of the economy. The Aprista leader further argued that only a strong state mechanism could effectively re-orient the national economy to serve the interests of the majority of the population. Classifying the national majority as the peasantry, the industrial proletariat, and the middle class, Haya strongly asserted that the governing of the country would have to fall to the middle groups, as both the rural and urban poor lacked the sufficient preparation and consciousness for the task. He minimized any conflict of interests between these groups by emphasizing their common oppression at the hands of foreign imperialism and the local oligarchy. A political union of the "oppressed" in Apra's *"Frente Unico"* or "United Front" of oppressed classes was, he declared, essential to gain the political control of the state. The concept of class cooperation, which Haya had repeatedly stressed in his original creation of a populist coalition during the 1920s, continued to receive heavy emphasis in the party program of 1931. In the second part of his speech Haya presented a vague outline of what courses of action he expected to take once elected to the presidency. The Aprista state, he affirmed, would be run as a kind of technocracy by recognized experts in each field of public endeavor.

More specific policies concerning the objectives of Aprista rule appeared in the party's official *programa mínimo* one month after Haya's August 23 speech. Filled with suggestions for government action, the program ranged from the area of bureaucratic decentralization to plans for special rates for students traveling on public transportation. Those sections of the *programa mínimo* most frequently echoed in the campaign included promises to end governmental corruption, to create an efficient public administration, to nationalize Peru's mining and petroleum industries in the near future, to insure the separation of church and state, and to establish a national social security system. Overall the document represented an interesting reflection of the basic coalition nature of the Aprista movement. Aprista leadership attempted to avoid potential conflict between the various segments of the coalition by emphasizing without distinction the alleviation of the economic problems of all those from whom votes might be forthcoming in the October election. Hence, direct appeals were pitched to the needs of urban industrial labor, the rural proletariat concentrated on coastal sugar and cotton plantations, small landowners, white collar workers, bureaucrats, professional people, and small businessmen. As one student of Apra has insightfully noted: "People of varying political positions and concerns . . . could find something appealing in Apra's program and they stressed one or another aspect of it according to their own inclinations.[8]

In their speeches, as well as in the official platform, Apra's top leaders demonstrated a deep concern for the creation and diffusion of a complex set of ideological tenets. Their continued insistence on the importance of Aprista doctrine contrasted sharply with the negligible use of ideology by the Sánchczccrristas. But that insistence plus the very volume of newspaper and magazine articles and pamphlets, written during and after the campaign which outlined Aprista doctrine, has led to an exaggerated emphasis of the difference between Apra and Sánchezcerrismo regarding the role of political ideology, particularly when considering its effect on mass participation. Specific Aprista doctrinal statements, nearly always encased in relatively sophisticated language, had little direct effect on the mobilization of a working class following in 1931. Discussions about the impact of imperialism on international and national politics or about the subtleties of Marxist-Leninist thought generally confused mass audiences rather than convincing them of the rightness of party precepts. Aware of the limited interest exhibited by the popular masses in his movement's ideology, Haya urged those who did not understand the doctrine to "feel" it.[9] And some years later Haya's second in command, Manuel Seoane, supported this view by affirming: "Therefore, we could almost say that we are less interested in how an Aprista *thinks* than knowing how an Aprista *feels*."[10]

While working class Apristas may in general have failed to understand many of their party's doctrinal statements, the ideology as an undifferentiated whole did, nevertheless, have an indirect impact on mass mobilization which was notably absent from Sánchezcerrismo. Above all, it gave individual Apristas a sense of political identity, of something concrete beyond the figure of the candidate to adhere to. Despite the difficulty the party's working class members might have experienced in reciting specific arguments about Peru's relationship to imperialist powers or about how the "Aprista state" differed from the Bolshevist state, they knew that those arguments existed and that they had been fashioned by a competent set of leadership figures. Indeed, the grandiloquent tone and complexity of Apra's ideological language reinforced the confidence of the rank and file in the party leaders, who possessed a high degree of intelligence in addition to the special intuition projected as much by Haya de la Torre as by Sánchez Cerro. Men with the ability to create and manipulate such an ideology were judged to be superior individuals who could not only direct Peru's destiny but who also could effectively interpret the world around them.[11]

The presentation of a somewhat complex body of political ideology was only one facet of Apra's use of rhetoric in the campaign. In addition to the sophisticated concepts and language of the maximum and minimum programs and other expositions of ideology, Aprista spokesmen spent considerable time in the presidential race in virulently attacking their political foes, a practice which had a more immediate impact on working class participation than the indirectly important elaboration and divulgation of doctrine. The use of negative reference rhetoric had also been a strident note of the Sánchezcerrista campaign. And although Apra's leaders clearly cared more about the elaboration of positive plans for government than the Sánchezcerristas, they too worked to build up their own movement by contrasting themselves favorably with their "evil" adversaries.

The most frequent targets of Aprista attacks were the oligarchy and the person of Sánchez Cerro. By denouncing Peru's traditional governing elite, the Apristas were able to draw on a deep wellspring of antioligarchical feeling that dated back to the first major schisms in the *República aristocrática* in 1908. More recently the hatred of the oligarchy had been exacerbated by Augusto Leguía, who had attempted to prolong the life of his own regime by actively vilifying all past administrations. With the demise of the *oncenio* in 1930 antielite sentiment did not markedly decrease but rather continued to be a potent political symbol throughout the 1931 electoral campaign. The Apristas, as had Leguía before them, classified the oligarchy under the rubric of Civilismo, a term which over the years had superseded its narrow application to the Partido Civil and had come to refer to an entire plutocratic class. During the presidential race, the Apristas attributed to that "Parasitic caste" the responsibility for all of Peru's past and present problems. The Civilistas, they argued, had made corruption and vice, the maintenance of mass poverty, the looting of the national treasury, and widespread political chicanery a way of life in order to retain their dominance over national affairs. The Apristas concluded that the only sure guarantee against the continued power of Civilismo was the victory of Haya de la Torre at the ballot box.[12]

Those who raised the specter of continued rule by the traditional elites claimed that Haya's election to the presidency was doubly important, for not only was the Aprista leader clearly the most anti-Civilista of the candidates, but also Sánchez Cerro, his strongest opponent, was portrayed to be the "dupe" of Peru's degenerate oligarchical caste. And what was worse, according to Aprista campaigners, the commandant-candidate was a totally evil and inferior human being. Using wildly abusive language, the spokesmen of Apra variously referred to Sánchez Cerro as an uncultured, illiterate, vain, smelly, dirty, cowardly thief whose supporters were similarly unlettered and unscrupulous vendors in the Lima market. He was also, in their words, a ridiculous, perverse, latent homosexual, mentally retarded and physically an epileptic, a fetid, Black-Indian half-caste whose primitive behavior and simian-like poses and attitudes suggested that a search for his origins would be like following the biological trail of a gorilla. In the most extreme of the Aprista attacks it was suggested that the key to Sánchez Cerro's repugnant character was indeed to be found in his origins but that his family tree did not include a monkey. Rather the readers of a nearly pornographic parable entitled *Sánchez Cerro or Excrement* were told that he was the unwanted fruit of the rape of his mother by an enormous pig: "That had to be his origin. A perversion of nature; passion's miscarriage; the fruit of a stolen and unexpected spasm; the product of a sexual aberration. . . ."[13]

The extreme abuse heaped on Sánchez Cerro by Apra's spokesmen did not always produce the desired result. Insults involving Sánchez Cerro's "racial inferiority," for example, were also indirectly insults to the majority of Lima's working class voters who shared his mixed ethnic background. Furthermore, attempts to criticize the commandant-candidate by calling him the leader of a shoddy retinue of culturally and racially backward *cholo* market vendors were considered by many to be a manifestation of implicit contempt toward the urban masses as a whole. When Sánchez Cerro's supporters struck back by calling Haya de la Torre and his fellow Aprista leaders a group of pale, perfumed *mocitos bien* ("little rich kids"), elegant in manner and dress but totally lacking in empathy for the working classes, their declarations found receptive ears.[14]

In fact, while more vehement than their opponents in the use of negative references, the Apristas increasingly found themselves on the defensive, forced to devote much of their campaign rhetoric to allaying Sánchezcerrista-spread fears of ominous consequences in the event of an Apra victory. One especially harmful accusation that the Apristas worked hard to refute was that they were fiercely anti-Catholic. Citing Haya de la Torre's participation in the Sacred Heart protest as evidence of the antireligious feelings that had impregnated Apra from its beginnings, the Sánchezcerristas warned that the election of the Aprista candidate would bring about the undermining of the family, the casting aside of marriage as a basic social institution, and the extensive practice of free love. They insisted that under these circumstances one could not be both a Catholic and an Aprista; for a truly religious person, therefore, it was simply a question of "Cristo sí, Apra no." The Catholic press and some individual clerics joined the attack, warning the faithful that Haya de la Torre was an enemy of Christ and that he advocated the burning of churches, the rape of nuns, and the execution of priests.

The Apristas answered these charges by protesting their neutrality vis-à-vis religion in Peru. They argued that the religious question was something of a red herring that was being used against them, and they advised the electorate to focus its attention on the solution of the more important economic problems facing the nation. Yet at the same time that the party largely remained silent on the subject of the church in an avowed attempt to avert the transformation of the campaign into a battle over religious beliefs, occasional pronouncements by Aprista leaders that religion was the opium of the masses and that schools must be built to replace convents, plus a platform plank calling for the definitive separation of church and state, lent a certain credibility to the Sánchezcerrista claims. In spite of their pledge that once in government they would respect all faiths, the Apristas appear to have lost the religious debate in many quarters. One indication of Apra's failure were the letters, usually written by women, that flooded into the campaign headquarters of Sánchez Cerro containing prayers for the triumph of the commandant-candidate in order to prevent the devil from reigning supreme in Peru.[15]

Another persistent charge against Apra involved the alleged ties of the movement and its leadership to the "henchmen" of ex-President Leguía. For their part, the Apristas had a difficult tightrope to walk in their relationship to Leguiísmo. On the one hand, they recognized that although Leguía himself no longer exerted any influence, his following, largely composed of middle sector professionals, businessmen, bureaucrats, white collar employees, and the wealthier artisans, continued to be a valuable political resource worth courting for the electoral contest. On the other hand, an explicit plea for Leguiísta support would clearly have been tantamount to political suicide in an atmosphere still charged with hatred for the men and politics of the *oncenio*. The Apristas attempted to solve this dilemma by privately enlisting the aid, especially economic, of various prominent Leguiístas while publicly going so far as to decry those who continued to malign the physically ailing and decrepit Leguía; they repeatedly criticized the Sánchezcerristas for trying to withhold political participation from a substantial sector of the population that continued to hold Peruvian citizenship. These private and public stances failed to convince the enemies of the ex-president that Apra had in fact taken a neutral position regarding Leguiísmo, but they did net a considerable amount of support for the party from Leguiísta factions. A large portion of the monies in Apra's campaign treasury came from the pockets of former supporters of Leguía, and numerous Aprista voters belonged to the ranks of the ex-president's followers, who presumed that a lukewarm Haya would be clearly preferable to a rabidly anti-Leguiísta Sánchez Cerro. Many of them also hoped that an Aprista victory might allow them continued access to the administrative posts and favors which they had acquired during the *oncenio*.[16]

Shortly after Haya de la Torre's first campaign appearance in Lima, the Apristas found themselves trying to refute still another imputation from the Sánchez Cerro camp, this time involving their lack of patriotism. The Sánchezcerristas accused their opponents of revealing an underlying contempt for Peru and things Peruvian by substituting their own flag and their own hymn for those of the nation. Apra's reply to these charges was again less than convincing: "And if we use a party flag, the ignorant editors of *El Comercio* should know that every political party in the world has one, except, of course, those occasional electoral groupings that do not have flags but just appetites. But *in addition* we carry the Peruvian flag. In all its meetings our party uses the Peruvian flag, and the demonstrators in the Plaza San Martín, *in addition* to the party songs, sang the National Anthem."[17] By stating that the Peruvian flag and hymn were present *in addition* to the Aprista flag and hymn, it did indeed seem that the symbols of the nation had taken second place to the symbols of the party.

Closely related to the imputation of antinationalist tendencies to Apra was the allegation that the movement represented a communist organization in disguise and that Haya de la Torre in reality planned to turn Peru into a Bolshevic dictatorship as soon as he was elected. The Sánchezcerristas reminded the electorate that Aprista speakers and writers frequently cited Marx, Engels, and Lenin, that the party referred to some of its branch organizations as cells, and that some of the most common themes of the movement's campaign rhetoric included opposition to united States imperialism, the defamation of the traditional elites, and the need for a complete renovation of Peruvian life. They concluded that a party with such radical tenets and inspiration, once in government, would undoubtedly destroy the principle of private property and force the population to work as slaves for the administrators of a communist state. In contrast to the ambiguity of their responses to other facets of the Sánchezcerrista negative reference campaign, the Apristas were quite unequivocal in their position on communism, totally rejecting the application of the communist label to their movement. They insisted that from its birth Apra had constituted a coalition between the oppressed middle and lower classes and therefore represented a clear repudiation of the basic communist concepts of the proletarian revolution and class conflict. Moreover, Haya and his fellow leaders condemned the official

Peruvian communist party as a bunch of *"communistas criollos"* or arm-chair radicals and classified the soviet experience as a reprehensible example of the tragic rise to power of a group of intellectual fanatics blinded by their class ambitions.[18]

Notwithstanding their rabid anticommunism, Apra was still regarded by Peruvian and foreign observers alike as a radical movement whose leaders were determined to carry out a major restructuring of the nation's economic, social, and political institutions. Yet an extensive review of the Apristas' written and spoken statements in 1931 reveals a striking lack of willingness to maintain firm radical stances on major issues of economic and social policy. Early in his political life Haya de la Torre had given indications of possessing revolutionary ideas with his statements about the imminence of a bloody onslaught on the exploitative capitalist class by the oppressed proletariat.[19] But by 1931 this inchoate radicalism had given way to a kind of flexible realpolitik, especially when it came to specific proposals for change. Haya himself explained his conversion from a revolutionary into a political pragmatist while still in exile:

> My plan for Latin America? It is difficult to explain it to you in this message. All I can promise you is a series of suggestions, the most realistic possible and the least possible "saturated with excessive goals." It seems that Europe's influence acts to keep men's thoughts on a realistic line, above all in politics. It seems as if those minds that have been inflamed by the intoxicating atmosphere of the tropics have cooled off and condensed themselves here; they work better not in the temperate zone that offers a proper climate but rather in the temperate zone of accumulated experience, of useful experience in the antisimplistic and practical atmosphere of peoples who know that social and political problems are not solved by axioms.[20]

During the campaign Aprista spokesmen demonstrated the same unwillingness as that of their *jefe máximo* to be pinned down on concrete plans for sweeping social or economic change. Manuel Seoane placed the party in between both "the extremes of Left and Right,"[21] and at the First National Aprista congress held two months before the 1931 election he added: "We represent, in general terms, the path to social justice. We cannot predict exactly what the stages of this fight will be and therefore, more than a specific program which would mean to point out the exact areas of the political battles, it is necessary that we indicate preferably a general plan to be followed."[22]

Apra's ambivalent radicalism becomes particularly apparent when the two most left-wing-sounding areas of party policy—opposition to capitalism and to imperialism—are closely studied. The movement's blanket indictment of capitalist economic systems for their exploitation of the masses coupled with the maximum and minimum programs' planks of nationalization, antimonopolism, and censure of Peru's capitalist elites seem to indicate a clear repudiation of the existing structure of the national economy. But on the questions of how fast that structure should be rectified and what kind of an economy should replace it, the extremism of the movement's anticapitalist posture pales significantly; the Aprista state would limit its fight against exploitation "as circumstances permit and in a gradual and slow manner."[23] Apristas referred to their brand of social justice as a protracted and evolutionary process and gave assurances that it did not include the expropriation by force of wealth or property from the upper classes. Towards the end of the campaign, the party faithful were told not to expect a frontal assault by an Aprista state on capitalism in Peru, but rather a controlling action which would result in higher salaries of employees and laborers. Aprismo in government, it was later pointed out, would neither defend the economic status quo nor march immediately down the path to socialism. Instead, the party would try to reach an essentially reformist middle ground which would combine the best elements of both capitalist and socialist systems in order to attain "merely a better stage. A stage in which men have less of today's egotism and a little more of tomorrow's integral humanism."[24] Perhaps one aspect of that combination in the campaign was that while Aprista leaders were ever ready to denounce Peru's decadent economic elites, they were not loath to receive considerable financial aid from prominent members of those elites. A case in point was the alleged contribution of 50,000 *soles* to the Apra effort by the wealthy Trujillo landowner and businessman Rafael Larco Herrera. Unlike other populist movements, notably Peronism, which apparently strained their relationship with the export sector in attempting to stimulate industrialization and augment the role of the state, Apristas hesitated to pursue an all-out attack on the powerful export oligarchy and indeed maintained strong ties with key components within it. Perhaps the relatively low level of mass political integration in Peru, compared to larger, more developed countries like Argentina, placed severe limitations on Apra's or any other populist movement's ability to seriously challenge entrenched privilege.[25]

Apra manifested an even greater flexibility on the consequences of imperialist economic expansion into Peru. From its founding in Mexico in 1924 the movement had identified its guiding principle, its very reason for being, as the fight against imperialism in Latin America. The first of the five points in its maximum program was "action against Yankee imperialism."[26] At various times in 1930-31 Haya de la Torre and other Aprista leaders explained that imperialist expansion was the greatest danger to Latin America in general and to Peru in particular. Classifying imperialism as the ruinous exploitation of the weak nations by the great powers, representatives of the party declared on various occasions that their major task was to resist its incursions. Yet this seemingly uncompromising opposition to foreign expansion was greatly tempered during much of the campaign. The *programa mínimo,* for instance, mentioned the word *antiimperialism* only once in relation to the signing of a pact with other Latin American nations "for the defense against any imperialist dangers," the focus being more on mutual defense against foreign invasion than on the question of economic penetration. Of even greater significance, from May through October Aprista spokesmen emphatically denied that their resistence to imperialism meant they were adverse to the continued flow of foreign capital into the country. On the contrary, they stressed that the activities of investors, businessmen, and industrialists from abroad were not only beneficial but essential to the economic progress of Peru. The Apristas surmised that given the dearth of investment capital, industrial infrastructure, and trained technicians in Peru, foreign economic interests should be welcomed as the indispensable elements of national modernization. They concluded that the nation's economic backwardness could only be overcome through the infusion of economic and human resources from the developed world. The Apristas recognized that foreign capitalists should derive a just profit for their endeavors and therefore concluded that the only restriction to be placed on those capitalists was that they pay an equitable amount of wages to their workers and taxes to the government. The Apristas did not even propose the abrogation of monopolies granted to foreign enterprises during the *oncenio,* but rather the revision of existing contracts to create a situation in which large foreign firms would "work hand in glove with the government" on terms fair to both parties.[27] Further evidence of the Apristas' willingness and in fact eagerness to live peacefully with foreign capital were the advertisements of "imperialist" companies that appeared almost daily in the party newspaper for products and services from Remington typewriters to Panagra Airlines.[28]

When directly confronted by the representatives of foreign capital and foreign governments fearful of Apra's original antiimperialist commitment, party leaders tried to accentuate their moderate image by giving assurance that they had forsworn all forms of antiforeignism. Manuel Seoane summed up his party's recantation from the more extreme positions of earlier years in an interview with *The West Coast Leader,* Lima's English-language newspaper, which represented the interests of the British and North American communities in Peru. Asked by the paper's correspondent, "But what about your slogan 'Let us present a united front against foreign imperialism?' That sounds rather alarming,"

Seoane replied, "More alarming in words than in fact. It is not intended to imply any attack on capital . . . The Aprista Party has no anti-foreign feeling."[29] Seoane was the same man who two weeks earlier had been referred to in a dispatch from United States ambassador to Peru, Fred Morris Dearing, as "the reddest of the red and a very dangerous man." After seeing the above interview, Dearing changed his mind about Seoane, characterizing him as a "sensible and realistic man." The American ambassador was to undergo a similarly dramatic change in attitude about the "danger" of the whole Aprista movement before the election campaign was over. It appears that Haya de la Torre himself was instrumental in altering Dearing's views. Previous to personally meeting Apra's leader, the ambassador had written that he was fully convinced that Haya was a communist "in the pay of the Soviets." Dearing termed the Aprista movement "subversive in character and not entitled to the freedom of a normal and natural political party . . . it is almost certain they are still under the influence of Moscow."[30] Anxious to dispel these apprehensions, Haya sought out Dearing and other United States officials to convince them that he had substantially softened his stands on Yankee imperialism and the nationalization of foreign enterprise. At Haya's request a meeting was arranged with Dearing, and judging by the ambassador's report of the event the Aprista leader succeeded admirably at portraying himself as a political moderate:

> Señor Haya de la Torre immediately impressed me by something warm and sympathetic in his character and by his apparent sincerity . . . He scouted the idea that he was destructive or ultra-radical and he seemed to have a sincere regard for our country which he has visited several times . . . Señor Haya de la Torre indicated clearly that if his party should ever be successful, he would expect as much understanding and helpfulness as possible from our government and a real cooperation between our two countries; he merely wishes it to be careful, considerate and fair . . . I am still uncertain as to whether I should say he is a man of destiny. From what I know up to this point, however, I should think that if he should become president of Peru, we should have nothing to fear and on the contrary might expect an excellent and beneficent administration of strongly liberal tendencies in which justice in the main would be done, and a period of confidence and well being be initiated.[31]

Haya also approached the executives of major foreign business concerns, such as the North American Cerro de Pasco Copper Corporation and the British Peruvian Corporation, to convince them that he wanted to reform, not revolutionize, the nation. In these meetings he also promised to tone down rhetoric that might be interpreted as antiforeign. On one occasion he was reported to have actively intervened in a mineworkers' strike, apparently on the side of the foreign owners, counseling the workers to abandon the use of extreme tactics and calmly accept the inevitable. Haya's success at blunting hostility from the foreign business sector was reflected in the views of one United States businessman, who wrote: "I met de la Torre, the real leader of the whole movement and found him to be a very moderate and reasonable fellow, educated at Oxford, and wide awake to everything that goes on in the world today. I don't think that there is much danger that the mob may run away from their present leaders."[32]

In sum, the general lines of Apra's campaign rhetoric justified the placement of the movement to the left of its major competitor in the 1931 election and were clearly adverse to the political principles of past *República aristocrática*-style rule. The concepts generated by Aprismo in the campaign suggested a greater willingness to adopt more drastic measures than the Sánchezcerristas to obtain for Peru's middle and working classes, as one Aprista song put it, "a better suit, a better dinner table, and a better place in which to live."[33] But the differences between the two movements might best be described as differences of degree rather than differences of kind. Apra's continued espousal in government of their essentially moderate plans for action regarding Peru's traditional oligarchy, capitalist enterprises, and foreign imperialism would probably have produced a modernizing regime with a new political style that, although interested in raising the standard of living of certain less fortunate sectors of the population, would have worked in cooperation with existing national and foreign economic elites and to the exclusion of any profound changes in social or economic structure. In projecting the political organization of an Aprista government the party's leaders suggested the creation of a corporatist state with a legislature composed of the delegates of functional interest groups. The executive branch and the public administration were to be run by technical experts whose job it would be to promote interest-group collaboration and to arbitrate between the representatives of different economic sectors on major questions of national policy. In the light of the high value placed on technical knowledge and class cooperation as well as the "family" configuration of Apra from its days as a worker-student front, it is not surprising that Haya and his fellow leaders proposed that the state be organized along the corporate lines of a so-called "functional democracy" in which the last word belonged to the specially qualified political technician at the top.

The conception of corporate government that Apra outlined in the 1931 campaign was strikingly similar in form and intent to various populist regimes that later exercised power in Latin America. As in the cases of Cárdenas's Mexico and Perón's Argentina, for example, the

Apristas envisioned an arbiter state that, standing above classes, would be society's most potent agent of class collaboration. Apra's populist state would flexibly juggle the various existing and potentially antithetical interest groups, applying pragmatism and technocratic know-how to the solution of any problems between them. This model posited the necessity not only of a more effectual state apparatus but also one sufficiently enlarged and strengthened so as to extend itself into wider areas of national concern while vigorously keeping the lid on possible internal conflict.[34]

Aprista ideological radicalism, or lack of it, functional corporatism, and technocracy, although essential to a notion about how the movement might have eventually governed Peru, were not fundamental aspects of the central question of popular participation in 1931. In terms of Apra's political mobilization of the urban masses, more than a united ideological front of issue-oriented voters, the party constituted a kind of moral crusade, above all for its followers of working class extraction. In 1931 and in subsequent years Apra strove to provide its adherents with a system of values and behavior patterns touching on every aspect of their lives. Aprista leaders insisted that they were concerned with the creation of a new Peruvian man characterized by moral purity, self-discipline, emotional control, and physical fitness. Once created, these men would form an exemplary "civilian army" dedicated to the destruction of the decrepit institutions, the personal hatreds, and the low passions that had made Peru a decadent nation.

The conception of Apra as a moral-cultural force was strongly reminiscent of the morals campaigns during the days of the Popular University. And the idea that there existed an almost familial bond between Apra's moral revolutionaries suggested an important facet of the initial development of the movement in the 1920s. In 1931, as previously, that bond was designed to make the individual Aprista "enjoy the gratification of feeling [himself] a member of a vast and intimate family of men"[35] while also functioning to preclude any serious threats to the unity of the party. Heedful of the moralistic and familistic fervor in Apra, outside observers commonly believed that the loyalty of Apristas to their party far surpassed all other loyalties, including those, for instance, to the nation, to a geographical region, or to a particular city. Haya de la Torre's description of the degree of solidarity that existed in Apra at the time of the 1931 election supports this belief: "We proved ourselves to each other with our sincerity . . . and with this, indestructible bonds of solidarity were established. There was no way to doubt one another . . . It was an emotional thing, a mystical thing, a creed."[36]

Haya may be faulted for exaggeration in his portrayal of the "inde-
structibility" of the Aprista bond, but his overall choice of words does
not seem excessive to describe the movement at the time of the 1931 campaign. The explicitly religious overtones of the idea of a "mystical credo"
are eminently appropriate to characterize a party that repeatedly called
itself "the new religion" and which had exhibited religious overtones
since the Popular University days. Apristas now identified their movement as a "religious" organization every time they sang the words of the
party hymn, the *"Marsellesa Aprista"*:

> Peruanos abrazad, la nueva religión
> LA ALIANZA POPULAR
> conquistará la ansiada redención![37]

> Peruvians embrace the new religion
> THE POPULAR ALLIANCE
> will conquer our longed-for redemption!

The heavy reliance on the themes and language of the New Testament to
symbolize Aprismo in party tracts and speeches indicates that the movement was represented as a brand of political Catholicism to its membership. Aprista spokesmen described their organization as a communion of
true believers, joined by a messianic faith and engaged in the sacred mission of purifying the nation and driving out the evil political pharisees
that had ruled in the past. *"Sólo el Aprismo salvará al Perú"* ("Only
Aprismo will save Peru") became the party salute to be used every time
two or more Apristas met.

Apparently the use of religious rhetoric had a significant impact on
Aprista followers, who began to refer to themselves as the dedicated
"disciples" of a predestined, Christ-like Haya de la Torre. On numerous
occasions rank-and-file party members pronounced themselves ready to
undergo great sacrifices in Haya's name for the good of the party and
ultimately of the nation. Two Aprista election posters illustrate well both
the prevalence of religious symbolism in the Apra campaign and Haya's
role as a saintly, religious-type leader. In the first (figure 20), the *jefe
máximo's* garlanded picture appears above what looks to be a Bible with
a Creation scene in the background that might have come out of Genesis.
The boldly lettered sign in the foreground alludes to Apra's salvationist
mission. The second (figure 21) presents a scene reminiscent of Dante's
Inferno in which a dramatically gigantic Haya seems to be pointing "the
way" above the outstretched hands of the naked and imploring masses.[38]

Apra's political religiosity grew out of several factors, not the least of
which was the influence of the movement's *jefe máximo*. A seminary stu-

Figure 20. Haya de la Torre in the Popular Mind. From AdHT.

dent in his youth, Haya has made reference at various times to his own
inclination towards the mystical aspects of religious faith, and he admits
that had he not become a politician, he would have entered the priesthood. When Haya eventually decided on a political career, he did so, according to his own words, in response to a quasi-religious call: "My cons-
cience told me: this greatness calls you, it calls you, I tell you thus."[39]
Haya infused all of his major ventures with a mystical tone. He classified
his participation in the university reform movement as service for a missionary cause. He fashioned the popular universities, which he called
"lay temples," along lines similar to the neighborhood church that
brought people together socially, culturally, and spiritually. The party's
successful continuation of these functions is one key to its resilience over
the years, despite persecutions and apparent radical deviations in
ideology; from the outset Apra was developed into much more than a
simple political party.[40]
      Haya's experiences in Europe during the exile years further reinforced
his conviction that the spiritual fervor of the membership was an important element in all serious political movements. Particularly in the context of Latin America, the communication of a "mystical sentiment" was,
in Haya's view, absolutely necessary for future political success. In addition to Haya's personal imprint of religiosity on Aprismo, the repression
of the original student-worker front by the Leguía regime and of the
party by Sánchez Cerro induced the likening of the movement to a

Figure 21. Aprista Election Poster. From AdHT.

persecuted sect with an evolution akin to that of early Christianity. As
one Aprista song put it, the followers of Haya de la Torre were:

> Hombres que sufren
> cruento dolor
> a formar
> del APRA la legión.
> Marchar! Marchar!
> hermanos todos del dolor!
> Luchar! Luchar!
> con la bandera del amor
> con fé y unión[41]

Men who suffer
a cruel pain
let us make
Apra a legion.
March! March!
brothers in pain!
Fight! Fight!
with the banner of love
with faith and unity. . .

And suffering in the future at the hands of oppressive governments would, according to one party notable, only strengthen Apra's religious unity: "Our enemies do not realize that Aprismo is a religion that grows with persecution and with the blood of its martyrs."[42]

The Apristas' fervent faith in their party resulted in large part from Haya de la Torre's effective projection of himself as a man of extraordinary personal qualities and abilities. In this respect he was no less successful than Sánchez Cerro. The vital cornerstone of the Aprista movement since its initial development as a worker-student alliance in the 1920s, Haya's dominance in the 1931 campaign was simply the logical expression in electoral politics of well-established tendencies. Almost echoing Sánchez Cerro in their belief that men were easier to understand and follow than words or ideas, the Aprista leadership declared that Haya de la Torre alone meant the salvation of the fatherland. His return to the country was called a special Peruvian Easter which marked the rebirth of the nation. He was, according to party advocates, the Apristas' "Supreme Guide" and the living incarnation of the Apra program. One of Haya's most enthusiastic lieutenants in the presidential race compared him to the "star of the great films when before they begin, appears alone and enormous on the screen, stimulating the romantic dreams of the young women."[43] The near deification of his person in the campaign was so pronounced that it sometimes embarrassed even Haya. But he never doubted its usefulness:

> When I think of the exaltation of the name Haya de la Torre I always think of the chief of our party, a rather ideal symbol and never of myself . . . I know that I am neither a genius nor a saint and that there are in the party many men and women who are superior to me in many ways. But although I know it I think that the faith that so many people have put in me as a leader may help very much to keep the unity of the party . . . So I extrovert my own personality and I put it to the full service of the common ideal, but never, never as a pedestal for my own vanity.[44]

Haya de la Torre's exalted image in the campaign was the product of his skillful combination of specific personality traits into a coherent political style. The major elements of that style had been developed well before the election, during the 1920s. Not unexpectedly, the Aprista leader built his political image for the 1931 presidential race through the dramatization of his past actions in the 1919 eight-hour strike, the consecration protest, and the Popular University. From the constant recounting of these episodes, two major personality characteristics emerged to constitute the basis of his political style: Haya the hero and Haya the educator. To emphasize the heroic Haya, the Apra camp reminded voters of his resolute confrontation of government troops in 1919 and 1923. And party spokesmen added that the bitter reward for this brave and devoted man who had created Apra was his lonely yet instructive exile from Peru. Apristas underscored these specific incidents of Haya's valor to depict their *jefe máximo* as preeminently a man of action. Like his opponent Sánchez Cerro, Haya was called a person of concrete accomplishments, ready to jump into the breach at any time to better the situation of his followers.[45]

The single most frequently cited past achievement of the Aprista leader in the campaign was his creation of the Popular University. And in the explicitly political Apra school of 1931 Haya was no less the *"maestro"* than he had been eight years earlier. Through his style of political oratory and his repeated emphasis of his personal educational mission, the *jefe máximo* revealed his continuing identification with the role of master teacher of the working classes. In contrast to the fierce harangues of Sánchez Cerro, Haya's lengthy and often complicated speeches resembled classroom lectures in which he marshaled evidence and logic to convince his listeners of the rightness of his position. Employing essentially the same terminology that abounded in the days of the workers' schools, he and other Aprista notables spoke of the need to "Saxonize the indiscipline and ignorance of the country" and to root out the "decadent sensualism" imbedded in the character of the still ignorant masses.[46] Haya and his fellow party chiefs concluded that since "one hundred years of oppression and illiteracy have kept the brain of the popular mass in a state of paralysis,"[47] Apra must constitute at bottom a great school dedicated to lifting the masses out of their traditional state of ignorance.[48]

Haya synthesized his images as heroic man of action and dedicated popular educator to emerge in the presidential race as a distinctive teacher-*caudillo*.[49] Physically the teacher-*caudillo* could not have differed more from his military-*caudillo* competitor. Haya, the tall, heavily built, white-skinned descendant of Spanish nobility, stood in sharp contrast to Sánchez Cerro, the short, wiry, *mestizo* army officer who had arisen from considerably more humble conditions. One British newspaperman, obviously impressed by Haya's aristocratic bearing, called him a man of "Oxford manner."[50] A photograph taken of Haya in 1931 exemplifies his distinguished air (see figure 22).

Despite their highly contrasting physical appearances and social demeanors, both Haya de la Torre and Sánchez Cerro made the adoption of the role of father figure toward their working class following a central element of their caudillistic charisma. The patriarchal posture was hardly new to the Aprista leader in 1931. Indeed, the only notable differences between "the father of the workers" in the 1920s and "the father of Apra" in the campaign were that in the latter period his "children" had grown in numbers far beyond a small group of union leaders, and in the electoral context there were political stakes to be won. The paternalism of the aristocratic Haya was clearly of the "great white father" variety, whereas Sánchez Cerro had demonstrated an uncanny ability virtually to integrate himself into the working class home as the head of the *cholo*

Figure 22. The Oxfordian Haya. From AdHT.

family. But beyond these obvious disparities, paternal affection and paternal authority constituted important parallels in the fatherliness of these two major political contenders. In Haya's case numerous observers remarked about his extraordinary personal warmth, his contagious smile, his generally pleasing disposition, and his prodigious memory for people and events of the past. Many of his person-to-person conversations with members of the Aprista faithful during the campaign revolved around the intimate problems of their daily lives, and Haya always seemed ready with sympathetic understanding and pertinent advice. Even his most avowed enemies could not help but comment enviously on the political benefits Haya gained from the paternalistic concern he was able to generate: "He possessed an ingenious and friendly loquacity that gave people the physical sensation of being loved, set apart individually from among the rest; he was acute at discovering and focusing on the immediate and small problems of the peoples and at treating them with a captivating friendliness, verbally showing interest in them."[51] The physical manifestation of Haya's personal warmth in the form of long handshakes, pats on the back, and above all fond embraces was a salient feature of these individual encounters. The Aprista leader's predilection for physical expression became an integral part of his paternalistic style. In the proud words of *La Tribuna,* the six million people that made up the Peruvian population in 1931 could feel embraced by the "affectionate and forgiving" arms of Haya de la Torre: "Proletarian Peru: Rise to your feet! Your guide has arrived: VÍCTOR RAÚL HAYA DE LA TORRE! His arms! . . . Those gigantic arms that never closed return open with the hunger of holding yours. . . ."[52]

But all was not fatherly benevolence from the Aprista patriarch. Like Sánchez Cerro, he was also ready to resort to harsh measures when the occasion warranted. Aprista literature portrayed Haya as a stern disciplinarian, equally quick to reproach bad conduct as he was to reward good actions. One campaign pamphlet declared that the *jefe máximo* was "sober and friendly . . . an exemplary and authoritarian *maestro*. Just and serene, he is inflexible in combating laziness, tardiness, sensualism . . . Thus he builds the foundations of this admirable discipline that today reigns in the Partido Aprista Peruano."[53] The coexistence of kindness and severity made for a dynamic counterpoint in the appeals of both Haya and Sánchez Cerro. At the same time that they maintained an intimate relationship with their followers, the two candidates were also able to set themselves apart as powerful and specially gifted leadership figures.

A revealing summary of the varied aspects of Haya de la Torre's political style in the 1931 election may be gained by studying the

Figure 23. The Respectable Haya. From *Biographía y graficos de Haya de la Torre* (Lima, 1931), unpaged.

photographs of the Aprista leader printed in a brief pictorial biography about him especially prepared for distribution during the campaign.[54] This graphic evidence shows that Apra wanted voters to see their *jefe máximo* as the offspring of what Peruvians would term a *familia decente,* or a "good family," headed by respectable and religious parents (figures 23, 24). While he had become a knowledgeable and experienced man of

Figure 24. The Moral Haya. From *Bibliographía y graficos*.

the world through his American and European travels (figure 25), Haya had not forgotten his "venerable parents," and he remained ever a loyal son (figure 26). Most significant, Haya was portrayed as a resolute leader of powerful character in the first photograph of the biography (figure 27). And he was a man who would never forget the needs of the popular masses (figure 28).

The impact of Haya de la Torre's political style was particularly notable in Apra's fight to capture working class votes. The Aprista campaign abounded with references made by Haya himself and by other

Figure 25. The Well-Traveled Haya. From *Biographía y graficos*.

Figure 26. Haya the "Family Man." From *Biographía y graficos.*

party notables to the Aprista leader's long history of collaboration with urban labor groups, collaboration which, it was promised, would result in the use of the power of the state to improve the conditions of the proletariat. Most important, Haya made the renewal of the ties of personal loyalty between himself and the capital's union leaders—ties forged from the eight-hour strike onwards—a top priority of his campaign. Labor leaders were invited to frequent face-to-face meetings with Haya, who was always quick to recall with affection specific instances of his past contacts with these individuals.

Haya's encounters with the leadership of Lima's organized workers bore abundant political fruit. Representatives of the largest unions gave their wholehearted support to their old friend and fellow combatant by participating in the Aprista Party Congress, and three eminent labor leaders—Arturo Sabroso of the Textile Federation, Luis Lopez Aliaga of the Trolley Car Workers, and Samuel Vasquez of the Chauffeurs' Union—were chosen to be Aprista congressional candidates for Lima. These and other first-line figures in the Lima labor movement sat prominently on the stage at nearly all Aprista gatherings. A high point of many such events was their testimonial of personal experiences with Haya de la Torre. They usually closed their remarks by assuring the audience that the same Haya de la Torre, at the head of Aprismo, would continue to lead the workers with a firm hand to the fulfillment of their just aspirations.[55]

Figure 27. The Resolute Haya. From *Biographía y graficos.*

The reminiscences of individual members of the capital's organized
labor force concerning how they came actively to support Apra confirm
the instrumentality of Haya the man to the success of his party in gaining
a working class following in the 1931 election. By their admission, they
stood behind Apra not because they thought that the party's victory
would mean power to the masses, but because of their long-standing personal acquaintance with and resultant faith in the movement's *jefe
máximo.* The words of the most prominent Aprista labor leader summarize well the ultimate political commitment of these men as a group to
the figure of Haya de la Torre: "Those who know me well know that I
was never an 'Hayista,' but they also know about my great admiration
for the work of Haya de la Torre. And precisely that work has been the
only thing that could bring me—as was the case with almost all the most
influential workers—to embrace the cause of a political party with the
same fervor that I struggle for the demands of my class: not withholding

Figure 28. Haya de la Torre, Friend of the People. From *Biographía y graficos*.

an ounce of my effort."[56] Memories of the "good days" of the early 1920s, still fresh, had been made all the fresher by the Aprista campaign. And now that their political mentor was actually a presidential candidate, there was no question as to whom to support or how much support to offer. Haya was eminently successful at using his ties with Lima union leaders to gain the organized labor vote in the 1931 election, and he was also able to secure much urban middle sector support that had previously been loyal to Augusto Leguía. However his popularity among these groups was not sufficient to offset Sánchez Cerro's overwhelming appeal among the more numerous urban *lumpenproletariat*. In 1931, at least, the Apristas would have to accept defeat.

8

The Election

EVERYONE SEEMED astounded, happily astounded. The day of the presidential election, October 11, 1931, had come and gone without the violence, without the bloodshed predicted so insistently in the previous weeks. The headlines of Lima's newspapers outdid themselves in paying tribute to the suffrage process. "Yesterday We Have Attended A New Kind Of Spectacle," affirmed Apra's daily *La Tribuna.* "The Secret Ballot Has Dignified Politics . . . There Have Never Been Elections So Orderly Yet So Hard Fought." *El Comercio,* favorable to Sánchez Cerro, was somewhat more discreet in its commendation: "The Voting Goes On In An Atmosphere Of Perfect Order In The City Of Lima."José María de la Jara y Ureta's paper, *El Perú,* on the other hand was ecstatic: "Not A Single Dissonant Note . . . The Great Democratic Conquest Of The Secret Ballot Has Been Achieved In Peru." And Arturo Osores's *Nuestro Diario* completed the chorus of praise: "We Are No Longer A Country Of Imposed Elections And Frauds . . . Civil Dignity Has Triumphed."[1]

The tranquil atmosphere surrounding the suffrage process, the exemplary behavior of the voters of all social strata, and the smooth functioning of the electoral machinery together prompted the strong approbation that filled the public statements on the day after the event. Election morning had dawned to find Lima's walls, shop windows, and public squares covered with posters and handbills scattered by the contending parties in last-minute efforts to build up their candidates. From early on the streets were filled with rapidly moving people attempting to reach their polling places before the voting was scheduled to begin at 8:00 A.M. Lines in front of the voting booths formed quietly, with a minimum of pushing and shoving. Everyone seemed determined that the business of electing a president proceed in an orderly fashion. As each voter reached the front of the line he showed his proof of registration to a public official and received an envelope containing various pieces of paper with the printed names of the individual candidates. In the voting booth he placed the papers with his choices in the envelope and then cast his vote by inserting it in a large ballot box placed on a table in front of the electoral officials. Some people remained at the polling places and entered in animated discussions about the political panorama, but most went home. At 5:00 P.M. the voting was over, and the ballot boxes were transported to the Chamber of Deputies, where the vote count would take place.[2] Months later when the official vote count was concluded, Sánchez Cerro had won decisively in the capital, amassing the support of 49.5 percent of the electorate with 29,131 votes. Haya de la Torre garnered 36.4 percent with 21,392 votes. Sánchez Cerro's margin of victory on the national level was also impressive: 50.7 percent (152,062 votes) to Haya's 35.4 percent (106,007 votes). Two minor candidates, José María de la Jara y Ureta and Arturo Osores divided the rest of the vote between them. In Lima they received 14 percent (8,291 votes) and countrywide 13.9 percent (41,574 votes).[3]

Despite the outward calm and widespread approbation that characterized the suffrage process, historians have generally considered the 1931 election to have been fraudulent. This view developed to a great extent from repeated claims by Apra of wrongdoing, claims that began to materialize eight days after the election when Haya fell behind in the unofficial vote count. The Apristas, who initially had joined the other parties in acclaiming the efficiency and neutrality of the electoral officials, soon changed their minds and to this day insist that the government took an active part in influencing the outcome of the election to prevent Haya's ascension to the presidency. The determination of the validity of Apra's claims is not only an important historiographical question but also essential to any accurate analysis of voting patterns in the election.[4]

Apra had history on its side in the allegation of government-sanctioned electoral malfeasance. Fraudulent elections had been the rule in Peru since the first suffrage process in the nation's history in 1850. Violence and vote-buying characterized these events in the nineteenth century, with candidates hiring mobs of retainers from the ranks of the urban poor to take balloting places by force. Once these balloting places, known as "electoral tables," were captured, usually following a bloody encounter between the armed and often drunken bands of opposing political aspirants, the victors would declare that their man had won all votes cast at that particular location. With the passage of a new electoral law in 1896, behind-the-scenes machinations perpetrated by the government replaced mob violence as the dominant means of engineering political succession; thereafter, a national electoral *junta* proclaimed the victory of individual candidates according to the dictates of the ruling regime. In 1913 still another variation was introduced into electoral politics when an assembly made up of the country's largest taxpayers, or in other words of Peru's economic oligarchy, together with the Supreme Court, replaced the national *junta* in the supervision of the "suffrage." This new approach, however, did not produce any major retreat from the fraudulent practices of the past. Elections continued to function mainly as a source of legitimacy and formal ratification for a political system controlled in nearly all its aspects by a small elite at the top. Votes were certainly an integral part of these occasions, but they were hardly a necesssary ingredient of political victory.[5]

The 1931 election marked a major departure from this tradition of government control. While Apra explained their failure at the ballot box by charging that fraud had been perpetrated by the "legal apparatus" at all levels in favor of Sánchez Cerro, a close examination of both the overt actions of the ruling *junta* and the political leanings of its members fails to support this position. The *junta* did not, as had been the common practice in the past, use the machinery of the state to produce the election of an "official" candidate. There were some indications that at one point the regime favored the return to a 1915-style party convention that would advance a single candidate, an alternative proposed early in the campaign by a coalition of moderate elite politicians called the Concentración Nacional. Later, when that possibility seemed doomed to failure, some members of the *junta* made a feeble attempt to reach another moderate solution by favoring the candidacy of José María de la Jara y Ureta, Peru's ambassador to Brazil, only to desist once again when it became apparent that La Jara would be unable to build a viable political movement in the face of the near political monopoly already shared by Sánchezcerrismo and Aprismo. It was also rumored that the minister of war in the *junta,* Gustavo Jimenez, had presidential ambitions and planned to declare himself chief of state in the event that no candidate won an absolute majority in the election.

Although Jimenez never publicly confirmed these suspicions, before and during the campaign he did display considerable animosity to the political aspirations of the man who ultimately obtained over 50 percent of the vote, Luis M. Sánchez Cerro. Initially close friends, Jimenez and Sánchez Cerro had a falling out in February 1931 over Jimenez's insistence that the "hero of Arequipa" not be allowed to stay in Peru to run for the presidency. In line with his stated purpose to keep his former comrade in arms out of politics, Jimenez later spearheaded attempts during Sánchez Cerro's exile to bar him from entering the country. And when it appeared that he could succeed in his efforts only at the risk of provoking a civil war, Jimenez grudgingly allowed Sánchez Cerro to return to Peru, but only after replacing all local authorities with men loyal to the *junta* in order to make sure that the ex-president would receive no governmental support in the coming election. Such was the minister of war's overt enmity toward Sánchez Cerro that certain commentators believed he actually favored the possibility of an Aprista regime as a workable alternative to the rule of the commandant-candidate.

Jimenez's position was particularly important considering that he was clearly the moving force of the governing *junta*. Notwithstanding Samanéz Ocampo's status as its titular president, his advanced age and physical decrepitude prevented him from assuming the functions of political leadership. He generally slept through the daily meetings of the *junta's* members and delegated nearly all of his authority to Jimenez. While none of the other members of the *junta* rivaled the minister of war in their hostility toward Sánchez Cerro, the *cholo* army officer was plainly far from being their presidential choice. The reason they took power in the first place had been to thwart Sánchez Cerro's continued rule through an *autoelección*. When the commandant-candidate won at the ballot box on October 11, they only allowed him to occupy the office of the presidency in keeping with their expressed promise to respect the results of a fair election. As José Gálvez, the *junta's* minister of justice and education who later became an Aprista sympathizer, remorsefully stated when asked about Sánchez Cerro's rise to the government palace: "Power was given up to the man whom the *junta* was very far from viewing with approval."[6] From Gálvez's remarks it appears that had the *junta,* and Jimenez in particular, detected any significant irregularities in the electoral machinery favoring Sánchez Cerro's candidacy, they might indeed have used them as a justification to keep him out of the presidency.

One man who had no doubt about where the political sympathies of the *junta* lay was Luis M. Sánchez Cerro; his vehement criticism of their handling of the electoral process up to October 12 rivaled Apra's criticism in the months and years following the event. Sánchez Cerro was justifiably skeptical of the possibility of fair treatment at the hands of the very men who had ousted him from power in February and who had subsequently made concerted efforts to thwart his candidacy by blocking his entry into the country. These same individuals, while calling on Apristas to contribute to the formulation of a new electoral statute at the beginning of the campaign, had systematically excluded Sánchezcerristas from the deliberations. Furthermore, shortly after taking power the *junta* had been thorough in its purge of the bureaucracy, removing Sánchez Cerro appointees on the local and national levels.

Sánchez Cerro's misgivings seemed confirmed when during the campaign the goverment consistently harassed his followers. The *junta* took determined measures to limit the size of Unión Revolucionaria demonstrations, closed down the Sánchezcerrista newspaper for a short time, and used the postal service to censor and on occasion confiscate letters between the party's national headquarters and local dependencies. Sánchez Cerro was even reported to have received warnings from ranking officers in the army and navy to renounce his candidacy. This atmosphere of repression prompted one Sánchezcerrista to complain privately: "We Sánchezcerristas are totally separated from the government *junta* for whom it is a greater crime to be a Sánchezcerrista than to be a Leguiísta."[7]

The Sánchezcerristas did not submit to these "arbitrary acts" of the *junta* without a fight. Daily the party press carried scathing accusations that the government was persecuting the followers of the commandant-candidate while at the same time preparing large-scale electoral fraud in order to either maintain itself in power or to favor an Aprista victory. Also in many of his public appearances Sánchez Cerro bluntly proclaimed that he did not expect the *junta* to treat him fairly and impartially when it came to the counting of votes. In part these angry denunciations of the government were designed to create a propitious atmosphere for a pro-Sánchezcerrista *coup d'état* should the commandant-candidate actually lose the election. And in fact, during the campaign and in the weeks between the balloting and the inauguration, both Sánchez Cerro and the Samanéz government maneuvered behind the scenes to gain military backing for what many observers considered an inevitable showdown. At various times Sánchez Cerro implied openly that he would take power by force were he denied a rightful victory, and he reached the point of writing a *Manifiesto* justifying a projected armed revolt to be led by him. It was unlikely that had he been able successfully to infiltrate the electoral authorities, as the Apristas alleged, Sánchez Cerro would have planned such drastic actions against the *junta* to assure what he considered his "rightful victory."[8]

This circumstantial evidence suggests that the Apristas were erroneous in their blanket indictment of the government for supporting Sánchez Cerro's election and perpetrating fraud to secure it. In addition, however, to their general imputation of the electoral process, the party professed to have found specific subversions of the suffrage machinery that directly prevented Haya's victory in the capital.[9] They censured the Lima results in the months immediately following the election by insisting that gross irregularities had occurred in the registration of voters which permitted certain individuals favorable to Sánchez Cerro to cast two or three ballots. Interestingly, the Apristas' condemnation of the registration process came over two months after that process had ended. During the formation of the voter roles they, together with the rest of the contending parties — with the notable exception of the Sánchezcerristas — warmly applauded the labors of the electoral authorities. When they finally made their formal complaint about malpractice in registering voters, it was based on the fact that the *junta* had been remiss in publishing the lists of electors in accordance with the formal provisions of the law. The Apristas presented few concrete examples of people who had in reality voted more than once. Finally, Haya's supporters argued that the Lima electoral jury had failed to annul the votes pertaining to a large number of ballot boxes that had, in their view, been tampered with. They identified a total of forty faulty boxes, which contained approximately 5,400 votes. Eleven of these, holding some 1,485 votes, had already been invalidated by the electoral jury, leaving more or less 3,915 votes at issue. Even if all of these ballots had been declared in Haya de la Torre's favor, they were still not nearly enough to offset Sánchez Cerro's winning margin of 17,765.[10]

More recently Aprista spokesmen have altered their version of how fraud was accomplished in 1931, contending that within the confines of the Lima electoral jury entire ballot boxes favorable to Sánchez Cerro were substituted for a number of those containing a majority of pro-Haya votes. The malefactors were said to have hidden the pro-Haya boxes behind a false wall in the fire station next to the National Congress building where the Lima jury functioned. The Apristas claim to have found these boxes some years later, and they tell that Haya made it a practice to give them away to illustrious foreign visitors as "souvenirs of Peruvian democracy."[11] A functionary of the National electoral jury who participated in the proceedings for the 1931, 1936, and 1939 elections has confirmed the Aprista account of ballot box switching but says that it occurred only on the latter two dates.[12] By his account the boxes found by the Apristas corresponded to the 1936 process, which was cancelled by incumbent President Oscar Benavides, and they contained votes that were never tallied.

In addition to the testimony of this public functionary, a close examination of the provisions and implementation of the 1931 election law that dealt with balloting and vote counting demonstrates the near impossibility of secretly carrying out the kind of extensive wrongdoing outlined by the Apristas. One important guarantee of fairness, for instance, was the law's stipulation that the representatives of the major political parties be present to oversee all stages of the electoral process. At individual polling places these representatives made sure that the local officials proceeded correctly. After the voting had ended, they supervised the covering of the ballot box with a heavy sheet of paper, and the representatives along with the local officials affixed their signatures to the paper covers. A signed copy of this paper cover traveled along with the ballot box to the electoral jury, and another was sent separately by mail or messenger to assure that no alterations had occurred during the journey. The boxes themselves were constructed of thick galvanized steel, and they could be opened at the top only by breaking a special lead seal. Any tampering with either the paper covering or the lead seal would have been immediately noticeable to the members of the electoral jury and to the party representatives. The Lima jury did, in fact, annul five boxes that showed signs of tampering. Under these conditions, any large-scale switching of ballot boxes would have entailed a massive and expert forgery effort involving thousands of signatures in order to produce official-looking substitute boxes. The immensity of such an enterprise made it a highly unlikely undertaking. Furthermore, in the case of Lima, fake boxes could only have been substituted within the Congress building where the departmental jury functioned, because on election day the head of each polling place in the capital personally delivered his respective ballot box to the jury in the company of the party representatives and under police guard. The shuffling of boxes in the Congress was doubtful since after each daily session of the jury they were stored in the cellar, and special signed seals were attached to all entries to detect any break-ins. Government troops surrounded the Congress day and night and took special precautions to bar the entry of anyone not on official business.[13]

Due in large part to these extraordinary precautions, all political groups, except the Apristas, commended the *junta* for its handling of the balloting and counting procedures. The anti-Sánchezcerrista press underscored the honesty of the electoral process and sharply criticized Apra for crying fraud. Opposition presidential and congressional candidates, including one Aprista, reluctantly conceded Sánchez Cerro's triumph with words of approval for the *junta's* exemplary administration of the suffrage process. Even the most rabid political enemies of Sánchez Cerro advised: "We should respect the results of the election with the hope that what the people have made will break up by itself."[14]

Among the strongest defenders of the fairness of the 1931 election were the members of the governmental *junta,* the individuals in the best position to know if fraud had been committed. Five of their number who have publicly passed judgment on the election — David Samanéz Ocampo (president), Gustavo Jimenez (minister of war), Francisco Tamayo (minister of government), José Gálvez (minister of justice and education), and Rafael Larco Herrera (minister of foreign relations and treasury) — were not only among the most powerful men in the *junta,* but also they were those most opposed to the candidacy of Sánchez Cerro. Because of their opposition to Sánchez Cerro, Jimenez, Tamayo, and Gálvez became the victims of government persecution after the election, suffering various fates including loss of work, imprisonment, deportation, and, in Jimenez's case, death. Despite their misfortunes, all have insisted that the *junta* maintained a hands-off policy, presiding over what Gálvez has called, "a truly exemplary electoral process."[15] Even the deeply embittered Jimenez, on his way to exile in 1932, tried to justify his having permitted the "hated" Sánchez Cerro to take office after the election by declaring that the *junta* had done its duty in "bringing the country with austere impartiality to the most pure and free elections ever seen in Peru." The fault, in Jimenez's estimation, lay not with the *junta* but with the politically immature Peruvian people, who had simply chosen the wrong man.[16]

In the light of powerful evidence that the election in Lima had been remarkably free of fraudulent practices, the Apristas' insistence on the existence of malfeasance would seem to have resulted from factors other than genuine surprise at losing the contest. Noting the antagonism of the most prominent *junta* members towards Sánchez Cerro, perhaps Haya and his fellow leaders hoped to provide a sufficient pretext for the government to abrogate the commandant-candidate's victory at the polls. Or failing that, possibly the Apristas felt that by continuing to impugn the election results they could prepare the country for the eventuality of an armed attempt against the Sánchezcerrista regime. One clearly positive effect of the Apristas' repeated charges of fraud was to increase popular sympathy for their "martyred and persecuted" party and to sustain the image, continually drawn in the campaign, that Apra spoke for the majority of Peruvians.

A more likely explanation than fraud for Apra's defeat in 1931 was that Haya failed to gain the visibility and public recognition to match that of Sánchez Cerro. While he was well known to organized labor and to certain sectors of the middle classes, the Aprista leader was unable to generate the kind of popular following that his opponent had fashioned through his spectacular overthrow of Leguía and his provisional presidency. In 1931 Sánchez Cerro was a known and widely admired quantity; Haya de la Torre was not to the same degree. On another level, the social groups from which Apra obtained backing were simply less numerous than the sectors of the population favorable to Sánchez Cerro. Contemporary observers and more recent analysts have generally agreed that Apra attracted the majority of its support in the capital from the middle sectors and from the ranks of organized labor, while Sánchezcerrismo was most successful among the artisanry and the urban *lumpenproletariat*. On the basis of extrapolations from occupational data in the 1931 Lima census, approximate numbers can be assigned to each of these categories. The male members of these four strata together constituted approximately 103,000 people. Of the total some 11,000 were organized laborers, 31,000 were middle sector individuals, and 61,000 belonged to the artisanry and the *lumpenproletariat*. In purely mathematical terms the sectors that were said to have been pro-Sánchezcerrista (61,000) clearly outnumbered those considered to have been the followers of Haya de la Torre (42,000). And although information is far too sparse and unreliable to make an exact correlation between the social position and the political orientation of the men that composed the Lima electorate in 1931, it is nevertheless interesting to note that Sánchez Cerro's and Haya's portions of the vote in the capital were quite close to the percentages of their supposed followers in the population[17] (see table 8.1).

It is impossible to make a truly accurate analysis of class voting patterns in 1931 because of the way the election machinery was set up. Instead of being assigned to polling places close to their domiciles, lists

Table 8.1. Social Class and Candidate Preference in Lima, 1931

	Number	Percentage
Lima's Population by Social Groups		
Organized labor	11,000	10.7
Middle sectors	31,000	30.1
Total	42,000	40.8
Artisans and *lumpenproletariat*	61,000	59.2
Grand Total	103,000	100
Votes for Populist Presidential Candidates		
Haya de la Torre	21,392	42.3
Sánchez Cerro	29,131	58.7
Grand Total	50,523	100

Sources: Perú, *Censo de Lima 1931,* pp. 197–201; Ricardo Martinez de la Torre, *Apuntes para una interpretación marxista de historia social del Perú.* (Lima: Empresa Editora Peruana, 1974), 3:141; and Perú, Jurado Nacional de Elecciones, "Libro de actas de sesiones públicas del Jurado Nacional de Elecciones" (Lima: Archivo del Jurado Nacional de Elecciones, 1931).

of names for each polling place were constructed using the order in which people appeared on the registration rolls. Hence, two neighbors might very conceivably vote at different ends of the city, making it impossible to construct a detailed social-political map for the election. Since voters did, however, generally register in the district where they resided, that is, Rimac, La Victoria, or Central Lima, a rough estimation of the sociogeographic support bases of the competing populist movements in the capital can be made by examining the breakdown of votes at individual polling places.[18]

In Lima's poorest and most traditional lower class district with the highest concentration of *lumpenproletariat* population, Rimac, Sánchez Cerro was a decisive victor over Haya de la Torre. The commandant-candidate carried ballot box after ballot box, with few exceptions, by a two to one margin (see table 8.2). The story was quite different in La Victoria, a less poverty-stricken, newer working class neighborhood that had a larger industrial laboring sector than Rimac. There at nearly every polling place Haya de la Torre fought a close battle, with Sánchez Cerro coming out on top, often by less then ten votes, in about 70 percent of the cases recorded (see table 8.3). The election was also extremely close in Central Lima, a mixed area of working class, middle, and a small percentage of upper class population, and there another interesting phenomenon emerged. In those ballot boxes that registered a relatively high proportion of votes for the two traditional elite candidates, La Jara and Osores — higher than in any of the other urban areas — Haya de la Torre almost invariably won a distinct majority from Sánchez Cerro. The coincidence of a high vote for the Aprista leader with a high vote for La Jara and Osores indicates two possibilities: that Haya attracted a generally more upper status voter than Sánchez Cerro and/or voting for traditional elite candidates cut into Sánchez Cerro's upper class support (see table 8.4). Sánchez Cerro scored his most convincing victories in Lima's rural districts, that is, Huaura, Huaral, Santa Eulalia, and San Mateo, where he usually won between 80 and 90 percent of the ballots cast at individual polling places (see table 8.5).

In sum, the Lima electorate in 1931 partitioned itself into a series of political micro-regions within the city and province. Each micro-region seems to have been the product of the specific social strata that composed it. The pattern that emerges from this division shows Sánchez Cerro successful in the traditional, poorer areas like Rimac and rural zones, while Haya de la Torre, although not always the winner, gained greater support in areas like La Victoria and Central Lima, which had a higher concentration of more privileged groups, namely, the upper reaches of the working classes and the middle sectors.

Table 8.2. Sample Returns from Rimac

	Votes cast			
Candidate	Box no. 3101	Box no. 3108	Box no. 3110	Box no. 3116
Sánchez Cerro	88	80	84	95
Haya de la Torre	38	44	47	39
La Jara	3	7	6	10
Osores	3	4	4	5

Sources: See above note 17 to this chapter.

Table 8.3. Sample Returns from La Victoria

	Votes cast			
Candidate	Box no. 3134	Box no. 3145	Box no. 3154	Box no. 3156
Sánchez Cerro	58	60	75	67
Haya de la Torre	66	54	48	63
La Jara	14	12	5	4
Osores	6	12	8	2

Sources: See above note 17 to this chapter.

One final revelation to be gained from studying the 1931 suffrage data was that the electorate was overwhelmingly lower and to a lesser extent middle class in social origin. The classification of the Lima voters by race shows that over 70 percent were either *mestizos* (62.9 percent), Indians (4.4 percent), or blacks (2.9 percent) and only 29.8 percent were classified as white. In terms of schooling the data painted a strikingly similar picture. Approximately 70 percent of the voters had received only primary schooling or less. The remaining 30 percent had attended or were attending secondary school, commercial school, or university.

Perhaps the single fact that most distinguished the 1931 urban electorate was its very size in comparison to previous voting populations. In the 1931 election 78,906 voters from the Lima-Callao area went to the polls, some 89 percent of those registered. Twelve years earlier, when Leguía won a freely contested election, the turnout in Lima-Callao amounted to only 16,372. The change was dramatic; the voting population had increased nearly fivefold. Moreover, the large turnout in the capital denoted its increased political importance on the national level. Whereas in 1919 the Lima vote accounted for only 9.7 percent of the countrywide total, in 1931 the proportion had risen to 28.2 percent.[19]

Judging by the racial composition, education levels, and size of the urban electorate, in one sense the fears of many members of Peru's traditional elites appeared to have indeed been justified: the popular masses and the middle sectors had risen to a position of true dominance in Peru's electoral politics.

Table 8.4. Sample Returns from Central Lima

Candidate	Votes cast			
	Box no. 3261	Box no. 3263	Box no. 3316	Box no. 3359
Sánchez Cerro	42	45	61	69
Haya de la Torre	48	63	61	49
La Jara	29	19	11	16
Osores	22	12	3	5

Sources: See above note 17 to this chapter.

Table 8.5. Sample Returns from Lima's Rural Districts

Candidate	Votes cast			
	Box no. 2852	Box no. 2940	Box no. 2963	Box no. 3043
Sánchez Cerro	112	38	81	109
Haya de la Torre	18	3	23	16
La Jara	2	0	11	0
Osores	0	0	0	1

Sources: See above note 17 to this chapter.

Not unexpectedly, Sánchez Cerro's electoral victory and subsequent sixteen-month presidency failed to bring calm to the Peruvian political scene. On the contrary, his brief term of office was racked by growing political instability and profound economic crisis. Immediately after the official tabulations became public, acts of violence between Aprista and Sánchezcerrista supporters escalated dramatically. Less than a week before the inauguration ceremony a band of Apristas cut the electrical current to the capital as a prelude to a hoped-for popular uprising that did not materialize. And the same day that Sánchez Cerro took office in Lima, in the northern provincial city of Trujillo, Haya de la Torre darkly predicted much greater violence in the future: "More Aprista blood will run. The immortal list of our martyrdom will grow, the terror will begin again its hateful task . . . *Compañeros:* Today a new chapter in the history of the Party begins for the Apristas. Pages of glory or shame will be written by us with blood or with mud."[20] Three months later, following an attempt on his life in which he was seriously wounded, Sánchez Cerro replied in kind:

My government cannot permit anyone to predicate doctrines of destruction and hatred in this country nor can Peru be the home of a sect of fanatics who come to the point of carrying out criminal acts . . . The government together with all the vital forces of the country will continue to direct this campaign of national defense with unabated force . . . My own spirit was formed in the heat of battle and to fight for my country is the only — the supreme aspiration of my life.[21]

In this highly charged atmosphere of political conflict, Peru tottered on the brink of civil war. The sixteen months of Sánchez Cerro's government reads like a long list of revolts: March 1932 an Aprista tried to assassinate the president while he was attending Sunday mass; in May the crews of two naval cruisers mutinied against the administration and eight sailors were subsequently executed; in June a group of Apristas failed to capture the military airfield near Lima; in July a mass Aprista revolt broke out in Trujillo and in its tragic aftermath thirty-four Army officers and men lay dead, many of their bodies horribly mutilated, while in retribution over one thousand suspected rebels faced firing squads (the violence of the Trujillo revolt was to create a seemingly unbridgeable chasm between the military and Aprismo for decades to come); in August another Aprista rebellion was put down in the provincial city of Huaraz; and in March 1933 a final attempt to overthrow Sánchez Cerro in the northern Department of Cajamarca met with defeat at the hands of superior government forces. To further complicate matters Peru had become embroiled in an armed conflict with Colombia in September 1932 over the possession of the Amazonian territory of Leticia. Finally in 1933 Sánchez Cerro's political foes had reason to rejoice. On an early April afternoon the president was leaving the Hippodrome after reviewing troops that were to fight against Colombia in the Leticia conflict. As his car slowly moved through the crowds on its way back to the government palace, a man bolted through the police lines and fired three shots at point blank range into Sánchez Cerro's body. This time the assassin, a member of the Aprista party, had been successful. The fatally wounded "hero of Arequipa" died minutes later.

In the context of such chaotic times it is difficult to evaluate Sánchez Cerro's performance as chief executive. It appears that most of his energy and attention was devoted to checking and ultimately attempting to destroy the political opposition. Frustrated at his inability to work more constructively, the president often commented: "These people won't let me govern."[22] In addition, Sánchez Cerro ran the country while it was in the throes of the Great Depression. The Treasury was nearly empty, pensions remained unpaid, the currency was devalued, public works were at a standstill, and unemployment increased daily to the point of almost doubling in the first year of Sánchez Cerro's government. Peru's political and social instability exacerbated its economic woes. The few domestic and foreign sources of credit that still existed were reluctant to invest in the country, and the generalized asphyxiation of all commercial activities due mainly to the lack of demand and contraction of the money supply coincided with the flight of national capital to "safer" markets abroad.

Throughout the civil insurrection, foreign war, and economic hardships that seemed to dominate his term of office, Sánchez Cerro continued to project as president the most salient feature of his political style as candidate: that of the stern yet benevolent caudillistic *patrón*. His stern side was clearly evident in his energetic response to Aprista insurgence. At the same time, paternalistic generosity, particularly with his working class followers, equally characterized Sánchez Cerro's brief period of rule. One of the most visible practices of his regime was the presidential audience. Large groups of the Lima poor daily invaded the government palace in search of favors, aid, and immediate material rewards. And the president, following the pattern he had established during the campaign, invariably appeared to come through with everything from notes of recommendation to hard cash. His personal secretary characterized Sánchez Cerro's presidential paternalism in straightforward terms: "The country was like a giant hacienda, and Sánchez Cerro, the *patrón* of the hacienda, did everything possible to provide benefits for his people so that they should be content."[23] While officially the chief executive was able to do little for "his people" beyond sponsoring a few public works programs and establishing a chain of popular restaurants run by the state to provide low cost meals to the needy, his continued ability to play a fatherly role towards the masses made for the persistence of a highly popular image until his life suddenly ended in 1933. "He understands the masses," wrote one of Sánchez Cerro's contemporaries, "and they understand him. He loves them, and he makes himself loved by them, guiding them and serving them. . . ."[24]

Sánchez Cerro appeared like a comet in the Peruvian political sky between 1930 and 1933. Few of those who so zealously supported or attacked him during his campaign and his term of office had ever heard of him before he gloriously flew into Lima to proclaim his victory over "the tyrant" Leguía. But in the short space between his triumphal Revolution of Arequipa and his tragic assassination, Sánchez Cerro the candidate and Sánchez Cerro the president was able to generate an enthusiasm for his person equaled by few men in Peruvian history. And although it would be difficult to find after his death even many of his loyal followers who could cite the concrete accomplishments of his regime — with the one exception of his constant battle with Apra — he continues, even today, to be lovingly remembered by working class men and women of his time. One still finds pictures of Sánchez Cerro alongside those of Jesus and selected saints adorning the walls of humble dwellings in the capital. And every year, on the anniversary of his death, the Lima cemetery is the scene of tearful gatherings of the working class faithful who, over forty years afterward, continue to venerate the figure of the "Hero of Arequipa."

For Haya de la Torre electoral defeat and subsequent persecution did not mark the end but the beginning of a political career. The Aprista leader was never to share Sánchez Cerro's honor of being president of Peru, yet he outlived the assassinated first executive to become the head of the nation's most important twentieth-century populist political organization. For Haya de la Torre, Sánchez Cerro's premature death meant the disappearance from the political scene of the only other politician with popular appeal that rivaled his own. Haya was prevented from personally competing for the presidency again until 1962 by a rabidly anti-Aprista military whose violent opposition to him had largely originated in the 1932 Trujillo massacre of army officers and was fed thereafter by oligarchical sectors that continued to fear the consequences of Apra rule. Notwithstanding his proscription from competing formally for high office, in the period between 1933 and the 1960s the *jefe máximo* of Apra took advantage of the lack of stiff competition to gain a strong hold over the working class vote in Peru for his political movement. Only in the last decade—particularly after the rise of the military's revolutionary government in 1968—has Haya's popularity among his proletarian following begun to show evident signs of decay. Nevertheless, he and his tightly organized party retained enough of a political following to win the largest number of votes in the 1978 elections for a constituent congress. Over fifty years after his first entry into politics Víctor Raúl Haya de la Torre showed his political staying power by becoming the president of that congress.

9

Populism and the Politics of Personal Dependence

IN 1931, under the banners of Sánchezcerrismo and Aprismo, the popular masses played a major role in national politics for the first time in Peruvian history. The study of the origins, styles, and internal dynamics of the political movements they supported is of importance not only in the understanding of the forms of their initial entry into politics, but also because these movements stand as material examples of aggregate mass political behavior. The analysis of how and why Sánchezcerrismo and Aprismo were successful in gaining working class followings was also implicitly an analysis of how and why the working classes participated in politics. The striking similarities between these two populist organizations makes them particularly appropriate for understanding various facets of the political orientation of the urban masses, including their fundamental assumptions regarding the nature of the political system and their role in it, their perceptions about the most effective methods for gaining access to authority, their expectations regarding the decision-making process, and their view of their own political capabilities vis-à-vis other actors in the system.

Both Sánchezcerrismo and Aprismo were vertical movements united by relationships of personal loyalty between leaders and followers. They differed appreciably from class or interest-based horizontal movements that consolidated around specific issues or an ideology. Unlike these generally horizontal organizations whose members come from roughly the same strata, Sánchezcerrismo and Aprismo cut across class and status lines to include individuals from various levels of Peruvian society. One important difference between the two movements in this regard was that Aprista verticality was usually expressed in the ties between specific social groups—such as unions, professionals, or employees—and the leadership, a tendency clearly expressed in the group-style organization of the party. Sánchez Cerro, on the other hand, generally avoided references to recognized occupational or social categories, emphasizing instead his one-to-one commitment to each and every Peruvian. But whether group- or individually-based, a primary element in the adherence of mass supporters to the two populist parties was the accessibility they provided to links with men above them on the social pyramid. For the working class populist such links seemed to afford a route to men with power who could help supply a degree of material welfare. An editorial in a Lima newspaper bitingly summarized this aspect of populist politics in 1931: "The best *caudillo* is the man from whom the most benefits may be expected. And the best party is that in which we can expect to find the largest number of accommodating friends."[1] For most people in the context of Peru's urban mass society of the early 1930s, the direct receipt of immediate rewards from those in power was unlikely. But that reality did not seriously detract from the populist image of personalized, "family" government, of government which, if unable to provide directly for all, still symbolized a generous force sympathetic to the suffering poor.

The political clientelism inherent in these early populist movements paralleled in many ways the kind of patron-client relationship that has permeated Peruvian and Latin American social life since colonial times.[2] Like the archetypical dyadic contract between the rural *hacendado* and the peon, the political tie between populist leader and follower was an individualistic, decidedly personal association between men from distinct social strata. Basic to the relationship was the reciprocal exchange of services and/or goods between those involved. For the political patrons, the exchange meant support in the streets and at the voting booth. For the clients, rewards could come in various forms from personal favors to material handouts. One working class voter in the 1931 election signally underlined the reciprocal aspects of the populist system when he explained: "Once politicians make it to the top the masses go to ask for jobs and a whole series of things. Nobody has watered the tree so that the seed will just sit there, nobody. Everybody went to take part in the harvest, that is all."[3] From the masses' point of view, therefore, populist clientelism developed as a realistic effort on their part to obtain a piece of a limited pie or simply to cope with a difficult, often threatening environment by forging ties to those who possessed greater access to the resources of the state. It is appropriate that one participant in the events of the 1930s chose the image of the traditional landed estate to describe the workings of populist politics: "The country was like a giant *hacienda,* and the *patrón* on the *hacienda* (referring to President Sánchez Cerro) did everything possible to provide benefits for his people so that they should be content."[4] Elite groups for generations had used clientelistic mechanisms to hold society together through the absorption or cooptation of other power contenders, rising middle sector individuals, and even upstart peasants. But in the mass society of the 1930s patronage could no longer proceed solely on a one-to-one basis. The populist movements that replaced the single patrons involved a whole series of clientelistic relations in which lesser party officials such as the Sánchezcerrista *capituleros,* as well as the top leaders, distributed rewards to "deserving" followers.

Notwithstanding the variety of clientelistic ties possible under populism, it was still the dominant presence of a charismatic leader that constituted the primary source of political cohesion. The formation of Sánchezcerrismo and Aprismo, their campaign styles, their rhetoric, their very reason for existence seemed to hinge upon providing a springboard for the rise of their maximum chiefs to political power. Central to the successful mass recruitment carried out by both parties was the effective glorification of the special personal qualities of their respective leaders. And despite the obvious differences between a military and a teacher-*caudillo,* each embodied basically similar qualities to the electorate. Accounts of past accomplishments, testimonials to present capabilities, and the personal appearances of each candidate ended in the communication of basically the same image: that of a big-hearted, affectionate, and above all protective father figure possessed of an extraordinary ability both to understand intimately the needs of his followers and through patronage to reward the faithful. It was primarily these leader-figures that gave the populist masses a sense of belonging to what otherwise might have been a relatively impersonal bureaucratic structure. In assessing the significance of Sánchez Cerro's personal charisma, for example, one of his top lieutenants stated: "The masses came to have political consciousness by loving Sánchez Cerro. The masses were conquered by embraces."[5]

For the members of the Lima working classes, the importance of these personal ties to the powerful increased enormously in times of augmented adversity or crisis. Perceiving even in normal times that they had few resources with which to confront their environment, crisis situations acted to make available resources even more scarce and accordingly heightened the tendency of the powerless to seek bonds of dependence with political patrons. Such a crisis situation was touched off in Peru by the Great Depression. In part the enthusiastic mass response to the two populist movements that emerged in the depression years of 1930 and

1931 occurred because the deepening impoverishment of the urban proletariat impelled them to see in the leaders of these movements, Sánchez
Cerro and Haya de la Torre, two powerful and apparently generous
patron figures with whom it was possible to forge valuable ties of personal dependence, at least on the symbolic level. Also, in a time of
general confusion and distress arising from the effects of rapid social
change, political crisis, and economic hardship, paternalistic populists
presented an extremely attractive image of strength and direction.
Hence, far from radicalizing the Peruvian working classes, the depression induced them to respond to populist alternatives as the most faithful
political embodiment of patrimonial social relations.[6]

The paternalistic leadership styles and vertical nature of both Sánchezcerrismo and Aprismo left little room for political self-assertion on
the part of their mass supporters. It is evident that the rank-and-file
followers of Sánchez Cerro and Haya de la Torre hoped to obtain
beneficial outputs from a government headed by their preferred candidate, but it was assumed that those outputs would accrue from the personal benevolence of the man in power. As one of Sánchez Cerro's top
assistants remarked about his movement:

> Among the poor there was the feeling that Sánchez Cerro would win, that he
> would reach the palace, without the feeling that in this way they would conquer
> the government or they would be the masters of the government palace. They
> were supporters of their commandant, and their commandant had to win and
> had to be the president of the republic. And from there the commandant would
> see, with everyone's help, how he would work things out. They had confidence
> in him.[7]

Under these "rules of the game" the working class populist abrogated all
pretense to influencing political policies by pressure from below. Instead,
it was assumed that positive rewards from the system could best be obtained by appealing to the considerateness of the political patron. If
granted, they invariably were interpreted as evidence of that patron's
personal magnanimity.[8]

The relatively uniform patterns of political behavior revealed by these
underlying parallels between the two competing populist movements in
1931 shed considerable light on the political culture of their mass followings. The study of political culture concerns the internalized feelings and
beliefs of the population as to how the political system operates, what
benefits the system does or should provide, and how to obtain those
benefits. To analyze the extent, direction, and limitations of real political
change, the intrinsic orientations of the voters towards political
movements, towards political leaders, and towards each other must be
taken into account.[9]

Mass political culture in Peru in 1931 may be defined as the politics of personal dependence. The political behavior of working class Sán-chezcerristas and Apristas revealed that they held their own political competence, either as individuals or as a group, in low regard. The urban masses undoubtedly were aware that they shared a common lot, but they fell short of translating that awareness into the formation of class-based political movements. Rather they placed their confidence in apparently powerful and sympathetic populist leaders. Real or imagined ties of personal dependence to these leaders were the major motivation in most cases for entering politics in the first place, and expectations held by mass supporters to gain something from their political participation hinged on those ties. The perception of the populist leader's dominance over populist follower precluded the possibility of demands from the rank and file to force specific courses of action on party directorates. In short, the observation of rank-and-file political behavior in Sánchezcerrismo and Aprismo indicates that Peruvian mass political culture in 1931 revolved around the interrelated values of belief in the hierarchy of political functions, loyalty to personalist leaders, and a low assessment of political self-efficacy.

While powerfully reinforced by the personalistic and clientelistic features of populism, the politics of personal dependence had first appeared in Peru long before the existence of either Sánchezcerrismo or Aprismo. In terms of political culture, the populist experience of the early 1930s stood as a clear continuation of past patterns of mass political behavior. Throughout the latter half of the nineteenth century and in the early part of the twentieth working class individuals had sustained extensive contact with electoral politics. The Lima poor took part in politics during this period mainly as members of clubs formed shortly before the balloting to promote the election of a particular candidate. Until an electoral reform in 1895 these clubs provided a tenuous organizational base for the forcible capture of the "electoral tables" or ballot boxes which were subsequently declared to favor the club's choice. The chief motivation for membership in a political club was the receipt of immediate material rewards in the form of money, food, and/or liquor distributed by the candidates through *capituleros*. Such was the mob violence that accompanied acts of suffrage in the nineteenth century that the "profession" of elector quickly became reserved for the male components of the Lima popular sectors. As one journalist who cavalierly called himself *"el Murciélago"* ("the Bat") remarked with regard to the 1855 election: "I have noticed, nevertheless, I the Bat, that the tables were surrounded solely by people of the color of mourning and that a small number of persons lighter in tone stood back at a certain distance like mere spectators of the great celebration."[10] With the 1895 electoral reform the violent capture of electoral tables, which had been the primary task of political clubs, came virtually to an end. Nevertheless, those clubs and the *capituleros* survived, transforming their activities into the buying of votes and the subsidizing of working class mobs to carry out street demonstrations for the purpose of showing the power capabilities of their respective candidates. As before, concrete remuneration for services rendered was the single stimulus for working class political participation. The only real choice exercised by the urban mass participant came in the field of economics: which candidate or *capitulero* would be most generous?[11]

This "commercial" view of politics went far beyond the specific instances of working class participation, penetrating to the roots of the political system. Traditionally a paramount function of the Peruvian state was the dispensing of political patronage in the form of jobs, personal services, and at times even direct monetary payoffs. Particularly from the vantage point of the majority of the populace that did not directly take part in the ruling of the country, politics seemed essentially a matter of individual favors, and regimes in power were often equated with exalted handout organizations. In the words of a popular saying Peru was not a "republic" but a "*res pública*" or a "public steer that has gone to the slaughter house and of which everybody can grab a piece."[12]

The central and most visible figure in the patronage mechanism was the president of the country. Especially in the popular mind, isolated from the workaday procedures of bureaucratic administration, the president was the government. To see the president as the ultimate authority and consequently the ultimate dispenser of favors was not unrealistic, given the high degree of centralization that had characterized governments in Peru since the latter half of the nineteenth century—a period that marked the revival of the patrimonial centralism of colonial administration—the considerable powers reserved by law and custom for the first executive, and the penchant of various Peruvian chiefs of state to intervene in matters as inconsequential as "the hiring of a doorman or the firing of a clerk because the national psychology requires that it be done that way."[13] Just previous to the appearance of populism this presidentialist tendency increased markedly, as Leguía during his eleven-year rule eliminated political parties, congressional independence, and the autonomy of local officials—in other words, most alternative sources of patronage. Individual presidents before and after Leugía placed emphasis on their political patron roles by devoting considerable time to person-to-person audiences with faithful followers. The "autobiography" supposedly written by president Augusto Leguía, for instance, asserts that he spent seven to eight hours every day listening to the requests of supporters and doling out money to the needy from his own pocket. And Sánchez Cerro's personal secretary echoed the Leguía experience, recalling the immediate and overwhelming rush for patronage after his chief's inauguration: "I say at times that the worst that can happen to one in politics is to win. Because the following day the winner is the first victim. Because one has his house filled with people, asking him for his card, calling him by telephone: 'Recommend me to this man.' 'Recommend me to that man; I want this, you are my friend.' "[14] Some presidents might have found distasteful this veritable invasion of the government palace by people competing for a part of the political barbecue, yet all seemed to recognize that it constituted a fundamental component of the political process.

The relative accessibility of Peruvian chief executives, their apparent omnipotence, and their attention to the most humble of petitioners inspired the attitude that presidential benevolence epitomized the best part of the political system, the part most sensitive to the needs of the common man. And this approach to politics held a certain logic, given the absence of interest or class organizations through which public benefits could be obtained. Political clientage simply constituted the most workable mechanism for popular mass individuals to gain some measure of welfare or security from the state. The political relationships generated were not unlike the ideal-type relations between father and son, teacher and pupil, saint and supplicant. Although authority was clearly concentrated in the man at the top, those at the bottom firmly expected that the proper show of deference and support might persuade him to utilize his power on their behalf. Hence, from the beginning of stable national government in Peru, the elaborate expression of obsequiousness towards the politically powerful became a principal form of mass political behavior, especially in situations involving appeals for favors from those occupying positions of political leadership.

That populist movements were part of a long tradition of patrimonial politics does not mean that they contributed nothing new to the national political equation. One immediately obvious innovation of both populist parties in 1930-31 was their mass constituency and their sensitivity to issues that affected their popular base. In their massive quality they stood in stark contrast to previous political organizations such as the Civilistas or the Demócratas that bore a closer resemblance to extended kinship groups than to political parties. With membership lists that contained only the names of the socially and economically prominent, their response to social issues was largely limited to support of various secular and religious charitable organizations in the large cities.

Each 1931 populist movement additionally provided its own special innovations to the political process. For Sánchezcerrismo, it was the elevation of a new socioracial type into the ranks of Peru's political leadership. A *mestizo* of lower middle class origin, in the years prior to his taking office Sánchez Cerro would certainly have been denied membership in those prestigious social clubs administered by the country's former upper class, white governing elite. Or as the famous Peruvian writer José Santos Chocano sarcastically remarked, the new president "has had his boots kissed by the grandchildren of men for whom his own grandfather daily performed the labor of shining their shoes."[15] Although Aprismo did not match Sánchezcerrismo in elevating a social outsider to a position of political leadership, it brought other changes to national politics. Perhaps the most significant of these was its elaborate organizational structure, typified by the party bureaucracy and the Aprista unions. Apra's tight organization has been a prime element in its nearly half-century survival as an active political entity and is perhaps what is most unique about Apra's special brand of populism. In contrast, Sánchezcerrismo's organizational looseness and reticence to institutionalize itself even during Sánchez Cerro's presidency made it virtually impossible for even the most loyal of leaders and followers to preserve the movement after the premature death of its founder and guiding force. Apra also reintroduced ideology as a basis for a sharp differentiation between itself and the other movements of the day, a political mode absent since the demise of the mid-nineteenth-century polemics between liberals and conservatives and almost nonexistent in the campaign of its populist rival.

The major break with the political past that accompanied the growth of populism was the conclusive abrogation of direct elite rule in Peru. More a circumstance of the fundamental social changes that occurred in the post World War I period than of populist pressures, national politics ceased to be monopolized by a limited number of upper class families. Throughout the nineteenth century the elites had used their wealth to insure political regimes favorable to their interests. And beginning in 1895 a close-knit group of frock-coated sugar and cotton planters, bankers, and large rural and urban property owners, not withstanding some internal quarreling, personally ran the affairs of state. With the domination of the 1931 presidential conflict by two powerful populist candidates, the *República aristocrática's* golden years of elite rule seemed to have run their course. To many, the election itself symbolized a new political path for Peru:

> Peru will have what it never had: elections. With their proportions of fraud and negligence. That does not matter. They will be elections. The moment which we

are living is characterized by the fact that we are liquidating the oldest and most serious of Peruvian problems: the predominance of the colonial caste, of a group of people that on the basis of their aristocracy, thought that Peru was their inheritance.[16]

Despite the euphoria of this editorialist, the "liquidation of the colonial caste" in the early 1930s constituted more a reorganization of the way in which political power was exercised than an abrupt shift in the locus of power to the newly politicized masses or to the rising populist counter-elites. Forced to relinquish the physical control of the state, the elites handed over active governing to other sectors in order to check the surge of what they considered to be the potential forces of mass revolution. But Peru's previous rulers continued to control basic social and economic institutions through their undisputed stewardship of the nation's export economy and international trade. Although no longer actively making political decisions, the representatives of the old order used their unbroken power in the social and economic spheres to insure themselves a significant voice in government policy and a veto power over those initiatives that directly affected their interests. It may in fact be something of an exaggeration to say that the elites abandoned active politics considering the high offices that prominent representatives of their caste continued to hold. The two presidencies of Manuel Prado a member of one of the country's most "aristocratic" families, constitute only the most dramatic case in point.

Despite the persistence of upper class individuals in the public sector, on the whole Peru's former governing elites showed a surprising willingness to hand over the reins of government to nonelite sectors so long as their economic and social privileges were not threatened. The two groups that mainly replaced the orderly oligarchy in the seat of power were the populists and certain sectors of the military. While the centralization of authority in populism's leader-figures appealed to the upper classes because it permitted them to deal with one man as opposed to masses of men, the prospect of military government held a particular attraction. The elites had lived with military rule for long stretches of the nineteenth century and had actively sought it in 1914 when President Billinghurst began to violate the established norms of political propriety. As the epitome of authority and order, the military appeared by nature to share their paramount concerns for economic and political stability and the defense of private property. The elites were able to reinforce this conservative orientation by playing on the military's anti-Aprista sentiments. Repeatedly flashing the symbol of the 1932 Trujillo massacre, for years they successfully convinced a large proportion of the officer class that the suppression of Apra was part of a larger battle against all those forces that could subvert the social order. Furthermore, upper class Peruvians were able to secure military cooperation by pandering to the middle class officers' aspirations for acceptance into the realm of high society.

The elites' acquiescence to indirect rule after 1930 added still another chapter to the historic Latin American pattern of adaptation by the existing system to new forces. Ready to exert behind-the-scenes influence, to temporize, to manipulate, the country's privileged caste was able to survive as a major national force. "No fights, no insults," appropriately wrote one critic of Peruvian politics. "The idea of accommodation, of adjustment, and standing aside at the fist sign of trouble is a basic part of the national organism. All of Peru's social and political history is composed of these compromises."[17] And even more revealing are the rules of the elite political game as reconstructed by Richard Stephens from his recent attitudinal surveys of upper class Peruvians: "Do not participate directly in politics, for reasons of prudence; do not be too visible, in order to avoid being a target; the essential is to get 'solutions' that favor one's clan, or at least conform to its preferences and interests."[18]

The integration of the masses into national politics under populism may not have fundamentally altered the distribution of power in Peru. But populist politics did contribute an important new modality to the Peruvian political system: the political massification of paternalism. Patron-client ties had been a conspicuous instrument of social control for centuries, and they have continued to fulfill that function in areas where the relatively small number of individuals to be served make face-to-face relations possible. But with the emergence of a mass society, especially in the cities, these one-to-one relationships could no longer fulfill their purpose. Populism arose to provide an enlarged framework through which to carry on patron-client relationships in the political sphere. Under populism, the party leader or the *capitulero* afforded an avenue in the urban context to the kinds of products and services that the *hacendado* had distributed in the countryside. And not only did the party functionaries act as brokers that connected the masses to the national power structure, but the populist party became the very focus of patronage. In an important sense the populists drew on old social norms and accommodated them to new social circumstances.

Following the first populist era of the early 1930s, nearly every Peruvian government has used populism's state paternalism to control socially and politically large segments of the country's masses. Without attempting a comprehensive reinterpretation of recent Peruvian history, the persistence of the populist style can be seen through the examples of the two regimes with the longest tenure of office since 1930: the eight-year rule of Manuel Odría from 1948 to 1956 and what is at the date of this writing the twelve-year rule of the Revolutionary Government of the Armed Forces from 1968 to 1980.

Both administrations appeared at times of social and political crisis similar to the social discontinuities that preceded the rise of populism. In the case of Odría the crisis was mainly political in nature, revolving around Apra's move to reenter national politics. Banished from the political stage since the early 1930s in the wake of their repeated attempts to take power by force, Apra regained the status of a legal party in 1945 and was allowed to participate in the elections of that year within a centrist coalition, the Frente Democrático Nacional (National Democratic Front). Thanks to Apra's support, the Frente's candidate, José Luis Bustamante y Rivero, won the election, but his years in office were plagued by an increasingly bitter battle for political supremacy between the Aprista majority in Congress and the president. Hesitant to assert decisive leadership, Bustamante proved unable to check the series of strikes and generalized instability that came to dominate the political scene. The chief executive's loss of legitimacy seemed to keep pace with the growing climate of political violence, culminating in an unsuccessful attempt by Apristas, both civilian and military, to overthrow Bustamante violently. Notwithstanding Apra's failure, the president had clearly lost the support of large segments of the populace, and the Aprista revolt was quickly followed by Alfonso Llosa's aborted movement in Juliaca and then Manuel Odría's successful coup in Arequipa.

Many of the same elements that prompted Odría to take power were present twenty years later when the armed forces ousted the government of Fernando Belaunde Terry in 1968. Elected in 1963 with open military support, Belaunde was the last great civilian hope for military men who had become extremely concerned with the direction of Peru's development. But, as during the Bustamante period, national politics arrived at an impasse during the Belaunde government, with a relatively weak president opposed by an Aprista-led Congress. The combined legislative forces of Apra and the Odría party representatives, with the support of powerful members of the traditional elites, effectively stymied nearly all of the president's half-hearted attempts at "peaceful" reform. With the additional stigmas of a smuggling scandal, an unpopular devaluation of the national currency, and Belaunde's deplorable handling of the nationalization of Peru's petroleum resources—long a hot political issue in the country—the chief executive, as had Bustamante two decades before and indeed as had Leguía nearly forty years earlier, seemed to lose all legitimacy to govern.

But by 1968 new forces had come into play which proved crucial to the military's decision to move against Belaunde. The 1950s and 1960s had been witness to profound social changes in Peru that in many ways paralleled yet clearly outpace the transformations of the post-World War I period. Massive waves of rural migrants fostered the growth of a myriad of slum settlements that ringed the major cities. Land invasion in both rural and urban areas appeared to threaten public order, not to mention the principle of private property. Strikes and student demonstrations were the order of the day. Rural guerrilla movements broke out in various parts of the interior during the mid-1960s, and urban guerrilla bands began to operate primarily in the capital city. All seemed to point to the fact that Peru was on the verge of the violent revolution predicted for all Latin America. Perceiving that the civilian government of Belaunde was patently unable to stem the "revolutionary" tide, the military took power, according to political analyst Julio Cotler, in "response to the much-proclaimed need to readjust the functioning of the Peruvian system, due to the threat posed by the political radicalization of the more organized sectors within the dominated clases."[19]

A major project of the Odría administration as well as of the post-1968 military government was the restoration of social harmony in a convulsed Peru, or in other words, the strengthening of social control. In their attempts to shore up the existing system both regimes drew upon the legacy of state paternalism introduced by the populists. Odría's brand of political clientelism was strikingly similar to the earlier version practiced by the Sánchezcerrista administration. Presidential charity was the earmark of Odría's attempt to blunt the Aprista threat by winning mass support for the government. Concentrating his efforts on the highly visible urban poor, incremented daily by massive post war rural-urban migration, the president's "charity" ran the gamut from various blanket wage increases for urban labor to the provision of large numbers of working class jobs under his active public works program. The most visible manifestation of state paternalism under Odría were the frequent highly publicized visits of his wife, María Delgado de Odría, in Eva Perón fashion, to the Lima slums bearing gifts of food and money. The terms used in a book sponsored by the Odría administration to describe her "good works for the people" have the familiar ring of the accolades directed at Sánchez Cerro and Haya de la Torre in the 1931 presidential campaign:

> Her hands, open, sincere, friendly extend towards the suffering of Lima, towards the afflicted of all the Peruvian provinces, towards every place there is the need for a spontaneous and understanding heart that holds back nothing. Her magnificent and tender figure radiates that contagious cheer that makes the poor of the fatherland so happy, given without limits to the young, the old, the sick, all that expect everything from her. To the poor of the fatherland she has

given shelter, medicines, food, advice and over everything else, love and more love. She has become the guide of the needy who will soon be calling her "Protector of the Humble."[20]

In addition, Odría exercised state paternalism by expediting the formation and legalization of squatter settlements to house Lima's growing lower class population. Often naming their settlements after the president or his wife, impressive numbers of the capital's popular masses filled the ranks of progovernment demonstrators in the largest plazas of the city. Acting reciprocally, they repaid the man who had "benevolently" looked after their needs. As David Collier pointed out in his groundbreaking study of relations between successive governments and Lima's squatter settlements: "Odría sought to build the idea that the poor enjoyed a special relationship with him. This was part of Odría's attempt to establish a dependent, paternalistic relationship between the president and the poor"[21] The purpose of Odría's paternalistic policy was plain: to undercut the popularity of Apra and generally to contain politically any working class groups seeking autonomously to organize and to place pressure on the status quo.

Even more directly than Odría, Peru's present military government has addressed itself to the question of social harmony and the masses' proper place in the system. This concern for the internal domination of the lower classes is hardly surprising in the light of the severe tensions of the 1960s. Using populism's theme of class conciliation in the name of the national family, the military regime has repeatedly insisted upon the notion that the common interests of all Peruvians plus an effective bureaucracy will supersede all potential social conflict. To channel demands from different social groups, the country's military rulers, particularly under President Juan Velasco Alvarado, proceeded to build a patrimonially administered state which, as did its populist and other predecessors, continued to deal in favors, jobs, and political patronage. But the regime brought patrimonialism a step futher by purposefully creating formal clientelistic institutions through which to tie working class constituents to the tutelary state. The foremost of these through 1975 was SINAMOS, an organization expicitly designed to provide a link between the government and the popular masses. SINAMOS sought to institutionalize political clientelism in various ways. All public and private welfare programs for the poor operated under its supervision. It became a formal broker between working class associations and individuals and the state. And it took primary responsibility for the direction of mass political participation. Each of these activities bears the indelible stamp of the politics of personal dependence practiced by the populists. In its treatment of Lima's large squatter settlement population, for exam-

ple, SINAMOS translated classic face-to-face patron-client relations into
individual-bureaucracy terms such that its offices were characteristically
filled with individuals seeking material aid for their settlements or
pleading for the legal recognition of their land titles. And despite the
institutional overlay, the behavior patterns of squatter clients seeking
benefits from the political patron (in this case the Dirección de Pueblos
Jovenes [DPJ] — a kind of agency for squatter settlements absorbed by
SINAMOS) are strongly reminiscent of Sánchez Cerro's supporters
crowding the halls of his campaign headquarters or the government
palace some forty years earlier. In a fascinating description by Henry
Dietz: "the individual presents himself as retiring (in the sense of not
being pushy or impatient), eager to listen and to please, and thankful for
the opportunity of coming to the DPJ . . . any display of belligerence or
hostility would normally be considered not only bad form, but also pre-
judicial and harmful to the undertaking. The basic attitude, then, is com-
pounded of respect for authority (probably real) and attentiveness and
willingness to cooperate (perhaps less real.)"[22] SINAMOS's mass
demonstrations in support of the regime also hark back to the Sánchezcerrista and Aprista efforts of the 1930s. Recruiting demonstrators
from its principal client groups, the organization defined *participation,*
the most recurrent term in the SINAMOS vocabulary, as the means by
which the people support their government. The most prominent banner
at a progovernment demonstration in the fishing port of Chimbote
suitably suggested the kind of passive, supportive "participation" that
SINAMOS encourages: "Tu Presencia es Revolución" ("Your Presence is
Revolution").[23]

Much has changed in Peru from the 1930s to the 1970s. The initial
massification of Peruvian society in the 1920s which lay the foundation
for the extension of political clientelism under populism pales before the
high rates of social and political mobilization and the economic modernization of recent decades. Along with the growth of a more complex
society in Peru has come a related increase in the numbers, sources, and
intensity of demands on the political system. In large part the military
government's attempts to institutionalize what had been essentially informal patron-client ties under populism and Odriísmo constitutes the adap-
tion of political clientelism to a changing Peru where structural modifica-
tion replaces symbolic rewards as a principle element of pacification. But
the basic motive — social control — and the methods — the patrimonial
state — remain the same. One Peruvian colonel's approach to the problems of mass political integration in the 1970s has an all too familiar ring:
"The masses in Latin America are starting to stampede. We the military

are the only ones who are capable of leading them — and us — onto safe ground."[24] His frank statement of preemptive politics is just another page out of the Brazilian Antonio Carlos Ribeiro de Andrada's forty-year-old book, "We must make the revolution before it is made by the people."

Notes
Bibliography

Notes

CHAPTER 1: POPULISM AND SOCIAL CONTROL

1 Various works have appeared in recent years which discuss the influence of patrimonialism in Latin American history. Chief among them is Howard J. Wiarda, ed., *Politics and Social Change in Latin America: The Distinct Tradition* (Amherst, Mass., 1974), especially chapters by Wiarda and Richard Morse. Other groundbreaking works in this area were the two anthologies edited by Claudio Veliz, *Obstacles to Change in Latin America* (London, 1965), and *The Politics of Conformity in Latin America* (New York, 1967). A good definition of patron-clientism is provided by Robert R. Kaufman, "The Patron-Client Concept and Macro-Politics: Prospects and Problems," *Comparative Studies in Society and History* 16, no. 3 (June 1974): 285. A thoughtful application of patron-clientism to recent Andean history is found in Frederick B. Pike, *The United States and the Andean Republics* (Cambridge, Mass., 1977), esp. pp. 5-9. Douglas Chalmers makes a provocative application of the patron-client concept to the larger political system in "The Politicized State in Latin America," in *Authoritarianism and Corporatism in Latin America,* ed. James M. Malloy (Pittsburgh, 1977), esp. pp. 33-34.
2 Prominent exceptions include Haiti, Nicaragua, and Paraguay.
3 Quoted by Francisco C. Weffort, "El populismo en la política brasileña," in Celso Furtado, et al., *Brasíl hoy* 2nd ed. (México, 1970), p. 62.
4 On the co-optation of the middle sectors see Veliz, ed., *Obstacles to Change,* esp. the "Introduction" and Helio Jaguaribe's chapter, "The Dynamics of Brazilian Nationalism," in which he discusses the concept of the *"Estado cartorial"*; Luis Ratinoff, "The New Urban Groups: The Middle Classes," in *Elites in Latin America,* ed. Seymour Martin Lipset and Aldo Solari (New York, 1967), pp. 61-93; and Charles W. Anderson, *Politics and Economic Change in Latin America: The Governing of Restless Nations* (Princeton, N.J., 1967). The first notable recognition of the importance of the middle sectors in Latin American society and politics came in John J. Johnson, *Political Change in Latin America: The Emergence of the Middle Sectors* (Stanford Calif., 1958).

5   James Malloy, "Authoritarianism and Corporatism in Latin America: The Modal Pattern," in *Authoritarianism and Corporatism,* ed. Malloy, p. 7. See also Ronald C. Newton, "Natural Corporatism and the Passing of Populism in Spanish America," in *The New Corporatism: Social and Political Structures in the Iberian World,* ed., Fredrick B. Pike and Thomas Stritch (Notre Dame, Ind., 1974), p. 45.

6   Kenneth Paul Erickson has convincingly emphasized the conservatizing nature of populism in the Brazilian case in his "Populism and Political Control of the Working Class in Brazil," in *Ideology and Social Change in Latin America* ed. June Nash, Juan Corradi, and Hobart Spaulding, Jr. (New York, 1977), pp. 200–236. In various articles Howard Wiarda has provided effective characterizations of the blend of new and old forces in modern Latin America. See his "Corporatism and Development in the Iberic-Latin World: Persistent Strains and New Variations," in *New Corporatism,* ed. Pike and Stritch, pp. 3–33, "Conclusion," in *Politics and Social Change,* ed. Wiarda, pp. 269–92, and "The Catholic Labor Movement," in *Contemporary Brazil,* ed. H. Jon Rosenbaum and William G. Tyler (New York, 1972), pp. 323–47.

7   Without attempting an exhaustive list, the following publications are useful studies of specific populist movements in Latin America. On Vargas see Francisco Weffort, "El populismo en la política brasileña," in Furtado et al., *Brasil hoy,* pp. 54–84; Erickson, "Populism and Political Control," and Philippe Schmitter, *Interest Conflict and Political Change in Brazil* (Stanford, Calif., 1971). Among the best works dealing with Peronist populism are Carlos S. Fayt, *La naturaleza del Peronismo* (Buenos Aires, 1967); Miguel Murmis and Juan Carlos Portantiero, *Estudios sobre los orígines del Peronismo,* vol. 1 (Buenos Aires, 1971); Samuel Baily, *Labor, Nationalism, and Politics in Argentina* (New Brunswick, N.J., 1967); Eva Perón, *La razón de mi vida* (Buenos Aires, 1951); and Peter Smith, "Social Mobilization, Political Participation and the Rise of Juan Perón," *Political Science Quarterly* 84, no. 1 (March 1969):30–49. On the Cárdenas period in Mexico see Arnaldo Córdova, *La ideología de la Revolución Mexicana: la formación del nuevo régimen* (México, 1973); Wayne Cornelius, "Nation Building, Participation, and Distribution: The Politics of Social Reform Under Cárdenas," in *Crisis, Choice and Change: Historical Studies of Political Development,* ed. Gabriel A. Almond, Scott L. Flanagan and Robert J. Mundt (Boston, 1973), pp. 392–498; and Evelyn P. Stevens, "Mexico's PRI; The Institutionalization of Corporatism?," in *Authoritarianism and Corporatism,* ed. Malloy, pp. 227–58. Another work of special interest on Latin American populism is Paul W. Drake, *Socialism and Populism in Chile 1932–52* (Urbana, Ill., 1978).

8   S.L. Andreski in Isaiah Berlin et al., "Populism: A Discussion," *Government and Opposition* 3, no. 2 (Spring 1968): 155.

9   Quoted ibid., p. 166. Populism's wide application matches the fuzziness of its definition. One contributing factor to that fuzziness is that, unlike socialism, communism, or anarchism, populist movements have no shared tradition. Social scientists, rather than populists themselves, have linked the movements together for analytical purposes. Two symposia that address themselves directly

to the problem of definition are Berlin et al., "Populism"; and Ghita Ionescu and Ernest Gellner, eds., *Populism* (New York, 1969). See also the introduction to Drake, *Socialism and Populism.*

10 My definition of populism is largely based on my Peruvian research. Also helpful were various works that have attempted to define populism in the Latin American context. The following were of particular value: Francisco C. Weffort, "Clases populares y desarrollo social (contribución al estudio del 'populismo')," *Revista paraguaya de sociología* 5, no. 3 (December 1968): 62–154; Weffort, "Populismo en la política brasileña"; Erickson, "Populism and Political Control"; Alistair Hennessy, "Latin America," in *Populism,* ed. Ionescu and Gellner, pp. 28–61; Gino Germani, Torcuato S. Di Tella, and Octavio Ianni, *Populismo y contradicciones de clase en Latinoamérica* (México, 1973); Jorge Basurto, "Populismo y movilización de masas en México durante el régimen cardenista," *Revista mexicana de sociología* 31, no. 4 (October 1969):853–92; Torcuato S. Di Tella, "Populism and Reform in Latin America," in Veliz, ed., *Obstacles to Change,* pp 47–74; Julio Cotler, "Crisis política y populismo militar en el Perú," (mimeographed, Lima, 1969); and Osvaldo Bayer et al., *El populismo en la Argentina* (Buenos Aires, 1974).

11 There are exceptions to this rule of urban populism—most notably Mexico's Revolutionary party, Bolivia's MNR, and Venezuela's Acción Democrática, all of which had large rural contingents.

12 This term is borrowed from Weffort, "Populismo en la política brasileña," p. 74.

13 These elitist, manipulative tendencies in populism are persuasively stressed in Malloy, "Modal Pattern," p. 10; and Norberto Rodriguez Bustamente, "Sociología del populismo," in Bayer, et al., *Populismo en la Argentina,* p. 140.

14 The term *authority-dependency relationship* is employed by Douglas Chalmers in his thoughtful discussion of the most common forms of political movements in twentieth-century Brazilian history. See his "Political Groups and Authority in Brazil: Some Continuities in a Decade of Confusion and Change," in *Brazil in the Sixties,* ed. Riorden Roett (Nashville, Tenn., 1972), pp. 51–76.

15 Real income data for Argentina may be found in Gilbert W. Merckx, "Sectoral Clashes and Political Change: The Argentine Experience," *Latin American Research Review* 4, no. 3 (Fall 1969): 97. On Mexico see James W. Wilkie, *The Mexican Revolution: Federal Expenditures and Social Change Since 1910* (Berkeley, Calif., 1970), p. 187.

16 An interesting outline of the major features of urban machines may be found in Kaufman, "Patron-Client Concept," pp. 303–4.

17 Erickson, "Populism and Political Control," p. 204.

18 Drake, *Socialism and Populism,* p. 9. See also Erickson, "Populism and Political Control," for an effective analysis of the transitory nature of populist gains.

CHAPTER 2: THE DESERTION OF THE ELITES

1 Oscar R. Benavides in *El Comercio,* July 10, 1931, p. 5.
2 Víctor Andrés Belaunde, *La realidad nacional* (Paris , 1931), p. 271.
3 *La Noche,* August 18, 1931, p.5.
4 An exception to mass political quiescence was the brief presidency of Guillermo Billinghurst (1912–14).
5 Juan Manuel Ugarte Eléspuru, *Lima y lo limeño* (Lima, 1966), p. 246; Germán Arenas, *Algo de una vida* (Lima 1941?), pp. 130–31; and Ricardo Martinez de la Torre, *Apuntes para una interpretación marxista de historia social del Perú,* 2d ed., vol. 1 (Lima, 1947), p. 190.
6 Víctor Andrés Belaunde, *Trayectoria y destino: Memorias completas,* vol. 2 (Lima, 1967), p. 1037.
7 Jorge Basadre, *Perú problema y posibilidad* (Lima, 1931), p. 192.
8 Frederick B. Pike, *The Modern History of Peru* (New York, 1967), p. 92. For further information on the guano era see Heraclio Bonilla, *Guano y burguesía en el Perú* (Lima, 1974); Pike, *Andean Republics,* pp. 85–87; and Carl F. Herbold, Jr., "Developments in the Peruvian Administrative System, 1919–1930: Modern and Traditional Qualities of Government Under Authoritarian Regimes" (Ph.D. diss., Yale University, 1973), pp. 31, 37, 40.
9 It is important to note that *"República aristocrática,"* while denoting the rule of the nation by a self-defined select class, does not imply that the elite was in any way a titled nobility or that its members necessarily pertained to families with ties to the titled nobility of the colonial period.
10 Mariano Nicolás Valcarcel, quoted by Arenas, *Algo de una vida,* p. 87. A similar characterization of the Peruvian elite during this period may be found in Gary Richard Garrett, "The Oncenio of Augusto B. Leguía: Middle Sector Government and Leadership in Peru 1919–1930" (Ph.D. diss., University of New Mexico, 1973), pp. 9, 53–54.
11 Enrique Echecopar, *Aptocracia* (Lima, 1930), p. 13. The following sources have been of particular value in the study of the *República aristocrática:* Carlos Miró Quesada Laos, *Radiografía de la política peruana,* 2d ed. (Lima, 1959), pp. 78, 80; *Autopsia de los partidos políticos* (Lima, 1961), p. 339; and *Pueblo en crisis* (Buenos Aires, 1946), p. 123; Pedro Ugarteche, interview, February 16, 1971; Jorge Basadre, *Historia de la República del Perú: 1822–1933,* 6th ed., vol. 10 (Lima, 1968–69), p. 5; Jorge Basadre and Rómulo Ferrero, *Historia de la Cámara de Comercio de Lima* (Lima, 1963), p. 69; and Yepes del Castillo, *Perú 1820–1920; Un siglo de desarrollo capitalista* (Lima, 1972), pp. 109, 173, 197, 263.
12 Candamo is quoted in Basadre and Ferrero, *Cámara de Comercio,* pp. 66–67. For biographical information on Candamo see ibid., pp. 63–64; and Ernesto Yepes del Castillo, *Un siglo de desarrollo capitalista,* pp. 192–93.
13 For a thoughtful discussion of the colonial carryovers in nineteenth- and twentieth-century Latin America in general see Stanley J. Stein and Barbara H. Stein, *The Colonial Heritage of Latin America* (New York, 1970).
14 For Rosas's remarks see Paulino Fuentes Castro, "La ratificación de la alianza

Piérola-Civilista," *Mundial* 2, no. 41, (February 4, 1921): 3. Piérola's statement was reprinted by Alfonso Benavides Correa, "Los partidos políticos del Perú," vol. 2 (Lima, 1947), p. 303. For further information on the coalition see Jesús Chavarría, "La desaparición del Perú colonial (1870-1919)," *Aportes,* no. 23 (January 1972): 130.

15 Quoted by Miró Quesada Laos in *Radiografía,* pp. 63-64.

16 This term is used by Rene Lemarchand and Keith Legg, "Political Clientelism and Development: A Preliminary Analysis," *Comparative Politics* 4, no. 2 (January 1972): 148-56.

17 The exception to this period of Civilista hegemony was the presidency of Guillermo Billinghurst (1912-14). It should be noted that notwithstanding Bilinghurst's ties to the Partido Demócrata, a large part of the Civilista party supported his quest for the presidency. On the decline of the Demócratas and the breaking of the alliance see Chavarría, "Perú colonial," p. 235.

18 The makeup of the Partido Civil is examined in fascinating detail in a letter of former Peruvian president Andrés Avelino Cáceres (1886-90) published by Miró Quesada Laos, *Autopsia de los partidos,* pp. 262-63.

19 Alejandro Deustua, quoted in Pedro Dávalos y Lissón, *Diez años de historia contemporánea del Perú (1899-1908)* (Lima, 1930), pp. 120-21.

20 The most detailed account of these events is Dávalos y Lissón, *Diez años,* pp. 118-23.

21 An example of this "distrust" in Leguía is found in the writings of one prominent Civilista, Germán Arenas, *Algo de una vida,* pp. 33-34.

22 On the developing split between Leguía and the Civilistas see José Carlos Martín, *José Pardo y Barreda, el estadista: un hombre, un partido, una época* (Lima, 1948), p. 36; Howard Lawrence Karno, "Augusto B. Leguía: The Oligarchy and the Modernization of Peru, 1870-1930," Ph.D. diss. (University of California, Los Angeles, 1970), pp. 122-25, 157-62; Arenas, *Algo de una vida,* pp. 51-53, 58; Basadre, *Historia de la República,* 12: 108, 116-18, 139; Luis Alberto Sánchez, *Raúl Haya del la Torre o el político. Crónica de una vida sin tregua* (Santiago, 1934), pp. 37-38; Miró Quesada Laos, *Autopsia de los partidos,* pp. 390, 396, 398-400; Aurelio Miró Quesada, *Don José Antonio Miró Quesada* (Lima, 1945), pp. 283-84; Belaunde, *Trayectoria y destino,* 1: 393; and Manuel A. Capuñay, *Leguía; vida y obra del constructor del gran Perú* (Lima, 1952), pp. 66, 76-79, 85-86.

23 Manuel González Prada, *Bajo el oprobio* (Paris, 1933), p. 64. See also David Matto, in José Galvez, *Nuestra pequeña historia* (Lima, 1966), p. 355; Miró Quesada Laos, *Autopsia de los partidos,* pp. 402-3; Basadre, *Historia de la República* 12: 129-30; Karno, "Leguía," pp. 164-65; Capuñay, *Leguía,* p. 139; and Chavarría, "Perú Colonial," p. 145.

24 Arenas, *Algo de una vida,* pp. 79, 84; and Alberto Ulloa Satomayor, *La organización social y legal del trabajo en el Perú* (Lima, 1916), p. 179. For information on the Billinghurst candidacy and presidency consult Miró Quesada Laos, *Autopsia de los partidos,* pp. 404-7; Karno, "Leguía, " pp. 166-67; Basadre, *Historia de la República,* 12: 207-19, 298; Belaunde, *Trayectoria y destino,* 1: 424; Belaunde, *La realidad nacional,* p. 281; Pike, *Modern*

History, pp. 198–99; and Yepes del Castillo, *Un siglo de desarrollo capitalista,* pp. 236–37.

25 Víctor Andrés Belaunde, "La crisis presente," in *Meditaciones peruanas,* 2d ed. (Lima, 1963), p. 100. See also Frederico More, *Una multitud contra un pueblo* (Lima, 1934), pp. 50–51; Basadre, *Historia de la República* 12: 299–300; and José Félix Aramburú, *Derecho electoral* (Lima, 1915), p. 15. A particularly good source on the elites' reaction to Billinghurst is Ulloa Satomayor, *Organización social,* pp. 177–79.

26 Arenas, *Algo de una vida,* p. 93.

27 *El Comercio,* March 29, 1915, p. 2.

28 For detailed information on the Convention see Ricardo R. Ríos, ed., *La Convención de los Partidos de 1915* (Lima, 1918), passim; Miró Quesada Laos, *Autopsia de los partidos,* pp. 429–30; Martín, *José Pardo,* pp. 88, 92–95; and Basadre, *Historia de la República* 12: 362–67.

29 José Fermín Herrera, "Con motivo del aniversario natal del Sr. Dr. Don José Pardo," in Colección de Hojas Sueltas, Biblioteca Nacional del Perú, Lima (hereafter referred to as CHS-BNP). On Pardo's second term consult Belaunde, *Meditaciones peruanas,* p. 242; Miró Quesada Laos, *Radiografía,* pp. 110–11; Miró Quesada Laos, *Autopsia de los partidos,* pp. 437–38; Abelardo Solís, *Once años* (Lima, 1934), pp. 13–14; Benavides Correa, "Partidos políticos," 2: 74; and Basadre, *Perú problema,* p. 174.

30 Belaunde, *Trayectoria y destino,* 1: 425, 774–75; Alberto Ulloa Sotomayor, *Don Nicolás de Píerola. Una época de la historia del Perú* (Lima, 1950), pp. 406–7, expresses a similar view.

31 On the Constitucionalistas see Basadre, *Historia de la República,* 10: 122; and Miró Quesada Laos, *Autopsia de los partidos,* pp. 337, 396. On the Partido Liberal see Manuel González Prada, *Horas de lucha* (Lima, 19??), p. 109.

32 Miró Quesada Laos, *Radiografía,* pp. 106, 111; and Capuñay, *Leguía,* p. 183.

33 A particularly interesting comment on the decadent state of elite politics in the period preceding the election of 1919 is José Carlos Mariátegui, in *Nuestra época,* June 6, 1918, quoted in Karno, "Leguía," p. 199. See also "El momento político y la opinión pública," in Manuel Vicente Villarán, *Páginas escogidas* (Lima, 1962), pp. 294–95.

34 The best treatment of the modernization of the state in Peru during this period is Herbold, "Peruvian Administrative System," passim. He summarizes his view in this statement: "The augmented administrative tasks represented by the service state then required the organization of new agencies, the incorporation of thousands of new employees, and the management of the collection and disbursement of enlarged fiscal resources" (p. 201). One of the first historians to take note of this process was Jorge Basadre, *Perú problema,* p. 185.

35 Information on the growth of public employment, agencies, and spending may be found in Perú, *Censo de las Provincias de Lima y Callao levantado el 13 de noviembre de 1931* (Lima, 1932), p. 206; and Herbold, "Peruvian Administrative System," pp. 153, 162.

36 The term *"Patria Nueva"* or "new nation," was used by Leguía and his supporters to characterize his three successive terms as president from 1919 to
1930. The "new nation" meant contempt for the past and the men of the past,
unconditional confidence in the figure of Leguía, and the assumption that he
alone could introduce Peru into an era of unparalleled progress.

37 Quoted by René Hooper Lopez, *Leguía* (Lima, 1964), pp. 139–40.

38 A valuable summary of Leguía's wide appeal in 1919 is contained in Garrett,
"Oncenio of Leguía," pp. 43–44; More, *Multitud,* pp. 124–25; Basadre,
Historia de la República, 10: 156; *El proceso electoral de Lima en la Cámara
de Diputados* (Lima, 1917), p. i; Julio Augusto and Espejo, "Leguía inaugura
una época," *Oiga* 9, no. 415 (March 19, 1971), p. 15.

39 Quoted by Tomás Meza, *40 años al servicio de los presidentes del Perú en la
Casa de Pizarro* (Lima, 1959), p. 32. Meza, who personally served in the
government palace, also reported that Leguía always carried a revolver for
purposes of self-defense in case of a *golpe.* Persuasive examinations of why
Leguía decided to take power by force in 1919 are presented by Garrett,
"Oncenio of Leguía," p. 52; and Herbold, "Peruvian Administrative System,"
pp. 93–94.

40 *The West Coast Leader,* April 3, 1928, p. 22. On Leguía's repressive acts see
Arenas, *Algo de una vida,* p. 134; Miró Quesada Laos, *Autopsia de los partidos,* pp. 452–53, 460; Felipe Barreda y Laos, "La crisis política del Perú: la
dictadura y la muerte de los partidos," *La Republica* (August 25, 1930), pp.
2–3; *El Comercio,* November 24, 1930, p. 2; More, *Multitud,* pp. 73–74; and
Enrique Chirinos Soto, *El Perú frente a junio de 1962. Síntesis de la historia
política de la República* (Lima, 1962), pp. 36–37. For lists of the most prominent figures deported by Leguía see Miró Quesada Laos, *Autopsia de los partidos,* p. 454; and Martín, *José Pardo,* p. 126. Leguía's repressive actions are
summarized in Garret, "Oncenio of Leguía," pp. 54–55.

41 Barreda y Laos, "Crisis política," p. 2. Similar sentiments were voiced by
Villarán, *Paginas escogidas,* pp. 291–92; *Variedades* 19, no. 797 (June 9,
1923); and Alberto Guillén, *El libro de la democracia criolla* (Lima, 1924), p.
42.

42 Garrett, "Oncenio of Leguía," pp. 57, 77–78.

43 Benjamín Roca, in *Mundial* 11, no. 538 (October 10, 1930): 30. For other expressions of this attitude see Francisco Echenique, president of the Banco
Internacional, in *Mundial* 11, no. 538 (October 30, 1930): 31 and *La revista
semanal* 4, no. 165 (October 30, 1930): 3. Another factor that might have
limited upper class spending on politics was the sharp drop of money in circulation which grew out of the economic crisis. In the banking sector, for example, the quantity of circulating paper and subsidiary currency dropped
from 25,513,080 *soles* in 1929 to 18,179,325 in 1930 and even lower to
8,299,672 in 1931. See Perú, Ministerio de Hacienda y Comercio, *Extracto
estadístico del Perú: 1939* (Lima, 1940), p. 372. This phenomenon was the
product of the austerity measures taken in response to the depression as well as

the decision of a large number of Peruvian capitalists, fearful of the effects of monetary instability, to retain funds in their possession or to send large sums abroad. One net effect of the reduction of the money supply seems to have been an increasing hesitance on the part of elite sectors to spend what monies were available on politics and on politicians that appeared to have lost their usefulness.

44 *El hombre de la calle* 1, no. 20 (January 31, 1931): 16.

45 José Matías Manzanilla and Manuel Vicente Villarán, "Los antiguos partidos han terminado su misión. El Partido Civil pertenece a la historia," *El Comercio,* September, 11, 1930, p. 3.

46 "Reportaje de caracter político," Biblioteca Nacional del Perú, E 1157. Others that commented on the death of the traditional parties include Barreda y Laos, "Crisis política," p. 2; Benjamín Chirinos Pacheco, *Hacia un Perú nuevo* (Arequipa, 1932), p. 83; Pedro Ugarteche, *Sánchez Cerro: Papeles y recuerdos de un presidente del Perú,* 4 vols. (Lima, 1969–70), 2: xvi–xxvii; Miró Quesada Laos, *Radiografía,* p. 63; and *Mundial* II, no. 545 (November 28, 1930): 38.

47 Belaunde, *Trayectoria y destino* 2: 763; "Boletín del Comité de Saneamiento y Consolidación Revolucionaria," November 1930, CHS-BNP; Mario Polar, *Viejos y nuevos tiempos: cartas a mi nieto* (Lima, 1969), p. 114; and *El Comercio,* September 27, 1930, p. 2; November 24, 1930, p. 2; February 20, 1931, p. 1.

48 Manzanilla and Villarán, "Los antiguos partidos," p. 3. Other sources of information in this regard include Pedro Ugarteche, interview, February 1, 1971; Pedro de Osma in *El Comercio,* September 16, 1930, p. 3; Federico More, *Zoocracia y canibalismo* (Lima, 1933), pp. 21–22; and Chirinos Pacheco, *Perú nuevo,* p. 22.

49 On congressional and judicial weakness see González Prada, *Horas de lucha,* p. 127; Basadre, *Perú problema,* pp. 180–81; More, *Zoocracia,* pp. 8–10; Carlos Sánchez Viamonte, *Jornadas* (Buenos Aires, 1929), pp. 74–75; Ugarteche, *Sánchez Cerro,* 2: xii–xiii; and Herbold, "Peruvian Administrative System," p. 111. An interview with Jorge Basadre on February 8, 1971, was also informative on this problem.

50 Augusto B. Leguía(?), *Yo tirano, yo ladrón* (Lima, 193?), p. 51.

51 Belaunde, *Meditaciones peruanas,* p. 257; Basadre, *Perú problema,* p. 188; Benavides Correa, "Partidos políticos," 1: 130; Hooper Lopez, *Leguía,* p. 184; Miró Quesada Laos, *Autopsia de los partidos,* pp. 468–70; Miró Quesada Laos, *Radiografía,* pp. 107, 110–11; Pike, *Modern History,* p. 218; More, *Multitud,* p. 55; Solís, *Once años,* pp. 16–17; and *La Crónica,* July 31, 1931.

52 A concise synthesis of the causes for the downfall of the *República aristocrática* is contained in David Scott Palmer, "The Politics of Authoritarianism in Spanish America," in *Authoritarianism and Corporatism,* ed. Malloy, p. 397.

CHAPTER 3: ENTER THE MASSES

1 See for example Tomás Escajadillo, *La revolución universitaria de 1930* (Lima, 1931), p. 113; and More, *Multitud,* p. 153.

2 Perú, Dirección de Salubridad Pública, *Censo de la Provincia de Lima (26 de junio de 1908),* vol. 1 (Lima, 1915), p. 315; Perú, Ministerio de Hacienda, *Resumen del censo de las Provincias de Lima y Callao levantado el 17 de diciembre de 1920* (Lima, 1927), p. 81; Perú, *Censo de Lima 1931,* pp. 44–46; and Perú, Ministerio de Hacienda y Comercio, Dirección Nacional de Estadística, *Censo nacional de población de 1940,* vol. 5 (Lima, 1948), p. 3. All figures for Lima are based on the Province of Lima as a whole, not only on the urban districts. This procedure was followed in order to make feasible calculations on the impact of migration on class and employment structure. Data on both of these areas are only available on the provincial level. This qualification does not present serious problems since 98.3 percent of Lima's population in 1931 was considered urban. If, however, the urban area comprising the districts of Lima, La Victoria, and Rimac is analyzed separately, the overall population growth is even more dramatic, from 191,408 in 1921 to 344,159 in 1931, nearly a 75 percent increase.

3 In addition to the official government statistics presented in Perú, Ministerio de Hacienda y Comercio, *Extracto estadístico del Perú, 1928* (Lima, 1929), pp. 58–110, two studies which trace in detail the effects of World War I on the Peruvian economy are Hernando de Lavalle, *La gran guerra y el organismo económico nacional* (Lima, 1919), esp. pp. 9, 15, 20; and Basadre and Ferrero, *Cámara de Comercio,* pp. 89–101, 104, 106–7.

4 Perú, *Extracto estadístico, 1928,* pp. 121, 129; Basadre, *Historia de la República* 12: 434–36; and Basadre and Ferrero, *Cámara de Comercio,* pp. 105–6.

5 Data on changes in Peru's import and export patterns may be found in Perú, *Extracto estadístico, 1928,* pp. 64, 74. On U.S. investment and other foreign investment in Peru in this period see Pike, *Andean Republics,* p. 199; and Herbold, "Peruvian Administrative System," pp. 45–46.

6 *The West Coast Leader,* May 24, 1919, p. 1.

7 Quoted in Garrett, "Oncenio of Leguía," p. 151. Garrett advances an interesting explanation of Leguía and the U.S. role on pp. 150–54.

8 Herbert Hoover and John Foster Dulles are quoted by William Appleman Williams, *The Tragedy of American Diplomacy* (Cleveland, 1959), p. 91. The whole area of increased U.S. investment in Latin America following World War I is extensively treated in Joseph S. Tulchin, *The Aftermath of War: World War I and U.S. Policy Toward Latin America* (New York, 1971).

9 Warren G. Harding is quoted in Williams, *Tragedy of American Diplomacy,* p. 93. The close relationship between the U.S government and U.S. investors is explained well by Pike, *Andean Republics,* p. 194.

10 *El hombre de la calle* 1, no. 43 (July 11, 1931): 28.

11 Yepes del Castillo, *Un siglo de desarrollo capitalista,* pp. 158–59; and Emilio Harth-Terre, *Orientaciones urbanas* (Lima, 1931), p. 6.

12 The most detailed source for information about the urbanization of Lima during the 1920s is *Ciudad y campo y caminos* (1924–29). See especially 1, no. 9 (August 1925): 21; 2, no. 15 (February 1926): 15–16; 2, no. 20 (August 1926): vi–viii; 3, no. 32 (August 1927): 21; and 3, no. 33 (September 1927): 47. An excellent summary of building in Lima during the *oncencio* is *Lima: 1919–1930* (Lima, 1935?), passim.

13 *Sierra,* literally meaning a mountainous area, is commonly used in Peru to refer to the country's Andean region.

14 On early migration see Henry E. Dobyns and Paul L. Doughty, *Peru: A Cultural History* (New York, 1976), pp. 175–76, 197, 212–13. The percentages of migrant population residing in Lima in 1931 by district are Lima, 40.9 percent, La Victoria, 34.3 percent; and Rimac, 37.2 percent. See Perú, *Censo de Lima 1931,* p. 187.

15 José María Arguedas, *Yawar fiesta* (Santiago, 1968), p. 63.

16 In addition to the work of Arguedas, another novelist, Pedro Reyes, *A la Capital* (Chiclayo, 1933), esp. pp. 7, 42, 48, portrays well the attraction of Lima for *provincianos.*

17 Alcides Carreño, interview, May 4, 1971. For discussion of the correlation between perceived economic betterment and migration see also Juan J. Ballón, "La realidad económica en el Perú," *El Comercio,* August 16, 1931, p. 15; Martinez de la Torre, *Apuntes para una interpretación* 1: 69, 72–74; and Leoncio M. Palacios, *Encuesta sobre presupuestos familiares obreros realizada en la ciudad de Lima en 1940* (Lima, 1944), p. 113. The analysis of data from a study of contemporary Lima squatter settlements made by Henry A. Dietz, "Becoming a *Poblador:* Political Adjustment to the Urban Environment in Lima, Peru" (Ph.D. diss., Stanford University, 1974) shows that a large proportion of the rural-urban migrants in the 1920s were atracted by a combination of better economic opportunities and a search for adventure. His data also show that few migrants (25 percent of the sample) had difficulty in obtaining work upon their arrival in Lima..

18 Quoted in *Ciudad y campo y caminos* 4, no. 46 (1929): 49.

19 To follow the thinking behind the *oncenio's* push for road building and the extent of the enterprise see *Ciudad y campo y caminos* (1925–29), esp. 5, no. 41 (August–September 1928): 44–74; 6, no. 46 (1929): 63, 87–89, 95, 102–3. A list of all major highways built by the Leguía government is contained in Capuñay, *Leguía,* pp. 197–99. The year-by-year evolution of construction is traced in Perú, Ministerio de Hacienda y Comercio, *Extracto estadístico del Perú: 1931–1932–1933* (Lima, 1935), p. 160. Leguía also undertook extensive railroad construction, building 1,038 kilometers between 1920 and 1929 as compared to the 280 kilometers built in the previous decade.

20 Arguedas, *Yawar fiesta,* pp. 64–65. See also Olinda Celestino, *Migración y cambio estructural: La comunidad de Lampián* (Lima, 1972), pp. 29–30; *Ciudad y campo y caminos* 2, no. 20, (August, 1926): vi–vii; and Basadre, *Historia de la República,* 13: 238.

21 Material on the cultural exchange produced by road building projects during the *oncenio* is found in "El proceso del gamonalismo" *Amauta* (Lima), no. 25 (July–August 1929): 79; Arguedas, *Yawar fiesta,* pp. 36–37, 64–65, 70; *Ciudad*

y campo y caminos 2, no. 13 (December 1925): 41; 3, no. 33 (September 1927): 32; 5, no. 41 (August-September 1928): 49; Gabriel Escobar Moscoso, "The Cultural Situation in Southern Peru: Institutional Factors and Their Relationship to Social and Economic Development Possibilities," in Perú, Comité del Plan Regional de Desarrollo del Sur del Perú, *Southern Peru Development Project,* vol. 22 (Lima, 1959), p. 47; Celestino, *Lampián,* p. 30; and Giorgio Alberti and Rodrigo Sánchez, *Poder y conflicto social en el valle del Mantaro* (Lima, 1974), p. 40.

22 An excellent summary of the general correlation between migration and the extension of communications networks is Julio Cotler, "Actuales pautas de cambio en la sociedad rural del Perú," in José Matos Mar et al., *Dominación y cambios en el Perú rural* (Lima, 1969), pp. 67-68. For specific references to this phenomenon in the 1920s see Arguedas, *Yawar fiesta,* pp. 63-64, 71; and Luis Alberto Sánchez, *Testimonio personal,* vol. 1 (Lima, 1969), p. 288.

23 The most extensive and carefully researched treatment of the *Concripción Vial* is Wilfredo Kapsoli, "El campesinado peruano y la ley vial," *Campesino* (Lima) 1, no. 2 (May-August 1969): 1-17. See also Thomas M. Davies, Jr., *Indian Integration in Peru: A Half Century of Experience, 1900-1948* (Lincoln, Nebr., 1974), pp. 82-85. Besides migration Indian revolts increased in response to the *Conscripción Vial.*

24 Julián Torres, Andrés Valero, and Vicente Valero to Ministro de Fomento, Todos los Santos, May 24, 1928, in *Amauta,* no. 12, (May-June 1928): 36. A similar statement may be found in a letter from the community of Coyllorqui to *Labor,* January 15, 1929, p. 6. On the structure of early-twentieth-century Indian communities and their decay see Celestino, *Lampián,* pp. 21-23; and Carlos Iván Degregori and Jurgen Golti, *Dependencia y desintegración estructural en la comunidad de Pacaraos* (Lima, 1973), pp. 14, 18. Dobyns and Doughty, *Peru,* pp. 210-12, describe the impact of population growth on the Indian communities and their decay. For further information on the upward revaluation of land and the race for new property see François Chevalier, "Temoignages littéraires et disparités de croissance: l'expansion de la grande propriété dans le Haut-Pérou au XX siécle," *Annales: économies, sociétés, civilisations* 21, no. 4 (July-August 1966): 818-21; Arguedas, *Yawar fiesta,* p. 25; Jean Piel, "A propos d'un soulèvement rural péruvien au début du vingtième siècle: Tocroyac (1921)," *Revue d'histoire moderne et contemporaine* 14 (October-December 1967): pp. 388-89, 394; Hildebrando Castro Pozo, *Del Ayllú al cooperativismo socialista,* 2d ed. (Lima, 1969), p. 205; and Eugene Hammel, *Power in Ica: The Structure of a Peruvian Community* (Boston, 1969), pp. 20-22. Discussions of the system of liberal legislation that facilitated *hacienda* growth include Chevalier, "L'expansion de la grande propriété," p. 829; and Carlos Iván Degregori, "Proceso histórico y desintegración estructural en la communidad de Pacaraos" (Lima, 1970), mimeographed, pp. 15, 17, 26-27. Two excellent descriptions of how land was actually transferred from *comunidades* to *latifundios* are José Antonio Encinas, *Contribución a una legislación tutelar indígena* (Lima, 1918), pp. 26-28; and Arguedas, *Yawar fiesta,* pp. 28-29.

25 In Encinas, *Legislación tutelar,* p. 22. The author does not name the *hacen-*

dado. See also Chevalier, "L'expansion de la grande proprieté," pp. 816, 824; Castro Pozo, *Del Ayllú,* pp. 202–3; Arguedas, *Yawar fiesta,* pp. 28–29; and Baltazar Caravedo Molinari, *Clases, lucha política y gobierno en el Perú (1919–1933)* (Lima, 1977), pp. 28–31.

26 On changes in *hacienda* ownership see Henry Favre, "Evolución y situación de las haciendas en la región de Huancavelica," in Favre, et al., *La hacienda en el Perú* (Lima, 1967), pp. 244–45; and José Matos Mar, "Las haciendas del Valle de Chancay," ibid., p. 344. Information on technological change is contained in Ricardo Bustamante Cisneros, "El urbanismo en el Peru," *Letras* (Lima) 1, no. 1 (1929): 86; "El proceso de gamonalismo," *Amauta* 25 (July–August 1929), p. 76; Julio Cotler, "Actuales pautas de cambio en la sociedad rural del Perú," in Matos Mar et al., *Dominación y cambios,* p. 79; and Matos Mar, "Las haciendas del Valle de Chancay," in Favre et al., *La hacienda en el Perú,* p. 346.

27 Un Pequeño Comerciante to *Labor,* January 15, 1929, p. 5.

28 Piel, "Tocroyoc," p. 388; Ballón, "La realidad económica," p. 15; and Degregori, "Proceso histórico," pp. 16, 31. The reaction of peasants to the rise of the large *hacienda* and the disintegration of the Indian community also took the forms of individual and community violence. Numerous former *comuneros* apparently found life on the *haciendas* intolerable and often reacted by committing criminal acts, including vandalism and physical assault. In a careful study of indigenous crime during the late nineteenth and early twentieth centuries a clear correlation was discovered between the increases in the rate of infractions committed by Indians and the encroachment of large *haciendas* on Indian communities. In part this correlation reflects the difficulties experienced by peasants in accustoming themselves to work on the *haciendas* and also by a rise in the number of personal feuds between men who were still *comuneros* over the distribution of the reduced amount of land still controlled by their communities. See José Antonio Encinas, *Causas de la criminalidad indígena en el Perú* (Lima, 1919), esp. pp. 18–19, 22, 76–78. Indian revolts also increased in areas of large-scale *latifundio* growth. Tensions that built from the turn of the century onward came to a head in the 1920s in various areas of rural Peru including Canas, Espinar, Ayacucho, La Mar, Ica, Tayacaja, Huancané, Lampa, Azángaro, and Quispicanchi. See Piel, "Tocroyoc," esp. pp. 392, 394–95; Wilson Reátegui, "Movimientos campesinos de La Mar e Ica," *Campesino* 1, no. 2 (May–August 1969): 18–30; and Robert Marett, *Peru* (London, 1969), p. 141.

29 Excellent descriptions of the *enganche* system are contained in Peter Klarén, *Modernization, Dislocation and Aprismo: Origins of the Peruvian Aprista Party, 1870–1932* (Austin, Tex., 1973), pp. 26–30; and Alberti and Sánchez, *Poder y conflicto social,* pp. 23, 51–52, 199–200. A good summary statement on the rise of mining in this period is contained in Caravedo Molinari, *Clases, lucha política,* pp. 25–27.

30 Perú, *Censo de Lima 1931,* pp. 43–44, 167–69, 183–91; and Roque García

Frías, "Intensidad absoluta y relativa de la emigración provinciana al Departamento de Lima," *Estadística peruana* 3, no. 5 (July 1947): 54-66. The natural population increase is determined by finding the difference between births and deaths in a specific time period. As large as the number of rural migrants seems, it is probably underestimated since the 1931 census did not account for the substantial migration flow from the rural areas of the Province of Lima.

31 García Frías, "Emigración provinciana," pp. 55-59; and Perú, *Censo de Lima 1931,* p. 188.

32 Perú, *Censo de Lima 1931,* pp. 183-85. The factor analysis was executed by John Cole and provided to me by Henry Dietz. It remains unpublished to date. Cole's development factor includes fourteen weighted variables. On the basis of those variables, he produced a ranking of all Peruvian provinces. Of course, infrastructural modernization, technological imports, and increased commercial exploitation of many areas in the thirty intervening years between the two censuses consulted make any exact calculations impossible. Yet certain trends do seem to predominate. It is interesting to note that in his study of migration to Lima during the contemporary period ("Poblador"), Henry Dietz finds a similar phenomenon of movement to the city from the middle ranges of Peruvian provinces.

33 Information on the importance of kinship and friendship ties in the migrants' decision to move are derived from data collected by Dietz, "Poblador." Arguedas, *Yawar fiesta,* pp. 72-73, contains an excellent description of the formation and functions of a regional association in Lima. Of the forty-four regional associations in existence in 1928, nearly two-thirds had been founded between 1922 and 1924, a fact that attests to the significant quantitative change in migration flow during the 1920s. A complete list of these associations, with information about the organizational structures, is contained in Cipriano A. Laos, *Lima "La Ciudad de los Virreyes"* (Lima, 1928), pp. 283-90. Evidence of their working class makeup is culled from Arguedas, *Yawar fiesta,* pp. 72-73, and the Lima newspapers of the 1920s that listed the activities of regional associations under the heading of *"Vida obrera"* (working class life"). See for example *La Crónica,* May 30, 1923, p. 11. An excellent description of their diverse functions is obtained in Dobyns and Doughty, *Peru,* pp. 214-15.

34 *El cancionero de Lima* (Lima), no. 1480, (n.d.), p. 5.

35 Calculations on the growth of the population and the labor force were made utilizing information from Perú, *Resumen del censo de Lima 1920,* pp. 147-57, 166-82; and Perú, *Censo de Lima 1931,* pp. 102-26, 197-201. For information on employment structure in Lima at the end of the nineteenth century see the incomplete yet interesting figures in Joaquin Capelo, *Sociología de Lima* (Lima, 1895), 1: 121; 2: 36-45. The use of data on professions presents various problems, including lack of clarity or honesty on the part of individuals in identifying their occupations; insufficient care in the classification of jobs by the census authorities; and the momentary shifting of employment brought on by a depression period, making a census taken at that time

somewhat misleading regarding the usual occupational mix of the area. These latter qualifications do not appear to have been of great importance in the 1920 census, which was taken in a time of nearly full employment. But in the 1931 census various occupational sectors appear to have considerably lower numbers of workers than they probably had throughout most of the *oncenio*. Notably the construction sector, the first to be hit by unemployment with the depression-caused drop in public works along with almost all forms of building, shows only a 77.97 percent gain over the 1920s. This figure probably falls far short of truly portraying the occupational importance of an area in which a large part of Lima's new proletariat found work. Similarly, "peddlers" shows an astronomical rise of 1,333.68 percent, also reflecting the conditions of underemployment and marginal unemployment created by the economic crisis.

36 Perú, *Censo de Lima 1931,* p. 93. Racial data alone are hardly a sufficient measure of working class growth due to the difficulties involved in the classification of race, particularly the differences of criteria applied by different censuses and even different census takers in the same census. Nevertheless, in the context of other measures, racial data reveal an important facet of lower class expansion.

37 Without specific economic data on diverse areas of the city the identification of working class districts presents special problems. Therefore, various procedures have been employed to gauge poverty in Lima *barrios,* and findings from specific types of data seem to reinforce each other. Racial composition of various districts is shown in Perú, *Censo de Lima 1931,* p. 94. For information on comparative population density see Alberto Alexander, *Las causas de la desvalorización de la propiedad urbana en Lima* (Lima, 1932), p. 5; and Bromley and Barbagelata, *Evolución urbana de Lima,* p. 117. Calculations on school attendance were computed utilizing material from Perú, *Censo de Lima 1931,* p. 163. Bromley and Barbagelata, *Evolución urbana de Lima,* p. 115, also present figures demonstrating that in 1931 the highest number of *callejones* and *solares* relative to the total number of buildings belonged to Rimac with 228 of 1,316. Another factor to be considered is that while certain working class areas definitely grew in population during the 1920s, other more traditional *barrios,* including parts of Rimac and Barrios Altos, exhibited a more moderate growth pattern. This phenomenon was due in part to the fact that the traditional zones were already filled up by 1920, and many new residents had to seek shelter elsewhere.

38 Perú, *Censo de Lima 1931,* pp. 194–95, 206; *The West Coast Leader,* March 21, 1933, p. 22; Magalí Sarfatti Larson and Arlene Eisen Bergman, *Social Stratification in Peru* (Berkeley, Calif., 1969), pp. 9, 111–12, 119; and Garrett, "Oncenio of Leguía," pp. 17–20.

39 Alejandro Garland, *El Perú en 1906* (Lima, 1907), pp. 209–10; J.P. Cole, *Estudio geográfico de la gran Lima* (Lima, 1957), chap. iv, pp. 17, 23; Martinez de la Torre, *Apuntes para una interpretación* 1: 190, 192, 243–44; Ricardo Mariátegui Oliva, *El Rimac: barrio limeño de abajo el puente (Lima, 1956),*

pp. 149-53; David Chaplin, *The Peruvian Industrial Labor Force* (Princeton, N.J. 1967), p. 97; *Lima, Ciudad de los Reyes en el IV centenario de su fundación* (Lima, 1935), pp. 243–46; Denis Sulmont, *El movimiento obrero en el Perú: 1900-1956* (Lima, 1975), p. 74; Garrett, "Oncenio of Leguía," pp. 136–37; and Herbold, "Peruvian Administrative System," p. 117. A list of industries in Lima in 1895 is contained in Capelo, *Sociología de Lima* 1: 127–30.

40 Lavalle, *La gran guerra,* pp. 39–41, 67–68; Basadre, *Historia de la República,* 12: 425, 440; Yepes del Castillo, *Un siglo de desarrollo capitalista,* pp. 168–69, 258; Perú, *Censo de Lima 1908* 2: 912; and *Perú, Censo de Lima 1920,* p. 173.

41 *Martinez de la Torre, Apuntes para una interpretación* 1: 61; Alexander, *Causas de la desvalorización,* p. 18; Chaplin, *Peruvian Industrial Labor Force,* p. 279; Sarfatti Larson and Eisen Bergman, *Social Stratification in Peru,* p. 104; Vicente Gay, *En el imperio del sol* (Madrid, 1925), pp. 232–33; and "La industria textil en Lima," *Ciudad y campo y caminos* 5, no. 39 (May 1928): i–ii. A striking example of the widespread preference for foreign industrial products was the suggestion by the government newspaper in 1926 that locally made products bear foreign labels in order to make them more saleable. See Herbold, "Peruvian Administrative System," p. 117.

42 See chapter 6.

43 An excellent summary of early labor organization is contained in Sulmont, *Movimiento obrero: 1900-1956,* pp. 68–73. Zitor (pseud.), "Historia de las principales huelgas y paros obreros habidos en el Perú," (Lima, 1946), BNP, No. E12221, esp. pp. 5, 8; *Estatutos y reglamentos de la Federación de Obreros Panaderos "Estrella del Perú"* (Lima, 1905); James L. Payne, *Labor and Politics in Peru* (New Haven, Conn., 1965), pp. 28–29, and 34–35; Sarfatti Larson and Eisen Bergman, *Social Stratification in Peru,* pp. 106–8; Luis Felipe Barrientos, *Los tres sindicalismos* (Lima, 1958), p. 148; and Luis Miró Quesada, *La cuestión obrera en el Perú* (Lima, 1904), pp 20–21. For lists of early labor organizations see Laos, *Lima,* pp. 270–83, which includes the dates of foundation and summaries of statutes of these institutions; and Miró Quesada, *La cuestión obrera,* pp. 50–51. Detailed descriptions of the port workers' strike of 1912 and its consequences are contained in César Lévano, *La verdadera historia de la jornada de las ocho horas en el Perú* (Lima, 1969); Martinez de la Torre, *Apuntes para una interpretación,* 1: 396–415; and Wilfredo Kapsoli Escudero, *Luchas obreras en el Perú por la jornada de las 8 horas (1900-1919)* (Lima, 1969), pp. 17–18.

44 Ulloa Sotomayor, *Organización social,* p. 149. See also p. 143.

45 Carlos Barba, "Memorias de una gesta," *Caretas* (Lima), no. 434 (April 28, 1971): 24. See also Basadre, *Historia de la República,* 12: 248; and Martinez de la Torre, *Apuntes para una interpretación,* 1: 405, 409.

46 Klarén, *Modernization and Aprismo,* pp. 95–96; Payne, *Labor and Politics,* pp. 34–35; Yepes del Castillo, *Un siglo de desarrollo capitalista,* p. 220; and Espejo, "Leguía inaugura," p. 15. For a detailed listing of the increasing number of labor disputes in 1917 see Federico Ortíz Rodriguez, "La crisis social," *La Prensa,* January 1, 1918, p. 11. A sharp correlation between a ris-

ing cost of living and labor protests is drawn by Sulmont, *Movimiento obrero: 1900–1956,* pp. 77–79.

47 See chapter 6 for details.

48 The eight-hour strike is treated at length in chapter 6. The most detailed information on the strike is contained in the Lima newspapers of the time, including *La Prensa* and *El Tiempo* (December 25, 1918–January 25, 1919).

49 A statement of the basic principles of the mutual aid societies is found in *Estatutos de la Sociedad de "Artesanos de Auxilios Mutuos," fundada el 26 de septiembre de 1860* (Lima, 1925), passim. Anarchist thinking was summed up by Manuel González Prada, *Anarquía* (Santiago, 1936), esp. p. 12–13. For details on anarchism, anarcho-syndicalism, and the labor movement see Piedad Pareja, *Anarquismo y sindicalismo en el Perú* (Lima, 1978); and Sulmont, *Movimiento obrero: 1900–1956,* pp. 83–84.

50 Interview, December 1970. Other sources on the move to syndicalism are Yepes del Castillo, *Un siglo de desarrollo capitalista,* pp. 219, 270–71; Ulloa Sotomayor, *Organización del trabajo,* p. 142; Basadre, *Historia de la República* 12: 489; and Payne, *Labor and Politics,* pp. 37–38.

51 This area is treated extensively in chapter 6.

52 Arturo Sabroso Montoya, interview, May 5, 1970; Arturo Sabroso Montoya, *Réplicas proletarias* (Lima, 1934), pp. 122–24; and Payne, *Labor and Politics,* pp. 40–41.

53 Martinez de la Torre, *Apuntes para una interpretación* 1: 245–46, 3: 38–39; José Carlos Mariátegui, *Ideología y política* (Lima, 1969), p. 199; and *Labor,* December 29, 1928, p. 6, February 2, 1929, p. 2.

54 The most complete source for the study of the effects of the depression on the Peruvian economy is the *Boletín Mensual de la Cámara de Comercio de Lima* (1930–32). For export and import data see Perú, *Extracto estadístico 1931–32–33, p. 67.* Other useful material on the depression in Peru may be found in *La revista semanal,* 4, no. 165 (October 30, 1930): 1–3, 4, no. 166 (November 6, 1930): 11; *Ultimas Noticias,* January 10, 1931, pp. 5–6; *The West Coast Leader,* January 26, 1932, p. 1; *El Comercio,* May 17, 1931, p. 3; *Mundial,* 11, no. 539 (October 17, 1930): 8, 11; no. 541 (October 31, 1930): 8.

55 An excellent breakdown of unemployment by profession and by migrants vs. nonmigrants is presented in Perú, *Censo de Lima 1931,* pp. 248–57. In addition see *La Tribuna,* July 7, 1931, p. 4; M. Montero Bernales and Alberto Alexander, "Contemplando la situación de los desocupados y la crisis de la vivienda," *El Perú* (January 23, 1931), p. 2; *El Comercio,* October 18, 1930, p. 4; February 9, 1931, p. 1; *El Perú,* August 4, 1931, p. 2; Martinez de la Torre, *Apuntes para una interpretación* 1: 111–13, 379; Junta Departamental de Lima Pro-Desocupados, *Memoria al 31 de diciembre de 1934* (Lima, 1935), pp. xvi–xxv; and Reyes, *A la Capital,* p. 44. There is some evidence that a moderate dip in employment preceded the depression by one year. See Martinez de la Torre, *Apuntes para una interpretación* 1: 111–13.

56 *La Noche,* August 25, 1931, p. 6; *El Perú,* January 20, 1931, p. 1; Amauta (pseud.), "Cartas al provinciano desconocido," *Mundial* 11, no. 540 (October

24, 1930): 32; and Martinez de la Torre, *Apuntes para una interpretación,* 1: 116.

57 El Comité Ejecutivo del Partido Comunista del Perú, *Manifesto del Partido Comunista* (March 14, 1931), CHS-BNP; Martinez de la Torre, *Apuntes para una interpretación* 1: 75, 2: 36; Sabroso Montoya, *Réplicas proletarias,* pp. 130–31; and Basadre and Ferrero, *Cámara de Comercio,* p. 134. The evolution of the transit strike is traced in *La Crónica,* August 3–9, 1931.

58 "Un estudio estadístico revela lo pavoroso que es la situación de la población escolar," *La Crónica,* August 14, 1931, p. 4; Montero Bernales and Alexander, "Contemplando la situación de los desocupados," p. 2; Alexander, *Causas de la desvalorización,* pp. 4–5; *El Comercio,* September 26, 1930, p. 1; *Libertad,* September 28, 1930, p. 7; and Perú, *Censo de Lima 1931,* p. 38. Another indicator of the suffering caused by the depression was the fall in the number of lower class marriages. In the working class district of La Victoria, for example, not one marriage was performed in November of 1930. See Amauta, "Cartas al provinciano desconocido," *Mundial* 11, no. 546 (December 5, 1930): 38. Notwithstanding the acknowledged difficulty of the situation in Peru, conditions there appear to have been less serious than in certain other Latin American countries, notably Chile. See the following for evaluations of Peru's position in relation to other areas: *El Comercio,* October 19, 1930, p. 2, December 10, 1930, p. 2.

CHAPTER 4: SÁNCHEZCERRISMO I
THE HERO APPEARS

1 *La Prensa,* August 24, 1930, p. 1.

2 Próspero Pereyra, interview, March 4, 1971; *El Comercio* (Extraordinary Edition), August 25, 1930, p. 1; and Carlos Miró Quesada Laos, *Sánchez Cerro y su tiempo* (Buenos Aires, 1947), pp. 75–80.

3 *El Comercio* (Extraordinary Edition), August 25, 1930, p. 1; Leguía, *Yo tirano,* pp. 49–50; Víctor Villanueva, *El militarismo en el Perú* (Lima, 1962), pp. 63–64; Miró Quesada Laos, *Sánchez Cerro,* pp. 77–79, More, *Zoocracia,* pp. 20–25; Ugarteche, *Sánchez Cerro,* 1: 147, 229; Basadre, *Historia de la República,* 13: 387, 389; *Noticias* (Arequipa), August 25, 1930, p. 1; Guillermo Thorndike, *El año de la barbarie* (Lima, 1969), p. 90; and Próspeɾo Pereyra, interview, March 4, 1971.

4 *La Prensa,* August 28, 1930, p. 2; *El Comercio,* August 28, 1930, pp. 1–3; and *La Crónica,* August 28, 1930, p. 1, all contain detailed accounts of Sánchez Cerro's reception in Lima.

5 Máximo Ortíz, interview, February 22, 1971.

6 Víctor Andrés Belaunde, *La crisis presente 1914–1939* (Lima, 1940), p. 146. Belaunde's feelings were echoed by other prominent men of the times, including Manuel Vicente Villarán, "La opinión del doctor Villarán sobre la situación política," *El Comercio,* September 11, 1930, p. 3; Arenas, *Algo de*

una vida, p. 188; Felipe Barreda y Laos, in *La República,* August 25, 1930, p. 1; and Polar, *Viejos y nuevos tiempos,* p. 114.

7 Meza, *40 años,* p. 19.

8 "Autógrafa de Sánchez Cerro" (September 27, 1919), in Ugarteche, *Sánchez Cerro,* 1: 27.

9 Ibid. For biographical data on Sánchez Cerro the following works were consulted: Miró Quesada Laos, *Sánchez Cerro,* esp. pp. 31–35; "Biografía del Tnte-Coronel don Luis M. Sánchez Cerro," *La Opinión,* December 8, 1931, p. 1; Elías Lozada Benavente, *Vaivenes de la política* (Lima, 1938), p. 145; Ugarteche, *Sánchez Cerro* 1: 3; Basadre, *Historia de la República* 14: 8; and Manuel Castillo Vasquez, "Semblanzas," *Revista policial del Perú* (Lima, August 30, 1932) p. 27. An interview with Pedro Ugarteche on February 13, 1971, also provided interesting information on Sánchez Cerro's early life.

10 Quoted by Eudocio Ravines, *La gran estafa* (Mexico, 1952), pp. 168–69.

11 Quoted in Miró Quesada Laos, *Sánchez Cerro,* pp. 31–32. For discussions of Sánchez Cerro's revolts in 1919 and 1922 see Miró Quesada Laos, *Sánchez Cerro,* p. 39; and Andrés Gallardo Echevarría, "1922: Motín en el Cuzco y las pretensiones del Tigre Leguía," *Oiga* 8, no. 369 (April 10, 1970): 44–45. On Sánchez Cerro's activities in the 1920s see Orazio A. Ciccarelli, "The Sánchez Cerro Regimes in Peru, 1930–1933" (Ph.D. diss., University of Florida, 1969), p. 24; and Miró Quesada Laos, *Sánchez Cerro,* pp. 37, 43.

12 Information on conspiracies previous to the revolt is derived from Alfonso Llosa G.P., interview, May 29, 1971; Pedro Ugarteche, interview, February 13, 1971; Andrés Gallardo Echevarría, "El regreso del Mayor Luis M. Sánchez Cerro," *Oiga* 8, no. 373 (May 8, 1970): 40, and "La Revolución de Arequipa del 22 de agosto de 1930," *Oiga* 8, no. 376 (May 29, 1970): 52–53. On the events in Arequipa the following were consulted: *La Noche,* July 21, 1931, p. 4; Jorge Maldonado Llosa, who took part in the revolt, interview, March 8, 1971; Basadre, *Historia de la República* 13: 383, 14: 12; Rafael Larco Herrera, *Memorias* (Lima, 1947), p. 122; *Noticias,* August 31, 1930, p. 1; Miró Quesada Laos, *Sánchez Cerro,* pp. 71–73; Chirinos Pacheco, *Perú nuevo,* pp. 11, 22; and Víctor Villanueva, *Así cayó Leguía* (Lima, 1977), pp. 110–14.

13 The *"Manifiesto de Arequipa"* has been reprinted in various places. Recently it was published in Ugarteche, *Sánchez Cerro* 1: 113–17. In the years since its appearance a lively controversy has developed concerning the identity of the writer of the *"Manifiesto de Arequipa."* Those most frequently named as its author include: José Luis Bustamante y Rivero, a prominent Arequipa attorney, a minister in one of Sánchez Cerro's cabinets, and later president of Peru (1945–48); Sánchez Cerro himself; Major Alejandro Barco, Sánchez Cerro's second in command during the revolt and also subsequent cabinet minister; and the whole group of officers that conspired together in Arequipa. On the basis of my own research, it appears that the truth is close to a combination of the above interpretations. At some time Sánchez Cerro seems to have asked Bustamante y Rivero to propose a draft declaration, and that draft may have provided the basis for the subsequent document. However, the final

"Manifiesto" was drawn up collectively by the officers that met weekly to plan the revolt, with specific sections assigned to different men. Each article was then debated by the group as a whole and a final form decided upon. The belief that Barco wrote the *"Manifiesto"* probably derives from the fact that he acted as the secretary of the group and was charged with writing up their deliberations. What is ultimately important is not who wrote each part of a document that presented in conventional terms a relatively conservative critique of the Leguía regime, but rather that Sánchez Cerro's tenacious planning inspired its writing in the first place and his perseverance and leadership gave it a place in history.

14 Dora Mayer de Zulén, *El oncenio de Leguía* (Callao, 1931), p. 3.

15 Mayer de Zulén presents an excellent discussion of Leguía's continued popularity in ibid. See especially pp. 1-4, 14-15. See also Sánchez, *Testimonio personal* 1: 281, 290-291; Basadre, *Historia de la República* 13: 371, 376-377; Basadre, *Perú Problema,* p. 173; Rafael Belaunde, "La dictadura del Perú su derrocamiento," *El Comercio,* November 19, 1930, p. 5; Waldo Frank, "Two Peruvians: Dictator and Poet," *The New Republic* 67, no. 871 (August 12, 1931), p. 332; Lawrence Dennis, "What Overthrew Leguía: The Responsibility of American Bankers for Peruvian Evils," *The New Republic* 64, no. 824 (September 17, 1930), pp. 117-18; Sarfatti Larson and Eisen Bergman, *Social Stratification in Peru,* pp. 9, 108-9; and Pike, *Andean Republics,* p. 181.

16 Basadre, *Historia de la República,* 13: 364-65; and Solís, *Once años,* p. 55. The widely read Lima daily newspaper *Libertad,* for example, published articles in nearly every issue from September to December 1930 describing Leguía's repressive tactics.

17 Alfonso Llosa G.P., interview, May 29, 1971; Jorge Maldonado Llosa, interview, March 8, 1971; Villanueva, *Militarismo,* p. 58; Chirinos Pacheco, *Perú nuevo,* pp. 34-35; Ugarteche, *Sánchez Cerro* 1: 107-8; Arnold Roller, "Revolt in Peru," *The Nation* 131, no. 3402 (September 17, 1930), pp. 292-94; Ernesto Galarza, "Debts, Dictatorship and Revolution in Bolivia and Peru," *Foreign Policy Reports* (May 13, 1931), p. 116; More, *Zoocracia,* pp. 13, 17-18; Karno, "Leguía," pp. 246-47; and Víctor Villanueva, *El Apra en busca del poder, 1930-1940* (Lima, 1975), pp. 31-32. The best treatment of the erosion of military support for Leguía is Villanueva, *Así cayó Leguía,* pp. 21-24.

18 An excellent discussion of Leguía's falling out with the economic elite is presented by Karno, "Leguía," pp. 234-41, 247. A public expression of the growing animosity between the president and these groups appeared in *Mundial* 9, no. 496 (December 20, 1929): 20. See also Garrett, "Oncenio of Leguía," pp. 201-2.

19 On the growing public dissatisfaction with Leguía see Garrett, "Oncenio of Leguía," pp. 211-12; *Mundial* 11, no. 564 (June 5, 1931): 30; Basadre, *Perú problema,* pp. 186-87; Basadre, *Historia de la República* 13: 375; More, *Zoocracia,* pp. 10-11; Belaunde, "La dictadura," p. 5; Roller, "Revolt in Peru," p. 293; Villanueva, *Militarismo,* pp. 61-62; and *La Prensa,* August 30, 1930, p. 1.

20 Oscar R. Benavides to Luis M. Sánchez Cerro, Nice, October 9, 1930, in Ugarteche, *Sánchez Cerro* 1: 232–33. See also *Libertad, El Comercio, La Prensa,* and *La Crónica* from September to December 1930 for examples of anti-Leguía muckraking.

21 "La palabra del Comandante Sánchez Cerro," *La Prensa,* October 6, 1930, p. 1; *El Comercio,* August 28, 1930, p. 2, February 23, 1931, p. 3; *La Prensa,* September 13, 1930, p. 1; Ugarteche, *Sánchez Cerro* 2: xxv–xxvi, 223–24; and Chirinos Pacheco, *Perú nuevo,* p. 17. In an interview on May 29, 1971, Alfonso Llosa G.P. also provided details on these events. The prevalence of this anticivilian bent among military officers and specifically their animosity towards civilian politics has been thoughtfully analyzed in Thomas M. Davies and Brian Loveman, eds., *The Politics of Antipolitics: The Military in Latin America* (Lincoln, Nebr., 1978), esp. pp. 10–11.

22 For an excellent summary of those acts which netted the most political capital for Sánchez Cerro during his presidency of the *junta* see the handbill printed in 1931, "Leguía y Sánchez Cerro," ASC. In an interview on March 4, 1971, Próspero Pereyra affirmed that the Lima working classes lived in constant fear that they would be forced to do road work under *Conscripción Vial.* Other sources of information on the application of *Conscripción Vial* in Lima include "La Conscripción Vial en Lima," *Ciudad y campo y caminos* 2, no. 19 (July 1926), iv; and Sabroso Montoya, *Réplicas proletarias,* pp. 111–13. The joyful reaction to Sánchez Cerro's abolition of the system is recounted in Sánchez, *Testimonio personal* 1: 328; Basadre, *Historia de la República* 14: 21; and Kapsoli, "La ley vial," p. 15.

23 *El Comercio,* September 18, 1930, p. 5.

24 *El Comercio,* September 18, 1930, p. 5.

25 *El Comercio,* September 18, 1930, p. 5. Other sources of information on the political effects of these measures are Eudocio Ravines, "El momento político peruano," *La Noche,* July 5, 1931, p. 6; Basadre, *Historia de la República,* 14: 49–50; *El Comercio,* October 18, 1930, p. 4; and *El Comercio* (afternoon edition), November 20, 1930, p. 1.

26 Eguiguren's activities are described in detail by the man himself in Luis Antonio Eguiguren, *En la selva política* (Lima, 1933), esp. pp. 4–6, 11, 14, 24–25. See also an interview of Eguiguren published in *Mundial* 11, no. 537 (October 3, 1930): 23.

27 "Boletín oficial emitido por el Teniente Coronel Luis M. Sánchez Cerro," (August 27, 1930), in Ugarteche, *Sánchez Cerro* 1: 152.

28 The initial support of labor leaders for Sánchez Cerro was revealed by Arturo Sabroso Montoya, interview, February 26, 1971. The decree dissolving the CGTP and the reply of the union federation are reprinted in Martinez de la Torre, *Apuntes para una interpretación* 3: 216–19. Student protests of this measure are chronicled in Escajadillo, *La revolución unversitaria,* pp. 224–27. Descriptions of mineworkers' strikes may be found in *The West Coast Leader,* September 16, 1930, p. 1, November 11, 1930, p. 1. Basadre, *Historia de la República* 14: 41–44, summarizes the labor disturbances and the government's reaction to them.

29 One exception to the conservative-leaning new cabinet members was José Luis Bustamante y Rivero, Sánchez Cerro's civilian collaborator in Arequipa who was appointed minister of justice and education.

30 Luis M. Sánchez Cerro to Antonio Sánchez Cerro, Arequipa, June 4, 1916, in Ugarteche, *Sánchez Cerro* 1: 17. Other sources on Sánchez Cerro's increasingly evident conservatism include Manuel O. Velasquez, "Carta que dirige al Presidente de la Junta de Gobierno, el Director de La Prensa, Sargento Mayor Manuel O. Velasquez," *La Prensa,* November 24, 1930, p. 1; and Ciccarelli, "The Sánchez Cerro Regimes," pp. 37–38, 58.

31 Sánchez Cerro's interest in finding experienced collaborators is described in Juan Pacheco Cateriano to Manuel Bustamante de la Fuente, Lima, September 27, 1931, AdBLF; and Ciccarelli, "The Sánchez Cerro Regimes," p. 27. For information on the conservatives' attempt to gain Sánchez Cerro's favor see Pedro de Osma to *La Nación,* Buenos Aires, September 10, 1930, in *El Comercio,* September 16, 1930, p. 3; and Escajadillo, *La revolución universitaria,* p. 75.

32 *El Comercio,* November 26, 1930, p. 1. Criticism of Sánchez Cerro was voiced in *La Hora* (Lima), November 25, 1930, p. 1.

33 David Samanéz Ocampo to Luis M. Sánchez Cerro, Cuzco, January 11(?), 1931, ASC.

34 *El Comercio,* February 7, 1931, p. 1.

35 Manuel Bustamante de la Fuente to Luis Alberto Sánchez, Lima, May 23, 1970, AdBLF. Bustamante de la Fuente's assertion that Sánchez Cerro was reluctant to give up power is substantiated by Víctor Andrés Belaunde in a letter to Bustamante de la Fuente, Lima, January 29, 1931, AdBLF, in which Belaunde tells of Sánchez Cerro's intransigence in an interview with him. The wording of Sánchez Cerro's acceptance of his candidacy is found in Ugarteche, *Sánchez Cerro* 2: 72–73. See also the description of these events in Ciccarelli, "The Sánchez Cerro Regimes," pp. 41–44, and "A la nación: Manifiesto de la Junta Directiva del Comité de Saneamiento y Consolidación Revolucionaria," (January 19, 1931), in Ugarteche, *Sánchez Cerro* 2: 69–70. Telegrams urging Sánchez Cerro's candidacy appeared in *El Comercio* and *La Prensa* from January 18 through February 22, 1931. Evidence that many of these telegrams were the product of official encouragement is found in letters from David Samanéz Ocampo to Luis M. Sánchez Cerro, Aplao, Cuzco, January 22, 1931, AdBLF; and José Falconí Solari to Manuel Bustamante de la Fuente, Aplao, January 23, 1931, AdBLF.

36 Much of Acción Republicana's opposition appeared in editorials in its newspaper. See *El Perú,* January 11, 1931, p. 2, and February 19, 1931, p. 2, for examples. See also *Mundial* 9, no. 549 (December 26, 1930): 11; *El Comercio,* January 19, 1931, p. 3; Basadre, *Historia de la República* 14: 53–54; and Ugarteche, *Sánchez Cerro* 2: xxvii.

37 *El Perú,* February 21, 1931, p. 2. For a detailed description of the revolt and its defeat see *El Comercio,* February 21, 1931, pp. 3–7; and "Los leguiístas pretendieron libertar a su jefe el Tirano para subirlo nuevamente al poder," CHS/BNP.

38 In *El Comercio,* February 21, 1931, p. 7.

39 Manuel Bustamante de la Fuente to Luis Alberto Sánchez, Lima, May 23, 1970, AdBLF.

40 The most detailed account of the events in Arequipa was written by one of the leaders of the movement: Manuel Bustamante de la Fuente, "Apuntes para la historia" (Lima, 193?), AdBLF. Other important primary documents include the minutes of a meeting of the Junta de Gobierno de Arequipa, March 3, 1931, AdBLF; "Manifiesto de la Junta Provisional de Gobierno," Arequipa, February 24, 1931, AdBLF; J. Alberto Cuentas to Manuel Bustamante de la Fuente, Puno, November, 1931, AdBLF; and Manuel Bustamante de la Fuente to Director of *El Deber,* Arequipa, March 17, 1931, in *Mundial* 11, no. 562 (March 27, 1931): 24.

41 Comandante Dianderas to Coronel González and Comandante Cabrera, Arequipa, February 22, 1931, in *El Pueblo,* February 23, 1931, p. 1. Other sources on the motives behind the growing opposition to Sánchez Cerro within the armed forced include Jorge Maldonado Llosa, interview, March 8, 1971; Moisés Pinto Bazurco, *Cuatro siglos y cuatro proletariados más japonización y lucha intestina* (Lima, 1935), passim; Andrés Gallardo Echevarría, "1930–1931 los tormentosos seis meses de la Junta de Gobierno," *Oiga* 8, no. 377 (June 5, 1970): 48; Ambassador Dearing to Secretary of State, Lima, September 13, 1930, in Ugarteche, *Sánchez Cerro* 2: 222; and Ciccarelli, "The Sánchez Cerro Regimes," pp. 44–45.

42 "Se deroga el decreto-ley sobre elecciones generales," *El Comercio,* February 24, 1931, p. 1; "La Marina de Guerra del Perú a la Nación," February 27, 1931, AdBLF; "Por acuerdo de la Junta de Gobierno se invita a una conferencia los representantes de la opinión pública," *El Comercio* (afternoon edition), February 28, 1931, p. 1; and "Texto de la renuncia del Presidente de la Junta de Gobierno," *La Prensa,* March 2, 1931, p. 1.

43 These events are chronicled in Basadre, *Historia de la República,* 14: 62–65. Telegrams between Jimenez and the *junta* in the South were reprinted in *El Pueblo,* March 6, 1931, p. 1. The impression in Lima that Jimenez would work for Sánchez Cerro's restoration was communicated to me by Alfonso Llosa G.P. in an interview, May 29, 1971, and is supported by Basadre, *Historia de la República,* 14: 62–63. Before coming to power, Samanéz had been something of a political chameleon, pledging his avid support to Sánchez Cerro's *"autoelección"* campaign at the same time that he incited numerous personal friends to plot the overthrow of the *caudillo*-president. See David Samanéz Ocampo to Luis M. Sánchez Cerro, Aplao, Cuzco, January 22, 1931, AdBLF; David Samanéz Ocampo to Manuel Bustamante de la Fuente, Cuzco, January 8, 1931, AdBLF; and David Samanéz Ocampo to Manuel Bustamante de la Fuente, Cuzco, January 26, 1931, AdBLF.

44 *El Comercio,* February 25, 1931, p. 1.

45 *The West Coast Leader,* March 3, 1931, p. 6.

46 Arenas, *Algo de una vida,* p. 190; Ugarteche, *Sánchez Cerro* 2: 100; and Miró Quesada Laos, *Sánchez Cerro,* pp. 99–100, 108–9.

47 Luis M. Sánchez Cerro, "Proclama del Presidente de la Junta de Gobierno a las tropas que marchan a Arequipa," in *El Comercio,* February 28, 1931, p. 7.
48 Luis M. Sánchez Cerro in Ugarteche, *Sánchez Cerro* 2: 110–11.
49 Luis M. Sánchez Cerro, "A la nación," *El Comercio,* March 8, 1931, p. 2. Other sources consulted on the public reaction to the ouster and Sánchez Cerro's maneuvers include *El Comercio* (extraordinary edition), February 23, 1931, p. 1, February 25, 1931, p. 4; and Basadre, *Historia de la República* 14: 59.
50 Manuel L. Hernani to Manuel Bustamante de la Fuente, Camaná, March 6, 1931, AdBLF.
51 *La revista semanal* 5, no. 184 (March 12, 1931), p. 1.

CHAPTER 5: SÁNCHEZCERRISMO II
THE HERO CAMPAIGNS

1 *The West Coast Leader,* June 30, 1931, supplement.
2 These events were reported at length in the Lima newspapers. See *La Tribuna,* July 3, 1931, p. 2; *El Comercio,* July 3, 1931, p. 2; *La Noche,* July 2, 1931, p. 2; *La Opinión,* July 3, 1931, p. 2; *La Crónica,* July 3, 1931, pp. 8–9; *Patria,* July 2, 1931, pp. 1–2; and *La Prensa,* July 3, 1931, p. 1. I also received two firsthand accounts from Próspero Pereyra, interview, March 4, 1971; and Máximo Ortiz, interview, February 22, 1971. The government's attempt to foil Sánchez Cerro's return to Peru was only one example of their deep-seated hostility toward him. Sánchez Cerro made various attempts to return earlier from his European exile only to be denied entry by the *junta.* They finally gave in due to pressure from various prominent men on his behalf and in the belief that his chances for electoral victory were slim. The maneuvering of both sides is revealed in letters found in the Sánchez Cerro Archive and is well summarized by Ugarteche, *Sánchez Cerro* 1: 125–47.
3 The primary importance of political style is certainly not a feature limited to Peru in 1931. An interesting discussion of the elements of political style is contained in Murray Edelman, *The Symbolic Uses of Politics* (Urbana, Ill., 1964), esp. pp. 31, 40.
4 Belaunde, *Trayectoria y destino* 2: 774, 789. *Cholo* is the commonly used term in Peru to denote a person of mixed European and Indian blood.
5 José Santos Chocano, "Elogio póstumo a Luis M. Sánchez Cerro; a la memoria de los Marqueses de Torre Tagle i de la Riva Agüero," Panamá, May 24, 1933, AdBLF.
6 Próspero Pereyra, interview, March 4, 1971. Various observers have commented on the importance of Sánchez Cerro's racial appearance in the campaign, including Pedro Ugarteche, interview, February 1, 1971; Basadre, *Historia de la República* 14: 156–58; *La Noche,* August 7, 1931, p. 2; Carlos Zavala Oyague, in ed. Alfredo Moreno Mendiguren, *Repertorio de noticias breves sobre personajes peruanos,* (Madrid, 1956), p. 524; and *Nuestro Diario,* September 14, 1931, p. 8.

7 Quoted by Máximo Ortiz, interview, February 22, 1971. For similar accounts see *The West Coast Leader,* September 1, 1931, p. 17; and *La Prensa,* July 5, 1931, p. 3. Almost every day between July and October, 1931, *El Comercio* printed long lists of visitors to Sánchez Cerro's headquarters.

8 A dance of coastal Peru of Afro-Hispanic origins performed by the urban and rural poor. For accounts of these parties the following were consulted: Máximo Ortiz, interview, February 22, 1971; and Miró Quesada Laos, *Sánchez Cerro,* p. 60.

9 Máximo Ortiz, interview, February 22, 1971.

10 Quoted by Jorge Maldonado Llosa, interview, March 8, 1971. Similar accounts were given by Pedro Ugarteche, interview, February 16, 1971; Alfonso Llosa G.P., interview, May 29, 1971; Máximo Ortiz, interview, February 22, 1971; Miró Quesada Laos, *Sánchez Cerro,* pp. 32–33; and Espejo, "Leguía inaugura," p. 17. Insight into the military side of Sánchez Cerro's paternalism was provided in personal conversations with Thomas Davies.

11 "A la mejicana," *Cancionero popular* (December, 1931?), p. 4.

12 Juan Pacheco Cateriano to Manuel Bustamante de la Fuente, Lima, October 12, 1931, AdBLF.

13 Máximo Ortiz, interview, February 22, 1971.

14 Sánchez, *Testimonio personal* 1: 327. See also Miró Quesada Laos, *Sánchez Cerro,* p. 45.

15 Accounts of Sánchez Cerro's violent outbursts include Meza, *40 años,* pp. 18, 84–86; Máximo Ortiz, interview, February 22, 1971; and *La Noche,* August 17, 1931, p. 2.

16 The particular attractiveness of a combined affectionate-stern father figure is not limited to the case of Sánchez Cerro in Peru. In his interesting study, *Sharecroppers of the Sertão: The Economics of Dependence on a Brazilian Plantation* (Stanford, Calif., 1971), Allen W. Johnson emphasizes the importance for rural landlords in northeastern Brazil of maintaining a status of superiority in relations with their peons. Comparing two specific landlords, he concludes that the one that insisted on and received deference, respect, and obedience from his tenants was held in considerably higher regard than the other, who disliked exercising authority and adopted a more liberal stance toward his workers. See pp. 124–28.

17 Luis Antonio Eguiguren, speech, September 12, 1930, in Ugarteche, *Sánchez Cerro* 1: 211; and Luis M. Sánchez Cerro, speech, in *El Comercio,* October 5, 1931, p. 3. Other examples include the addresses of Sánchez Cerro published in *La Prensa,* August 30, 1930, p. 1, October 26, 1930, p. 1; and *El Comercio,* December 14, 1930, p. 5.

18 Quoted by Pedro Ugarteche, interview, February 13, 1971.

19 Sánchez Cerro, speech, in *El Comercio,* November 25, 1930, p. 1. See also his speech of August 22, 1931, in Ugarteche, *Sánchez Cerro* 2: 178–81.

20 Luis M. Sánchez Cerro, speech, August 22, 1931, in Ugarteche, *Sánchez Cerro,* 2: 181.

21 Information on Sánchez Cerro's speaking style has been culled from various sources including the speeches themselves. Of particular help were the personal impressions of many of those who actually saw the commandant-candidate speak, including Próspero Pereyra, interview, March 4, 1971; Pedro Ugarteche, interview, February 16, 1971; Alfonso Llosa G.P., interview, May 29, 1971; and Jorge Maldonado Llosa, interview, March 8, 1971. Printed sources that comment on Sánchez Cerro's speechmaking include Miró Quesada Laos, *Sánchez Cerro,* pp. 46–47, 85; Manuel R. Layseca, "El ideal de los reprobos y Sánchez Cerro," *La Prensa,* August 29, 1930, p. 4; *El hombre de la calle 1,* no. 44 (July 18, 1931): 25; Pike, *Modern History,* p. 251; José Matías Manzanilla, in Moreno Mendiguren, ed., *Repertorio de noticias,* p. 523; and *El Comercio,* December 14, 1930, p. 5. For an interesting analysis of the important aspects of political oratory, see the article of Richard Nixon's speechwriter, William Safire, in "The Nixon Style," *San Francisco Chronicle,* October 30, 1971, p. 19.

22 Max Weber, *The Theory of Social and Economic Organization* (Glencoe, Ill., 1947), p. 358.

23 The view of Sánchez Cerro as a father figure was expressed in various speeches by Sánchezcerrista club presidents. See, for example, speech by president of Club Bolívar Sánchez Cerro Ancashino No. 2, in *La Prensa,* July 11, 1931, p. 9; speech by president of Centro Político Lealtad y Firmeza No. 4, in *El Comercio,* July 23, 1931, p. 8; "Acta de Fundación del Sub-Comité Nacional Obrero Sánchez Cerro No. 1," ibid., July 31, 1931, p. 2; and Comité Sánchezcerrista to Luis M. Sánchez Cerro, ibid., July 20, 1931, p. 3. See also Ugarteche, *Sánchez Cerro* 2: xlvii.

24 Comité Nacional Obrero Sánchez Cerro No. 1 to *El Comercio,* in *El Comercio,* July 2, 1931, p. 4; Club Vanguardia Bellavista Comandante Luis M. Sánchez Cerro to *El Comercio,* ibid., July 19, 1931, p. 11; and Comité Departamental de Ancash-Sánchez Cerro to *El Comercio,* ibid., August 26, 1931, p. 15.

25 F. J. de Santillana to Luis M. Sánchez Cerro, Lima, December 9, 1931, ASC. See also the following statements in the same tone: Comité Político Chosicano to *El Comercio,* in *El Comercio,* July 2, 1931, p. 4; "Acta de fundación del Club Triunfo de la Opinión del Mercado de la Aurora Sánchez Cerro No. 1," ibid., July 6, 1931, p. 4; "Acta de fundación del Club Lealtad y Firmeza Sánchez Cerro No. 1," ibid., July 14, 1931, p. 8; speech by Secretary General of Partido Regionalista Ancashino, in *La Opinión,* July 31, 1931, p. 6; "Acta de Fundación del Club Unión y Firmeza Luis M. Sánchez Cerro," in *El Comercio,* August 12, 1931, p. 2; Club Libertad No. 1 Pro Elección Sánchez Cerro to *El Comercio,* ibid., August 19, 1931, p. 13; Club Pro Juventud Lima Sánchez Cerro No. 2 to *El Comercio,* ibid., August 28, 1931, p. 17; Juventud Revolucionaria de Lambayeque, "Manifiesto a los pueblos del Departamento de Lambayeque," (September 2, 1931), in Ugarteche, *Sánchez Cerro* 2: 171–72; Club Sánchez Cerro No. 1 de Lince y Lobatón to Luis M. Sánchez Cerro, in

La Opinión, December 10, 1931, p. 6; Club Unión Mercado Central y la Parada No. 1 Pro Candidatura Sánchez Cerro, to *La Opinión,* ibid., December 10, 1931, p. 4; and Modesto Soto, "Los dos grandes factores de la popularidad de Sánchez Cerro," ibid., Janaury 8, 1932, p. 7.

26 "CREDO CERRISTA," 1931, CHS/BNP.

27 Club Sánchez Cerro No. 1 Huancavelica to Luis M. Sánchez Cerro, in *El Comercio,* December 9, 1931, p. 14. See also "Manifiesto de la Colectividad Piurana," ibid., August 4, 1931, p. 4; ibid., August 13, 1931, p. 2; and speech by María Luisa de Revoredo, president of Club Femenino Lobatón Sánchez Cerro No. 1, ibid., October 4, 1931, p. 3.

28 *La Opinión,* October 5, 1931, p. 2.

29 Máximo Ortiz, interview, February 22, 1971. Similar feelings were expressed by Próspero Pereyra, interview, March 4, 1971; and Pedro Ugarteche, interview, February 16, 1971. See also Belaunde, *Crisis presente,* p. 146; and Miró Quesada Laos, *Autopsia de los partidos,* p. 475.

30 Sánchez Cerro, in *The West Coast Leader,* September 1, 1931, p. 17.

31 Manuel Bustamante de la Fuente to Luis Alberto Sánchez, Lima, May 23, 1970, AdBLF.

32 The following discussions of the symbolic value of ideology and platforms in the understanding of political movements were consulted: François Bourricaud, *Ideología y desarrollo: el caso del Partido Aprista Peruano* (México, 1966), passim.; Edelman, *Symbolic Uses of Politics,* p. 116; Angus Stewart, "The Social Roots," in *Populism,* ed. Ionescu and Gellner, p. 191; and Kenneth Minogue, "Populism as a Political Movement," ibid., p. 205.

33 "L.M. Sánchez Cerro," and "El Triunfo de la Revolución de Arequipa," *Cancionero popular* August, 1931?), pp. 1–3.

34 *La Opinión,* October 11, 1931, p. 1. See also Luis M. Sánchez Cerro, *Programa de gobierno del Comandante Luis M. Sánchez Cerro* (Lima, 1931), pp. 3–4.

35 "Hechos y no palabras" (1931), ASC; "La obra de Luis M. Sánchez Cerro," *El Día,* July 18, 1931, p. 1; *La Opinión,* June 10, 1931, p. 6, June 12, 1931, p. 5, July 7, 1931, p. 4; and *La República,* July 14, 1931, p. 6.

36 Sánchez Cerro, *Programa de gobierno,* p. 4; "La Revolución de agosto está incompleta," "Declaraciones del Comandante Sánchez Cerro," (September 3, 1931), in Ugarteche, *Sánchez Cerro* 2:211–12; and *El Comercio,* September 23, 1931, p. 3.

37 Sánchez Cerro, *Programa de gobierno, passim.*

38 *Ibid., pp. 30–36.*

39 The term "negative reference" is borrowed from Lee Benson, *The Concept of Jacksonian Democracy* (Princeton, N.J., 1961).

40 Luis M. Sánchez Cerro, speech, in *El Comercio,* October 5, 1931, p. 3; "Obreros recordad!!" (1931), ASC; "El Leguiísmo y el Apra," *El Comercio,* August 26, 1931, p. 6; "Pueblo alerta," *La Tribuna,* August 25, 1931, p. 1; *La Opinión,* December 25, 1931, p. 6; and Ciccarelli, "The Sánchez Cerro Regimes," pp. 117–19.

41 Probably the single most important document in this vein was "El

Anti-patria," *El Comercio,* August 19, 1931, p. 1. Pedro Ugarteche, interview, February 13, 1931, explicitly said that the central Sánchezcerrista headquarters constantly spread rumors about the horrors of an Apra victory. For interesting commentary on the negative reference campaign and its effects see Manuel Bedoya, *El otro Caín* (Lima, 1933?), pp. 10–11; and Basadre, *Historia de la República,* 14:155.

42 Luis M. Sánchez Cerro, speech in *El Comercio,* August 23, 1931, p. 5.

43 Ibid., p. 16. See also Sánchez Cerro, *Programa de gobierno,* pp. 6–7; *El Perú,* August 3, 1931, p. 6; "Partido Unión Revolucionaria principios fundamentales" (1931?), ASC; and Ciccarelli, "The Sánchez Cerro Regimes," p. 104.

44 Luis M. Sánzhez Cerro, interview, in *The West Coast Leader,* March 3, 1931.

45 Juan Pacheco Cateriano to Manuel Bustamante de la Fuente, Lima, October 12, 1931, AdBLF.

46 Luis M. Sánchez Cerro to Luis Humberto Delgado, Colón, Panamá, June 16, 1931, ASC. Whether friend of foe of Sánchez Cerro, there was general agreement that he would have the majority of the *lumpenproletariat* vote. For pro-Sánchez Cerro analyses see F.J. Pinzas to Luis M. Sánchez Cerro, Lima, May 31, 1931, ASC; Eguiguren, *Selva política,* p. 38; *El Comercio* (afternoon ed.), July 22, 1931, p. 2, August 25, 1931, p. 5; and *La Opinión,* July 31, 1931, p. 6. Specific working class institutions directly pledged their support to the commandant-candidate. See Hermandad de Cargadores y Zahumadores del Señor de los Milagros de Nazarenas to *La Opinión,* ibid., October 7, 1931, p. 7; and Confederación de Artesanos Union Universal del Perú to Luis M. Sánchez Cerro, Lima, June 18, 1932, ASC. Aprista sources that also attest to Sánchez Cerro's popularity among the urban poor include Víctor Raúl Haya de la Torre, interview, December 11, 1970; *La Tribuna,* July 8, 1931, p. 8, July 9, 1931, p. 7, September 8, 1931, p. 2, October 11, 1931, p. 3; Rómulo Meneses, *Aprismo femenino peruano* (Lima, 1934), pp. 39–40, 53; Manuel Seoane, in Pedro Muñiz and Carlos Showing, *Lo que es el Aprismo,* (Bogotá, 1932), p. 138; and Sánchez, *Testimonio personal* 1: 352, 355. Other observers who concur on the makeup of Sánchezcerrismo are Jorge Basadre, interview, January 11, 1971; Víctor Andrés Belaunde, *Meditaciones peruanas,* 2d ed., (Lima, 1963), p. 259; and Alfredo Hernandez Urbina, *Nueva política nacional* (Trujillo, 1962) pp. 75–76.

47 The reticence of the elites to support either major candidate is reflected in both their public expressions and private writings of the time. See Belaunde, *Trayectoria y destino* 2: 773; Enrique Bustamante y Ballivián to César A. Rodriguez, Lima, September 12, 1931, Víctor Andrés Belaunde to Manuel Bustamante de la Fuente, Lima, September 19, 1931, A. Rodriguez to Manuel Bustamante de la Fuente, Lima, September 29, 1931, and Juan Pacheco Cateriano to Manuel Bustamante de le Fuente, Barranco, October 8, 1931, AdBLF; *La revista semanal* 5, no. 204 (July 30, 1931): 28; *El Comercio,* July 31, 1931, p. 1; *Nuestro Diario,* September 8, 1931, p. 8; *Mundial* 11, no. 580 (September 25, 1931): 17; Pike, *Modern History,* pp. 251–52; and Luis Alberto Sánchez, *Haya de la Torre y el Apra* (Santiago, 1955), p. 258.

48 Private correspondence is the best source for tracing the elite's swing over to

Sánchez Cerro. See Lima to Cayaltí, August 20, 1931 and Cayaltí to Ramón Aspillaga, October 27, 1931 in Lorenzo Huertas Vallejos, *Capital burocrático y lucha de clases en el sector agrario* (Lambayeque, Peru, 1920–1950) (Lima, 1974), pp. 75–77; Felipe Barreda y Laos to Luis M. Sánchez Cerro, Buenos Aires, March 21, 1931, Luis M. Sánchez Cerro to Ignacio Brandaríz, Paris, April 13, 1931, and Luis Humberto Delgado to Luis M. Sánchez Cerro, Lima, June 17, 1931, ASC; Juan Pacheco Cateriano to Manual Bustamante de la Fuente, Lima, September 1, 1931, and October 12, 1931, AdBLF. Of great interest in this regard are the notes of José de la Riva Agüero (October 7, 1931), Manuscript Collection of the Biblioteca Nacional del Perú (hereafter referred to as BNP), E1157; and Arenas, *Algo de una vida,* pp. 195, 199.

49 Pedro Ugarteche, interview, February 13, 1971. See also Juan Pacheco Cateriano to Manuel Bustamante de la Fuente, Barranco, September 5, 1931, AdBLF.

50 For information on Sánchez Cerro's cabinet ministers consult Felipe Barreda y Laos to Luis M. Sánchez Cerro, Buenos Aires, November 16, 1931, ASC; *The West Coast Leader,* December 8, 1931, p. 17; More, *Zoocracia,* pp. 52–53; More, *Multitud,* pp. 131–32; and Ciccarelli, "The Sánchez Cerro Regimes," p. 157. Evidence of the extent of Civilista influence, over Sánchez Cerro is contained in Oscar Miró Quesada to Luis M. Sánchez Cerro, Lima, April 19, 1932, ASC.

51 Jorge Basadre, interview, February 1, 1971; Alfonso Llosa G.P., interview, May 29, 1971; Eguiguren, *Selva política,* p. 35; Club Nacional to Luis M. Sánchez Cerro, Lima, October 3, 1930, ASC; More *Zoocracia,* p. 52; José Raúl Cáceres, *El pasmo de una insurgencia* (Lima, 1942), p. 53; Víctor Raúl Haya de la Torre, *Construyendo el Aprismo. Artículos y cartas desde el exilio (1924–31)* (Buenos Aires, 1933), pp. 143–44; Miró Quesada Laos, *Sánchez Cerro,* p. 34; *La Tribuna,* July 5, 1931, p. 2; *The West Coast Leader,* September 1, 1931, p. 17; *Nuestro Diario,* September 17, 1931, p. 4; and Espejo, "Leguía inaugura," p. 16.

52 Most of my information on the formative period of the right-wing nationalists is from personal interviews of one of them, Pedro Ugarteche, February 13 and 16, 1931. The "declaration of war" was published in *La Prensa,* July 22, 1924, p. 3. For examples of this group's nationalism see Pedro Ugarteche, *La política internacional peruana durante la dictadura de Leguía* (Lima, 1930), esp. pp. 14, 22–23, 36, 38–44, 48; and "Memorial del Comité Universitario de Defensa de los Derechos Internacionales del Perú" (August 26, 1922), CHS-BNP. Biographies of prominent young Sánchezcerrista leaders were published in *La Opinión,* October 8, 1931, p. 3, and October 10, 1931, pp. 4–5.

53 Pedro Ugarteche, interview, February 16, 1971.

54 Pedro Ugarteche, interview, February 13, 1971. See also "Posturas falsas," *Claridad* 2, no. 7 (November 1–15, 1924): 11; "Nuestras cuestiones internacionales," *Evolución* (September 12, 1923), in Ugarteche, *Sánchez Cerro* 1: 273; Sánchez, *Testimonio personal* 1: 145, 315, and Basadre, *Historia de la República* 13: 71–72.

55 Alfredo Herrera, in Moreno Mendiguren, *Repertorio de noticias,* p. 523. Pedro Ugarteche, interviews, December 3, 1970, and February 13, 1971, expressed similar views. See also Ugarteche, "El deber de la hora actual," *El Comercio,* February 23, 1931, p. 3; Ugarteche, *La política internacional,* pp. 42–43; and Ugarteche, *Sánchez Cerro* 2: xix.

56 Pedro Ugarteche, interview, February 16, 1971.

57 El Amauta, "Cartas al provinciano desconocido," *Mundial* 11, no. 575 (August 21, 1931): 30 Próspero Pereyra, interview, March 4, 1931, reinforced the view that there were wide differences between socioeconomic groups within Sánchezcerrismo: "They had very little contact with the masses. Because they were always, what shall I say, very despotic. They thought they were big men," The following were consulted regarding the beginnings of Sánchezcerrista organization: Pedro Ugarteche, interviews, February 1, 13, 16, 1971; Ugarteche, *Sánchez Cerro* 2: xxviii, xliv-xlviii; *El Comercio,* September 7, 1930, p. 17, October 4, 1930, p. 4. Lists of the members of the Directing Council and Central Committee of the Unión Revolucionaria and the editorial board of *La Opinión* may be found in *El Comercio,* August 18, 1931, p. 5; "Junta Central Directiva de la Unión Revolucionaria," ASC; Ciccarelli, "The Sánchez Cerro Regimes," p. 93; and Miró Quesada Laos, *Sánchez Cerro,* p. 152. The functioning of the party organization was described by Pedro Ugarteche, interviews, February 13, 16, 1971; "Estatutos del Partido Unión Revolucionaria," ASC; Eguiguren, *Selva política,* p. 39; Basadre, *Historia de la República* 14: 159–61; *El Comercio,* July 31, 1931, p. 4; and Espejo, "Leguía inaugura," p. 17.

58 Except for *El Comercio* and *La Opinión,* the six other Lima daily papers and the three most widely read weekly publications strongly opposed Sánchez Cerro. Sánchez Cerro's ties with *El Comercio* are outlined by Pedro Ugarteche, interview, February 16, 1971; and Basadre, *Historia de la República* 14: 162–63. On Eguiguren's contributions to Sánchez Cerro's campaign see Eguiguren, *Selva política,* pp. 3, 32–36, 38, 42–44; *El Comercio,* July 30, 1931, p. 8; *La Opinión,* August 4, 1931, p. 7; and *La Noche,* August 17, 1931, p. 4.

59 Máximo Ortiz, interview, February 22, 1971.

60 For accounts of the Sánchezcerrista demonstrations see *El Comercio,* August 23, 1931, pp. 5, 16, October 5, 1931, p. 3; *La Opinion,* October 5, 1931, p. 1; *The West Coast Leader,* October 6, 1931, p. 10; Federico Ortiz Rodriguez, "Página del pueblo," *Mundial* 11, no. 575 (August 21, 1931): 40; and Amauta, "Cartas al provinciano desconocido," ibid., 11, no. 576 (August 28 1931): 5. Information on the groundwork laid for demonstrations is available from *El Perú,* August 11, 1931, p. 2; *La Noche,* August 11, 1931, p. 3; *El Comercio,* August 13, 1931, p. 4, August 29, 1931, p. 2; *La Opinión,* October 4, 1931, p. 7; and "Rodear al Comandante Sánchez Cerro. . ." (1931), ASC.

61 Máximo Ortiz, interview, February 22, 1971.

62 Although the use of alcohol at club meetings was roundly denied by the Sánchezcerristas in 1931, Máximo Ortiz, interview, February 22, 1971, told the author that in his political club "there were always drinks for the meetings. We

never lacked for someone who would buy a bottle of *pisco* (grape brandy)."
Much of the information about the makeup and activities of the clubs was
provided to the author in interviews with Máximo Ortiz, February 22, 1971;
Próspero Pereyra, March 4, 1971; and Pedro Ugarteche, February 13, 1971.
Also, newspapers carried extensive reports on these clubs, showing their independent organization: *El Comercio,* July 12, 1931, p. 11, August 31, 1931, p.
4; and *La Opinión,* August 30, 1931. Each club had its own membership card.
Pictures of these documents were printed in *La Tribuna,* September 1, 1931, p.
6, September 13, 1931, pp. 6–7, October 11, 1931, p. 10.

63 This figure may, of course, be incorrect. It is difficult to know how many of
the institutions listed were in reality paper organizations, created to impress
the populace with Sánchez Cerro's strength. Also, it is impossible to know
how many people each club contained. Nevertheless, given the mass turnouts
at Sánchezcerrista demonstrations and Sánchez Cerro's final vote in Lima (29,
131), the above calculation may not be far from correct.

64 The figure of 155 was reached on the basis of a day-by-day study of the an-
nouncements of club meetings printed in *El Comercio* and *La Opinión* between June and November 1931. The most complete listings of Sánchezcerrista
organizations in existence appeared in the following issues of *El Comercio:*
August 21, 1931, p. 8; August 22, 1931, p. 15; August 23, 1931, p. 4; October
4, 1931, p. 1. An interesting description of how clubs received their name is
contained in "Acta de Fundación del Club Paz Orden y Trabajo Sánchez
Cerro No. 1," *El Comercio,* July 14, 1931, p. 11: "The whole membership and
each individual member together are working towards the single goal of the
well-being of the Fatherland which we understand to be: Work, order, and
peace constitute our banner."

65 The number of *provinciano* clubs was calculated from the lists cited in note 67
below. For specific information on these organizations see "A los Piuranos,"
El Comercio, July 12, 1931, p. 1; "Los hijos de Huancayo en la casa particular
del Comandante Sánchez Cerro," *La Opinión,* July 31, 1931, p. 7; and *El
Comercio,* August 28, 1931, p. 10. Information was also provided by Próspero
Pereyra, interview, March 4, 1971.

66 Details on what functions the clubs fulfilled in the campaign were provided by
Máximo Ortiz, interview, February 22, 1971; and *El Comercio,* July 13, 1931,
p. 2, August 21, 1931, pp. 3, 13, August 29, 1931, p. 13. During the campaign
the Sánchezcerristas were accused of using *capituleros* on various occasions.
See *La Tribuna,* May 18, 1931, p. 1; *Nuestro Diario,* September 7, 1931, p. 8;
and *The West Coast Leader,* September 15, 1931, p. 17. See also Sánchez,
Testimonio personal 1: 354. The Sánchezcerristas always denied these allegations. See, for instance, "Protestado de una falsedad," *El Comercio,* August
28, 1931, p. 17. But interviews with Sánchezcerristas I carried out show that
the accusers were closer to the truth: Pedro Ugarteche, February 13, 1971; and
Máximo Ortiz, February 22, 1971.

CHAPTER 6: APRA I
THE BIRTH OF AN ALLIANCE

1 Unificación Obrera Textil Vitarte to Textile Workers, Vitarte, December 23, 1918, in Martinez de la Torre, *Apuntes para una interpretación* 1: 417–18.

2 According to Haya de la Torre, interview, November 4, 1970, the laborers who contacted him after the publication of his proposal in *La Prensa,* August 20, 1918, p. 7, were Arturo Sabroso Montoya, Fausto Posada, Adelberto Fonkén, Fausto Navarro, and Delfín Lévano. Sabroso was to be the most important link between Haya and anarchist leaders. His stature within the labor movement is evidenced by his role as co-founder of the most influential labor publication of the 1920s, *El obrero textil.* Haya's initial meetings with strike leaders are described in Víctor Raúl Haya de la Torre, "La jornada de 8 horas," *APRA* 14, no. 5 (February 22, 1946): 26; Ricardo Temoche Benites, *El APRA y los trabajadores* (Lima, 194?), p. 4; Felipe Cossío del Pomar, *Víctor Raúl,* 2 vols. (México, 1961, 1969), 1: 94; and Lévano, *La verdadera historia,* p. 38. For information on the contacts between the strikers and the students see the series of letters reprinted in Martinez de la Torre, *Apuntes para una interpretación* 1: 422–24, 436–37.

3 *La Prensa* (afternoon edition), January 13, 1919, p. 1; and "1919: la tempestad obrera," *Caretas,* no. 477 (May 21, 1973): 46–48.

4 Quoted by Arturo Sabroso Montoya, interview, December, 1970. Cossío del Pomar, *Víctor Raúl* 1: 99, reprints similar statements of Haya on the same occasion.

5 On the anarchists' reaction Arturo Sabroso Montoya, interview, February 26, 1971, was consulted. For information on Haya's role as intermediary the following were useful: Víctor Raúl Haya de la Torre, interview, November 4, 1970; Haya de la Torre, "La jornada," pp. 28–29; Cossío del Pomar, *Víctor Raúl* 1: 97–99; Martinez de la Torre, *Apuntes para una interpretación* 1: 442–45; Barba, "Memorias de una gesta," p. 26; *La Prensa,* January 14, 1919, p. 4; *Variedades* 15, no. 568 (January 18, 1919): 46; Guillermo Thorndike, *El año de la barbarie* (Lima, 1969), pp. 76–77; and Sánchez, *Testimonio personal* 1: 146.

6 Haya de la Torre, "La jornada," p. 29; Sánchez, *Haya y el Apra,* p. 56; and *Haya de la Torre: su vida y sus luchas* (Lima, 1957), p. 24. Valuable information on Haya's rise to leadership in the eight-hour movement was obtained from Arturo Sabroso Montoya, interview, December 1970; Cossío del Pomar, *Víctor Raúl* 1: 95, 98, 100–101; and Haya de la Torre, "La jornada," pp. 27–28.

7 The scene of the eight-hour victory was described by Haya de la Torre, "La jornada," p. 30; Haya de la Torre, interview, November 4, 1970; *La Prensa,* Janaury 16, 1919, p. 3; Cossío del Pomar, *Víctor Raúl* 1: 103–5; Arturo Sabroso Montoya, interview, December 1970; and Martinez de la Torre, *Apuntes para una interpretación* 1: 450. An excellent short summary of the

events of the strike is contained in Basadre, *Historia de la República* 12:486–47.

8 For detailed data on Haya's family background see the family tree and other information presented by Eugenio Chang-Rodriguez, *La literatura política de González Prada, Mariátegui y Haya de la Torre* (Mexico, 1957), esp. pp. 213–14. Also useful in this regard have been Luis Eduardo Enriquez, *Haya de la Torre: La estafa más grande de América* (Lima, 1951) p. 62; Espejo, "Leguía inaugura," p. 17; Víctor Raúl Haya de la Torre, interview, December 12, 1970; Cossío del Pomar, *Víctor Raúl* 1: 17–36, passim; and Sánchez, *Haya y el Apra,* p. 25.

9 Víctor Raúl Haya de la Torre, "Mis recuerdos de González Prada," *Repertorio americano* (San José, Costa Rica) 15, no. 6 (August 13, 1927): 84–85. Also reprinted in Sánchez, *Haya o el político,* p. 53; Sánchez, *Haya y el Apra,* p 37; and Klarén, *Modernization and Aprismo,* p. 94.

10 Víctor Raúl Haya de la Torre, interview, December 12, 1970.

11 Some of González Prada's most suggestive writings in this regard include "Propaganda y ataque," in his *Páginas libres* (Lima, 1966) 2: pp. 154, 158–59; *Horas de lucha,* esp. pp. 47–51, 70; and *Anarquía,* pp. 16, 133. Haya confirmed González Prada's influence over him in an interview, December 12, 1970.

12 Víctor Raúl Haya de la Torre, interview, May 20, 1971. Other references to this game may be found in Cossío del Pomar, *Víctor Raúl* 1: 33; and Haya de la Torre, *Haya de la Torre luchas,* p. 6.

13 Víctor Raúl Haya de la Torre, interview, December 1970.

14 Felipe Destefano, quoted by Arturo Sabroso Montoya, interview, December 1970.

15 Quoted by Arturo Sabroso Montoya, interview, December 1970.

16 In the reconstruction of the events surrounding the foundation of the Federación Textil the following sources were particularly valuable: Víctor Raúl Haya de la Torre, interview, November 24, 1970; Arturo Sabroso Montoya, interviews, May 5, 1970, December 1970, February 26, 1971; Haya de la Torre, "La jornada," pp. 26, 30; *La Prensa,* January 17, 1919, p. 1; *El obrero textil* 3, no. 33 (February 1, 1922): 2; Ricardo Temoche Benites, *El Apra y los trabajadores,* (Lima, 194?), pp. 4–5; Barrientos, *Tres sindicalismos,* pp. 156–57; Cossío del Pomar, *Víctor Raúl* 1: 105; and Basadre, *Historia de la República* 12: 488. For a copy of the "Act of Foundation" of the Federación Textil see *La Tribuna,* January 1, 1946, p. 11.

17 Demetrio Flores, *Medio siglo de vida sindical en Vitarte* (Vitarte, 1961), p. 50. For further information on Haya's campaign see Jeffrey Klaiber, S.J., "The Role of the González Prada Popular Universities in the Development and Formation of the Peruvian Aprista Movement" (M.A. thesis, Loyola University, 1968), p. 54. On Haya's activities in Lima see Víctor Raúl Haya de la Torre to *El obrero textil,* Lima, July 1, 1920, in *El obrero textil* 1, no. 13 (July 1, 1920): 3; and Cossío del Pomar, *Víctor Raúl* 1: 129–30, 142.

18 The foundation, evolution, and impact of the Universidad Popular has been comprehensively covered by Jeffrey L. Klaiber, S.J., "The Popular Universities and the Origins of Aprismo, 1921–1924," *Hispanic American Historical*

Review 55, no. 4 (November 1975): 693–715; and also in his "González Prada Popular Universities," passim. On the student assembly see *Primer Congreso Nacional de Estudiantes reunido en la sede universitaria del Cuzco del 11 al 20 de marzo de 1920* (Lima, 1920), passim, esp. pp. 12, 24, 37; Sánchez, *Haya o el político,* p. 67; and Klaiber, "González Prada Popular Universities," pp. 41–42. The idea of the Universidad Popular was not original to Haya. Previously in Great Britain, France, and Soviet Russia similar institutions had been created. Also the Latin American University Reform movement had sponsored popular universities in Argentina and Chile. In Peru these schools were preceded by "popular lectures" and university extension courses. Haya's first experience with the idea of a popular university was during his youth in the provincial city of Trujillo. In an interview on December 11, 1970, Haya stated in this regard: "In Trujillo in the year 1916 the idea of a popular university came to me. I read some books about the popular universities in France. I used to say to my father, 'The problem of this country is ignorance.' This was my first discovery. I don't know how I came to it . . . The Popular University of Trujillo was a failure. There I gained experience in the things you should not do." Sources consulted on his search for teachers include: Víctor Raúl Haya de la Torre, interviews, November 12, 1970, December 11, 1970; Enrique Cornejo Koster, "Crónica del movimiento estudiantil peruano," in *La Reforma Universitaria,* ed. Gabriel del Mazo, (Lima, 1968), 2: 20; Martinez de la Torre, *Apuntes para una interpretación* 2: 257; and Klaiber, "González Prada Popular Universities," p. 52.

19 On the students' original support of Leguía see Karno, "Leguía," p. 212, Basadre, *Historia de la República* 15: 110–13; and "Federación de Estudiantes del Perú," in Pedro Parra, *Bautismo de fuego del proletariado peruano* (Lima, 1969), p. 32. The falling out of the students with Leguía is traced in Cáceres, *Pasmo insurgencia,* pp. 18–19. Although most students supported the ideals of the university reform, the majority in 1919–20 were far from being "political radicals," and only a few of their number would actually become opposition politicians in 1930–31. This was nowhere more evident than at the Congreso del Cuzco, which had a more patriotic than social-minded atmosphere. The best treatments of the causes and evolution of the Reform movement include José Carlos Mariátegui, *7 ensayos de interpretación de la realidad peruana,* 7th ed. (Lima, 1969), esp. pp. 121–25, 138–39; Martinez de la Torre, *Apuntes para una interpretación* 2: 248–53; Carlos Enrique Paz Soldán, *De la inquietud a la revolución: diez años de rebeldías universitarias (1909–1919)* (Lima, 1919), pp. 115, 121, and *De la revolución a la anarquía universitaria* (Lima, 1922), pp. 12, 26–27; and Jesús Chavarría, "A Communication on University Reform," *Latin America Research Review* 3, no. 3 (Summer 1968): 192–95.

20 Expressions of youthful confidence by prominent members of the student counter-elite include Víctor Raúl Haya de la Torre, in José Ingenieros and Haya de la Torre, *Teoría y táctica de la acción renovadora antimperialista de la juventud en América latina* (Buenos Aires, 1928), pp. 24–25; Mariátegui, *7*

ensayos, p. 144; Antenor Orrego, "Prólogo," in Alcides Spelucín, *El libro de la nave dorada* (Trujillo, Peru, 1926), pp. 17–21; and Spelucín, "Haya de la Torre en mi recuerdo," *APRA* 14, no. 3 (February 22, 1946): 14, 19. On the effects of war and revolution on the formation of a youthful counter-elite in Peru, I consulted Mariátegui, *7 ensayos,* pp. 122–23, 126; Manuel Seoane, "La nueva generación peruana," *Claridad* 2, no. 7 (November 1, 1924): 9; Haya de la Torre, "La jornada," p. 26; Víctor Raúl Haya de la Torre, *A dónde va Indoamérica?* 2d ed. (Santiago, 1935), p. 190. The influence of Gonzalez Prada and other similar-thinking intellectuals on the students has been traced by Basadre, *Historia de la República* 13: 340; and Luis Alberto Sánchez, interview, February 16, 1971.

21 The most articulate expression of this position is presented by Peter Klarén in his *Modernization and Aprismo,* esp. xvi, 148. See also a similar statement in Lorca, *Apra sombra,* pp. 148–49. One Aprista statement that seems to support this view may be found in the editorial of *La Tribuna,* August 28, 1931, p. 1.

22 Principal among those leaders from well-off families with political connections were Manual Seoane, Carlos Manuel Cox, Luis Heysen, Pedro Muñiz, and Enrique Cornejo Koster. Information on the backgrounds of these and other leaders was obtained from Luis Alberto Sánchez, interview, February 16, 1971; Víctor Raúl Haya de la Torre, interviews, November 4, 1970, December 12, 1970; Jorge Basadre, interview, November 19, 1970; *The West Coast Leader,* May 5, 1931, p. 4; Fergac (pseud.), *Aprismo* (Lima, 1933?), p. 3; Polar, *Viejos y nuevos tiempos,* p. 113; *APRA,* no. 2 (October 20, 1930), p. 16; Luis Alberto Sánchez, *Aprismo y la religión* (Lima, 1933), pp. 28–29; and Manuel Seoane, "Prologo," in Juan de Dios Merel, *Principios del Aprismo* (Santiago, 1936?), p. 1. A similar view of the openings in the establishment available to the young Aprista leaders may be found in Sarfatti Larson and Eisen Bergman, *Social Stratification in Peru,* pp. 127–28.

23 Quoted by Cossío del Pomar, *Víctor Raúl* 1: 144. For information on other aspects of the inauguration ceremony see *Mundial* 2, no. 40 (January 28, 1931): 21; *El Comercio,* January 24, 1921, p. 1; *La Prensa,* January 24, 1921, p. 4; Klaiber, "González Prada Popular Universities," p. 50; and Cossío del Pomar, *Víctor Raúl* 1: 142–43. Some two weeks later a Universidad Popular was established in Vitarte and in succeeding months various branches were set up in other areas of Lima with a high concentration of union organizations. See Muñiz and Showing, *Aprismo,* pp. 9–10.

24 In *El obrero textil* 4, no. 43 (March, 1923): 2. Further data on the early stages of the Universidad Popular were obtained from Cornejo Koster, "Movimiento estudiantil," p. 20; Arturo Sabroso Montoya, interview, December 1970; *El obrero textil* 2, no. 28 (November 1, 1921): 4; 2 no. 31 (December 15, 1921): 4; and Klaiber, "González Prada Popular Universities," pp. 56–58, 66. *La Crónica* and *El Tiempo,* 1921–22, passim, almost daily published the class schedules and summarized the most important lectures in the Universidad Popular.

25 For lists of the courses and professors in the Universidades Populares see Cossío del Pomar, *Víctor Raúl* 1: 147; *Claridad* 1, no. 1 (May 1, 1923): 9–10; Cornejo Koster, "Movimiento estudiantil," p. 22; and Humberto Tejera,

Maestros indoíberos (México: 194?), p. 256. The practical and moralist aspects of the U.P.'s curriculum were emphasized by Luis Alberto Sánchez, interview, May 20, 1971; Klaiber, "González Prada Popular Universities,"pp. 62, 65-66, 117-18; *El Tiempo,* January 25, 1922, p. 7; Luis Carnero Checa, "Haya de la Torre y la U.P.G.P.," APRA 14, no. 3 (February 22, 1946): 4; and John A. Mackay, *The Other Spanish Christ* (New York, 1933), p. 194. For a description of one Fiesta de la Planta see Cornejo Koster, "Movimiento estudiantil," p. 23.

26 Víctor Raúl Haya de la Torre, interview, November 12, 1970. Klaiber, "González Prada Popular Universities," pp. 53, 55-56, claims that as many as 1,000 workers attended bi-weekly lectures in Lima by Haya de la Torre and 400 saw and head the young instructors from San Marcos in Vitarte. For further information on the establishment of Popular Universities see Jeffrey L. Klaiber, *Religion and Revolution in Peru* (Notre Dame, 1977), p. 125.

27 *La protesta* 9, no. 95 (May 1921): 2.

28 Víctor Raúl Haya de la Torre, interview, November 12, 1970. This analysis has also been echoed by Arturo Sabroso Montoya, interview, December 1970; Klaiber, "González Prada Popular Universities," pp. 61-66, 128-29; and Cossío del Pomar, *Víctor Raúl* 1:145.

29 Luis Lopez Aliaga, in *La Tribuna,* November 11, 1931, p. 5.

30 *El obrero textil* 3, no. 42 (January 1923): 3. For a similar statement see *El obrero textil* 3, no. 39 (October 1922): 1.

31 *El obrero textil* 3, no. 44 (May 1923): 3; Arturo Sabroso Montoya, interviews, December 1970, February 26, 1971; and Cossío del Pomar, *Víctor Raúl* 1:177, 179.

32 Klaiber, "Origins of Aprismo," p. 703, mentions that in personal interviews with Haya the Aprista leader stressed the importance of the Universidad Popular in the development of his political style.

33 Haya's behind-the-scenes activities in arranging the protest are chronicled by Cornejo Koster, "Movimiento estudiantil," p. 25. The first editorials against the consecration appeared in *Variedades* 19, no. 793 (May 12, 1923): 1149-50, no. 794 (May 19, 1923): 1213-14, and no. 795 (May 26, 1923): 1277-78. Information on the Universidad Popular's role in the protest was obtained from Víctor Raúl Haya de la Torre, interview, December 12, 1970; and Sánchez, *Haya y el Apra,* pp. 118-19. The March 19th handbill is reprinted in Martinez de la Torre, *Apuntes para una interpretación* 2: 265.

34 Quoted by Sánchez, *Haya y el Apra,* p. 124.

35 Ravines, *Estafa,* p. 75.

36 *El Tiempo,* May 26, 1923, p. 4. An excellent example of the nearly unanimous support for the movement after the events of May 23 may be found in *La Cronica,* May 25, 1923, p. 11. The most valuable sources of information on the events surrounding the consecration attempt are the Lima newspapers. The above summary was mainly derived from the following newspapers: *La Crónica,* May 16-29, 1923; *El Tiempo,* May 21-28, 1923; *La Prensa,* May 24-29, 1923. An excellent summary of the events of May is Cornejo Koster, "Movimiento estudiantil," pp. 25-29. An interview with a participant in the

protest, Arturo Sabroso Montoya, in December 1970, was also useful in tracing the movement.

37 Mariátegui, *7 ensayos,* p. 141.

38 Víctor Raúl Haya de la Torre, interview, November 12, 1970. See also *El obrero textil* 5, no. 69 (October 1, 1924): 3.

39 In *El Tiempo,* July 6, 1924, p. 3. Similar sentiments were expressed in *Claridad* 1, no. 2 (September 1, 1923): 1.

40 Arturo Sabroso Montoya, interview, December 1970.

41 "Himno de la Universidad Popular," provided to me by Arturo Sabroso Montoya, December 1970.

42 Quoted by Víctor Raúl Haya de la Torre, interview, November 24, 1970. Haya named the following leaders as having made the above proposition: Sabroso, Otazú, Fonkén, Fajardo, and Guerrero Quimper. His version is supported by Jorge Del Prado, *40 años de lucha, Partido Comunista Peruano 1928–1968* (Lima, 1968?), p. 7; Arturo Sabroso Montoya, interview, December 1970; and Cossío del Pomar, *Víctor Raúl* 1: 179.

43 Víctor Raúl Haya de la Torre, interview, November 24, 1970. These same sentiments were expressed in a series of letters written by Haya to *La Crónica,* May 30, 1923, p. 5, June 1, 1923, p. 3.

44 Arturo Osores to Raúl Haya de la Torre, Guayaquil, July 7, 1923, ASC.

45 For a thorough summary of these events see *El obrero textil* 5, no. 51 (November 1, 1923): 1. For Haya this incident occurred at a lucky time when he was about to be defeated in an election for the presidency of the Federación de Estudiantes by Manual Seoane. But anti-Hayismo among the students was quickly forgotten when they saw him being shipped out of the country.

46 Víctor Raúl Haya de la Torre to "los estudiantes y obreros," San Lorenzo, October 4, 1923, in *El obrero textil* 5, no. 50 (October 15, 1923): 1. Klaiber, *Religion and Revolution,* pp. 135–36, calls Haya's posture Catholic-style political messianism. The martyr image has been a feature of many Latin American populists' political styles. Perhaps the most famous example is Getulio Vargas's 1954 suicide note that expresses sentiments strikingly similar to those of Haya. The note is published in Louis Hanke, ed., *History of Latin American Civilization* (Boston, 1973), 2: 432–33.

47 Union organization and the Universidad Popular had passed through various stages in their relations with the state during the decade from 1917 to 1927. In the beginning they were allowed to subsist, and in the case of the Universidad Popular, even encouraged by the state. Through 1922 into 1923 the government began to watch their activities more closely, considering them a possible threat. After the Sacred Heart protest various measures were adopted to make their existence difficult, and finally after 1924 every effort was undertaken to close them down permanently. On the evolution from tolerance to repression of these organizations see Arturo Sabroso Montoya, in *La Tribuna,* August 15, 1931, p. 9 (originally written in 1925); *La Prensa,* August 9, 1918, p. 2, August 17, 1918, p. 2, August 20, 1918, p. 3, January 23, 1921, p. 6; Klaiber, "González Prada Popular Universities," pp. 74, 84, 91–93; Barrientos, *Tres sindicalismos,* pp. 164–65, 169; Cornejo Koster, "Movimiento estudiantíl," p.

31; Martinez de la Torre, *Apuntes para una interpretación* 2: 270; Sánchez, *Haya y el Apra,* pp. 155-56; La Crónica, May 24, 1924; *El obrero textil* 5, no. 77 (February 1, 1925): 1; (March 15, 1925): 2; *Claridad* 1, no. 1 (May 1, 1923): 9, 1, no. 3 (September 15, 1923): 20; and Muñiz and Showing, *Aprismo,* pp. 10-11. Arturo Sabroso Montoya, interview, December 1970, was also extremely helpful in tracing these events. On the raid of 1927 see Alejandro Bravo de Rueda, "La verdad sobre el complot comunista fraguado por la policía en junio de 1927," *Libertad,* October 3, 1930, p. 2.

48 Víctor Raúl Haya de la Torre, interview, December 12, 1970.

49 "Vals ideal," in *Cancionero aprista* (Lima, 193?), p. 19.

50 There are numerous sources of information detailing Haya's gains with the organized labor movement as a result of their common experience of suffering. Most prominent among them are Haya's elevation in the labor press. See *El obrero textil* 5, no. 51 (November 1, 1923): 1, 5, no. 60 (March 15, 1924): 3, 5, no. 77 (February 1, 1925): 3; *La protesta* 12, no. 121 (December, 1923): 1; and *La Tribuna,* June 11, 1931, p. 6. This trend is also reflected in Haya's own writings. See Víctor Raúl Haya de la Torre to Julio Barcos, London, June 20, 1925, in Víctor Raúl Haya de la Torre, *Ideario y acción apprista* (Buenos Aires, 1930), pp. 85, 149; Haya de la Torre, *Construyendo el Aprismo,* pp. 72, 75, 97. In personal interviews with me on November 12, 1970, December 12, 1970, Haya continued to express a similar opinion. In various interviews in December 1970 and January 29, 1971, labor leader Arturo Sabroso Montoya also testified to the profound effects of common suffering on the unity between workers and Haya.

51 The form of these communications was described by Luis Alberto Sánchez, interview, May 20, 1971. Some of the most characteristic examples of Haya's letter writing style may be found in printed sources. They include Víctor Raúl Haya de la Torre to "Los Compañeros de la Universidad Popular Gonzalez Prada," Havana, November 4, 1923, in *El obrero textil* 5, no. 55 (February 1924): 2; Víctor Raúl Haya de la Torre to "Los Obreros de Lima," Colón Panamá, no date, in *Claridad* 1, no. 4 (January 1, 1924): 2; Víctor Raúl Haya de la Torre to "Grupo Redactor de Claridad," San Angel, México, February 1924, in *Claridad* 1, no. 5 (March 1924): 19; Víctor Raúl Haya de la Torre, Leysin, Switzerland, March 1925, in Ricardo Luna Vegas, "Lealtad de Haya de la Torre y del Aprismo," *APRA* 14, 3 (February 22, 1946): 7; Víctor Raúl Haya de la Torre to *Amauta,* London, November 2, 1926, in Haya de la Torre, *Ideario,* pp. 105-6; and Víctor Raúl Haya de la Torre to "Compañeros Trabajadores Manuales e Intelectuales de las Universidades Populares González Prada," London, November 1926, in *Amauta,* no. 6 (February 1927): 35.

52 The best source on these events has been Luis Alberto Sánchez, interview, May 20, 1971. Haya himself corroborated Sánchez's analysis in an interview on December 12, 1970; "We had a very well established communications network . . . when in exile I wrote letters to workers . . . I carried on a correspondence of hundreds of letters . . . We had quite good, efficient information organization." On the founding of Apra I consulted Víctor Raúl Haya de la Torre, interviews, November 4, November 24, 1970; Arturo Sabroso Mon-

toya, interview, December 1970; Temoche Benites, *Apra y trabajadores,* p. 15; and Cossío del Pomar, *Víctor Raúl* 1: 5, no. 50.

53 Octavio Carbajo, in *El obrero textil* 5, no. 50 (October 15, 1923).

54 "Un Discípulo" [pseud.] ibid., 5, no. 69 (October 1, 1924).

55 Lucinda Podio, ibid., 5, no. 76 (January 15, 1925).

56 *El obrero textil* 5, no. 74 (December 15, 1924): 1. For additional examples of newspaper articles dedicated to Haya de la Torre see *El obrero textil* 5, no. 59 (May 1, 1924): 3, 5, no. 61 (June 1, 1924): 2, 5, no. 67 (September 1, 1924): 1; *Claridad* 1, no. 4 (January 1, 1924): 2; and *Solidaridad* 2, no. 19 (May 1927), passim. One of the handbills widely distributed in 1925 was entitled "La Federación Obrera Local de Lima al proletariado en general en el segundo aniversario de la jornada por la libertad de conciencia," May 23, 1925, in CHS/BNP.

57 Víctor Raúl Haya de la Torre, interview, December 15, 1970. On the cell organization of Apra the following have been consulted: Luis Alberto Sánchez, interview, May 20, 1971; Martinez de la Torre, *Apuntes para una interpretación* 1: 240; Basadre, *Historia de la República* 14: 34; and Klaiber, "González Prada Popular Universities," p. 95. Mackay, *That Other Spanish Christ,* p. 196, describes a meeting between Haya and several military officers who proposed that he head a revolution.

58 *El obrero textil* 3, no. 43 (March 1923): 2.

59 *El obrero textil* 2, no. 31 (December 15, 1921): 1. Information on the anarchists' dislike of politics and their classification of Haya and his fellow students as ambitious future politicians was obtained from the following sources: *La Acción Popular* November 3, 1912, p. 1; *La Prensa,* January 14, 1919, p. 1; *El obrero textil* 1, no. 3 (December 20, 1919): 2, 1, no. 6 (March 6, 1920): 4, 2, no. 25 (August 1, 1921): 3 *La protesta* 9, no. 95 (May 1921)): 2; Sabroso Montoya, *Réplicas proletarias,* pp. 15–16; Sabroso Montoya, interview, December 1970; and Barba, "Memorias de una gesta," p. 26. For a lively exposition of the anarchist position vis-à-vis politics and politicians see the declarations of Peru's leading anarchist, Manuel González Prada, in his book, *Anarquía,* p. 72.

60 Víctor Raúl Haya de la Torre, interview, December 11, 1970.

61 Information on Haya's "apolitical" stance and his appeal to the anarchists was obtained from Víctor Raúl Haya de la Torre, *Dos cartas de Haya de la Torre* (Lima, 1923), p. 18: Haya de la Torre, interview, May 20, 1971; Klaiber, "González Prada Popular Universities," pp. 60–64; Arturo Sabroso Montoya, interviews, May 5, 1970, December 1970; José Carlos Mariátegui, *La organización del proletariado* (Lima, 1967), pp. 211–12; and Martinez de la Torre, *Apuntes para una interpretación* 2: 257.

62 "Un compañero de Santa Catalina" in *El obrero textil* 3, no. 43 (March 1923): 2. A valuable discussion of the impact of the May 1919 strike on the Lima workers is presented by Sulmont, *Movimiento obrero,* pp. 89–91.

63 *La protesta* 12, no. 115 (June 1923): 1. See also p. 4 in the same issue.

64 *La protesta* 12, no. 118 (November 1923): 1, 14, no. 126 (June 1924): 1. Other sources on Haya's ultimate victory over the anarchists include Víctor Raùl Haya de la Torre to the U.P.G.P.S. of Peru, in *El obrero textil* 5, no. 55 (February 1924): 2; *El obrero textil* 1, no. 18 (February 15, 1921): 1, 3, no. 37 (July 15, 1922): 1, 5, no. 57 (April 1, 1924): 1; and Parra, *Bautismo de fuego,* pp. 90–91, 102.

65 On Mariátegui's introduction to the labor movement and his role in the 1920s the following sources were of use: Basadre, *Historia de la República* 13: 349–50; Klaiber, "González Prada Popular Universities," p. 90 and "Origins of Aprismo," pp. 708–9. The effects of the antiimperialist conference in Brussels on Haya and Mariátegui are detailed in Víctor Raúl Haya de la Torre, *El antiimperialismo y el APRA,* 3d ed. (Lima, 1970), p. 82; Barrientos, *Tres sindicalismos,* p. 173; Sánchez, *Testimonio personal* 1: 309; and Sánchez, *Haya y el Apra,* p. 208.

66 Haya's proposals were part of his so-called "Plan de México," The plan is reprinted in Martinez de la Torre, *Apuntes para una interpretación* 2: 290–93. For Mariátegui's critique of the plan see José Carlos Mariátegui to the "Célula Aprista de Méjico," Lima, April 16, 1928, and "Carta colectiva del grupo de Lima," 1928, in ibid., 2: 296–98 and 299–302. For the best treatments of the whole affair see Martinez de la Torre, "De la Reforma Universitaria al Partido Socialista," in his *Apuntes para una interpretación* 2: 212–375, passim; and Ricardo Luna Vegas, *Mariátegui, Haya de la Torre y la verdad histórica* (Lima, 1978), passim. Also useful in the analysis of Haya's PNL is Víctor Raúl Haya de la Torre to César L. Mendoza, Berlin, September 29, 1929, in Partido Aprista Peruano, *El proceso de Haya de la Torre,* 2d ed. (Lima, 1969), esp. pp. 139–41; and Klaiber, *Religion and Revolution,* p. 137.

67 Luis Alberto Sánchez, interview, May 20, 1971.

68 Manuel Seoane to Luis Alberto Sánchez, no date, in Sánchez, *Haya o el político,* p. 165.

69 José Carlos Mariátegui to "Célula Aprista de Méjico," Lima, April 16, 1928, in Martinez de la Torre, *Apuntes para una Interpretación* 2: 296–98.

70 Víctor Raúl Haya de la Torre to José Carlos Mariátegui, México, May 20, 1928, in Martinez de la Torre, *Apuntes para una interpretación* 2: 298–99.

71 See, for example José Carlos Mariátegui to Eudocio Ravines, Lima, December 31, 1928, in Martinez de la Torre, *Apuntes para una interpretación* 2: 335–37; and *Labor,* December 8, 1928, p. 2. Víctor Raúl Haya de la Torre to "Célula del Apra del Cuzco," Berlin, February 25, 1930, in Partido Aprista Peruano, *Proceso Haya,* esp. pp. 146–50; and Víctor Raúl Haya de la Torre to César L. Mendoza, Berlin, September 29, 1929, in Partido Aprista Peruano, *Proceso Haya,* p. 141.

72 Juan de Dios Merel, interview, January 14, 1971.

73 Ricardo Martinez de la Torre Nerval, Lima, June ?, 1929, in Martinez de la Torre, *Apuntes para una interpretación* 2: 349.

74 Comité Aprista Peruano, Brigada de Organización, *Organización Vertical del Partido Aprista Peruano* (Santiago, 1937), p. 1. This document, which is the

best example of early Aprista organizational principles, was originally drawn up on May 18, 1931, and later reprinted in 1937. It was supplied to the author by Thomas Davies. See also Haya de la Torre, *Antimperialismo y APRA,* p. 114.

75 *La protesta* 9, no. 95 (May 1921): 2; and "Un Compañero de Santa Catalina" in *El obrero textil* 3, no. 43 (March 1923): 2.

76 Arturo Sabroso Montoya, interview, January 29, 1971. The most important justification from the middle and upper class leadership for this unequal division of power was in the Aprista platform of 1931, written by Haya de la Torre and entitled, *El plan del Aprismo* (Lima, 1931), pp. 15, 19–21.

77 Partido Aprista Peruano, *Proceso Haya,* p. 16.

78 Sánchez, *Testimonio personal* 3: 970. See also Bourricaud, *Poder y sociedad,* pp. 259–60; and Alberto Hidalgo, *Por que renuncié al Apra* (Lima, 1954), p. 20, in which this angry former Aprista calls the party a monarchy.

79 Víctor Raúl Haya de la Torre, interview, December 15, 1970. See also Klaiber, *Religion and Revolution,* p. 146.

80 Manuel Seoane, "Por qué celebramos los Apristas el cumpleaños de Haya de la Torre," *APRA* 14, no. 3 (February 22, 1946): 8.

81 Haya de la Torre, *Plan del Aprismo,* p. 12.

82 Víctor Raúl Haya de le Torre, *Política aprista,* 2d ed. (Lima, 1967), p. 110.

83 Víctor Raúl Haya de la Torre, interview, December 12, 1970. For other statements of Haya on paternalism in Trujillo see the following published interviews of the Aprista leader: "75 años en la vida de un líder," *La Prensa* (Suplemento), February 22, 1970, p. 44; and "Las nostalgias de Haya," *Caretas,* no. 432 (March 22, 1971): 18. An Aprista leader who also has observed Haya's paternalism is Luis Alberto Sánchez, *Testimonio personal* 2: 828. On the family spirit of Apra the following were consulted: Víctor Raúl Haya de la Torre, interview, December 15, 1970; *La Tribuna,* August 5, 1931, p. 1, August 12, 1931, p. 5; Seoane, "Por qué celebramos," p. 8; Arturo Sabroso Montoya, interview, December 1970; Sánchez, *Testimonio personal* 2: 772; Haya de la Torre, in *Cartas de Haya de la Torre a los prisioneros apristas,* ed. Carlos Manuel Cox (Lima, 1946): pp. 63, 78–79, 84; Basadre, *Historia de la República* 14: 137; Jorge Basadre, interview, February 8, 1971; "Nostalgias Haya," p. 18; Esmaro Salas to Víctor Raúl Haya de la Torre, March 16, 1934, in Esmaro Salas, *Proceso aclaratorio de la traición de Esmaro Salas al Partido Aprista Peruano* (Lima, 1942), p. 153; and Bourricaud, *Ideología y desarrollo,* pp. 36–37. Haya may have also been inspired in part by the elitist tenets of Arielismo, a popular intellectual trend of the day.

84 The concept of class vs. following in the analysis of political movements is borrowed from Benno Galjart, "Class and Following in Rural Brazil," *América latina* 6, no. 3 (July–September 1964): 3–23. Galjart views Brazil's peasant leagues in similar terms, emphasizing the traditional patron-client character of the relations within these movements.

CHAPTER 7: APRA II
THE ALLIANCE IN THE CAMPAIGN

1 Haya de la Torre, *Construyendo el Aprismo,* pp. 150–51; and Haya de la Torre, *A dónde va Indoamérica?,* p. 134.
2 Víctor Raúl Haya de la Torre, quoted by Sánchez, *Haya o el político,* p. 174.
3 On initial attempts at Aprista organization see Luis Eduardo Enriquez, *Haya de la Torre: La estafa más grande de America* (Lima, 1951), pp. 82–83; Manuel Seoane,*Obras apristas de 1931 a 1948* (Lima, 1957?), pp. 8–9; Luis Alberto Sánchez, "El deber de hacer política," *Mundial* II, no. 537 (Octobeɪ 3, 1930): 10; and "Hay que definirse," ibid., no. 538 (October 10, 1930): 6; *La Prensa,* October 26, 1930, p.l; and Klarén, *Modernization and Aprismo,* pp. 120–21. Concerning the government's repression of Apra consult Luis Eduardo Enriquez to President of the Junta de Gobierno, Lima, December 9, 1930, CHS/BNP; *El Perú,* February 20, 1931, p. 2; *The West Coast Leader,* May 5, 1931, p. 4; and Sánchez, *Testimonio personal* 1: 345.
4 Reflections of Haya's preoccupation with organization are found in Haya de la Torre, *Antimperialismo y APRA,* pp. vi–vii, 149–50; *Biografía y gráficos de Haya de la Torre* (Lima, 1931), p. 22; and Basadre, *Historia de la República,* 14: 134. For a list of the members of the original National Executive Committee see *La Tribuna,* May 18, 1931, p. 5. The Aprista newspaper *La Tribuna,* May–October 1931, passim, coordinated and published in daily columns information about the activities of local organizations. For descriptions of specific meetings see *La Tribuna,* July 20, 1931, p. 6, and August 6, 1931, p. 3.
5 *La Tribuna,* June 20, 1931, p. 4. The basic tenets of party discipline were outlined in Comité Aprista Peruano, *Organización vertical,* pp. 3, 8. *La Tribuna* is the best source of information on the day-to-day discipline exercised within the Aprista party during the campaign. See especially the following issues: June 9, 1931, p. 4; August 9, 1931, p. 1; August 19, 1931, p. 1; and August 23, 1931, p. 1. Also, in Haya de la Torre's celebrated trial by the Sánchez Cerro regime in 1932, party discipline was a major theme of his testimony. See Partido Aprista Peruano, *Proceso Haya,* esp. pp. 188–90, 192–94, 239.
6 For information on preparations made for Aprista demonstrations see the following issues of *La Tribuna:* August 2, 1931, p. 1; August 4, 1931, p. 4; August 5, 1931, p. 4; August 7, 1931, p. 8; August 13, 1931, p. 2; August 15, 1931, p. 7; and October 7, 1931, p. 2. Two publications which made particularly glowing comments about the orderliness of Aprista demonstrations were *The West Coast Leader,* August 25, 1931, p. 4; and Amauta, "Cartas al provinciano desconocido," *Mundial* 11, no. 575 (August 21, 1931): 30.
7 Descriptions of Aprista rallies and estimates of size were obtained from both pro- and anti-Aprista sources. The most detailed pro-Aprista source is *La Tribuna.* See the following issues: August 8, 1931, p. 5; extraordinary edition, August 15, 1931, p. 1; August 16, 1931, pp. 1–2; and September 5, 1931, p. 2. Commentaries with a less favorable stance toward the party include Enriquez,

Estafa política, p. 114; Ravines, *Estafa,* p. 178; and Marett, *Peru,* p. 157. Two observers who have noted striking parallels between the atmosphere and planning of these events and Nazi rallies and who also speculate that Haya might have been inspired by what he saw in Germany in 1930 regarding political demonstrations are Jorge Basadre, interview, February 8, 1971; and Miro Quesada Laos, *Pueblo en crisis,* p. 183. A somewhat blurred yet impressive photograph of an Aprista demonstration appeared in *La Tribuna,* August 17, 1931, p. 1.

8 For the full text of Haya's August 23 speech see Haya de la Torre, *Plan del Aprismo,* pp. 1–37. The *programa mínimo* is reprinted in Haya de la Torre, *Plan del Aprismo,* pp. 38–56. In spite of the importance attributed to the *programa mínimo* following its publication, in the eyes of some contemporary observers its creation was an afterthought in response to critics who accused Apra of lacking a concrete program. See *The West Coast Leader,* September 22, 1931, p. 4.

9 Haya de la Torre, *Plan del Aprismo,* p. 34.

10 Manuel Seoane's statement, made in 1944, was published in *Radiografía de Haya de la Torre* (Lima, 1946), p. 20. Similar assertions concerning the difficulty experienced by working class Apristas in understanding their party's doctrine come from *La Tribuna,* September 5, 1931, p. 2; and Sánchez, *Testimonio personal* 1:356–57. Some of the Aprista writings published around the time of the 1931 election which underline the importance of Party doctrine were Haya de la Torre, *Ideario, Plan del Aprismo,* and *Teoría y táctica del Aprismo* (Lima, 1931). Various scholars have reinforced the notion of the importance of Aprista ideology by discussing the movement largely in terms of its ideological components. See, for example, Harry Kantor, *The Ideology and Program of the Peruvian Aprista Movement* (Berkeley, Calif., 1953); and Robert J. Alexander, ed., *Aprismo; the Ideas and Doctrines of Víctor Raúl Haya de la Torre* (Kent, Ohio, 1973).

11 An interesting analysis of the function of ideology in the Aprista movement is contained in Bourricaud, *Ideología y desarrollo,* esp. pp. 7, 19.

12 Almost from the first day of its publication in May 1931 the Aprista newspaper *La Tribuna* was the major organ of anti-civilista rhetoric. For examples of that rhetoric see *La Tribuna,* May 1931–November 1931, passim, esp. July 21, 1931, pp. 4–5; August 21, 1931, p. 1; August 23, 1931, p. 1; August 26, 1931, p. 1; and September 7, 1931, p. 1. Other examples of Apra's antioligarchical attack include Magda Portal, *Frente al momento actual* (Lima, 1931), passim; "Travesuras," in *Cancionero aprista,* p. 24; Bedoya, *Otro Caín,* passim; Víctor Rodrigo Alva, *El mito de la revolución de agosto* (Lima, 1933), p. 11; and Merel, *Principios del Aprismo,* p. 69.

13 Alberto Hidalgo, *Sánchez Cerro o el excremento,* originally published in 1931 and reprinted in Alberto Hidalgo, *Diario de mi sentimiento (1922-1936)* (Buenos Aires, 1937), pp. 149–55. At one point in this tract Hidalgo listed 188 epithets to describe Sánchez Cerro. Similar terminology used in the campaign to denigrate Sánchez Cerro may be found in numerous issues of *La Tribuna,* including July 2, 1931, p. 2; July 3, 1931, p. 1; July 6, 1931, p. 1; July 17,

1931, pp. 3, 6; July 22, 1931, p. 3; July 24, 1931, p. 7; and October 10, 1931, p. 5.

14 *La República*, July 14, 1931.

15 The large quantity and the contents of the pro-Catholic mail received by Sánchez Cerro were described to me by Pedro Ugarteche, interview, February 16, 1971. The anti-Catholic accusations against Apra are summarized in Sánchez, *Aprismo y religión, esp. pp. 9, 27, 39; Aprismo—anticatolicismo* (Lima, 1934), esp. pp. 3, 13, 21, 24, 25; and Klaiber, *Religion and Revolution*, p. 139. For Apra's replies and occasional "slips" into anticlericalism see *La Tribuna,* August 12, 1931, p. 1; *Biografía y gráficos,* p. 13; Sánchez, *Aprismo y religión,* esp. p. 30; Manuel Seoane, in Muñiz and Showing, *Aprismo,* pp. 88–89; andKlaiber, *Religion and Revolution,* pp. 140–41. During and after the campaign the Apristas complained bitterly about the necessity to constantly be on the defensive. See, for example, Luis Alberto Sánchez, *Carta a una indoamericana* (Quito, 1932), p. 3; Sanchez, *Haya y el Apra,* pp. 128–29; and Cossío del Pomar, *Víctor Raúl* 1: 326–27.

16 Examples of Apra's position on the issue of Leguiísmo include "Peruanos sin patria," *Mundial* 11, no. 575 (August 21, 1931): 12; and *La Tribuna,* February 7, 1932, p. 1. Observers who have commented on Apra's winning of Leguiísta support in the 1931 election include Víctor Andrés Belaunde, *Meditaciones peruanas,* p. 259; Chirinos Pacheco, *Perú nuevo,* p. 163; and Garrett, "Oncenio of Leguía," pp. 213–14. An excellent summary of the various forms Leguiísta aid took, including economic, may be found in Thomas M. Davies, Jr., "The *Indigenismo* of the Peruvian Aprista Party," *Hispanic American Historical Review* 51, no. 4 (November 1971): 635–36.

17 *La Tribuna,* August 19, 1931, p. 1; *mine.* See also *La Noche,* July 29, 1931, p. 3; and Sánchez, *Haya o el político,* p. 193. Under the heading of lack of patriotism, Haya was also accused of having sold out to Chilean gold, of being a Soviet pawn, and of being an agent of British imperialism. See Sánchez, *Haya y el Apra,* pp. 130, 209.

18 A harsh indictment of Apra's "communism" is *El verdadero plan de la Alianza Popular Revolucionaria Americana* (Lima, 193?), esp. pp. 23, 26, 28, 30. Examples of Apra's response during the campaign to the affirmations of its communist orientation include Manuel Seoane, *Nuestros fines* (Buenos Aires, 1931), pp. 21–22; *Biografía y gráficos,* p. 17; and *La Tribuna,* July 6, 1931, p. 6. Before and after the presidential race prominent Apristas devoted considerable effort to attacking the Latin American communist parties. See Haya de la Torre, *Antimperialismo y Apra,* passim; and Manuel Seoane, *Comunistas criollos* Arequipa, 1964), passim. An excellent treatment of the Aprismo vs. communism question is contained in Basadre, *Historia de la República* 14: 139.

19 Haya de la Torre, *Dos cartas,* esp. pp. 7–8, 11, 17; Víctor Raúl Haya de la Torre, *Por la emancipación de América latina; artículos, mensajes, discursos 1923–1927* (Buenos Aires, 1927), passim; and Eliseo Flores V., "Víctor Raúl Haya de la Torre," *Claridad* 1, no. 5 (March 15, 1924): 10.

20 Víctor Raúl Haya de la Torre to José María Zeledón, México, December 29, 1927, in *Repertorio americano* 16, no. 4 (January 28, 1928): 63.

21 Sánchez, *Carta a indoamericana,* p. 39.

22 Manuel Seoane, in Muñiz and Showing, *Aprismo,* pp. 72–73. Other statements in a similar vein include Antenór Orrego, "Por que y como se ataca al Aprismo," in Partido Aprista Peruano, *Llamamiento a la Nación por el Comité Ejecutivo Nacional* (Lima, 1931), p. 20; and *Variedades* 27, no. 1219 (July 15, 1931): 1.

23 Haya de la Torre, *Política aprista,* p. 10.

24 Alfredo Saco, *Síntesis aprista* (Lima, 1934), p. 144.

25 Information on Larco Herrera's contribution may be found in Davies, *"Indigenismo,"* 633. There is evidence that Apra also received aid from the powerful Piedra family in the Trujillo area. See Aspillaga to Ramón Aspillaga, Cayaltí, October 27, 1931, in Huertas Vallejos, *Capital burocrático,* p. 77. Sources dealing with the "evolutionary" characteristics of Aprista radicalism include *La Tribuna,* September 11, 1931, p. 1, October 7, 1931, p. 4; and Manuel Seoane, in Fergac, *Aprismo,* p. 22.

26 Haya de la Torre, *Antimperialismo y APRA,* p. 3. Later the adjective Yankee was dropped as Apra saw itself as combating the imperialism of all nations. For other strong statements concerning antiimperialism see Haya de la Torre, *Antimperialismo y Apra,* p. 83; and Luis E. Heysen, *El A.B.C. de la peruanización* (Lima, 1931), p. 16. The early concern of Haya and other Aprista leaders with the threat of imperialism developed out of their student days when they were involved with the university reform movement. In Peru, as well as in its initial stages in the rest of Latin America, the university reform had included antiimperialism as a major ideological postulate. See Federación Universitaria Argentina, "Al pueblo de la República," Buenos Aires, October 11, 1920, in Martinez de la Torre, *Apuntes para una interpretación* 2: 241–42; and Primer Congreso Internacional de Estudiantes, "Resoluciones," México, September–October 1921, in Mazo, *Reforma universitaria* 2: 81–83.

27 Manuel Seoane, quoted in *The West Coast Leader,* May 5, 1931, p. 4.

28 Favorable statements by Haya with regard to foreign capital may be found in Haya de la Torre, *Política aprista,* pp. 49–50; and Haya de la Torre, *Plan del Aprismo,* pp. 10–12. For various statements of this position in *La Tribuna* consult the following issues: May 26, 1931, p. 1; June 12, 1931, p. 3; August 10, 1931, p. 1; and September 11, 1931, p. 1.

29 Manuel Seoane, quoted in *The West Coast Leader,* May 5, 1931, p. 4.

30 Fred Morris Dearing, quoted in Davies, *"Indigenismo,"* pp. 643, 643–44, 642.

31 Ibid., pp. 643–44.

32 Davies, *Indian Integration in Peru,* p. 111n. An excellent account of Haya's contacts with the representatives of foreign governments and businesses is contained in Davies, *"Indigenismo,"* esp. pp. 642–45. In addition see Haya's statements to the United Press reprinted in *La Tribuna,* July 11, 1931, p. 1.

33 "Canción aprista," *Cancionero aprista,* p. 13. Other examples of Apra's intention to provide immediate material benefits to the middle sectors and the masses may be found in the pages of *La Tribuna;* July 8, 1931, p. 4; July 15, 1931, p. 1; July 16, 1931, p. 4; July 19, 1931, p. 4; and September 16, 1931, p.

5. Haya's writings also mirrored this concern: Haya de la Torre, *Ideario,* pp. 35, 128, and *Teoría y táctica,* p. 93.
34 For the most definitive statements about Apra's "functional democracy" see Haya de la Tore, *Plan del Aprismo,* pp. 20-21, 38; and Julio Valdéz Garrido, *De Bolívar a Haya de la Torre* (Lima, 1947), pp. 62-65.
35 Manuel Seoane, in *Radiografía de Haya de la Torre* (Lima, 1946), p. 20.
36 Víctor Raúl Haya de la Torre, interview, December 12, 1970. Excellent discussions of the "spiritual" aspects of Apra during and after the 1931 election include Bourricaud, *Ideología y desarrollo,* esp. p. 17; and François Bourricaud, *Poder y sociedad en el Perú contemporáneo,* trans. Roberto Bixio (Buenos Aires, 1967), esp. p. 158. Direct expressions of Aprista moral fervor in the campaign may be found in various articles from *La Tribuna.* See the following issues: July 6, 1931, p. 1; August 5, 1931, p. 1; August 15, 1931, extraordinary edition, p. 8; and September 6, 1931, p. 1. See also Haya de la Torre, *Plan del Aprismo,* pp. 30-31; Haya de la Torre, *Ideario,* p. 56; Haya de la Torre in Muñix and Showing, *Aprismo,* p. 32; Sánchez, *Aprismo y religión,* p. 47, Manuel Seoane, in *Radiografía de Haya,* p. 19; and John A. Mackay, *That Other America* (New York, 1935), p. 106.
37 In *Cancionero aprista,* p. 2.
38 For examples of the religious tone of the Aprista campaign see *La Tribuna,* May-October 1931. As was the case of the *"Marsellesa Aprista,"* religion was a common theme in Aprista songs. See, for example, "Elecciones," *Cancionero aprista,* p. 14; and "La bandera del Aprismo," in *La Tribuna,* November 29, 1931, p. 12.
39 Víctor Raúl Haya de la Torre to Alberto Hidalgo, Berlin, March 11, 1931, in Hidalgo, *Diario,* p. 315. Haya's interest in the priesthood was expressed in an interview with me on November 4, 1970. On Haya's early religious background and his feelings of predestination see also "Las nostalgias de Haya," p. 18; Mackay, *Other Spanish Christ,* p. 194; and Víctor Raúl Haya de la Torre to John Mackay, Lima, 1932?, in Mackay, *That Other America,* p. 109.
40 Víctor Raúl Haya de la Torre, interviews, November 4, November 12, 1970; Haya de la Torre, *Dos cartas,* pp. 23-25, 28; Partido Aprista Peruano, *Proceso Haya,* p. 79; and Klaiber, *Religion and Revolution,* p. 146.
41 "Marcha aprista," *Cancionero aprista,* p. 1.
42 Serafín Del Mar (pseud.), in Reynaldo Bolaños, *El año trágico* (Lima, 1934), p. 43. Others who have commented on the relationship between persecution and spiritual sentiment in Apra's early days are Bourricaud, *Poder y sociedad,* p. 178; and Cossío del Pomar, *Víctor Raúl* 1: 327. The equation of suffering and religious unity in Apra becomes even more clear when viewing the development of the movement after the 1931 election. Forced underground by Sánchez Cerro and later during Oscar Benavides's two terms as president (1933-39), Apra's religiosity increased markedly, as evidenced by the numerous party tracts filled with comparisons of Christ's suffering with that of Haya de la Torre plus descriptions of the martyrdom of Apra's fallen. One of the best sources in this regard is a collection of Haya's letters written during

the 1930s: *Cartas de Haya de la Torre,* ed. Cox, esp. pp. 12–15, 24, 33, 69–70. The religious streak in Apra is a highly complex and important part of the movement. Two recent studies which bear on the issue and differ somewhat from my view are Fredrick B. Pike's "Religion, Collectivism, and Intrahistory: The Peruvian Ideal of Dependency," *Journal of Latin American Studies* 10, no. 2 (November 1978): 239–62; and Klaiber's *Religion and Revolution.* Pike affirms that Apristas consciously appropriated Catholic symbolism to trade on some of the church's legitimacy with the lower and middle classes. Klaiber, esp. pp. 145–46, argues that the transfer of Catholic symbolism to Apra allowed party members to "express religious sentiments within the Aprista movement."

43 Hidalgo, *Diario,* pp. 145–46.

44 Víctor Raúl Haya de la Torre to John Mackay, Lima, 1932?, in Mackay, *That Other America,* pp. 110–11. Another example of Haya's belief in the importance of great leader figures in bringing about progress is an interview of him reprinted in Sánchez, *Haya y el Apra,* p. 112. For some of the most striking examples of Haya's exaltation in the campaign, consult the following issues of *La Tribuna:* July 13, 1931, pp. 3, 6; July 15, 1931, p. 1; July 19, 1931, p. 1; July 20, 1931, p. 5; August 12, 1931, p. 6; August 15, 1931, pp. 8–9; and August 15, 1931, extraordinary edition, p. 3.

45 Examples of Haya's heroic campaign image may be found in *La Tribuna,* May 16, 1931, p. 3; May 20, 1931, extraordinary edition, p. 1; June 25, 1931, p. 1; July 20, 1931, p. 6; and August 15, 1931, p. 9. For characterizations of Haya as a man of action see Samuel Vasquez F., "Mi palabra," *La Tribuna,* August 15, 1931, p. 9; and Magda Portal, "Haya de la Torre y José Carlos Mariátegui," *APRA,* no. 2 (October 20, 1930): 4. According to a childhood acquaintance of Haya, he played the role of hero for his peers from an early age: Alcides Spelucín, "Haya de la Torre en mi recuerdo," *APRA* 14, no. 3 (February 22, 1946): 14. Haya also visualized himself as a hero on occasion, as was evident in Haya de la Torre, *Construyendo el Aprismo,* pp. 101–2.

46 Manuel Seoane, in *The West Coast Leader,* May 5, 1931, p. 4.

47 Antenor Orrego, in Partido Aprista Peruano, *Llamamiento,* pp. 13–15. This is just one example of Apra's essentially elitist critique of Peruvian national and especially working class culture during the campaign. The Apristas' belittling of the popular masses through the application of labels such as ignorant, decadent, etc., probably lost them working class votes in the long run to Sánchez Cerro, who never publicly indulged in similar kinds of rhetoric. For further examples of this tendency in Apra see the following works of Haya de la Torre and other leaders: *Antimperialismo y APRA,* pp. 31–32; *Ideario,* pp. 33, 128; Heysen, *A.B.C.,* p. 13; and Elias Avarado Z., *Notas políticas de actualidad. Folleto anti-centralista* (Pacasmayo, 1931), pp. 27–30, 65–66.

48 *La Tribuna* was a major propagator of the idea that Apra was a school. See the following issues for statements of the metaphor: August 3, 1931, p. 4; August 5, 1931, pp. 1, 3; August 9, 1931, p. 1; August 12, 1931, p. 4; September 6, 1931, p. 1; and October 12, 1931, p.1.

49 "Teacher-*caudillo*" is my term and was not used by Apristas to describe Haya.

In fact, the Apristas explicitly rejected the use of the label *caudillo* to describe Haya de la Torre. But at the same time that they rejected it and called him a simple soldier of Aprismo, they also referred to Haya as the *"caudillo* of *anti-caudillismo."* The apparent contradiction is resolved by viewing the Apristas' definition of a *caudillo* as an ambitious, false, opportunistic, and demagogic traditional politician. Most of the time that they used the term it was in reference to their major opponent, Sánchez Cerro. For examples of Apra's ambiguous stance on the *caudillismo* of their leader see articles from *La Tribuna* dated June 25, 1931, p. 1; July 13, 1931, extraordinary edition, p. 1; July 16, 1931, p. 8; August 15, 1931, p. 1; and August 16, 1931, p. 1. An interesting early integration of the concepts teacher and hero in describing Haya may be found in *Claridad* 1, no. 4 (January 1, 1924): 14.

50 *The West Coast Leader,* August 25, 1931, p. 4. An excellent collection of pictures of Haya from his infancy through 1931 is *Biografía y gráficos,* passim. For a physical description of Haya in the same work see p. 7. An interesting comparison to be made between Haya and Sánchez Cerro in physical terms is that the military *caudillo,* while less "revolutionary" in his program, was certainly more "revolutionary" regarding his appearance than the teacher-*caudillo.* Haya racially and socially resembled the archetype elite politician of the past, while Sánchez Cerro was a kind of new socioracial man on the political scene.

51 Ravines,, *Estafa,* p. 102. See also pp. 100–101.

52 *La Tribuna,* August 15, 1931, p. 8. See also *La Tribuna,* July 13, 1931, p. 3.

53 *Biografía y gráficos,* p. 26. For examples of the individual and mass expressions of Haya's paternalism in the 1931 campaign see descriptions of the man in the following issues of *La Tribuna:* July 18, 1931, p. 6; July 21, 1931, p. 2; and August 16, 1931, p. 12. Valuable information in this regard may also be found in *La Noche,* July 20, 1931, p. 6, and August 17, 1931, p. 3; "Sensacionales declaraciones de Haya de la Torre," *Mundial* 11, no. 575 (August 21, 1931): 13; and Hidalgo, *Diario,* p. 144.

54 *Biografía y gráficos,* passim. The photographs selected may be found on the following pages of the work: Figure 27, p. 8; Figure 28, p. 12; Figure 29, p. 27; Figure 30, p. 4; Figure 31, p. 3; and Figure 32, p. 23. Given Haya's supreme importance to the Aprista movement, it is not surprising that at least since the 1940s Apra has held its major annual demonstration to celebrate Víctor Raúl's birthday. As Manuel Seoane put it in "Por qué celebramos," p. 8: "We celebrate his birthday because it is ours, since it is his. He has been an example for all, those who are today twenty years old and those who have been with him for twenty years."

55 For examples in Haya's speeches where he promoted his identification with labor see *La Tribuna,* August 24, 1931, p. 6, and September 5, 1931, p. 2; and Haya de la Torre, *Política aprista,* p. 43. See also *Biografía y gráficos,* pp. 9, 11; Temoche Benites, *Apra y trabajadores,* pp. 5, 8–9; Seoane, *Nuestros fines,* p. 22; and Sánchez, *Carta a indoamericana,* p. 12. Various labor leader testimonials appeared in *La Tribuna;* May 24, 1931, p. 1; June 1, 1931, p. 8; July 25, 1931, p. 2; August 3, 1931, p. 3; August 5, 1931, p. 3; August 14,

1931, p. 3; August 16, 1931, p. 4; August 24, 1931, p. 2; and September 17, 1931, p. 1. Individuals who have attested to Haya's success in wooing labor leaders include Parra, *Bautismo de fuego,* pp. 17–18, 103–4; article from *El Trabajador,* no. 6, in Martinez de la Torre, *Apuntes para una interpretación* 3:164; Arturo Sabroso Montoya, interview, December 1970; Víctor Raúl Haya de la Torre, interview, November 24, 1970; Jorge Basadre, interview, January 11, 1971; and Flores, *Medio siglo en Vitarte,* p. 56. For a list of the unions which appear to have been the major supporters of Haya in the labor movement see Sabroso Montoya, *Réplicas proletarias,* pp. 122–24.

56 Sabroso Montoya, *Réplicas proletarias,* pp. 14–15, and see also in the same work pp. 13, 16–19. Sabroso expressed a similar point of view to mine in an interview in December 1970. Other laborers who have concurred with this position include Fausto Posada in *Mundial* 11, no. 537 (October 3, 1930): 25; Temoche Benites, *Apra y trabajadores,* esp. pp. 8–9; Walter García, in *La Tribuna,* May 23, 1931, p. 3; Pedro Valle A., in *La Tribuna,* July 6, 1931, p. 3; Manuel Palomino Zeza, ibid., July 17, 1931, p. 7; Manuel Arenas, ibid., July 23, 1931, p. 5; ? Marchand, ibid., July 26, 1931, p. 3; and Gavroche (pseud.) (Arturo Sabroso Montoya?), August 6, 1931, p. 5. It is interesting to note that one area in which Apra filed to win the vote of organized labor was the Port of Callao. One explanation of the Apristas' failure there is that all the major strikes and labor victories had occurred in Callao previous to Haya's first contact with the union movement in 1919. It is also possible that their early attainment of the eight-hour work day and relatively good material benefits had made the workers in Callao into a conservative "aristocracy of labor," more responsive to the traditional figure of Sánchez Cerro than the more radical Haya de la Torre.

CHAPTER 8: THE ELECTION

1 Headlines and favorable reports on the election-day atmosphere are contained in *La Tribuna,* October 12, 1931, pp. 1, 4–5; *El Comercio,* October 12, 1931, pp. 5 ff; *El Perú,* October 12, 1931, pp. 1–2; *Nuestro Diario,* October 12, 1931, p. 1; and *La Cronica,* October 12, 1931, pp. 2, 8–9.

2 *El Perú, La Crónica, El Comercio, La Tribuna,* and *Nuestro Diario,* October 12, 1931.

3 For Lima election results I consulted Lima, Jurado Departamental de Elecciones, "Acta general de escrutinio de los votos emitidos en las elecciones practicadas el 11 de octubre ultimo en el Departamento de Lima," November 6, 1931, Anexo I, Archivo del Jurado Nacional de Elecciones. For the national results see Basadre, *Historia de la República,* 16: 168–70.

4 For examples of Apra's charges of fraud see *La Tribuna,* October 20, 1931, p. 1; October 22, 1931, pp. 1, 2; October 23, 1931, p. 8; and November 2, 1931, p. 2.

5   Published material on electoral wrongdoings in the nineteenth and twentieth
    centuries in Peru is abundant. The best single treatment of this phenomenon is
    Villarán's "Costumbres electorales," in his *Páginas escogidas,* p. 197–205, and
    see also pp. 227–44 in the same work. Other excellent summaries may be found
    in Jorge Basadre, *La multitud, la ciudad y el campo en la historia del Perú,* 2d
    ed. (Lima, 1947), pp. 232–33; and Basadre, *Perú problema,* pp. 178–80. A
    particularly useful nineteenth century source is Manuel A. Fuentes, *Aletazos
    del Murciélago,* 2d ed. (Paris, 1866), esp. 1: 75, 86, 91, 99, 106, 114–17, 2: 344.
6   José Galvez, in Luis Guerrero, "El inolvidable 'Zorrito' Jimenez," February 15
    (Lima?, 1959), ASC. Other members of the *junta* that echoed Galvez's dislike
    for Sánchez Cerro included Herrera, *Memorias,* pp. 123–24, 135–37; and
    Manuel A. Vinelli to Manuel Bustamante de la Fuente, Lima, December 10,
    1931, AdBLF. The minister of government, Francisco Tamayo, who organized
    and supervised the election, is also reported to have been an enemy of Sánchez
    Cerro in Ugarteche, *Sánchez Cerro* 2:xxi. Evidence of Jimenez's animosity
    towards Sánchez Cerro may be found in "Conversación telegráfica entre
    Gustavo Jimenez y David Samanéz Ocampo," *El Pueblo,* March 6, 1931, p. 1;
    Juan Pacheco Cateriano to Manuel Bustamante de la Fuente, Barranco,
    September 12, 1931, AdBLF; Meza, *40 años,* p. 76; and *La Noche,* August 29,
    1931, p. 2. On Jimenez's favorable attitude towards Aprismo see *La Noche,*
    July 20, 1931, p. 2; and Juan Pacheco Cateriano to Manuel Bustamante de la
    Fuente, Barranco, October 8, 1931, AdBLF. I also discovered in an interview
    with Manuel Bustamante de la Fuente on November 4, 1970, that Haya's
    second in command, Manuel Seoane, was strongy considered to head a
    ministry in the Samanéz *junta* and was at one point unanimously approved for
    the post by the civilian and military rebels in Arequipa in February of 1931.
    The *junta's* replacement of Sánchez Cerro-appointed local authorities is
    discussed in *El Pueblo,* February 24, 1931, p. 1; and Manuel Bustamante de la
    Fuente to David Samanéz Ocampo, Arequipa, June 15, 1931, AdBLF. The
    government's effort to forward the candidacy of La Jara y Ureta is chronicled
    in Arturo Osores, "Manifiesto al electorado del Perú," in *El Comercio,*
    September 27, 1931, p. 3. Sources consulted on Jimenez's presidential preten-
    sions include J. Antonio Docarmo and A. Aguirre Morales to Manuel
    Bustamante de la Fuente, Lima, n.d., AdBLF; *La Noche,* August 14, 1931, p.
    2; and *El hombre de la calle* 1, no. 45 (July 27, 1931): 4, no. 66 (December 19,
    1931): 32. On Samanéz's role within the *junta* and Jimenez's domination, the
    following were consulted: Bustamante de la Fuente, "Apuntes para la
    historia," pp. 6–7; Manuel Bustamante de la Fuente to Carlos Beytía, Are-
    quipa, March 8, 1931, AdBLF; Manuel Bustamante de la Fuente, interview,
    October 10, 1970; Alfonso Llosa G. P., interview, May 29, 1971; and Arenas,
    Algo de una vida, p. 193.
7   F.J. Pinzas to Luis M. Sánchez Cerro, Lima, May 31, 1931, ASC. Sánchez
    Cerro intiated a similar purge of Samanéz officials shortly after his inaugura-
    tion. See Herbold, "Peruvian Administrative System," pp. 270–71.

8 Sánchez Cerro's personal secretary, Pedro Ugarteche, outlined the plans for a *golpe* to me in an interview on December 20, 1971. According to Ugarteche, Sánchez Cerro was particularly concerned to maintain the support of the Lima garrison and remained constantly in contact with the commander of the powerful 7th Infantry Regiment, Colonel Cirilio Ortega, to maintain a military support base. Aprista leader Luis Alberto Sánchez has provided interesting detail on the movements from within the *junta* to prevent Sánchez Cerro's rise to power. He affirms that not only was the minister of goverment, Francisco Tamayo, ready to begin a revolt, but he also planned to give the Apristas arms to fight on the *junta*'s side. See Sánchez, *Testimonio personal* 1: 363. For examples of Sánchezcerrista published criticism and suspicion of the *junta* see, in *La Opinión,* June 5, 1931, p. 1; July 5, 1931, p. 1; August 4, 1931, pp. 2, 4; September 22, 1931, p. 1; and October 4, 1931, p. 2; and a widely circulated handbill, "El escrutinio departamental en el Perú significa la burla del sufragio y el escarnio de la voluntad popular," September 26, 1931, ASC.
9 As this study is devoted to the analysis of political participation in Lima, the discussion of electoral fraud will be limited to that city.
10 Each ballot box was to contain 150 votes, but because a small percentage of the registered voters failed to vote on election day, the boxes averaged 135 votes. The above computations are made on the basis of 135 votes per box and are therefore approximate. The Apristas' charges of wrongdoing in the Lima election are contained in Crisólogo Quesada Campos to the President of the Jurado Departamental de Elecciones, Lima, November 7, 1931, Archivo del Jurado Nacional de Elecciones. On the anulling of ballot boxes and the electoral jury's response to Apra's allegations see Jurado Departamental de Elecciones de Lima, "Acta de escrutinio," 1931 in Archivo del Jurado Nacional de Elecciones, esp. pp. 1–3, and Anexo 1. The smoothness and fairness of the registration machinery was attested to by various antiSánchezcerrista sources including *El Perú,* July 18, 1931, p. 1; *La Crónica,* July 21, 1931, p. 4, July 22, 1931, p. 5, and July 26, 1931, p. 5; *Mundial* 11, no. 569 (July 10, 1931): 12; *Variedades* 27, no. 1222 (August 5, 1931): 1; Apra's request for the anullment of the election nationwide was published in *La Tribuna,* November 19, 1931, pp. 1–3.
11 This interpretation may be found in Thorndike, *Barbarie,* pp. 138–39.
12 This individual prefers to remain anonymous. He was interviewed on March 17, 1971.
13 For the provisions of the law and the regulations governing its implementation see Perú, *Estatuto electoral y reglamento para su aplicación* (Lima, 1931), passim, esp. pp. 39, 47–61; and Jurado Departamental de Elecciones de Lima, "Información oficial," October 11, 1931, CHS/BNP.
14 Federico More, in *El hombre de la calle* 2, no. 58 (October 24, 1931): 27; see also p. 29.
15 José Galvez, in Guerrero, "'Zorrito' Jimenez."
16 Gustavo Jimenez, "A las conciencias libres del Perú," Callao, February 15, 1932, CHS/BNP. Samanéz attested to the honesty of the suffrage process in

his address to the constituent congress upon turning over the government to Sánchez Cerro in Ugarteche, *Sánchez Cerro,* 2: 252–53. Tamayo's statement is contained in Ciccarelli, "The Sánchez Cerro Regimes," p. 132. For Larco Herrera's remarks see his *Memorias,* p. 136. Anti-Sánchezcerrista publications that unhappily admitted the fairness of the election included the pro-La Jara *El Perú,* October 23, 1931, p. 2; and the pro-Osores *La revista semanal* 5, no. 215 (October 15, 1931): 1. Opposing candidates that testified to the legitimacy of Sánchez Cerro's victory included José María de la Jara y Ureta to Luis M Sánchez Cerro in *La Opinión,* November 30, 1931, p. 4; and Toribio Sierra M., "Manifiesto a mis electores Apristas y no Apristas y al público en general," Callao, November 1, 1931, CHS/BNP.

17 The numbers assigned to each social group are based on figures in Perú, *Censo de Lima 1931,* pp. 197–201; and Martinez de la Torre, *Apuntes para una interpretación* 3: 41. Martinez de la Torre lists 14,941 union members in 1929, and I subtracted 3,336 from that amount, which corresponds to the number of workers in the port of Callao and from the rural areas of the Province of Lima, men who therefore did not vote in Lima. The respective proportions of the Lima vote were calculated from statistics contained in Jurado de Lima, "Acta de escrutinio," Anexo I. Both from the evaluations of contemporary and other observers and the tone of much of Apra's campaign rhetoric, there appears to be little doubt that the Aprista party won a majority of the urban middle sector vote. For a detailed study of Apra's social base, especially at the leadership level, see Liisa North, "The Origins and Development of the Peruvian Aprista Party" (Ph.D. diss., University of California, Berkeley, 1973), esp. pp. 110, 195–200.

18 The electoral results by individual ballot box were published in *El Comercio,* October–November 1931, and *La Tribuna,* October–November 1931. All calculations and examples are based on that information. The total number of votes differs from box to box because not all of the registered voters cast ballots.

19 Racial and educational data was obtained from Perú, Dirección Nacional de Estadística, *Extracto estadístico y censo electoral de la República* (Lima, 1933), pp. 136–37. The educational statistics may be somewhat inflated, as apparently many respondents exaggerated their level of schooling. Figures on voter turnout are found in ibid., p. 135.

20 Haya de la Torre, *Construyendo el Aprismo,* pp. 172–75. Haya's December 8, 1931, speech has been termed everything from a call for revolution to an attempt to hold back his more hotheaded followers by taking a radical line. The speech alone is not as important as the light it sheds on the extent to which Haya himself was ready to adopt violent measures to gain power. In the most recent addition to the polemic, Víctor Villanueva's *El Apra en busca del poder,* the author argues that Haya himself always attempted to avoid violent confrontation, preferring to achieve power electorally. Villanueva places the responsibility for much of the violence of the 1932–33 period on the remains of anarcho-syndicalist thinking in the Apra faithful. See esp. pp. 7–8, 55–56.

21 Sánchez Cerro, speech, March 25, 1932, in Ugarteche, *Sánchez Cerro,* 3: 82-83.
22 Quoted by Pedro Ugarteche in a letter to Jorge Basadre, Lima, August 22, 1968, ibid., 4: 347.
23 Pedro Ugarteche, interview, February 16, 1971.
24 José Matías Manzanilla, in Pedro Ugarteche ed., *Homenaje a Sánchez Cerro, 1933-1953* (Lima, 1953), p. 3. For information on Sánchez Cerro's presidency consult Ugarteche, *Sánchez Cerro,* vols. 3,4; Basadre, *Historia de la República,* vol 16; Miró Quesada Laos, *Sánchez Cerro;* and Thorndike, *Barbarie.*

CHAPTER 9: POPULISM AND THE
POLITICS OF SOCIAL CONTROL

1 Editorial from *Patria,* reprinted in *El Comercio,* August 24, 1931, p. 6. An excellent discussion on the importance of vertical vs. horizontal groups in Latin American politics is contained in Douglas A. Chalmers, "Political Groups and Authority in Brazil: Some Continuities in a Decade of Confusion and Change," in *Brazil in the Sixties,* ed. Roett, pp. 55-57.
2 The definition of the patron-client relationship and political clientelism is derived from John Duncan Powell, "Peasant Society and Clientelistic Politics," *American Political Science Review* 62, no.2 (June 1970): 411-25; Lemarchand and Legg, "Political Clientelism," passim; and Eric Wolf, "Kinship, Friendship and Patron-Client Relations in Complex Societies," in *The Social Anthropology of Complex Societies,* ed. Michael Banton, (London, 1966), pp. 16-17.
3 Próspero Pereyra, interview, March 4, 1971.
4 Pedro Ugarteche, interview, February 16, 1971.
5 Pedro Ugarteche, interview, December 3, 1970. A similar view was expressed about Haya de la Torre by Enrique Chirinos Soto, *Actores en el drama del Perú y del Mundo* (Lima, 1961), p. 121.
6 The connection between economic crisis and the populist type of political response was implicitly traced by Federico Ortíz Rodriguez, "Página del pueblo," *Mundial* 11, no. 543 (November 14, 1930): 33-34; Martinez de la Torre, *Apuntes para una interpretación,* 1: 129; and *La Crónica,* July 19, 1931, p. 7. The tendency to seek closer ties with patron figures in times of crisis has also been discussed in relation to the success of charismatic leadership. See Max Weber, *On Charisma and Institution Building* (Chicago, 1968), pp. xii-xiii, 25.
7 Pedro Ugarteche, interview, February 1, 1971.
8 Various political scientists have presented interesting analyses of the relationship between the political system, political behavior, and feelings of political competence in the above terms. See Gabriel Almond and Sidney Verba, *The Civic Culture,* 2d ed. (Boston, 1965), esp. pp. 17-18, 118, 138, 169; Peter Merkl, *Modern Comparative Politics* (New York, 1970), p. 226; and Alain

Touraine and Daniel Pecaut, "Working Class Consciousness and Economic Development in Latin America," *Studies in Comparative International Development* 3, no. 4 (1967): 72–73.

9 An excellent source on the major features of political culture is *Political Culture and Political Development,* ed. Lucian W. Pye and Sidney Verba (Princeton, 1965). See especially in this volume: Lucian W. Pye, "Introduction: Political Culture and Political Development," pp. 7–8, 22–23; and Sidney Verba, "Conclusion: Comparative Political Culture," pp. 513, 554. Also useful are: Almond and Verba, *Civic Culture,* pp. 13, 16–18; Samuel Beer in Beer et al., *Patterns of Government* (New York, 1962), p. 32; and Richard E. Dawson and Kenneth Prewitt, *Political Socialization* (Boston, 1969), pp. 26, 33. For an interesting discussion of the persistence of traditional political culture in spite of major innovations in political institutions see Robert Levine, "Political Socialization and Culture Change," in *Old Societies and New States,* ed. Clifford Geertz (Glencoe Ill., 1963), pp. 280–304, esp. p. 289.

10 Fuentes, *Aletazos del Murciélago* 1: 97. Fuentes is an excellent source on the beginnings of electoral clubs in Peruvian politics. See also ibid., 1: 85, 95, 104–5, 111–12. The most detailed descriptions of the formation and functioning of these clubs were written in satirical form by Clemente Palma under the pseudonym Juan Apapucio Corrales. See "De toros," *Variedades* 8, no. 213 (March 30, 1912): 396–99; no. 214 (April 6, 1912): 428–31; no. 215 (April 13, 1912): 458–61; no. 216 (April 20, 1912): 496–97; no. 220 (May 18, 1912): 612–15; and no. 224 (June 15, 1912): 742–45.

11 On vote buying see Villarán, *Páginas escogidas,* p. 228; *El hombre de la calle* 2, no. 56 (October 10, 1931): 16; and *La Acción Popular,* April 26, 1913, p. 1. Two extremely interesting descriptions of the preparation of mass demonstrations and their importance in showing a candidate's power capabilities are Arenas, *Algo de una vida,* pp. 19–20; and Meza, *40 años,* pp. 16–18.

12 Guillén, *Libro de democracia criolla,* p. 98. See also Miguel A. Sardón, *Las sentencias de un peruano* (Lima, 1945), p. 11.

13 Pedro Dávalos y Lissón, *La primera centuria,* 4 vols. (Lima, 1919–26), 1: 60. An excellent discussion of Peru's tradition of administrative centralism is contained in Herbold, "Peruvian Administrative System," esp. pp. 20, 177, 180–85.

14 Pedro Ugarteche, interview, February 13, 1971; and Leguía, *Yo tirano,* pp. 129–30. Peruvian historical literature is filled with allusions to the president's traditional role as the supreme dispenser of patronage. Some prominent examples include Guillén, *Libro de democracia criolla,* pp. 26, 45–47; Dávalos y Lissón *Primera centuria* 1: 59–62; Belaunde, *Meditaciones peruanas,* p. 58; and *La Acción Popular,* February 8, 1913, p. 2. Specifically on the presidentialism of Leguía see Mayer de Zulén, *Oncenio de Leguía,* pp. 82–83; Garrett, "Oncenio of Leguía," pp. 94, 105–6, and 111–12; and Herbold, "Peruvian Administrative System," p. 91.

15 Chocano, "Elogio póstumo," no page given.

16 *La revista semanal* 5, no. 201 (July 9, 1931): 2.

17 Alberto Ulloa Sotomayor, *Reflexiones de un cualquiera* (Buenos Aires, 1943), p. 236.
18 Richard Stephens, *Wealth and Power in Peru* (Metuchen, 1971), pp. 110–11. Carl Herbold, "Peruvian Admnistrative System," p. 130, supports this view of the shift from direct to indirect rule writing: "Significantly, our survey of the biographical data for political and bureaucratic leaders during the 1895–1945 period indicates that by the 1930s, the elite no longer exercised their power directly through ministerial posts and seats in the legislature. The 'great institutions' they controlled were primarily economic and social ones. There was a notable shift in tactics from overt dominance to more covert, subtle control."
19 Julio Cotler, "The New Mode of Political Domination," in *The Peruvian Experiment: Continuity and Change Under Military Rule,* ed. Abraham Lowenthal (Princeton, N.J., 1975), p. 46. On the crisis that precipitated the military action in 1968 see also Abraham Lowenthal, "Peru's Ambiguous Revolution," in *Peruvian Experiment,* ed. Lowenthal, pp. 26–30. On Odría's rise to power See David Collier, *Squatters and Oligarchs: Authoritarian Rule and Policy Change in Peru* (Baltimore, Md., 1976), p. 134.
20 Percy MacLean y Estenós, *Historia de una revolución* (Buenos Aires, 1953), pp. 205–7, 219.
21 Collier, *Squatters and Oligarchs,* p. 60. See also pp. 58, 59, and 61. An excellent series of descriptions of the methods used by Odría to manipulate a mass following and stage mass demonstrations is found in Mario Vargas Llosa's novel on the period, *Conversación en la Catedral,* 2 vols. (Barcelona, 1969).
22 Henry A. Dietz, "Bureaucratic Demand-Making and Clientelistic Participation in Peru," in *Authoritarianism and Corporatism,* ed. Malloy, p. 421. Dietz's article, pp. 413–58, is an informative analysis of those institutions designed to establish an "organizational relationship of the citizen to the state." Also consult his larger study of the Lima squatters, *Poverty and Political Participation Under Authoritarian Rule: The Urban Poor in Lima, Peru* (Austin, Tex., 1979); and David Scott Palmer, "The Politics of Authoritarianism in Spanish America," in *Authoritarianism and Corporatism,* ed. Malloy, esp. p. 404.
23 Collier, *Squatters and Oligarchs,* p. 110. The notion of the military regime's corporate nationalism is shared by various authors, including Cotler, "New Modes of Domination"; Lowenthal, "Ambiguous Revolution"; James M. Malloy, "Authoritarianism, Corporatism and Mobilization in Peru," in *New Corporatism,* ed. Pike and Stritch, pp. 52–84; and Wiarda, "Corporatism and Development" in ibid. Recent events in Peru indicate that the military government's attempts at clientelistic control have fallen far short of expectations. The replacement of Juan Velasco Alvarado by Francisco Morales Bermudez as president in 1975 marked a move away from military populism. But more important in the failure of clientelistic institutions has been their evident inability to fulfill the mass expectations created by the government's own propaganda, which promised true popular liberation. Because of the gap between mass expectations and governmental performance, the authorities have begun

to resort increasingly to open repression in order to control popular pressures. On this change in orientation see Julio Cotler, "Concentration of Income and Political Authoritarianism in Peru," in *Antipolitics,* ed. Davies and Loveman, esp. pp. 296-97.

24 Quoted by Wiarda, "Corporatism and Development," p. 31. Authors who have called attention to the adaptability of clientelism to changing circumstances are Lemarchand and Legg, "Political Clientelism," passim.

Selected Bibliography

INTERVIEWS

The following individuals contributed substantially to the information and ideas developed in this study. Formal and informal conversations with these people took place many times between January 1970 and July 1971. Precise dates of specific interviews and given in the appropriate note references.

Basadre, Jorge
Carreño, Alcides
Gunther, Juan
Haya de la Torre, Víctor Raúl
Llosa G.P., Alfonso
Maldonado Llosa, Jorge
Merél, Juan de Dios
Ortíz, Máximo
Pereyra, Próspero
Sabroso Montoya, Arturo
Sánchez, Luis Alberto
Ugarteche, Pedro

ARCHIVES

Archivo Sánchez Cerro (ASC). Lima, Peru.
Archivo de Manuel Bustamante de la Fuente (AdBLF). Lima, Peru.
Archivo de Víctor Raúl Haya de la Torre (AdHT). Vitarte, Peru.
Archivo de Arturo Sabroso Montoya. Lima, Peru.
Archivo del Jurado Nacional de Elecciones. Lima, Peru.
Manuscript Collection of the Biblioteca Nacional del Perú (BNP). Lima, Peru.
Colección del Hojas Sueltas of the Biblioteca Nacional del Perú (CHS/BNP). Lima, Peru.

MANUSCRIPT SOURCES

Bustamante de la Fuente, Manuel. "Apuntes para la historia." Lima, 1931? AdBLF.

Chocano, José Santos. "Elogio póstumo a Luis M. Sánchez Cerro. A la memoria de los Marqueses de Torre Tagle i de la Riva Agüero." Panamá, May 24, 1933. AdBLF.

Guerrero, Luis. "El inolvidable 'Zorrito' Jimenez." Lima?, 1959. ASC.

Perú. Jurado Nacional de Elecciones. "Libro de las actas de sesiones publicas del Jurado Nacional de Elecciones." Lima, 1931. Archivo del Jurado Nacional de Elecciones.

Riva Agüero, José de la. "Reportaje de carácter político de letra y firma de José de la Riva Agüero." Lima, 1930. BNP, no. E1157.

Vela, José. "La jornada de ocho horas." Lima, 19??. BNP, no. E1110.

Zitor (pseud.). "Historia de las principales huelgas y paros obreros habidos en el Perú." Lima, 1946, BNP, no. E1221.

DISSERTATIONS AND THESES

Benavides Correa, Alfonso. "Los partidos políticos del Perú." 2 vols. B.A. thesis, Universidad Nacional Mayor de San Marcos, Lima, 1947.

Ciccarrelli, Orazio A. "The Sánchez Cerro Regimes in Peru, 1930–1933." Ph.D. diss., University of Florida, 1969.

Dietz, Henry A. "Becoming a Poblador: Political Adjustment to the Urban Environment in Lima, Peru." Ph.D. diss., Stanford University, 1974.

Garrett, Gary Richard, "The Oncenio of Augusto B. Leguía: Middle Sector Government and Leadership in Peru, 1919–1930." Ph.D. diss., University of New Mexico, 1973.

Herbold, Carl F., Jr. "Developments in the Peruvian Administrative System, 1919–1930: Modern and Traditional Qualities of Government Under Authoritarian Regimes." Ph.D. diss., Yale University, 1973.

Jaquette, Jane S. "The Politics of Development in Peru," Ph.D. diss., Cornell University, 1971.

Karno, Howard Lawrence. "Augusto B. Leguía: The Oligarchy and the Modernization of Peru, 1870–1930." Ph.D. diss., U.C.L.A., 1970.

Klaiber, Jeffrey, S.J. "The Role of the González Prada Popular Universities in the Development and Formation of the Peruvian Aprista Movement." M.A. thesis, Loyola University, 1968.

Palmer, David Scott. "Revolution from Above: Military Government and Popular Participation in Peru, 1968–1972." Ph.D. diss., Cornell University, 1973.

PRINTED GOVERNMENT SOURCES

Boletín de la Dirección de Salubridad Pública. Lima, 1926.

Comité del Plan Regional de Desarrollo del Sur de Perú. *Southern Peru Development Project.* Vol. 22. Lima: Servicio Cooperativo Peruano Norteamericano de Educación, 1959.

Oficina Nacional de Planeamiento y Urbanismo. *Lima metropolitana: Algunos aspectos de su expediente urbano y soluciones parciales varias.* Lima: ONPU, 1954.

Perú. *Anteproyecto de una ley de elecciones. Exposición de motivos. Votos discordantes.* Lima: Empresa Periodística Hermanos Faura, 1931.

Perú. *Censo de la Provincia Constitucional del Callao de 20 de Junio 1905.* Lima: Imp. de San Pedro, 1906.

Perú. *Censo de las Provincias de Lima y Callao levantado el 13 de noviembre de 1931.* Lima: Torres Aguirre, 1932.

Perú. Dirección de Salubridad Pública. *Censo de la Provincia de Lima (26 de junio de 1908).* 2 vols. Lima: Ministerio de Fomento, 1915.

Perú. Dirección de Salubridad. Ministerio de Fomento. Inspección Técnica de Urbanizaciones y Construcciones, "Primer informe anual sobre el Registro Sanitario y Catastro de la Propiedad Urbana de Lima." *Ciudad y campo y caminos,* no. 38 (March–April, 1928): 25–28.

Perú. Dirección de Salubridad. Ministerio de Fomento. Inspección Técnica de Urbanizaciones y Construcciones. *Segundo informe sobre el Registro Sanitario y Catastro de la Propiedad Urbana de Lima.* Lima: Talleres Gráficos de la Prensa, 1928.

Perú. Dirección de Salubridad. Inspección Técnica de Urbanizaciones y Construcciones. "Catastro del Distrito de la Victoria," *Ciudad y campo y caminos,* no. 44 (1929): 45–56.

Perú. Dirección de Salubridad. Ministerio de Fomento. Inspección Técnica de Urbanizaciones y Construcciones. *Cuarto informe sobre el Registro Sanitario de la Vivienda—Catastro de la Propiedad Urbana de Lima.* Lima: Talleres Graficos de la Prensa, 1929.

Perú. Dirección Nacional de Estadística. *Extracto estadístico y censo electoral de la República.* Lima: Linotipiá. 1933.

Perú. *Estatuto electoral y reglamento para su aplicación.* Lima: Librería e Imprenta Gil, 1931.

Perú. Ministerio de Hacienda. *Resumen del censo de las Provincias de Lima y Callao levantado el 17 de diciembre de 1920.* Lima: Imprenta América, 1927.

Perú. Ministerio de Hacienda. *Estadística de precios y números indicadores.* Lima: Imprenta Americana, 1938.

Perú. Ministerio de Hacienda y Comercio. *Extracto estadístico del Perú: 1928.* Lima: La Opinión Nacional, 1929.

Perú. Ministerio de Hacienda y Comercio. *Extracto estadístico del Perú: 1931–1932-1933.* Lima: Imprenta América, 1935.

Perú. Ministerio de Hacienda y Comercio. *Extracto estadístico del Perú: 1939.* Lima: Imprenta América, 1940.

NEWSPAPERS

El Comercio. Lima, 1910–32.
La Crónica. Lima, 1915–31.
El Deber. Arequipa, 1931.
El Día. Lima, 1931.
La Hora. Lima, 1931.
Labor. Lima, 1928–29.
Libertad. Lima, 1930–31.
La Noche. Lima, 1931.
Noticias. Arequipa, 1931.
Nuestro Diario. Lima, 1931.
La Opinión. Lima, 1931–32.
Patria. Lima, 1931.
El Perú. Lima, 1930–31.
La Prensa. Lima, 1910–71.
El Pueblo. Arequipa, 1931.
La República. Lima, 1930–31.
El Tiempo. Lima, 1917–23.
La Tribuna. Lima, 1931–67.
Ultimas Noticias. Lima, 1931.
Variedades. Lima, 1910–31.
The West Coast Leader. Lima, 1930–33.

PERIODICALS

Amauta. Lima, 1926–30.
APRA. Lima, 1930–46.
Boletín de las Universidades Populares González Prada. Lima, 1946.
Campesino. Lima, 1969.
El cancionero de Lima. Lima, 1914–45.
Cancionero popular. Lima, 1931.
Caretas. Lima, 1960–71.
Ciudad y campo y caminos. Lima, 1924–29.
Claridad. Lima, 1923–24.
El hombre de la calle. Lima, 1930–32.
Mundial. Lima, 1920–31.
El obrero textil. Lima, 1920–25.
Oiga. Lima, 1965–71.
La Protesta. Lima, 1916–24.
La revista semanal. Lima, 1930–31.
Solidaridad. Lima, 1927.

BOOKS AND PAMPHLETS

Alberti, Giorgio and Julio Cotler. "Estructura social, relaciones sociales y personalidad." Mimeographed. Lima, 1969.

Alberti, Giorgio, and Rodrigo Sánchez. *Poder y conflicto social en el valle del Mantaro.* Lima: Instituto de Estudios Peruanos, 1974.

Alexander, Alberto. *Estudio sobre la crisis de la habitación en Lima.* Lima: Imprenta Torres Aguirre, 1922.

Alexander, Alberto. *Los problemas urbanos de Lima y su futuro.* Lima: Ministerio de Fomento, Dirección de Salubridad Pública, 1927.

Alexander, Alberto. *Las causas de la desvalorización de la propriedad urbana en Lima.* Lima: 1932.

Alvarado Z., Elias. *Notas políticas de actualidad. Folleto anticentralista.* Pacasmayo: La Unión, 1931.

Aprismo = anti catolicismo. Lima: Verdades, 1934.

Arenas, Germán. *Algo de una vida.* Lima: Sanmarti, 1941?.

Arguedas, José María. *Yawar fiesta.* Santiago: Editorial Universitaria, 1968.

Barrientos, Luis Felipe. *Los tres sindicalismos.* Lima: Ediciones Continente, 1958.

Basadre, Jorge. *Perú problema y posibilidad.* Lima: Rosay, 1931.

Basadre, Jorge. *La multitud, la ciudad y el campo en la historia del Perú.* 2d ed. Lima: Editorial Huascarán, 1947.

Basadre, Jorge. *Historia de la República del Perú: 1822-1933.* 6th ed. 16 vols. Lima: Editorial Universitaria, 1968-69.

Basadre, Jorge. *Introducción a las bases documentales para la historia de la República del Perú con algunas reflexiones.* 2 vols. Lima: P.L. Villanueva, 1971.

Basadre, Jorge, and Rómulo Ferrero. *Historia de la Cámara de Comercio de Lima.* Lima: Santiago Valverde, 1963.

Bayer, Osvaldo et al. *El populismo en la Argentina.* Buenos Aires: Editorial Plus Ultra, 1974.

Bedoya, Manuel. *El otro Caín.* Lima: Editorial "Llamarada," 1933?.

Bedoya, Manuel. *La argolla negra.* Lima: La Epoca, 193?.

Belaunde, Víctor Andrés. *La realidad nacional.* Paris: Editorial "Le Livre Libre," 1931.

Belaunde, Víctor Andrés. *La crisis presente 1914-1939.* Lima: Ediciones Mercurio Peruano, 1940.

Belaunde, Víctor Andrés. *Meditaciones peruanas.* 2d ed. Lima: P.L. Villanueva, 1963.

Belaunde, Víctor Andrés. *El debate constitutional.* 2d ed. Lima: P.L. Villanueva, 1966.

Belaunde, Víctor Andrés. *Trayectoria y destino: Memorias completas.* 2 vols. Lima: Ediventas, 1967.

Biografía y gráficos de Haya de la Torre. Lima: Editorial "APRA", 1931.

Bonilla, Heraclio. *Guano y burguesía en el Perú.* Lima: Instituto de Estudios Peruanos, 1974.

Bourricaud, François. *Ideología y desarrollo: el caso del Partido Aprista Peruano.* México: El Colegio de México, 1966.

Bourricaud, François. *Poder y sociedad en el Perú contemporáneo.* Translated by Roberto Bixio. Buenos Aires: Sur, 1967.

Bourricaud, François, Jorge Bravo Bresani, Henri Favre, and Jean Piel. *La oligarquía en el Perú.* Lima: Instituto de Estudios Peruanos, 1969.

Bromley, Juan, and José Barbagelata. *Evolución urbana de la ciudad de Lima.* Lima: Editorial Lumen, 1945.

Cabré, Francisco P.F.M. *La unión de la clase obrera.* Arequipa: Círculo de Obreros Católicos, 1918.

Cáceres, José Raúl. *El pasmo de una insurgencia.* Lima: Editorial Perú, 1942.

Camacho, Diego. *La revolución de agosto de 1930.* Lima: Vasquez, 193?.

Cancionero aprista. Lima: Editorial Aprista, 193?.

Capuñay, Manuel A. *Leguía: Vida y obra del constructor del gran Perú.* Lima: Cía. de Impresiones y Publicidad, Enrique Bustamante y Ballivián, 1952.

Caravedo Molinari, Baltazar. *Clases, lucha política y gobierno en el Perú (1919–1933).* Lima: Retama Editorial, 1977.

Carta réplica a los manifiestos del Sr. Haya de la Torre por un peruano. Dated August 29, 1933. No publisher, no place.

Cartilla aprista No. 1. Preguntas y respuestas. Lo que todo hijo del pueblo debe saber. Lima: n.p., 1931?.

Cartilla aprista. Ecuador: n.p., 1933.

Castro Pozo, Hildebrando. *Nuestra comunidad indígena.* Lima: El Lucero, 1924.

Castro Pozo, Hildebrando. *Del Ayllú al cooperativismo socialista.* 2d ed. Lima: Librería Editorial Juan Mejía Baca, 1969.

Catolicismo y aprismo. Lima: Imprenta Minerva, 1939.

Celestino, Olinda. *Migración y cambio estructural: La comunidad de Lampián.* Lima: Instituto de Estudios Peruanos, 1972.

Chang-Rodriguez, Eugenio. *La literatura política de González Prada, Mariátegui y Haya de la Torre.* México: Ediciones de Andrea, 1957.

Chaplin, David. *The Peruvian Industrial Labor Force.* Princeton, N.J.: Princeton University Press, 1967.

Chaplin, David, ed. *Peruvian Nationalism: A Corporatist Revolution.* New York: Dutton, 1974.

Chirinos Pacheco, Benjamín. *Hacia un Perú nuevo.* Arequipa: Rumbos, 1932.

Chirinos Soto, Enrique. *Actores en el drama del Perú y del mundo.* Lima: Ediciones de Divulgación Popular, 1961.

Chirinos Soto, Enrique. *El Perú frente a junio de 1962. Síntesis de la historia política de la República.* Lima: Ediciones del Sol, 1962.

Ciccarelli, Orazio A. "Militarism, Aprismo and Violence in Peru: The Presidential Election of 1931." SUNY-Buffalo, Council on International Studies, Special Study no. 45, 1973.

Cole, J. P. *Estudio geográfico de la gran Lima.* Lima: ONPU, 1957.

Collier, David. *Squatters and Oligarchs: Authoritarian Rule and Policy Change in Peru.* Baltimore, Md.: Johns Hopkins University Press, 1976.

Comisión Gráfica de Organización y Propaganda Sindical. *Manifiesto a los obreros gráficos.* Lima: Imp. Carlos Vásquez, 1930.

Comité Aprista Peruano, Brigada de Organización. *Organización vertical del Partido Aprista Peruano.* Santiago de Chile: n.p., 1937.

Cossío del Pomar, Felipe. *Víctor Raúl.* 2 vols. México: Editorial Cultura, 1961, 1969.

Cotler, Julio. "La mecánica de la dominación interna y del cambio social en el Perú." Mimeographed. Lima, 1967.

Cotler, Julio. "Crisis política y populismo militar en el Perú." Mimeographed. Lima, 1969.

Cotler, Julio. *Clases, estado y nación en el Perú.* Lima: Instituto de Estudios Peruanos, 1978.

Cox, Carlos Manuel. *Ideas económicas del aprismo.* Lima: Atahualpa, 1934.

Cox, Carlos Manuel, ed. *Cartas de Haya de la Torre a los prisioneros apristas.* Lima: Editorial Nuevo Día, 1946.

Dandler H., Jorge. *El sindicalismo campesino en Bolivia.* México: Instituto Indigenista Interamericano, 1969.

Dávalos y Lissón, Pedro. *La primera centuria.* 4 vols. Lima: Imprenta Gil, 1919–26.

Dávalos y Lissón, Pedro. *Diez años de historia contemporánea del Perú. (1899–1908).* Lima: Librería e Imprenta Gil, 1930.

Davies, Thomas, M., Jr. *Indian Integration in Peru: A Half Century of Experience, 1900–1948.* Lincoln, Nebr.: University of Nebraska Press, 1974.

Davies, Thomas M., and Brian Loveman, eds. *The Politics of Antipolitics: The Military in Latin America.* Lincoln, Nebr.: University of Nebraska Press, 1978.

Dawson, Richard E., and Kenneth Prewitt. *Political Socialization.* Boston: Little, Brown, 1969.

Degregori, Carlos Iván. "Proceso histórico y dependencia en dos comunidades del Valle de Chancay," Mimeographed. Lima, 1970.

Degregori, Carlos I., and Jurgen Golti. *Dependencia y desintegración estructural en la comunidad de Pacaroas.* Lima: Instituto de Estudios Peruanos, 1973.

Del Mar, Serafín (pseud. for Reynaldo Bolaños). *El año trágico.* Lima: Editorial Cooperativa Aprista Atahualpa, 1934.

Dietz, Harry A. *Poverty and Political Participation Under Authoritarian Rule: The Urban Poor in Lima, Peru.* Austin, Texas: University of Texas Press, 1979.

Dobyns, Henry E., and Paul L. Doughty. *Peru: A Cultural History.* New York: Oxford University Press, 1976.

Drake, Paul W. *Socialism and Populism in Chile: 1932–52.* Urbana, Ill.: University of Illinois Press, 1978.

Echecopar, Enrique. *Aptocracia.* Lima: La Prensa, 1930.

Eguiguren, Luis Antonio. *En la selva política.* Lima: Sanmarti, 1933.

Encinas, José Antonio. *Contribución a una legislacion tutelar indígena.* Lima: C. F. Southwell, 1918.

Encinas, José Antonio. *Causas de la criminalidad indígena en el Perú.* Lima: Universidad Mayor de San Marcos, 1919.

Enriquez, Luis Eduardo. *Haya de la Torre. La estafa más grande de América.* Lima: Ediciones del Pacífico, 1951.

Escajadillo, Tomás. *La revolución universitaria de 1930.* Lima: Sanmarti, 1931.

El esfuerzo libertador del comandante Jimenez. 1933?.

Estatutos de la Bolsa de Trabajo anexo de la Confederación de Artesanos "Unión Universal" aprobados por el Supremo Gobierno por decreto de 13 de febrero de 1915. Lima: Imprenta de Víctor A. Torres, 1915.

Estatutos de la Sociedad "Artesanos de Auxilios Mutuos." Lima: Imprenta Seminario, 1925.

Estatutos y reglamentos de la Federación de Obreros Panaderos "Estrella del Perú. Lima: n.p., 1905.

Favre, Henry, Claude Collin Delavaad, and José Matos Mar. *La hacienda en el Perú.* Lima: Instituto de Estudios Peruanos, 1967.

Fergac (pseud.). *Aprismo.* Lima: n.p., 1933?.

Flores, Demetrio. *Medio siglo de vida sindical en Vitarte.* Vitarte, n.p., 1961.

Fuentes, Manuel A. *Aletazos del Murciélago.* 3 vols. 2d ed. Paris: Imprenta de A. D. Laine y J. Havard, 1866.

Furtado, Celso, et al. *Brasil hoy.* 2d ed. México: Siglo XII, 1970.

García Calderón, Francisco. *En torno al Perú y América.* Lima: Juan Mejía Baca y P.C. Villanueva, 1954.

Garland, Alejandro. *El Perú en 1906.* Lima: Imprenta "La Industria," 1907.

Germani, Gino, Torcuato S. Di Tella, and Octavio Ianni. *Populismo y contradicciones de clase en Latino-américa.* México: Ediciones Era, 1973.

Gómez, Luis E. *Reflexiones sindicalistas.* Lima: n.p., 193?.

González Prada, Manuel. *Horas de lucha.* Lima: Editores Latinoamericanos, 19??.

González Prada, Manuel. *Anarquía.* Santiago de Chile: Ediciones Ercilla, 1936.

González Prada, Manuel. *Propaganda y ataque.* Buenos Aires: Ediciones Imán, 1939.

González Prada, Manuel. *Páginas libres.* 2 vols. Lima: Fondo de Cultura Popular, 1966.

González Prada, Manuel. *Figuras y figurones.* 2d ed. Lima: Editorial Gráfica Labor, 1969.

Guillén, Alberto, *El libro de la democracia criolla.* Lima: Imp. Lux, 1924.

Hammel, Eugune A. *Power in Ica: The Structure of a Peruvian Community.* Boston: Little, Brown, 1969.

Harth-Terre, Emilio. *Orientaciones urbanas.* Lima: Imp. Torres Aguirre, 1931.

Hauser, Phillip M., ed. *Urbanization in Latin America.* New York: International Documents Service, 1961.

Haya de la Torre, Víctor Raúl. *Dos cartas de Haya de la Torre.* Lima: El Inca, 1923.

Haya de la Torre, Víctor Raúl. *Por la emancipación de la América latina; articulos, mensajes, discursos 1923-1927.* Buenos Aires: Gleizer, 1927.

Haya de la Torre, Víctor Raúl. *Ideario y acción aprista.* Buenos Aires: N. Ferrari, 1930.

Haya de la Torre, Víctor Raúl. *El plan del Aprismo*. Lima: Editorial Libertad, 1931.

Haya de la Torre, Víctor Raúl. *Teoría y táctica del Aprismo*. Lima; Editorial Cahuide, 1931?.

Haya de la Torre, Víctor Raúl. *Ante la historia y ante la América y el mundo*. Buenos Aires: Editorial Libertad, 1932.

Haya de la Torre, Víctor Raúl. *Construyendo el Aprismo. Artículos y cartas desde el exilio (1924–31)*. Buenos Aires: Claridad, 1933.

Haya de la Torre, Víctor Raúl. *A dónde va Indoamérica?* 2d ed. Santiago: Ediciones Ercilla, 1935.

Haya de la Torre, Víctor Raúl. *Ex-combatientes y desocupados*. Santiago de Chile: Ercilla, 1936.

Haya de la Torre, Víctor Raúl. *Fundamentos filosóficos del Aprismo*. Santiago: Centro de Estudios Sociales APRA, 1945.

Haya de la Torre, Víctor Raúl. *El pensamiento político de Haya de la Torre*. 5 vols. Lima: Ediciones Pueblo, 1961.

Haya de la Torre, Víctor Raúl. *Política aprista*. 2d ed. Lima: Editorial-Imprenta Amauta, 1967.

Haya de la Torre, Víctor Raúl. *El antimperialismo y el APRA*. 3d ed. Lima: Editorial-Imprenta Amauta, 1970.

Haya de la Torre, Víctor Raúl. *Obras completas*. 7 vols. Lima: Juan Mejía Baca, 1977.

Haya de la Torre: su vida y sus luchas. Lima: Editorial Andimar, 1957.

Hernandez Urbina, Alfredo. *Nueva política nacional*. Trujillo: Ediciones Raíz, 1962.

Heysen, Luis E. *El A.B.C. de la peruanización*. Lima: Editorial APRA, 1931.

Heysen, Luis E. *El comandante de Oropesa*. Lima: Editorial APRA, 1931.

Hidalgo, Alberto. *Diario de mi sentimiento (1922–1936)*. Buenos Aires: Excelsior, 1937.

Homenaje a la memoria del héroe de Arequipa. Lima: n.p., 1933?.

Hooper Lopez, René. *Leguía*. Lima: Ediciones Peruanas, 1964.

Huertas Vallejos, Lorenzo. *Capital burocrático y lucha de clases en el sector agrario (Lambayeque, Perú, 1920–1950)*. Lima: Seminario de Historia Rural Andina, Universidad Nacional Mayor de San Marcos, 1974.

Ingenieros, José, and Víctor Raúl Haya de la Torre. *Teoría y táctica de la acción renovadora y antiimperialista de la juventud en América latina*. Buenos Aires: Centro Estudiantes de Ciencias Económicas, 1928.

Ionescu, Ghita, and Ernest Gellner, eds. *Populism, its Meaning and National Characteristics*. New York: MacMillan, 1969.

Johnson, Allen W. *Sharecroppers of the Sertão. The Economics of Dependence on a Brazilian Plantation*. Stanford, Calif.: Stanford University Press, 1971.

Johnson, John J. *Political Change in Latin America: The Emergence of the Middle Sectors*. Stanford, Calif.: Stanford University Press, 1958.

Kantor, Harry. *The Ideology and Program of the Peruvian Aprista Movement*. Berkeley, Calif.: University of California Press, 1953.

Kapsoli Escudero, Wilfredo. *Luchas obreras en el Perú por la jornada de las 8 horas (1900–1919).* Lima: UNMSM-Centro de Estudiantes de Historia, 1969.

Klaiber, Jeffrey L. *Religion and Revolution in Peru.* Notre Dame, Ind.: University of Notre Dame Press, 1977.

Klapp, Orrin E. *Symbolic Leaders.* New York: Minerva Press, 1964.

Klarén, Peter. *La formación de las haciendas azucareras y los orígenes del APRA.* Lima: Moncloa Campodónico, 1970.

Klarén, Peter. *Modernization, Dislocation and Aprismo: Origins of the Peruvian Aprista Party, 1870–1932.* Austin: University of Texas Press, 1973.

Laos, Cipriano A. *Lima: "La ciudad de los Virreyes,"* Lima: Editorial Perú, 1928.

Larco Herrera, Rafael. *Memorias.* Lima: Editorial Rimas, 1947.

Lavalle, Hernando de. *La gran guerra y el organismo económica nacional.* Lima: Librería E Imprenta Gil, 1919.

Leguía (?), Augusto B. *Yo tirano, yo ladrón.* Lima: Editorial Ahora, 193?.

Leguía. Lima: Imp. Minerva, 1926.

Lévano, César. *La verdadera historia de la jornada de las ocho horas en el Perú.* Lima: n.p., 1969.

Lévano, Delfín. *Mi palabra.* 2d ed. Lima: n.p., 1934.

Lima: 1919–1930. Lima: n.p., 1935?.

Lowenthal, Abraham, ed. *The Peruvian Experiment: Continuity and Change Under Military Rule.* Princeton, N.J.: Princeton University Press, 1975.

Lozada Benavente, Elías. *Vaivenes de la política.* Lima: Imp. Minerva, 1938.

Luna Vegas, Ricardo. *Mariátegui, Haya de la Torre y la verdad histórica.* Lima: Retama Editorial, 1978.

Mackay, John A. *The Other Spanish Christ: a Study in the Spiritual History of Spain and South America.* New York: Macmillan, 1933.

Mackay, John A. *That Other America.* New York: Friendship Press, 1935.

MacLean y Estenós, Percy. *Historia de una revolución.* Buenos Aires: Editorial E.A.P.A.L., 1953.

Malloy, James M., ed. *Authoritarianism and Corporatism in Latin America.* Pittsburg, Pa.: Pittsburg University Press, 1977.

Marett, Robert. *Peru.* London: Ernest Benn Ltd., 1969.

Mariátegui, José Carlos. "La crisis universitaria." *Claridad* 1, no. 2 (September 1923): 2–3.

Mariátegui, José Carlos. *7 ensayos de interpretación de la realidad peruana.* 17th ed. Lima: Empresa Amauta, 1969.

Mariátegui, José Carlos. *Ideología y política.* Lima: Empresa Editora Amauta, 1969.

Martín, José Carlos. *José Pardo y Barreda, el estadista: un hombre, un partido, una época.* Lima: Cía. de Impresiones y Publicidad, 1948.

Martinez de la Torre, Ricardo. *Apuntes para una interpretación marxista de historia social del Perú.* 2d ed. 4 vols. Lima: Empresa Editora Peruana, 1974.

Matos Mar, José, et al. *Dominación y cambios en el Perú rural.* Lima: Instituto de Estudios Peruanos, 1969.

Mayer, de Zulén, Dora. *El oncenio de Leguía.* Callao: Tip. Peña., 1931.

Mazo, Gabriel del, ed. *La Reforma Universitaria.* 3 vols. Lima: Universidad Nacional Mayor de San Marcos, 1968.

Meneses, Rómulo. *Por el Apra.* Lima: Atahualpa, 1933.

Meneses, Rómulo. *Aprismo femenino peruano.* Lima: Atahualpa, 1934.

Merel, Juan de Dios. *Principios del Aprismo.* Santiago: Ediciones ULAM, 1936?

Meza, Tomás. *40 años al servicio de los presidentes del Perú en la Casa de Pizarro.* Lima: n.p., 1959.

Miró Quesada, Luis. *El contrato de trabajo.* Lima: Librería Escolar e Imprenta de E. Moreno, 1901.

Miró Quesada, Luis. *La cuestión obrera en el Perú.* Lima: n.p., 1904.

Miró Quesada Laos, Carlos. *Pueblo en crisis.* Buenos Aires: Emece, 1946.

Miró Quesada Laos, Carlos. *Sánchez Cerro y su tiempo.* Buenos Aires: Librería "El Ateneo" Editorial, 1947.

Miró Quesada Laos, Carlos. *Radiografía de la política peruana.* 2d ed. Lima: Páginas Peruanas, 1959.

Miró Quesada Laos, Carlos. *Autopsia de los partidos políticos.* Lima: Ediciones Páginas Peruanas, 1961.

More, Federico. *Zoocracia y canibalismo.* Lima: Editorial Llamarada, 1933.

More, Federico. *Una multitud contra un pueblo.* Lima: n.p., 1934.

Morse, Richard M., ed. *The Urban Development of Latin America 1750–1920.* Stanford, Calif.: Stanford Center for Latin American Studies, 1971.

Muñiz, Pedro, and Carlos Showing. *Lo que es el Aprismo.* Bogotá: Publicaciones del P.A.P., 1932.

Muñoz, José, and Diego Robles. *Estudio de tugurios en los distritos de Jesús María y La Victoria.* Lima: Oficina Nacional de Planeamiento y Urbanismo, 1968.

Nash, June, Juan Corradi, and Hobart Spaulding, Jr., eds. *Ideology and Social Change in Latin America.* New York: Gordon and Breach, 1977.

Palacios, Leoncio M. *Encuesta sobre presupuestos familiares obreros realizada en la ciudad de Lima en 1940.* Lima: Ed. Lumen, 1944.

Pareja, Piedad. *Anarquismo y sindicalismo en el Perú.* Lima: Ediciones Rikchay, 1978.

Parra V, Pedro. *Bautismo de fuego del proletariado peruano.* Lima: Editorial Linotipo los Rotarios, 1969.

Partido Aprista Peruano. *4 aspectos importantes del Aprismo.* Lima: Editorial Manco Capac, 1933.

Partido Aprista Peruano. *40 preguntas y 40 respuestas sobre el Partido Aprista Peruano.* 2d ed. Lima: Atahualpa, 1946.

Partido Aprista Peruano. *El proceso de Haya de la Torre.* 2d ed. Lima: Ed. Amauta, 1969.

Partido Unión Revolucionaria. *Era el más patriota! Era todo corazón: Abrid soldados de la U.R.!* Lima: Editorial Inca, 1934.

Partido Unión Revolucionaria. *Estatutos del Partido Unión Revolucionaria del Perú.* Lima: Imp. Hispano-América, 1932.

Payne, James L. *Labor and Politics in Peru*. New Haven, Conn.: Yale University Press, 1965.

Paz Soldán, Carlos Enrique. *De la inquietud a la revolución: diez años de rebeldías universitarias (1909-1919)*. Lima: Biblioteca de "La Reforma Médica," 1919.

Paz Soldán, Carlos Enrique. *De la revolución a la anarquía universitaria*. Lima: Biblioteca "La Reforma Médica," 1922.

Pike, Frederick B., *The Modern History of Peru*. New York: Frederick A. Praeger, 1967.

Pike, Frederick B. *The United States and the Andean Republics: Peru, Bolivia and Ecuador*. Cambridge, Mass.: Harvard University Press, 1977.

Pike, Frederick B., and Thomas Stritch, eds. *The New Corporatism: Social and Political Structures in the Iberian World*. Notre Dame, Ind.: University of Notre Dame Press, 1974.

Polar, Mario. *Viejos y nuevos tiempos: Cartas a mi Nieto*. Lima: Moncloa-Campódonicio, 1969.

Portal, Ismael. *Del pasado limeño*. Lima: Librería e Imprenta Gil, 1932.

Portal, Magda. *Frente al momento actual*. Lima: Secretaría de Organización del Comité Departamental de Lima, 1931.

Portal, Magda. *El Aprismo y la mujer*. Lima: Atahualpa, 1933.

Primer Congreso Nacional de Estudiantes reunido en la sede universitaria del Cuzco del 11 al 20 de marzo de 1920. Lima: Secretaría de la Federación de Estudiantes del Perú, 1920.

Quijano, Aníbal. *Imperialismo, clases sociales y estado en el Perú: 1890-1930*. Lima: Mosca Azull, 1978.

Radiografía de Haya de la Torre. Lima: Ediciones "Páginas Libres," 1946.

Ramírez Castilla, Samuel. *La tiranía se desencadena*. Lima: Panfletos Políticos, 1932.

Ravines, Eudocio. *La gran estafa*. México: Libros y Revistas S.A., 1952.

Revoredo, Alejandro. *Apuntes de historia política y financiera*. Lima: Librería e Imprenta Gil, 1939.

Ríos, Ricardo R., ed. *La Convención de los Partidos de 1915*. Lima: Imp. Torres Aguirre, 1918.

Rodrigo Alva, Víctor. *El mito de la revolución de agosto*. Lima: Imprenta Minerva, 1933.

Roett, Riorden, ed. *Brazil in the Sixties*. Nashville: Vanderbilt University Press, 1972.

Romero, Emilio. *Historia económica del Perú*. Buenos Aires: Editorial Sudamericana, 1949.

Romero Rodriguez, Rosa. *Historia de la Revolución de Arequipa*. Lima: La Lira Limeña, 1930.

Sabroso Montoya, Arturo. *Réplicas proletarias*. Lima: Atahualpa, 1934.

Saco, Alfredo, *Síntesis aprista*. Lima: San Cristobal, 1934.

Sánchez, Luis Alberto. *Carta a una indoamericana. Cuestiones elementales del Aprismo*. Quito: n.p., 1932.

Sánchez, Luis Alberto. *Elementos del Aprismo*. Quito: n.p., 1932.

Sánchez, Luis Alberto. *Aprismo y religión*. Lima: Editorial Cooperativa Aprista Atahualpa, 1933.

Sánchez, Luis Alberto. *Raúl Haya de la Torre o el político. Crónica de una vida sin tregua*. Santiago: Biblioteca América, 1934.

Sánchez, Luis Alberto. *Principios de economía política aplicada al Perú*. Lima: Editorial "Librería Peruana," 1934.

Sánchez, Luis Alberto. *Dialéctica y determinismo*. Santiago: Ercilla, 1938.

Sánchez, Luis Alberto. *Haya de la Torre y el Apra*. Santiago: Editorial del Pacífico, 1955.

Sánchez, Luis Alberto. *Testimonio personal*. 3 vols. Lima: Edit. Villarán, 1969.

Sánchez, Luis Alberto. *Apuntes para una biografía del Apra*. Lima: Mosca Azul, 1978.

Sánchez Cerro, Luis M. *Programa de gobierno del Comandante Luis M. Sánchez Cerro, candidato a la presidencia de la República del Perú*. Lima: 1931.

Sánchez Viamonte, Carlos. *Jornadas*. Buenos Aires: J. Samet, 1929.

Sarfatti Larson, Magalí, and Arlene Eisen Bergman. *Social Stratification in Peru*. Berkeley, Calif.: Institute of International Studies, 1969.

Seoane, Manuel. *Nuestros fines*. Buenos Aires: Publicaciones del P.A.P., 1931.

Solís, Abelardo. *Once años*. Lima: Sanmarti, 1934.

Sulmont, Denis. *El movimiento obrero en el Perú: 1900–1956*. Lima: Pontificia Universidad Católica del Perú, 1975.

Sulmont, Denis. *Historia del movimiento obrero en el Perú (de 1890 a 1977)*. Lima: Tarea, 1977.

Temoche Benites, Ricardo. *El Apra y los trabajadores*. Lima: 194?

Thorndike, Guillermo. *El año de la barbarie*. Lima: Editorial Nueva América, 1969.

Ugarte Eléspuru, Juan Manuel. *Lima y lo limeño*. Lima: Editorial Universitaria, 1966.

Ugarteche, Pedro. *La política internacional peruana durante la dictadura de Leguía*. Lima: Imp. C.A. Castrillos, 1930.

Ugarteche, Pedro. *Sánchez Cerro. Papeles y recuerdos de un presidente del Perú*. 4 vols. Lima: Editorial Universitaria, 1969–70.

Ulloa Cisneros, Abel. *Escombros (1914–1930)*. Lima: CIP, 1934.

Ulloa Sotomayor, Alberto. *La organización social y legal del trabajo en el Perú*. Lima: "La Opinión Nacional," 1916.

Ulloa Sotomayor, Alberto. *Reflexiones de un cualquiera*. Buenos Aires: Rodriguez Giles, 1943.

Valdéz Garrido, Julio. *De Bolívar a Haya de la Torre*. Lima: Imp., 1947.

Veliz, Claudio, ed. *Obstacles to Change in Latin America*. London: Oxford Press, 1965.

Veliz, Claudio, ed. *The Politics of Conformity in Latin America*. New York: Oxford University Press, 1967.

El verdadero plan de La Alianza Popular Revolucionaria Americana. Lima: Editorial Pachacutec, 193?

Villanueva, Víctor. *El militarismo en el Perú.* Lima:. T. Scheuch, 1962.

Villanueva, Víctor. *El Apra en busca del poder, 1930–1940.* Lima: Editorial Horizonte, 1975.

Villanueva, Víctor. *Así cayó Leguía.* Lima: Retama Editorial, 1977.

Villarán, Manuel Vicente. *Páginas escogidas.* Lima: P.L. Villanueva, 1962.

Weber, Max. *The Theory of Social and Economic Organization.* Translated by A.M. Henderson and Talcott Parsons. Glencoe: The Free Press, 1947.

Weber, Max. *On Charisma and Institution Building.* Chicago: University of Chicago Press, 1968.

Wiarda, Howard J., ed. *Politics and Social Change in Latin America: The Distinct Tradition.* Amherst: University of Massachusetts Press, 1974.

Yepes del Castillo, Ernesto. *Perú 1820–1920; un siglo de desarrollo capitalista.* Lima: Instituto de Estudios Peruanos-Campodónico, 1972.

ARTICLES

Alexander, Alberto, to Director de Salubridad. In *Boletín de la Dirección de Salubridad Pública,* no. 2 (1926): 183–87.

"Alojamiento para la clase obrera en el Perú." *Boletín del Ministerio de Fomento, Dirección de Salubridad* 2, no. 1 (January 31, 1906): 53–83.

A.P.E. (pseud.). "Sánchez Cerro y la revolución que derrocó a Leguía." *Oiga,* no. 130 (June 25, 1965): 32–35.

"Así como el hábito no hace al monje, el voto secreto no hará la elección." *El hombre de la calle* 2, no. 56 (October 10, 1931): 16–17.

Barba, Carlos. "Memorias de una gesta." *Caretas,* no. 434 (April 28, 1971): 24–26, 36.

Barreda y Laos, Felipe. "La crisis política del Perú: la dictadura y la muerte de los partidos." *La República,* August 25, 1930, pp. 1–3.

Basadre, Jorge. "La emoción social." *Claridad* 2, no. 5 (March 15, 1924): 11–13.

Basurto, Jorge. "Populismo y movilización de masas en México durante el régimen cardenista." *Revista mexicana de sociología* 31, no. 4 (October 1969): 853–92.

Bedoya, Manuel. "Viejas oligarquías y 'gente improvisada.'" *Mundial* 4, no. 181 (November 2, 1923): 3.

Belaunde, Rafael. "La dictadura del Perú y su derrocamiento." *El Comercio,* November 19, 1930, p. 5.

Berlin, Isaiah, et al. "Populism A Discussion," *Government and Opposition* 3, no. 2 (Spring 1968): 137–79.

Bravo de Rueda, Alejandro. "La verdad sobre el complot comunista fraguado por la policía en junio de 1927." *Libertad,* October 3, 1930, p. 2.

Bustamante de la Fuente, Manuel. "La elección departamental." *El Derecho* 16, no. 118 (June 1931): 115–116.

Carnero Checa, Laureano. "El 'viejo' don Arturo." *Revista central sindical* 2, no. 19 (March 1968): 15–19.

Carnero Checa, Luis. "Haya de la Torre y la U.P.G.P." *APRA* 14, no. 3 (February 22, 1946): 4.

Chavarría, Jesús. "La desaparición del Perú colonial (1870–1919)." *Aportes* no. 23 (January 1972): 120–53.

Chevalier, François. "Témoignages littéraires et disparatés de croissance: L'expansion de la grande propriété dans la Haut-Pérou au XXe siècle." *Annales économies, sociétés, civilisations* 21, no. 4 (July–August 1966): 815–31.

"Cinco (5) de octubre – Día del Camino." *Ciudad y campo y caminos,* no. 41 (August–September 1928): 44–74.

Clement, Juan Bautista. "Haya de la Torre y el Aprismo." *La Tribuna,* July 30, 1962, p. 5.

"La Conscripción Vial en Lima," *Ciudad y campo y caminos* 2, no. 19 (July 1926): iv–v.

Cornejo Koster, Enrique. "Hombres y sombras," *Claridad* 1, no. 4 (January 1924): 14.

Davies, Thomas M., Jr. "The *Indigenismo* of the Peruvian Aprista Party." *Hispanic American Historical Review* 51, no. 4 (November 1971): 626–45.

"El deber de todos." *Mundial* 11, no. 578 (September 11, 1931): 14–15.

Espejo, Julio Augusto (pseud.). "Leguía inaugura una época." *Oiga* 9, no. 415 (March 19, 1971): 14–17.

"Un estudio revela lo pavoroso que es la situación de la población escolar." *La Crónica,* August 14, 1931, p. 2.

Fuentes Castro, Paulín. "La ratificación de la alianza Piérola-Civilista." *Mundial* 2, no. 41 (February 4, 1921): 3.

Galjart, Benno. "Class and Following in Rural Brazil," *América latina* 6, no. 2 (July–September 1964): 3–23.

Gallardo Echevarría, Andrés. "1922: Motín en el Cuzco y las pretensiones del Tigre Leguía." *Oiga* 8, no. 369 (April 10, 1970): 44–45.

Gallardo Echevarría, Andrés. "El regreso del Mayor Luis M. Sánchez Cerro." *Oiga* 8, no. 373 (May 8, 1970): 40–42.

Gallardo Echevarría, Andrés. "La Revolución de Arequipa del 22 de agosto de 1930." *Oiga* 8, no. 376 (May 29, 1970): 52–54.

Gallardo Echevarría, Andrés. "1930–1931 los tormentosos seis meses de la Junta de Gobierno." *Oiga* 8, no. 377 (June 5, 1970): 48–51.

Gallardo Echevarría, Andrés. "La Junta de Gobierno de Samanéz Ocampo." *Oiga* 8, no. 378 (June 12, 1970): 47–48.

Gallardo Echevarría, Andrés. "Los nueve meses de Samanéz Ocampo y el regreso de Sánchez Cerro." *Oiga* 8, no. 379 (June 19, 1970): 45–46.

García Frías, Roque. "Intensidad absoluta y relativa de la emigración provinciana al Departamento de Lima." *Estadística peruana* 3, no. 5 (July 1947): 54–66.

Garro, J. Eugenio. "Caridad humana." *Claridad* 1, no. 4 (January 1, 1924): 17–18.

Haya de la Torre, Víctor Raúl. "Mis recuerdos de González Prada." *Repertorio americano* 15, no. 6 (August 13, 1927): 84–85.

Haya de la Torre, Víctor Raúl. "La jornada de 8 horas." *APRA* 14, no. 5 (February 22, 1946): 26–30.

"La industria textil en Lima." *Ciudad y campo y caminos,* no. 39 (May 1928): I-II.

Kapsoli, Wilfredo. "El campesinado peruano y la ley vial." *Campesino* (Lima) 1, no. 2 (May–August 1969): 1–17.

Kaufman, Robert R. "The Patron-Client Concept and Macro-Politics: Prospects and Problems." *Comparative Studies in Society and History* 16, no. 3 (June 1974): 284–308.

Klaiber, Jeffrey L. "The Popular Universities and the Origins of Aprismo, 1921–1924." *Hispanic American Historical Review* 55, no. 4 (November 1975): 693–715.

Lemarchand, Rene, and Keith Legg. "Political Clientelism and Development: A Preliminary Analysis." *Comparative Politics* 4, no. 2 (January 1972): 148–65.

Luna Vegas, Ricardo. "Lealtad de Haya de la Torre y del Aprismo." *APRA* 14, no. 3 (February 22, 1946): 7.

Mackay, John A. "Intelectuales de panteón." *Claridad* 1, no. 1 (May 1, 1923): 6–7.

Manzanilla, José Matías, and Manuel Vicente Villarán. "Los antiguous partidos han terminado su misión: El Partido Civil pertenece a la historia," *El Comercio,* September 11, 1930, p. 3.

Montero Bernales, M., and Alberto Alexander. "Contemplando la situación de los desocupados y la crisis de la vivienda." *El Perú,* January 23, 1931, pp. 2–3.

"Las nostalgias de Haya." *Caretas,* no. 432 (March 22, 1971): 17–21.

"El ocaso del Apra." *Caretas* 10, no. 211 (December 22, 1960): 11.

Orrego, Antenor. "La defensa del Aprismo." *Últimas noticias,* January 10, 1931, pp. 8–9.

"Peruanos sin patria." *Mundial* 11, no. 575 (August 21, 1931): 12.

Piel, Jean. "A propos d'un soulèvement rural péruvien au début du vingtième siècle: Tocroyoc (1921)." *Revue d'histoire moderne et comtemporaine* 14 (October–December 1967): 375–405.

Pike, Frederick B. "Religion, Collectivism, and Intrahistory: The Peruvian Ideal of Dependency," *Journal of Latin American Studies* 10, no. 2 (November 1978): 239–62.

Portal, Magda. "Haya de la Torre o el héroe." *APRA* 14, no. 3 (February 22, 1946): 4–5.

"Posturas falsas." *Claridad* 2, no. 7 (November 1, 1924): 11–13.

Powell, John D. "Peasant Society and Clientelistic Politics." *American Political Science Review* 62, no. 2 (June 1970): 411–25.

"El proceso del gamonalismo." *Amauta* 62, no. 25 (July–August 1929): 69–80.

Ravines, Eudocio. "El momento político peruano." *La Noche,* July 5, 1931, p. 6.

"La realidad actual y los partidos políticos." *Mundial* 11, no. 533 (September 5, 1930: 17.

Roger, Gastón. "Fuegos fatuos." *Mundial* 11, no. 532 (August 29, 1930): 14.

Safire, William. "The Nixon Style," *San Francisco Chronicle,* October 30, 1971, p. 19.

Sánchez, Luis Alberto. "El deber de hacer política." *Mundial* 11, no. 537 (October 3, 1930): 10.

Sánchez, Luis Alberto. "Hay que definirse." *Mundial* 11, no. 538 (October 10, 1930): 6.

Sánchez, Luis Alberto. "Del caudillo a la idea." *Mundial* 11, no. 539 (October 17, 1930): 13–14.

Sánchez, Luis Alberto. "75 años en la vida de un líder." *La Prensa* (Suplemento, February 22, 1970), pp. 41–47.

"Sensacionales declaraciones de Haya de la Torre," *Mundial* 11, no. 575 (August 21, 1931): 13.

Seoane, Manuel. "La nueva generación peruana," *Claridad* 2, no. 7 (November 1, 1924): 0–11.

Seoane, Manuel. "Por qué celebramos los Apristas el cumpleaños de Haya de la Torre," *APRA* 14, no. 3 (February 22, 1946): 8.

Spelucín, Alcides. "Haya de la Torre en mi recuerdo." *APRA* 14, no. 3 (February 22, 1946): 14, 19.

Temoche Benites, Ricardo. "Lucha heróica por la jornada de 8 horas en el Perú." *La Tribuna,* January 15, 1959, p. 4.

Ugarteche, Pedro. "El deber de la hora actual." *El Comercio,* February 23, 1931, p. 3.

Vasquez F., Samuel. "Mi palabra." *La Tribuna,* August 15, 1931, p. 9.

Veraz, Justo. "Puñado de verdades," *La revista semanal* 5, no. 202 (July 16, 1931): 16–17.

"La vialidad en el Perú." *Ciudad y campo y caminos,* no. 20 (August 1926): vi–viii.

Weffort, Franciso C. "Clases populares y desarrollo social (contribución al estudio del 'populismo')." *Revista paraguaya de sociología* 5, no. 3 (December 1968): 62–154.

Index

293

JACKET BY PHILL THILL DESIGN
COMPOSED BY LANDMANN ASSOCIATES, MADISON, WISCONSIN
MANUFACTURED BY CUSHING MALLOY, ANN ARBOR, MICHIGAN
TEXT IS SET IN TIMES ROMAN, DISPLAY LINES IN OPTIMA

ᗯ

Library of Congress Cataloging in Publication Data
Stein, Steve.
Populism in Peru.
Bibliography: p. 276.
Includes index.
1. Peru — Politics and government — 1919-1968.
2. Populism — Peru. 3. Labor and laboring classes —
Peru — Political activity. 4. Partido Aprista Peruano.
5. Haya de la Torre, Víctor Raúl, 1895- 6. Sánchez Cerro,
Luis M., 1889-1933. I. Title.
F3448.S73   985'.063   80- 8315
ISBN 0-299-07990-2